NATION BUILDING

The Geopolitical History of Korea

Walter B. Jung

University Press of America,® Inc.
Lanham • New York • Oxford

Copyright © 1998
University Press of America,® Inc.
4720 Boston Way
Lanham, Maryland 20706

12 Hid's Copse Rd.
Cumnor Hill, Oxford OX2 9JJ

Library of Congress Cataloging-in-Publication Data

Jung, Walter
Nation Building : the geopolitical history of Korea / Walter B. Jung.
p.   cm.
Includes bibliographical references and index.
1. Korea—Foreign relations. 2. Geopolitics—Korea. I. Title.
DS910.18.J86 1998   951.9—dc21   98-39911 CIP

ISBN 0-7618-1273-3 (cloth: alk. ppr.)
ISBN 0-7618-1274-1 (pbk: alk. ppr.)

⊖™ The paper used in this publication meets the minimum
requirements of American National Standard for Information
Sciences—Permanence of Paper for Printed Library Materials,
ANSI Z39.48—1984

Contents

Preface

No nation can entirely escape the dynamics of its relative location factors in its nation building process. Particularly for small nations surrounded by larger, powerful neighbors, geopolitical dynamics tend to yield significantly greater influence, for a nation's history is formed and shaped by its interactions to key external powers.

The Korean peninsular, sharing borders with China, Russia, and Japan (across the Korea Strait), is a host of unique geopolitical properties. As a result, its nation building process has been heavily swayed by its momentous contacts with regional powers which in the past have been aggressive and imperial in nature. Korea's precarious endeavors in defending the national identity in the early periods and the division of the nation into two parts at the outset of the cold war era can be comprehensible only through adequate understanding of the dynamics of the regional geopolitics.

In this book my focus is on the mechanisms and consequences of the regional geopolitics that Korean states have had to deal with throughout the long nation building process. In doing so, it became necessary to limit the discussion of some domestic developments, which, though important , were considered to have less direct bearing on the process and direction the Hahn nation has followed for the last two millenia. It has been my intention to review the region's geopolitical developments that directly influenced Korea's evolution in nation building so that the backdrop of contemporary Korean history appears more transparent.

I must express here my deep appreciation to several individuals for their invaluable assistance. My dear friend, Dr. Don Duffy, generously lent his expertise in editing the manuscript. He made numerous valuable suggestions for its improvement. Dr. Xiaobing Li, an outstanding colleague and historian, supplied much needed advice and encouragement. Mr. Terry May, a friend and mentor, furnished unconditional, warm encouragement. Mr. Zhong Xue was instrumental in preparing the final manuscript. His professionalism, energetic drive, and careful attention to details is exemplary.

My deepest gratitude must go to my wife Young who provided unfailing encouragement and support. Without her unselfish devotion the work should have been much too lonely and demanding. I also owe a great deal of appreciation to my son Dorian and my daughter Nina for their understanding and support. They have been and will remain the source of my inspiration and pride.

W. B. Jung

Chapter 1

The Founding Period: Gohchosun to Silla

1. The Land and the People

Contemporary Korea, made up of the Korean peninsula and its accessory islands, about 85,500 square miles in total area, is located on the eastern edge of the Asian mainland trailing off into a southerly direction. The nation shares its northern border with China and Russia; the Amrok (Yalu) and Tuman (Tumen) rivers separate the peninsula from Chinese Manchuria and the Russian Far East, respectively. It is separated from mainland China by the Yellow Sea and from the Japanese archipelago by the East Sea and the Korea Strait. The narrowest distance across the Korea Strait is 130 miles.

The Korean peninsula lies between 33 and 43-degrees north latitude and between 124 and 131-degrees east longitude. Its physical dimensions are approximately 620 miles in north-south length and 130 miles wide at its narrowest. The peninsula's total size is equivalent to that of Great Britain. At present, it remains divided into two parts: the northern part (People's Democratic Republic of Korea) comprises fifty-five percent of the total land area while the southern part (Republic of Korea) is slightly smaller, forty-five percent.[1] The land is mountainous, formed mainly of ancient Archean rocks. Farm lands are limited and largely located in the south. The nation's mineral resources, diverse in kind but paltry in quantity, are more heavily concentrated in the north.

The peninsula has a heavily indented coastline more than 10,000 miles in total length. Its east coast is rocky and rugged, providing only a few good harbors; the south and west coasts are low but more indented, providing most of the nation's major harbors.

The Koreans, the ethnic Hahns, are descendants of the Mongolian tribes which migrated from Central Asia's Mongolian plain to Manchuria and later to the Korean peninsula.[2] The people are homogeneous, essentially unrelated to either the Chinese or the Japanese, their geographic neighbors. Their spoken language, Korean, is also entirely different from either Chinese or Japanese; the written language, the Hahngul, is their own, unrelated to that of neighbors. Contemporary Koreans, however, use some two thousand Chinese characters as a part of their written language. Nevertheless, words made up with Chinese characters are all Koreanized in pronunciation, and thus often not interchangeable with Chinese usage.

2. Northeast Asia's Tenacious Power

The Hahn people of Korea began their long journey of nation building from the remote Northeast Asian plain. Most of the Manchurian Plain and the adjacent region in northern Korea were widely inhabited by Korean tribes as early as the tenth century B.C. These tribes entered the region during the Paleolithic Age some thirty thousand years ago. They share a common racial origin with the Mongols, the Manchus, and the Siberian tribes, as indicated by their common language family, the Altaic language of northern Asia.[3]

Korean tribes moved out of the central Asian highlands, reaching the Manchurian plain first and then slowly expanding their domain along the coastal areas of the Korean peninsula. The number of these early Hahn settlers did not exceed one million in the tenth century B.C. During this early period they maintained a nomadic life style, improvising foods and shelter and wandering the large, sparsely populated area.

Gradually the livelihood of the early Korean settlers evolved from simple hunting and gathering methods to subsistence farming. This early transformation was slow and tedious. Yet over the period the settlers developed stationary farming suitable for the region's physical limitations: mountainous topography and a shorter growing season. They grew mostly wheat and barley during this early period, unlike the contemporary Chinese settlers, who by then had undertaken flourishing rice farming in the Yangtze and Yellow River basins.

Early Korean settlers made the southern Manchurian plain and northern Korea their primary domain. Yet they steadily expanded their settlements into the southern part of the Korean peninsula, evidently in search of milder weather and richer farmland. By the fifth century B.C. their domain   extended to include most of southern Korea although the new territories were still sparsely and irregularly inhabited. In spite of their penetration into the southern part of the peninsula, the Koreans maintained their power base in southern Manchuria and northern Korea upon which they exercised   dominating control. It was in this region that the Hahn Koreans founded, during the fourth century B.C., their first clan-oriented state, Gohchosun.

The Kingdom of Gohchosun ruled the greater portion of Northeast Asia, a territory between the Liao River in southern Manchuria and the Dandong River in northern Korea. The kingdom of Yen, one of the Han Chinese states of the period located just west of the Liao River, shared the common but ill-defined border with the Korean kingdom.[4] Even in this early period the Koreans encountered the hostility of much larger Yen China. Gohchosun offered stiff competition, and as a result it not only managed to forestall the Chinese attempts for regional domination but gradually consolidated its power and emerged as the ruler of the rich Liao River basin in southern Manchuria.

Yen China had encountered intermittent, destructive raids by its northern neighbor, the Hsiung-nu, a group of nomadic tribes roaming the steppes of the north-central Asian highlands. To Yen, an early Han state, Gohchosun posed even more serious threats to its regional hegemony since Gohchosun was more stationary and thus territorial. Yen's bitter experience with Hsiung-nu's incessant and destructive raids had already led it to believe that all non-Han races, including the Koreans, were dangerous and barbaric. By this time the Han state had already acquired the "Middle Kingdom" bearing toward its smaller neighbors.[5] Gohchosun's geographic juxtaposition to this powerful kingdom was ominous from the very beginning.

Han China was anxious to conquer the Korean state, the most serious rival that competed against the Middle Kingdom in the region. Both China's imperialistic bid to put Gohchosun under its control and the Koreans' resolute endeavor to defend their domain were intense. A wave of military campaigns launched by Yen around 200 B.C. exacted a heavy toll of the large but lightly populated Korean kingdom. At the end, Gohchosun had to surrender the Liao River basin to Yen but still maintained its domain in northeastern Manchuria.

Gohchosun's ruling classes were believed to have had some access to the Chinese culture. At this stage the cultural exchanges between these two ancient neighbors might have been one-sided: with its advanced and basically self-contained civilization, China had more to give than to receive from the Korean peninsula. Mainly through commercial exchanges, the Gohchosun society had made contacts with diverse elements of the Chinese culture. As a result, the cultural transfer between the two states was done piecemeal; there were no systematic efforts between these militant neighbors.

Notwithstanding its cultural and military backwardness, the Kingdom of Gohchosun was successful in containing China's territorial ambition in the region for a prolonged period. It had even made successful raids on the Chinese state at times, extending its rule into northern China. Although its territory reached as far as the present day Beijing region, Korea's penetration had never threatened the Chinese states even when Han China was in serious trouble internally.[6] Unlike the nomadic Hsiung-nu or the predatory Mongols or the opportunistic Manchurian tribes that had challenged Han China for control of the Middle Kingdom, Koreans had no apparent ambition to rule China itself. They were content with control of southern Manchuria and the Korean peninsula.

Regardless of Gohchosun's desire to remain at peace in its remote domain, the Chinese did not cease in making periodic attempts on the Korean territory. In 202 B.C. Han China emerged as the first Chinese dynasty to lay a foundation for a continental power with highly developed administrative systems and military might. On the other hand, Gohchosun still remained an ancient clan state. As a defense against the numerically superior China, the Koreans maintained highly motivated and mobile fighting forces to protect their large but sparsely populated territory.

Although the early Koreans zealously protected their territories from unrelenting Chinese attempts, they were quite open in adopting various elements of the Chinese culture; Koreans adopted Chinese practices such as a centralized ruling structure based on a highly authoritarian monarch. Still, their early experimentation with the Chinese practices was selective and limited in scope. Aside from both having strong monarchies, there were fundamental differences in the status of the monarch in the two countries. From the early stage of its nation building, China had embraced a political succession scheme in which an eventual victor of a power struggle, which was bound to erupt in the waning period of a dynastic era, would become the next ruler. The Son of Heaven, more commonly known as "emperor" and acknowledged as having received a heavenly mandate, reigned over "kings," or regional warlords, who exercised varying degrees of autonomous power in the region under his control. The Koreans were never comfortable with such an arrangement but preferred a monarch who assumed absolute power as the leader of the strongest tribe in a federation. Political process in Korea in this early period was often heavily influenced by ubiquitous factional rivalry. Nevertheless, the fact that the much advanced Chinese culture did not overwhelm the Korean state was an indication that Gohchosun's adoption of the Chinese systems was deliberate and selective.

The military strength of Gohchosun reached its pinnacle in the second century B.C., when it defeated and expelled a Han force from Manchuria. However, the Korean kingdom scored this military success when Han China was still heavily involved in internal squabbles and unable to achieve political consolidation. Because of its population, which may have been 40 to 50 million around the second century B.C., and because of its chronic political factionalism, Han China needed a considerable time to prepare itself for power politics in the region. When it was finally able to unify warring factions and turned its attention to external matters, many of its neighbors felt the perils of geographic proximity to such a powerful state. Korea was no exception but a major target. When the Chinese had secured the regions at its rear, southern China and Annam (Vietnam), Han launched its full scale military invasion of Gohchosun.

The invasion, launched by a land and sea-borne force of 50,000 men in 109 B.C., was an embarrassing fiasco for the Middle Kingdom. Han invading forces were soundly defeated by resourceful Korean defenders at their well-defended fortresses on the Liaodong peninsula.[7] Chinese invaders could not overrun the Korean forces despite their vast numerical advantage and presumably time-tested military tactics. This first full-scale Chinese-Korean military contest ended in the Koreans' decisive victory. Yet the victory was short-lived. Not discouraged by the defeat, Han China managed within a few years to subjugate the Korean kingdom. In an attempt to integrate the conquered territory into its administrative system, Han China organized four counties in the territory of Gohchosun. Placing Chinese officials in charge, Han began to rule not only southern Manchuria but most of the Northwestern and west-central regions of the Korean peninsula. Only the Korean tribal states of the southern and mountainous northern regions remained free of Han control.

It was a major setback for the Koreans that Gohchosun, admittedly a small tribal state with greatly limited resources, collapsed so soon after its impressive military success. Among others, two factors were most responsible for the sudden turn of fortune. First, Han's sophisticated culture had won powerful followers in the Korean court, a development that led to active rebellion and eventually forced Hahn submission to the Chinese. In the process, the court's nationalist officials were defeated by the proponents of accommodation. It was an ominous portent of Korean toadyism that would inflict incalculable damage on the Hahn peoples' nation building process in the succeeding Koryo and Chosun period. Second, the faction of realists in the court may have sided with nearsighted Han supporters in an attempt to appease the Chinese onslaught. The Korean realists came to realize that all-out warfare against immense and powerful China would have been disastrously expensive for the small, relatively less advanced Korean kingdom, in both economic and, even more importantly, psychological costs. They might have preferred appeasement to continued confrontation to avoid a certain defeat.

The submission of their first national state to China served as a dire warning to the Korean people of the dangers posed by China, the only foreign power known to the Koreans at the time. Han's eventual rout of the Korean kingdom represented the beginning of Chinese dynasties' interminable quest to dominate the Korean peninsula. It also illustrated the nascent pattern of the geopolitical mechanism that was to remain long the dominant political process in the region.

Han's conquest of southern Manchuria, northern Korea, Mongolia, central Asia, and the tropical regions on the south served a dual purpose: pacification of the unstable border regions and demonstration of China's growing military and political power over its neighbors. It was a typical behavior often repeated by Chinese states throughout history.

Unlike other conquered areas in which Han often chose to install infiltration posts protected by military garrisons, the Han installations in the territory of Gohchosun were more like colonial administrations. Han's objective in Manchuria and Korea was not mere political subjugation of the unruly border states but the establishment of permanent colonies. Two considerations may have motivated the Han court to pursue this course: colonization of the Gohchosun territory could stabilize China's northeastern border by neutralizing the region's hostile but elusive nomadic tribes, and it also could secure Chinese trade interests in the region.[8]

The Han court's desire to colonize the Korean territory may have also been caused by its growing concerns with the Japanese. Han may have intended to build a buffer zone against that little-known maritime kingdom, whose nature Han perceived as hostile and aggressive. The location of its colonies in the Gohchosun territory indicates that their choice was based on well-developed strategic considerations: Hyundo in southern Manchuria and northern Korea, Laklang in Northwestern Korea close to China's Shantung peninsula, Limdun in northeastern Korea, and Chinbun in the southwestern region of the peninsula, where Korean tribes had conducted periodic commercial dealings with Japan.[9]

The Han colonies could have been effective in blocking possible Japanese advance toward China through the Korean peninsula. The colonized Korean territory would have been China's other "Wall" -this one against a perceived enemy on the east. Japan did not, however, pose any direct threat to the Han court during this period, and Han may simply have been concerned with protecting its already substantial sea-borne trade with Korea. Japanese piracy, which was inflicting heavy damages along coasts of both China and Korea during the period, may have been another factor that caused Han China to establish its colonies in Korea.

The Han colonies in Korea were dismantled by the Korean tribal states after only a short period because they had failed to gain the support of the Koreans, who refused to submit to the Chinese attempt to colonize their land and instead went south to the area then dominated by the Hahn tribes.[10] Nonetheless, the colonies had served as an effective conduit for further propagation of the Chinese culture in Korea. Although the transfer of Chinese culture to Korea was still carried out by a limited number of members of the nobility, the impact was increasingly substantial. Artifacts and other items found at the sites of the colonies show that the Koreans were recipients of highly refined Chinese culture during this period.[11] Although Chinese culture was introduced into the Korean kingdom through rather unorganized commercial exchanges even before the establishment of the Han colonies, the Han presence in the region undoubtedly accelerated the process to a significant extent.

Even before the large-scale adoption of Chinese systems, Gohchosun had practiced an effective governing system, including highly centralized political control and a universal penal system. Three Gohchosun penal codes known today indicate that the kingdom was ruled by an aristocracy committed to strict legalism.[12] Similar penal codes were adopted by the Kingdom of Buyeo, a tribal kingdom formed in Northern Manchuria by the Koreans during the later period of Gohchosun. The penal codes of both Korean kingdoms reveal that the law was designed primarily to protect citizens from murder and bodily injury, to guard private property, and to discourage women from committing adultery and extreme acts of jealousy. The codes also manifested that the society was heavily dominated by the ruling classes of nobility, whose lives and properties were considered high priorities to be protected through harsh punishment imposed on the commoners. It appears that by the time the penal codes (not yet a fully developed legal system) were adopted around the Seventh to Fifth Century B.C., the nomadic Korean tribes had been transformed into a society of law and order, though the codes were not intended to protect the common people. In their severity and their simplicity the Gohchosun penal codes were substantially dissimilar to the contemporary Chinese penal codes. It is highly likely that the Korean courts were aware of the existence of more sophisticated Chinese penal systems, yet they apparently chose to adhere to their simpler system probably to preserve their unique class society.

During the Gohchosun period Korean society had departed from a nomadic life style. Such momentous evolution replaced the old practice of communal property with a concept of private ownership and brought about the formation of social classes, which had led to a widening gap between rich and poor. The society of the first Hahn state was divided into the noble class of rulers, common people, farmers, and slaves. Rigid class barriers restricted upward mobility in the lower classes. An individual's class status was strictly hereditary with only minor exceptions, such as elevation to the nobility of persons who had unusual merit or who had made significant contributions to the court. On the other hand, downward mobility was open and easy: members of the nobility and commoners became slaves if they committed certain major crimes specified by the penal codes. Reflecting a male-oriented class society, the early Korean penal codes distinctly favored men and the rich. Wealthy perpetrators of crimes escaped harsh punishment through monetary compensation. The compensation might involve substantial fines, but this loophole available to men of means represented the Korean society's preference for the welfare of the upper class to broad social justice during this early period.

The harsh and discriminatory punishment that Gohchosun's penal codes imposed on women indicates that the early Korean society was based on a male-dominant family system. The codes also manifested that the noble classes were widely practicing polygamy - perhaps an inevitable consequence in a society that was ruled by complex tribal coalitions formed and maintained through liberal exogamy. As polygamous marriages became a common practice in the kingdom's ruling class, family problems caused by jealous and adulterous wives might have mounted to an extent that harsh punishment was meted out. This may have been the beginning of the tradition continuing throughout history that Korean women are expected to observe strict fidelity. In contrast, issues of male fidelity were largely ignored in Korean society until very recent times.

The penal codes of Gohchosun somewhat resembled the characteristics of legalism that were popular in China during the third and fourth centuries B.C. Yet other aspects of the kingdom's political systems generally lacked such a spirit. Even more pronounced was the absence of Confucian influence during the period. Although the teachings of Confucius and his disciples had prevailed over traditional Chinese thought since the Fourth and Fifth Century B.C., there is little evidence that Confucianism had penetrated Korean social life to any meaningful extent. Shunning highly complicated Confucian teachings of ritual behavior and moral reflection, the Korean state opted to maintain a simplistic ruling structure mainly designed to foster internal collaboration. Only a few members of the nobility dared to adopt Chinese systems of writing and learning, displaying the kingdom's concerns about the culture the Chinese represented and its desire to maintain interference-free external relations.

In the process of transforming its primitive tribal coalition into a cohesive feudal state, Gohchosun successfully resisted Chinese interference. Repeated Chinese attempts to subjugate the Korean tribes only hardened their resolve to stay free. Until it met a sudden fall, Gohchosun managed to keep alive its tradition of an independent warrior-nation. Unfortunately, the spirit of a sovereign nation the Korean kingdom displayed so eloquently in that early stage of national development carried with it an unavoidable drawback - a passivity toward the Chinese culture on the whole. Reluctance to adopt the advanced Chinese culture later cost the nation dearly. On the other hand, that precaution was an effective defense against Chinese expansionism - not only in a military but also in a psychological sense. Resisting Chinese influence thus helped to long preserve the smaller and less advanced Korean state.

The fall of Gohchosun and the subsequent installation of four Han colonies were a severe setback to the Koreans' independent spirit. Han China managed to dash the Koreans' desire to maintain a state that was strong enough to withstand the powerful Chinese Empire. Nevertheless, the aspirations of the Korean people were not completely lost, for the Chinese occupation prompted an intense nationalistic resistance that ultimately led to the birth of three Korean kingdoms: Koguryo, Paeckche, and Silla.[13] During the ensuing period of the Three Kingdoms, the Korean people for the first time realized their potential of building culturally-refined, politically-sophisticated states which were strong enough to defeat waves of Chinese onslaughts. Most of all, they were to create and preserve a magnificent cultural foundation for the Korean nation.

3. Emergence of the Three Kingdoms

Toward the end of the first century B.C., Han China's territorial expansion in the northeast ceased. In 68 B.C. Han was forced to abandon all its military garrisons beyond the Great Wall and to reduce its political sphere to south-central China. The Han Dynasty's political fortunes continued to decline until the usurper Wang Mang replaced the Han court in 9 A.D. Although the Han Dynasty was restored as Later Han after Wang's brief reign, it never regained its former prestige or power. Instead, China fell into a long, painful period of internal struggles plagued by military dictatorships and anarchy until the middle of the sixth century. As a result, the Korea-China relations were relatively quiescent for a long period. China's presence on the Manchurian plain amounted to the establishment of only two minor colonies during the period, both in North Wei.

Neither the Korean tribal states that had remained beyond the political control of the Han colonies nor Korean citizens restless under the Han occupation missed this opportunity to eradicate Han's colonial apparatus from the Korean territory. Having rejected Chinese colonial power even during the prime of the Han Dynasty, the Korean tribes were caught up in a fever of nation building when they succeeded in driving the Han colonies out from their territory. As a result, the political map of Korea was drastically changed during the late first century B.C. In place of the Han colonies there emerged three Korean kingdoms with cohesive and centralized political structures. Unlike Gohchosun, the three new kingdoms effectively occupied the territory, extending from the Manchurian plain to the southern part of the Korean Peninsula. Although this territory was divided among the three rival kingdoms, this momentous development represented an auspicious beginning for the Hahn people's arduous journey in laying out the foundation for one of the most successful civilizations in the region.[14]

Silla was the first of the three kingdoms to emerge in this period of strong nation-building energy. It was founded in 57 B.C. in the southeastern corner of the Korean peninsula, the land of the Saro-Kuk tribal state. Unlike the rulers of the two contemporary kingdoms, the rulers of Silla came from ruling families of local Saro-Kuk tribes. Silla's early leadership demonstrated an uncommon ability to overcome the complicated problems of unifying many different tribal interests in its nation-building process. Its practice of reaching amicable compromises and avoiding destructive tribal confrontations greatly helped Silla achieve the nation-creating transformation quickly and also effectively eliminated opportunities for the Chinese to interfere or exercise influence. Silla's early administrative and political structures did not reflect Chinese systems very much. The fact that the Saro-Kuk region was beyond the direct control of any Han colony must have helped Silla remain free of Chinese influence during the period.

Because of its relatively isolated location, Silla among the three kingdoms was in the best position to develop an indigenous system not contaminated by external interferences. Long sheltered from foreign incursions, it utilized the period of tranquility effectively for its nation-building process, although a dearth of Chinese impact was a reason its transformation took a longer period than did its two rival kingdoms. In spite of its loose coalition of diverse tribal interests, Silla soon achieved the state of a functioning monarchy by wisely managing the succession to the throne without suffering disruptive dissension. Without having to commit national resources for major military conflicts, the kingdom's economy fared well. By the late forth century Silla's nation-building had evolved to form the new political system, a centralized monarchy that discarded a loose tribal coalition. By the sixth century it further strengthened the power of the monarchy by adopting an extensive legal system.

In spite of its slower development and dependence on essentially indigenous governing systems, Silla not only survived five centuries of intensive military and political competition but eventually prevailed over its more militaristic and "cultured" rivals. Silla's harmonious political process, a stable economy, and a well-trained, highly motivated military force were the sources of its strength. Yet these could not have given the small, isolated kingdom enough edge to defeat its more powerful rivals. Relentless invasions launched by both the Sui and Tang courts of China drastically altered the balance of power on the Korean peninsula and the Manchurian plain.

Koguryo, the second of the Three Kingdoms, emerged during the first century B.C.[15] It was founded by exiled military leaders of old Buyeo, a loosely built Korean tribal state that ruled northern Manchuria. Koguryo, the most militant and aggressive kingdom the Korean people ever founded, conquered a number of tribes in the region and soon occupied most of the Manchurian plain and the northern half of the Korean peninsula. In terms of territory Koguryo was not only the largest of the three kingdoms but also the largest state in Korea's history. With a strong military force and expansion-oriented leaders, Koguryo became a formidable Korean state capable of checking China's advance into the region. Sharing its poorly defined territorial border with the Chinese states, it maintained from the early period a policy of steadfast defiance. It also adopted a posture of arrogance and militancy toward the rival kingdoms in the south. Both in spirit and in strength Koguryo was the most competent power in northeast Asia.

Having succeeded to the traditions of Gohchosun and Buyeo, Koguryo quickly and firmly consolidated its power in the region. During the early part of its nation building, Koguryo managed to establish firm control over most of the Manchurian plain, taking advantage of troubled Han China, which remained preoccupied by domestic instability and thus hardly in a position to challenge Koguryo's military might. Nevertheless, like its spiritual predecessor Gohchosun, an increasingly powerful Koguryo inevitably came into conflict with the Chinese states. The first military contest between Koguryo and Han erupted in the early third century over the control of the Liaodong peninsula, a resource-rich region of southern Manchuria regarded as the natural passage for a Chinese advance into the region and therefore a key defense line for the Koguryo kingdom. When a military confrontation became unavoidable, Koguryo launched a preemptive strike against Wi China in 242.[16] The campaign was inconclusive but provided an excuse for Wi China to launch an attack against Koguryo. Two years later, Wi sent a force of 20,000 men against Koguryo and forced the Hahn kingdom to retreat to the Yalu River. The first military confrontation was a bitter setback for Koguryo, but it never conceded the territory to the Chinese, and in 313 Koguryo's King Michon launched successful military campaigns against vastly more populous China. Through this campaign Koguryo not only avenged its earlier defeat but also conquered the remnant of the Chinese colonies, Laklang, and ended four centuries of Chinese presence in Korea. Eradication of the Chinese colonies brought Koguryo and its southern neighbor, the Paeckche kingdom, into direct contact. Militant Koguryo and the suspicious Paeckche kingdoms were natural rivals who came to share a common border. Relations between the two kingdoms deteriorated rapidly.

While its southern border was still unstable, Koguryo also faced Earlier Yen China, the kingdom that replaced Wi in northern China along its northwestern frontier. This new adversary, founded by a nomadic tribe of central Asia, was an aggressive power that inflicted a severe military defeat on Koguryo in 342. During this period Koguryo not only had to stand against superior forces of Chinese states but also had to cope with the increasingly competent and bold Paeckche kingdom along its southern border. Paeckche was equally determined to subdue Koguryo and caused it a humiliating defeat in 371. In spite of these costly losses, Koguryo survived and managed to build a military force capable of resisting Chinese incursions and challenging its southern rivals for supremacy on the Korean peninsula.

Paeckche was the last kingdom to emerge in this period of nation building. It was founded by leaders of an exiled Koguryo ruling class in the west-central region of the peninsula. Like Koguryo, Paeckche was a distant descendant of the Buyeo Kingdom of northern Manchuria and harbored a desire to recover the vast Manchurian plain. Paeckche's location afforded it fertile agricultural land and an easy access to Korea's western sea. It shared common borders with two hostile neighbors, Koguryo on the north and Silla on the east. Nevertheless, benefiting from Koguryo's preoccupation with the Chinese states and Silla's slow development, Paeckche continued to expand its domain to the southwest, where it commanded the peninsula's richest agricultural region and long shorelines. In the latter part of the fourth century growing national strength and pressure from the competing Korean kingdoms prompted Paeckche to extend relations to East Chin China and Japan.[17] By then Paeckche had built a state strong enough to enter a three-way competition for the right to rule the entire Korean peninsula and the Korean territory in Manchuria.

All three kingdoms had arisen from small but progressive tribal states that had successfully conquered other tribes in the process. In a sense it was the same process of elimination when the three kingdoms plunged into military contests among themselves. When they had solidified their political domains, the three kingdoms were to compete for rule of a unified Korea. Intense, quickly formed rivalry among the three Korean states overshadowed strategic needs to present a common front against mighty China. They were yet to form a sense of common fate, a unity as one nation rather than three quarreling states that would have enabled the Hahn people to withstand Chinese incursions and maintain their own national identity.

The major combatants of the long unification struggle were not just the Korean kingdoms. The deep involvement of China made the Hahn people's domestic struggle profoundly more consequential. The war of unification was not like the military confrontation between Gohchosun and Han China, which was filled with nationalistic fervor for control of the Manchurian plain. The unification contest was in essence a war of survival in which the participants did not hesitate to import foreign forces and to seek alliances with neighbors.

Fundamental incompatibility among the three kingdoms was more emotional and political than anything else. Emotional cleavages among the three kingdoms can be traced back to their myths about the founding of the kingdoms. According to the myths, Koguryo and Paeckche were founded by military heroes of the old Buyeo Kingdom, while Silla was founded by a man given by Heaven to a ruling family of Gohchosun. Thus each of the three kingdoms laid claim to being a direct descendant of the Korean states of Gohchosun and Buyeo, and thus each was compelled to recapture the old glory by unifying the Korean peninsula and reclaiming the Manchurian plain. Furthermore, the three kingdoms passed through the stages of nation-building at different periods of time, which made it difficult for them to maintain an equilibrium of power. Koguryo, with ready access to Chinese culture and to the remnants of the Han colonies, as well as its huge size and militant character, had the best opportunity to unify the peninsula. The confident Koguryo was openly contemptuous of Silla, calling it an "eastern barbarian," and tried to install itself over its smaller southern rivals. As the legitimate ruling group of old Korean territory in the Manchurian plain, Koguryo was the dominant power during the early part of the unification contest.

Both the Paeckche and the Silla kingdoms also shared the aspiration for predominance in the struggle. Utilizing its geographic advantages, Paeckche made itself a formidable contender; it traded with China along the sea routes while building national wealth and military power on a rich agricultural economy. It also maintained a close relationship with Japan, sharing with the island nation its sophisticated culture. Silla, owing to its distant and isolated location and lacking Koguryo's militarism and Paeckche's diplomatic arts, lagged behind the two rivals during the early period of the struggle. But motivated by its precarious position in the three-way struggle, Silla aggressively developed various indigenous political systems which later proved to be critical to its ultimate victory over its more powerful rivals. One of Silla's invaluable educational institutions was the Hwa-Rang-Do, a highly effective training program for promising young men of the kingdom. The program, which emphasized the Five Rules, produced not only many elite military leaders but also a highly motivated ruling class.[18] As a political organ Silla invented the Hwa Baek system, a decision-making practice requiring unanimous consent which helped hold the feudal kingdom together. In addition, because of its unfavorable location Silla came to comprehend the regional geopolitics better and readily went along with strategic alliances to achieve its objectives.

By the fourth century the stage was set for the most brutal upheaval the Korean peninsula had ever experienced. The strife continued through three periods: the first was the fourth to fifth century, dominated by militarily superior Koguryo; the second was the sixth century, during which Silla made giant strides to become a legitimate contender; and the third was the seventh century, ending in unification and during which unified China periodically interceded in the conflict.

The Three Kingdoms(7th century)

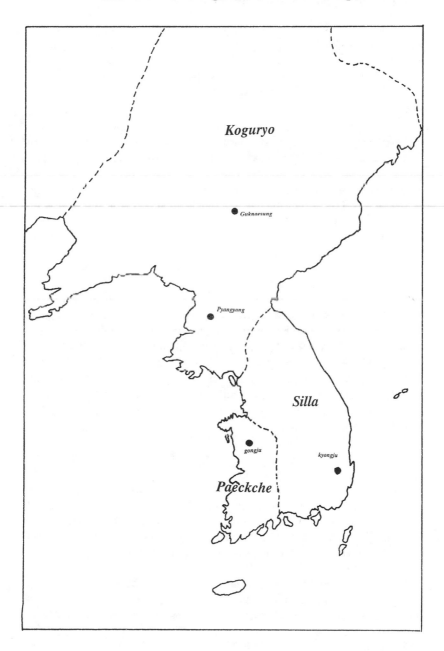

4. Koguryo's Spirited Stand against China

Koguryo's glory began in 391 A.D. with the enthroning of a young ruler posthumously named King Gwanggaeto.[19] The king, an ambitious military genius, commenced a large-scale military campaign the very year he came to the throne. He first neutralized Paeckche's threat by successfully attacking and taking some Paeckche territory along the Limjin River. Having secured his southern border, the king led his army to subjugate troublesome neighboring nomadic tribes in northern Manchuria. Koguryo's highly mobile horse-mounted army was unstoppable, and it soon pacified the northern border region. In 396 the king led another campaign against Paeckche, pursuing a total subjugation of his southern rival. On this expedition the Koguryo army appropriated Paeckche territory north of the Limjin River and gained Paeckche's formal pledge of loyalty to the Koguryo court. King Gwanggaeto's failure to incorporate the entire Paeckche territory but instead to be content with a pledge from the defeated Paeckche monarch offers no logical explanation. In spite of the setback, a formal submission to the Koguryo king, Paeckche had neither a solid nor long-lasting loyalty to the arrangement and remained a valid contender in the unification contest.

In 397 the three-way struggle became even more complicated by Paeckche's use of a Japanese force in its invasion of Silla. Koguryo responded to the development by sending its forces to help Silla. Paeckche's joint military venture with Japan was counterproductive because it encouraged the rapprochement between Koguryo and Silla, leaving Paeckche even more vulnerable. After securing Silla's friendship and defeating Paeckche's attempt on Silla, Koguryo was ready to turn its attention to Eastern Chin, a Chinese state with which it shared a long but ill-defined border.

In 398, Koguryo launched a large-scale military expedition against Eastern Chin. After the highly successful campaign the Koguryo king moved a large number of Koreans to the conquered northern Chinese territory. Koguryo intended to establish a buffer zone populated by its own people to discourage Chinese incursions. In 402, King Gwanggaeto led another successful campaign, this one against the Chinese state of the Later Yeon, and established more border garrisons. As Koguryo's military penetration reached northern China, the entire region of Liaodong was firmly under the Korean control.

The Koguryo king continued to conquer nomadic tribes on the Mongolian-Manchurian plain until his death in 414. King Gwanggaeto realized the dream of the Hahn people, regaining all territories that had once belonged to the Gohchosun and Buyeo kingdoms. His territory extended to the Amur River on the north, the Limjin River on the south, and the Inner Mongolian Plain and northern China on the west. Koguryo had refused to be confined to the congested Korean Peninsula but had extended its territories throughout northeast Asia. This feat, accomplished in such a short period, is unique in the history of Korea and has never been duplicated. Had successive Hahn states managed to hold on to the territory, Korea would have remained one of the major powers of northeast Asia, one that could have challenged China and Japan for leadership of the region.

Koguryo's dominance in northeast Asia continued even after the death of King Gwanggaeto, a truly remarkable Korean hero. His able son, King Jangsoo, upheld the nation's proud military tradition by maintaining an effective military force which he utilized to protect Koguryo's vast territory. In spite of its continued militancy, however, Koguryo's China policy underwent a major revision after the death of King Gwanggaeto. For the first time in history it adopted a policy of appeasement to complement its militant confrontation; it initiated diplomatic relations with both the Northern and Southern dynasties.[20] Although Koguryo's steadfast stand against Chinese ambitions over the Manchurian plain remained in place for a while, the kingdom's strategic position in the region was increasingly undermined by the initiatives taken by King Jangsoo.

Among many initiatives Koguryo undertook during the post-King Gwanggaeto period, its ill-conceived transfer of its capital to Pyongyang was the most puzzling and had far-reaching consequences. The former capital, Kungnaesung, in the present day Jinan in the mountainous upper Yalu region in Manchuria, was far more suitable as a field headquarters for the ever-active Koguryo military machine in the Manchurian plain than as a capital for a stable nation.[21] Nevertheless, the new site for the court, Pyongyang, located in a fertile farming plain on the Daedong River in northern Korea, was a questionable choice as the capital for Koguryo, which had to administer a vast territory extending from the Manchurian plain to northern Korea. The transfer signified the fact that Koguryo had drastically revised its strategic posture in relation to China and also to its southern rivals. The capital change served as a formal statement that Koguryo's territorial expansion in the north had reached its limits and that the kingdom had chosen a defensive stance. It was a tacit but unmistakable message to China that Koguryo no longer intended to continue its territorial expansion along China's northeastern frontier. Koguryo's vast territorial gains on the Manchurian and Mongolian plains had been achieved by a small force of highly mobile and ferocious cavalry. Koguryo might have realized that its national strength could have ill afforded full-scale military conflicts with China. In any event, Koguryo, by transferring its capital to Pyongyang, in effect declared a truce with China. Meanwhile, it was an open declaration for a new front on the south. Koguryo was to utilize its potent energy in southward expansion and in the unification contest.

Whether Koguryo simply became complacent about its relations with its northern nomadic neighbors after King Gwanggaeto's unchallenged successes or whether it hoped to maintain a status quo with China, it soon learned its grave mistake. China quickly adopted an aggressive policy toward the Pyongyang-based Koguryo kingdom. Destructive China-Koguryo confrontations that overwhelmed the Manchurian Plain and northern Korea for decades were an eloquent testimony that Koguryo's territorial interests could have been better served by a transfer of its capital to a location in northern Manchuria, from which it could have governed the conquered territory more effectively. Koguryo based in Pyongyang became the most formidable power in the Korean peninsula but lost its effective control over the strategic Manchurian plain.

From its new capital in Pyongyang, Koguryo directed its energies toward restructuring its domestic governing systems and strengthening the power of its monarchs. For these domestic purposes the transfer of the capital proved to be highly beneficial: it enhanced the power of the monarch by neutralizing the political power of five tribes based around the old capital. To facilitate its political reform, Koguryo undertook a large-scale political purge of "old guards" while encouraging the rise of new bureaucratic aristocracies. Furthermore, taking advantage of Pyongyang's excellent geographic features, Koguryo tried to build a comprehensively functional capital. The kingdom of relentless military energy was seeking to become a nation of cultural taste with a stable governing body. In a sense, Koguryo undertook an ambitious task of transforming a military government into a balanced and stable civilian government similar to those already developed by its southern rivals.

Naturally, the actions taken by the Koguryo court alarmed both Silla and Paeckche. Their reaction to Koguryo's apparent intention to become the foremost power on the Korean peninsula was formation of a defensive alliance. This Paeckche-Silla alliance, signed in 433, was effective in keeping the ambitious Koguryo at bay for several decades. It was not until 475 that Koguryo was able to mount its first major campaign against Paeckche. When the offense was launched, however, Koguryo's powerful military quickly defeated Paeckche, conquering a large part of Paeckche's northern territory. By this conquest Koguryo gained control of the largest part by far of Hahn territory, which included most of the central part of the peninsula.

In the following decades, although Koguryo maintained military pressure on its southern neighbors, the Paeckche-Silla alliance stood firm and was generally effective in preventing Koguryo from expanding farther south. The balance of power between Koguryo and the Paeckche-Silla alliance prevailed for the next half century. China still had to recover from internal turmoil before it could attempt a campaign against Koguryo. The rare tranquillity that settled over the quarrelsome kingdoms of the Korean peninsula was not, however, a blessing for militant Koguryo. Instead of capitalizing on a period of peace and calm, Koguryo's ruling class allowed itself to plunge into fatal political infighting, revealing its critical vulnerability to its opportunistic enemies.

The Paeckche-Silla alliance seized the opportunity presented by Koguryo's domestic squabble by launching an attack in 551; Koguryo, the strongest military power in the peninsula, had to surrender a large territory along the Hahn River. Once the common enemy was checked, however, the Paeckche-Silla alliance crumbled, and the old rivalry between them resumed; Silla launched its campaign against its former ally, seizing the Koguryo territory that Paeckche had occupied. Paeckche retaliated to the attack by initiating its own crusade against Silla, only to be badly defeated. As the power of wounded Koguryo and battered Paeckche was significantly reduced, Silla came to emerge as the strongest of the three kingdoms.

The shift in the balance of power among the three contenders led to another realignment, an alliance between Koguryo and Paeckche, former mortal enemies. The new alliance was a clear indication that Silla was a rising power in the peninsula. Silla benefited from its newly acquired farmlands in the central section of the peninsula for its food supply and its new west-coast territory, which provided the kingdom a direct sea route to China. Unlike the quarreling Koguryo and Paeckche courts, the Silla court was run by highly nationalistic leaders under its unique, consensus-oriented governing system. Silla was mostly beyond the direct influence of China during the early unification struggle and had yet to develop a cultural dependency on China or an "inferiority complex"; Silla considered itself the equal of the Chinese states. Geographic isolation from both China and the other Korean kingdoms during its early nation-building stage allowed Silla to develop a critical edge over its rivals, a national unity that was hardened by an independent spirit. Growing military strength, adept diplomatic maneuvering, and the peninsula's unique geographic characteristics were to bestow upon Silla an overwhelming advantage in the final stage of the contest for the unification of the peninsula.

In 589, after a hard-fought internal struggle that lasted for more than two centuries, China was once again united by the Sui court. Inevitably the emergence of an aggressive Sui compounded the already complex political landscape in northeast Asia. Silla quickly sought an alliance with the new Chinese state, which alarmed Turks in northern Asia, Koguryo and Paeckche on the Korean peninsula, and Japan. These groups sought to establish a common defense by forming a coalition, which never materialized. Soon all the major powers in the region were involved to some degree in the new power game. The outcome of this grand contest affected the political configuration of the region for a long time to come.

As expected, the new regional conflict was ignited with Sui's resumption of Han China's campaign against Koguryo. Sui invaded the Korean kingdom in 598 with an army of 300,000 men. The numerically outnumbered Koguryo forces utilized various defensive tactics, and after a protracted war of attrition they eventually succeeded in forcing the invaders to retreat with heavy casualties. The first invasion was fought in the Liaodong region, and the Sui forces failed to advance to the Koguryo territory in Manchuria or on to the Korean peninsula. Nevertheless, the resolute Sui launched a second Korean campaign in 612 with an army of more than one million men. Mindful of its previous failure, Sui launched both land and sea borne attacks; while the army was invading the Liaodong region, the sea borne force crossed the Western Sea and attacked Pyongyang. Sui's all-out attack was intended to subjugate the stubborn Koguryo once and for all. However, the skillful Koguryo defenders prevailed over the invaders again. The invasion forces that managed to penetrate north of the Pyongyang castle were wiped out at the Salsoo River by the Koguryo forces led by General Elzimunduk, the commander of Koguryo forces.[22] Single-minded Sui launched successive invasions on Koguryo in 613 and 614, but its invading forces met a similar fate. The Koguryo forces were at a relative disadvantage in numbers, but they overcame it with resourceful tactics and steely determination to defend their territory.

The costly and disastrous military campaigns against Koguryo brought Sui domestic turmoil. Peasant revolts erupted as a result of abusive requisitions imposed upon them to support the unpopular invasions. The Sui Dynasty, which had committed much of its national energy to the unsuccessful conquest of Koguryo and had been further weakened by costly public works projects and campaigns against other neighbors, was toppled in 618. However, the collapse of Sui did not mean that Koguryo was free of

Chinese territorial ambitions. On the contrary, Sui China was replaced by another dynasty, Tang, which shared basically the same view of relations between the Middle Kingdom and its smaller neighbors. Koguryo was to learn that Tang China was equally determined to pursue military conquest of the Korean peninsula. China, regardless of the dynasty that was in control, intended to conquer the Korean states, and only Koguryo was strong enough to challenge its avaricious behavior.

Relations between Koguryo and Tang China were calm, however, during the period in which the new dynasty was preoccupied with immediate tasks of political consolidation. Koguryo was too well aware of the danger of provoking the greatest land power of the region, and Tang no doubt understood the risk of invading the determined Korean state that had largely caused the downfall of the Sui Dynasty. As a result, a status quo prevailed for a time. Nevertheless, by then Koguryo was all too familiar with Chinese behavior. It did not become complacent but proceeded to build a new defensive wall in preparation for the next onslaught. Meantime, Koguryo's ambitious Yeongaesomun seized extraordinary power and appointed himself as the wartime military dictator. He pursued a militant policy against Silla, Tang's Korean ally, escalating a Koguryo-Silla confrontation. Koguryo repeatedly sent expedition forces to recover its old territory, now held by Silla. Eventually Koguryo's repeated campaigns against Silla provided Tang an excuse to intervene. By then Tang had achieved the greatest military expansion in the history of China, having conquered nomadic tribes along its western and northern borders. Tang China became the third major Chinese dynasty to attack a Korean state when it invaded Koguryo by both land and sea forces in 644. Tang's allies, the Turks and Silla, participated to the invasion, and Koguryo had to fight all these adversaries simultaneously. Again the Koguryo defenders faced numerically superior Tang forces in the strategic Liaodong region. Again they were resolute in blocking the invader's advance, waging gallant resistance at the Ansisung castle under the leadership of General Yang Man Chun. In the castle Koguryo forces endured a ten-month-long Tang siege but managed in the end to defeat the attackers. China had suffered yet another bitter defeat at the hands of determined Koguryo defenders.

Notwithstanding its failure to unify the Korean peninsula, Koguryo's triumph against both the Sui and Tang dynasties was the glory of the Korean people and one of the memorable events in Korean history. Not only did it crush the Chinese ambitions to annex the peninsula, but also it gave the Hahn people the confidence that Korea could overcome Chinese attempts. If the Sui or Tang invasions had been successful in conquering Koguryo, it would have been easier for Chinese states to subdue the weaker and less militant Silla and Paeckche kingdoms. Although Koguryo eventually collapsed, exhausted by years of warfare against powerful invaders, its crucial role in defending the Korean peninsula from the Chinese can hardly be exaggerated. Without Koguryo's valorous resistance, Korean history might have become a part of Chinese history some thirteen centuries ago.

Once Tang's invasion was repelled, the unification struggle resumed. First Paeckche took the initiative and attacked its rival Silla, seeking to isolate Silla from Tang by denying Silla access to the west coast ports. Paeckche's belligerence compelled Silla to seek an ally. It approached both Japan and Koguryo. Failing to form an alliance with these neighbors, Silla then turned to Tang, which was still smarting from defeat by Koguryo. Naturally Tang did not miss this excellent opportunity and entered a formal military alliance with Silla. When the contest resumed, Koguryo and Paeckche proved to be too weak and dispirited to resist the rising power of Silla and the still mighty Tang China. By the late seventh century the end of the Three Kingdoms era was approaching. The Tang-Silla forces attacked and defeated Paeckche in 660, ending a reign that had lasted for 679 years. After Paeckche was subdued, Tang forces proceeded to attack Koguryo without the participation of Silla, which, weakened by internal problems and the Paeckche campaign, was not ready to challenge Koguryo. Again Tang experienced a setback as Koguryo mustered the strength to defeat the invaders. By that time, however, the political fortunes of Koguryo had begun a rapid decline. The process was even more swift after the death of its dictatorial leader, Yeongaesomun. In 668, Silla and Tang forces invaded Koguryo and brought down that proud kingdom which had ruled the Manchurian plain and repeatedly defeated military attempts of powerful Chinese dynasties for nearly seven centuries.

If Silla's intention in bringing Tang into the Korean struggle was no more than to gain military assistance, Tang apparently had a grander scheme in mind. Tang seized the opportunity to conquer the whole peninsula under the pretext of aiding its ally. After Koguryo's defeat, Tang created colonial prefectures throughout the Korean peninsula, including Silla itself. Tang China had finally achieved its territorial ambition in the Korean peninsula by manipulating the Hahn people's inability to settle domestic squabbles among themselves.

It was Silla's turn to confront Tang China's territorial ambitions and regain the territorial integrity of the Hahn people. With help from forces still loyal to the defeated Paeckche and Koguryo kingdoms, Silla waged long, hard campaigns against the Chinese occupation forces. Still Silla had to wait until 676 to claim sovereign power over the unified territory as Tang's last colonial prefecture command was evacuated from Pyongyang.[23] It had taken the Hahn people more than seven hundred years to unify the three kingdoms under a single government. Although the unification was a momentous event in Korean history, Silla was unable to claim control of all of the three kingdoms' former territories; Koguryo's old territories in Manchuria and northern Korea remained beyond Silla's control. Silla's inability to recapture the entire Koguryo territory might have been a direct cause for the Hahn people's eventual losing the control of the Manchurian plain.

Notwithstanding the political reality, the Koreans' emotional and historic attachment to the Manchurian plain was steadfast; they refused to relinquish their claim to the old Koguryo territories. In 698 Dae Jo Young, a Koguryo general, founded the Balhae Kingdom in present-day Jilin in northern Manchuria. Unlike other small rebellions staged by former Koguryo citizens who refused to submit to Silla and remained beyond its control for a prolonged period, the Balhae Kingdom was a fully independent state committed to rebuilding Koguryo. At the peak of its power Balhae ruled the vast northern Manchurian plain and much of eastern Siberia. Although Balhae's population included a large number of Tartars and other nomadic tribes, its ruling classes were largely descended from those of Koguryo. Balhae pursued territorial expansion in the north and in the south, where it encountered Tang. Initially Tang was conciliatory to Balhae as it was with other minor states founded by Koguryo descendants and conferred a regional kingship on the Balhae monarch in 713. Yet when Balhae continued to expand its territory, Tang again allied with Silla to check Balhae, which responded by establishing friendly relations with the Turks and the Japanese.

Balhae failed to evolve into a mature power that could replace Silla in spite of its control of vast territories and its Tang-style culture, which flourished particularly during the ninth century. It floundered in channeling its considerable energy into building a stable nation, unable to overcome serious disadvantages, such as sparse, nomadic population and limited food supply. Balhae's collapse was sudden; the new power of the region, Khitan, crushed Tang and Balhae in 907 and in 927 respectively.[24] Balhae was the last Hahn state to dominate the old territory of Gohchosun and Koguryo. In this strategic region Koreans had stood against numerically superior Chinese forces time after time with determination and confidence. But as Balhae collapsed and Silla confined itself to the south of the Pyongyang region, the old Koguryo territory held by the Hahn people for more than ten centuries was finally lost.

5. Geopolitics of the Unification

The eventual unification of the Korean peninsula was to be expected, considering its homogeneous population and its small size. Yet the unification came much later than it might have been. Compared to developments in China, which realized its first continent-size dynasty in 221 B.C., Korea's unification was a prolonged struggle. When it finally came about, the unification provided the Hahn people an invaluable opportunity to develop a sense of oneness as a nation for the first time in their history. Identity as a single nation with a common fate began to be instilled in the minds of Koreans who had fought each other for the entire period of their existence. Still, the wounds of that bloody rivalry were deep and slow to heal. Reconciling centuries-old ill feelings was extremely difficult, as evidenced by strong reactions in the old territories of Koguryo and Paeckche. In spite of Silla's various gestures of appeasement toward former citizens of Paeckche and Koguryo, many chose to rebel against the Silla court and tried to create separate states. Widespread dissension in the defeated kingdoms made the national reconciliation time-consuming. Nevertheless, Silla's political control was firm and effective, albeit over a much smaller territory than the one occupied by the three kingdoms. The sporadic rebellions were in general contained, although they remained troublesome throughout the entire period of the unified Silla. Even in the highly cultured Silla society the emotional divisions produced by seven centuries of rivalry were not banished quickly. The unification came almost too late for the emotional chasms to close quickly. It was quite different from the Chinese experience; although factionalism often swept through it, China always managed to reunite under a new dynasty after a fairly short period of disorder. China would not have survived as a cohesive empire without the periodic reassurance of oneness.

Silla's eventual triumph in the unification race was possible because of its ability and willingness to skillfully manipulate geopolitics of the peninsula. The outcome depended not so much on which kingdom was most capable in terms of leadership and military skill as on the ability to survive. In the long and costly struggle the ultimate survivor became the victor. China made a profound contribution to this outcome by forcing the mightiest kingdom, Koguryo, into exhaustion from repeated warfare. At the end no kingdom, even victorious Silla, was strong enough to prevent Chinese occupation of the peninsula. If there had been no Chinese invasion of Koguryo, the outcome of the unification struggle might have been entirely different. Koguryo's ambition to unify the peninsula under its leadership was undermined by never-ending Chinese hostility. Koguryo, preoccupied with the Chinese, had no time or resources to devise and carry out an effective plan to subdue its southern rivals. Sui and Tang China's relentless assaults on Koguryo gave Paeckche and Silla breathing room to build their kingdoms so that eventually they could face Koguryo on equal footing. Koguryo had to face three rivals, one of which happened to be China. In the end, Koguryo was defeated by the Chinese Empire, not by its southern brothers.

Koguryo committed some strategic blunders in its struggle with its southern rivals. First, it consistently underestimated their strength. As a result its expeditions against them failed to produce a gradual unification but only achieved minor territorial gains and pledges of friendship or elusive subordination. Koguryo's last expedition against Paeckche was victorious enough to annex Paeckche to Koguryo. Yet Koguryo demanded only minor territorial concessions and Paeckche's loyalty to its court. Paeckche recovered from this setback and later inflicted a major blow on Koguryo. The construction of the defensive wall in the Liaodong region by Yeongaesomun proved immensely costly but ineffective. The transfer of the capital to Pyongyang may have been detrimental. the court located in Pyongyang was too far from the Liaodong front, where most military engagements took place. While Pyongyang was too distant to provide a timely leadership in the front, it was not immune from China's sea borne attacks.

Perhaps a more fundamental strategic error committed by Koguryo was its profound inclination to surround itself with hostile rivals. Koguryo could have formed an effective alliance with one of its southern rivals, thereby neutralizing the other while it was engaged against the Chinese. Koguryo's mastery of military tactics, demonstrated so plainly in its wars with the Sui and Tang dynasties, was not matched by its dexterity in political maneuvering. Koguryo, built and maintained by spectacular military successes against numerically superior forces, failed to outgrow its rigid militarism and to develop flexible political strategies. Nonmilitary considerations, such as the welfare of its people, were ignored by rulers perpetually absorbed in military matters. In the end the lack of a comprehensive understanding of its unique geopolitics cost Koguryo the opportunity to unify the peninsula and the Manchurian plain under its banner.

Paeckche's performance in the tripartite struggle was relatively insignificant. Considering its more favorable geopolitical position, Paeckche's early abandonment of unification aspirations was puzzling. The Paeckche society had not only displayed a highly dynamic and enterprising personality as manifested by its willingness to import and adopt Chinese culture, but it also employed at times the most refined and sophisticated diplomacy among the three kingdoms. In contrast, Koguryo was resolutely militaristic and uncompromising, while Silla was isolated and intensely inward. With flexibility no other kingdom was able to master, Paeckche maintained a fairly amiable relationship with Chinese empires most of time and made pivotal contributions to the cultural development of Japan. Unlike its two rivals, Paeckche enjoyed the friendship of its two distant neighbors, although neither shared a common border with it.

Paeckche's advantageous geopolitical position was not restricted to international relations; it ruled a rich, densely populated agricultural region. With these advantages Paeckche might have had as much opportunity to unify the three kingdoms as the others, if not more. A complete comprehension of Paeckche's poor performance in the unification drive remains unattainable owing to the lack of written records. Nevertheless, the prime reason appears to have been its geography and its foreign policy, the very factors commonly considered to have been its advantages.

Paeckche's territory was a serious liability. It was difficult to defend, particularly against the highly mobile Koguryo horsemen. The territory, the west-central plain of the peninsula, extended to Koguryo's northwest plain with no major natural obstacles between the two kingdoms. In a sense, Paeckche's northern front remained open to Koguryo forces. Of course, the same point can be made about Koguryo's southern front. Naturally, the geography favored the more militaristic Koguryo. Under constant pressure from aggressive Koguryo, Paeckche never really enjoyed a tranquil period during which it could gain sufficient national strength to win the unification race. On the other hand, its eastern border, which separated it from Silla, was a natural obstacle to its advance on Silla. The mountain range shielded Silla from Paeckche intrusion. In fact, Paeckche's geography was such that it was open to stronger Koguryo but closed to weaker Silla, a formidable prescription for being conquered but not to conquer.

Paeckche's close ties with Japan was a negative factor in its unification struggle. Because of Japan's notorious piracy with its repeated raids on the region's seacoasts, it was shunned not only by the Korean kingdoms but also by the Chinese states. Paeckche's de facto alliance with Japan was viewed with suspicion and contempt by the other Korean kingdoms. Moreover, Japan's military assistance to Paeckche proved to be inconsequential. In spite of Paeckche's contributions, Japan's insular culture was yet to develop the military might capable of effectively intervening in Korean politics. It had to wait a long while to do so.

Silla's ability to unify the peninsula was the result of its deliberate cultivation of national power and foreign alliances during a period when its rivals' political power was at a low ebb. Neither the exhausted Koguryo nor the confused and dispirited Paeckche was capable of matching the rising power of Silla. The irony was that the intense unification struggle went on so long that the initially weaker Silla eventually caught up with the other two kingdoms. Silla's quest for a unified Korea under its banner benefited most by its seemingly disadvantageous location, the southeast corner of the peninsula. That remote location, particularly in a sense that "civilization" entered the peninsula from the north, was responsible for Silla's delayed cultural development. On the other hand, the location, bordered by rough mountain ranges on both the northern and the western fronts, was highly advantageous for defending the kingdom from the rival kingdoms. In spite of repeated attempts, both Koguryo and Paeckche invasion forces had difficulty reaching the capital of Silla. Its location was also an obvious hindrance to Silla's desire to maintain close relations with China. But, ironically, the lack of foreign cultural influence gave Silla's indigenous culture time to mature and thus to make an orderly transition from a tribal state to centralized monarchy. Moreover, the long tranquillity Silla experienced, mainly owing to its isolated location, made possible the establishment of civilian control over national affairs, in contrast to Koguryo, where civilian control was never established owing to constant military pressure from Chinese states.

Silla was deliberate and patient in the unification contest, while Koguryo and Paeckche were aggressive and impulsive. While Koguryo and Paeckche were involved in costly but inconclusive border clashes, Silla concentrated its energy on building a stronger and wealthier nation. It was not until 562 that Silla demonstrated its military might, conquering the Kaya Kingdom, which had been a source of long and bitter dispute between Paeckche and Silla. Silla was circumspect until it was ready to emerge as a power capable of competing with its rivals for the long-coveted leadership of the peninsula.

To opportunistic and imperialistic Tang China, Silla's ascendancy over the rival kingdoms represented its best opportunity to realize its long-frustrated ambition, the subjugation of the Korean states. Silla was perceived neither as the formidable military power that Koguryo had been nor as the master of diplomacy as Paeckche had been. Tang's low esteem of Silla was abundantly clear in its rude treatment of the kingdom after Tang and Silla's joint military expeditions brought the other two kingdoms to submission.

Korea's physical and cultural characteristics were detrimental to early unification. Separated by mountain ranges and independent cultural heritages, inhabitants of the peninsula did not develop a sense of oneness during the Three Kingdoms period. Indeed, for all the kingdoms the three-way contest was more for survival than for unification of the Hahn people; motivation to unify the Hahn people for the betterment of all the people was conspicuously absent.

The conflict, which lasted off and on for more than five centuries, caused severe impoverishment of the peninsula as a whole. Even after the Unified Silla gained control, the peninsula continued to suffer from dissension and violence. Moreover, one third of the peninsula remained beyond the control of Silla, which was able to exercise power over only a small portion of the territory the three kingdoms had once dominated, and the control of the strategic Manchurian plain escaped the Hahn people's grip forever. Silla brought a unified government to the Korean people but tragically failed to secure the whole territory.

6. The Unified Silla

The Unified Silla Kingdom ruled the Korean peninsula for 240 years. As the name of the kingdom implies, the Unified Silla was not much different from the old Silla except that it controlled a larger territory and more subjects. It failed to evolve into a new dynasty with new visions and nation-building energy. Rather, it was a disappointing product of a centuries-old political struggle in which a sense of nationalist mission never materialized. Nonetheless, the unification ended the devastating warfare and brought to the Korean peninsula a rare period of peace. The court, which was eager to stabilize the war-torn kingdom, took steps to appease the citizens of the defeated Koguryo and Paeckche kingdoms. Many members of the nobility of the fallen kingdoms were absorbed into the new ruling class, and lands obtained through war were redistributed to its members. In the end, it was the ruling classes who benefited the most, while the common people were generally ignored. The court itself underwent reform, adopting an absolute monarchy system; royal power was greatly enhanced, while the power of the political advisory committee, the Hwa Baek, was reduced.[25] The court's administrative functions were revised along the line of Tang's six department system.[26]

Tang, an exceedingly successful Chinese dynasty in both cultural advances and influence abroad, found Unified Silla a docile neighbor, unlike the defiant and militant Koguryo. Since most of Koguryo's northern territory was occupied by Tang and Balhae, Unified Silla was hardly in a position to challenge the power of Tang. As a result, a fairly stable equilibrium developed in the region, and normal relations between two states were restored. As exchanges between the two nations increased, Tang's cultural influence in Silla became even more pervasive. Korea's cultural sinicization had begun in earnest; sending offspring to Tang for study became popular in the ruling classes of the Unified Silla.

Not every aspect of Tang culture was readily accepted in Unified Silla, however. Serious conflicts erupted between systems imported from Tang and indigenous systems.[27] Silla's young intellectuals advocated adoption of Tang's civil service examination system, which was designed to assure a learned and able man a government post. The system was rejected by the Silla court, which continued to practice traditional nepotism. Such conflicts were responsible for growing public discontent. It was also during this period that Confucianism was formally introduced into Korea, which further weakened the kingdom's Buddhist-oriented governing structure. In spite of the long period of tranquillity and the cultural regeneration stimulated by a close association with Tang, the Unified Silla never realized its potential in revitalizing the Hahn nation.

By the late ninth century the Unified Silla was suffering from many social and political disorders. An enlarged nobility - the result of rewards to war heroes and the absorption of the Koguryo and Paeckche ruling classes - created severe strains on the kingdom's landholding system. Members of the nobility and powerful regional leaders amassed huge portions of the nation's farmland, forcing peasant farmers to fall into slave status or to join rebel groups. Tax burdens became increasingly heavy as farmers had to pay excessive taxes to support the central government and the local warlords. Rebellions led by displaced farmers and slaves swept the countryside. As the court became unable to restore order, a few rebel groups controlling the kingdom's peripheries grew into a major political force with a large number of followers. The disintegration of the Unified Silla had begun. Among the splinter groups two major states emerged, Later Paeckche in 892 and Later Koguryo in 901, opening a new era in the Korean political landscape that came to be known as the period of the Later Three Kingdoms. The Korean peninsula was once again divided into three kingdoms and was swept by another unification war.

The war of the second unification of the Korean peninsula lasted about forty years. Later Paeckche dominated the initial period of the struggle but soon submerged into destructive domestic disputes and surrendered the initiative to Later Koguryo. Later Koguryo, shortly renamed Koryo or

The United Silla and Balhae Kingdoms (8th Century)

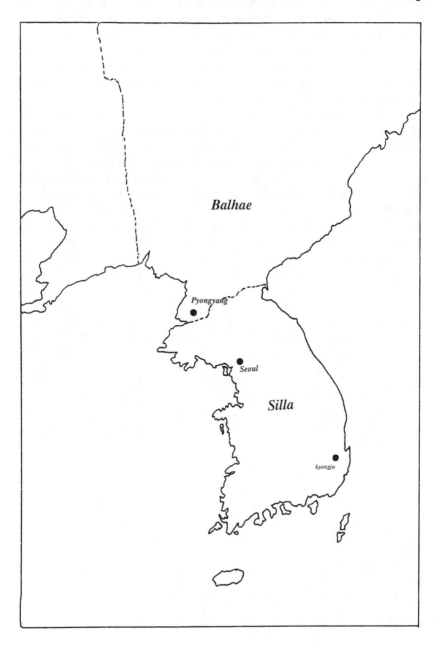

Korea, as it came to be called in the Western world, emerged as the most powerful state under the leadership of Wang Ghun and pursued aggressive military campaigns to unify the three kingdoms. Being exhausted, the Unified Silla quickly surrendered, and Later Paeckche was subdued militarily by the Koryo forces in 936. Koryo kingdom had risen to become the second Hahn state to rule the entire Korean peninsula. As the kingdom's name implies, Koryo leaders were committed to reviving the glory of Koguryo. At the end, the Unified Silla had proved to be no more than a weak transitional state, and Koryo was the first Korean state committed to governing all of the Hahn people under the new leadership and with new vision. Whether the geopolitics of the region would allow Koryo to achieve its ambition was another matter.

Three major dynasties dominated the Chinese mainland while the three Hahn kingdoms were immersed in their wars of survival. All three Chinese states sought to colonize the peninsula and time after time sent massive expeditions to Korea. Han China was able to establish colonies. Sui China was ruined primarily by its costly and unsuccessful Korean campaigns. Tang China turned the army it sent to help Silla into an occupation force after the other two Korean kingdoms collapsed. Although Silla managed to fight back and expelled the occupation force, it never seriously attempted to recover Koguryo's vast northern territory. The Unified Silla survived some two centuries essentially as a caretaker, but not as the heir of either Gohchosun or Koguryo. Throughout Korea's long unification struggle China's imperial intention toward the Korean peninsula never abated; at the end the unrelenting invasions weakened the militant Koguryo so thoroughly that it became easy prey for the Tang-Silla allied force. Ironically, China was so strong that it managed to ruin Koguryo even in China's own defeat. Another irony was Silla's ability to unify the peninsula even while it served the interests of imperial China. Although it failed to colonize Korea, China was fairly successful in sinicizing Korea during the Unified Silla era.

The China-Korea contest during its first thousand years thus produced mixed result: Koreans were resolute in defending their peninsula, but not the Manchurian plain. They violently opposed China's territorial ambitions but tolerated significant cultural sinicization. Nevertheless, the Korean peninsula under the Three Kingdoms remained politically independent but highly militant toward their dominant neighbors. The Three Kingdoms lost an invaluable opportunity to build a large nation across Manchuria and the Korean peninsula, but they did not surrender either their home base or their soul to ever-imperialistic China, even under massive and devastating pressures.

Notes

1. In 1998 South Korea's population is estimated to be 45.5 million, while North Korea's is 23.5 million.
2. Hahn is also spelled Han. In this book Hahn is used to distinguish it from Han, the ethnic Chinese, with whom Korea's Hahn people have no blood relation.
3. The Ural-Altaic language includes the Lappish of Lapland and Samoyed speech of Siberia, the Finish language, Magyar, Turkish or Tartar, Manchu, and Mongol. There is an opinion that it might not include the Korean language. Some have argued that the Korean language has a close relation to the Dravidian language of the Indo-European family. (Wells, 127)
4. The period was contemporary with the period of the Warring States in China, which lasted from 453 B.C. to 220 B.C.
5. The Han Chinese considered their state the center of the world, construing its cultural superiority as national supremacy. They envisioned that the virtue of the Son of Heaven, the Emperor, would spread in time beyond the borders. The world the early Chinese understood is hardly the entire world, for they were only dimly aware of India and the Roman world. Surrounded by Hsiung-nu, Tibetans, and other aboriginals, the Han Chinese were convinced of their own primacy.(Garraty and Gay, 128)
6. Han China was in perpetual struggle to survive. Most dynasties did not last long as never-ending warfare weakened them. Although it achieved unification in 221 B.C. for the first time in history, neither internal warfare nor Hsiung-nu incursions stopped for long.
7.The fortresses on the Liaodong peninsula are commonly quoted in the Korean literature as "castles."
8. The Chinese exacted fish, salt, iron, timber, and farm products from the colonies in Korea.
9. Among the colonies Laklang, located around the present-day Pyongyang, was the most powerful and also the longest lasting. It was the center of Chinese culture and influence in Korea.
10. Laklang, the last surviving Chinese colony, was driven out by Koguryo in 313 A.D.
11.Personal ornaments of gold and silver filigree and wood or brick lacquer ware were found.
12. The concept of capital punishment and private property was firmly established. However, the practice may not be considered a fully developed legal system, for it mostly came out of tribal customs intended mainly to protect the upper classes.
13. Some scholars include the Kingdom of Kaya in this group. Kaya, located in the southern coastal region between Silla and Paeckche, was the smallest kingdom. It was governed by a tribal system, and unlike the other kingdoms, failed to develop a stable central government. Kaya, taken by Paeckche and Silla during the sixth century, did not participate in the Hahn nation's unification competition. It is a general practice in Korea not to include Kaya in the Three Kingdoms period.

14. Han colonies were abandoned: Chinbun and Limdun in 82 B.C., Hyundo in 75 B.C. Laklang lasted until 313 A.D. but occupied a relatively small area near northeastern Korea and southwestern Manchuria. Because of its border location and the declining influence, Laklang did not interfere with the emergence of the Three Kingdoms.

15. The exact date is not known.

16. Wi was one of the three kingdoms that succeeded Han China. It ruled northern China during the Three Kingdoms period.

17. Founded in 317, the East Chin kingdom lasted till 420.

18. Hwa Rang Do's Five Rules are as follows: 1) to serve the King with loyalty, 2) to serve one's parents with filial piety, 3) to be faithful to one's friends, 4) not to retreat in battle, and 5) not to kill indiscriminately.

19. The official titles of Korean kings were all given after the king passed away. During the king's reign the titles this book is using were not used.

20. The Southern Dynasty of Sung was established in 420 and the Northern Dynasty of Northern Wei was founded in 439.

21. Jinan is located along the Yalu River in Jilin Province, northeast China.

22. The Salsoo River is the old name for the Daedong River or its branch.

23. Customarily from this time on Silla is called the Unified Silla. In this book such a title is used to avoid a confusion.

24. Khitan was a Manchurian-Mongolian tribe which founded the Khitan kingdom in northern China in 916.

25. The Hwa Baek was an advisory institution to the monarchy. It was an old tribal conference, a meeting of all the important men of the ruling class who considered important political matters. The king was not obliged to accept the Hwa Baek's political proposals.

26. The system divided the court's administrative functions into six departments.

27. An example is Buddhism. The importation of Tang's Buddhism caused extensive division in the religion.

Chapter 2

The Koryo Dynasty and the Northern Tribes

1. The Rise of the Koryo Dynasty

The founder of the Koryo Dynasty, Wang Ghun, was a military leader from a rich merchant family in Gaesung in central Korea. In the early tenth century when he joined the rebel faction that claimed itself the Late Koguryo, he was already a man of unusual background and experience.[1] After having replaced the faction's leadership, Wang Ghun founded the Koryo Dynasty in 918 at his stronghold, Gaesung. For the next seventeen years he waged the nation's second unification war with astute diplomacy and shrewd military campaigns. His unification drive was completed by the surrender of exhausted Silla in 935. In this war, unlike the first unification war, no contestants sought the help of China because the Tang Dynasty, a Silla ally in the earlier race, had fallen in 907. Han China, suffering from serious internal conflicts, was unable to field Tang's successor until the founding of Sung in 960. Meanwhile, highly divided Chinese states were too preoccupied with domestic squabbles to interfere in political developments in Korea.

Considering the fatal state of disintegration that the Unified Silla was undergoing, Koryo's emergence was the salvation of the Hahn nationhood. Unlike the first unification war, the Late Koguryo, renamed later as Koryo, represented a dynastic change that was needed to ensure the national drive for continuing reconciliation and rejuvenation.

The most urgent priority Wang Ghun's Koryo Dynasty faced was the restoration of political stability in the nation's hinterland, which the waning Silla had been unable to achieve. The new court put the nation under effective central control and arrested the rampant social disorder by applying both military and civil tactics. Wang Ghun eradicated the epidemic revolts in the countryside with military means but at the same time instituted various policies designed to achieve national harmony. He was eager to placate the Silla aristocracy and sought its cooperation by granting various concessions.

King Taejo, Wang Ghun's posthumous title by which he is known in history, refrained from wholesale dismantling of the Silla ruling system. Such a move was chosen primarily to secure a measure of legitimacy for his new dynasty and to provide continuity for the nation. In so doing, however, he lost an opportunity to neutralize the extensive political power of the nation's nobility, who had become a serious national economic burden and political obstacle for any reform movements. The restraint that Wang Ghun employed, seeking not to be a conqueror but rather an alternative ruler for fallen Unified Silla, caused serious difficulties for the new court. His deliberate effort to appease rather than conquer the conservative ruling classes of Silla meant that power remained basically intact in the new court. The fact that the new court was still dominated by the same corrupt, ineffective ruling class was, however, an inauspicious omen.

King Taejo's efforts to consolidate his political power over the entrenched ruling class were largely ineffective. Consequently, his desire to undertake a series of political reforms suffered a mortal setback from the outset. One of his early goals was the relocation of the capital to Pyongyang, where Koguryo had its court. His desire to transfer the court to Pyongyang represented Taejo's far-reaching desire to recover the Koguryo territory lost during the era of the Unified Silla. The new regime was also mindful of another potential benefit: relocation of the capital would help break the political grip of the nation's conservative nobility, who was centered around Gaesung, the current capital. Through the relocation King Taejo could have weakened the political power of the nobility and at the same time put his northward policy into effect. Naturally the relocation attempt was met with vehement objections by the nobility, which successfully derailed it. King Taejo's ambitious plan to recover the northern territory was for all practical purposes doomed from its inception not by foreign adversaries, but by selfish and shortsighted court officials. In general, Koryo's political system was more sophisticated and progressive than that of the Unified Silla. Koryo continued Silla's tradition of selectively adopting China's political and social systems that included the educational

The Koryo Kingdom(11th century)

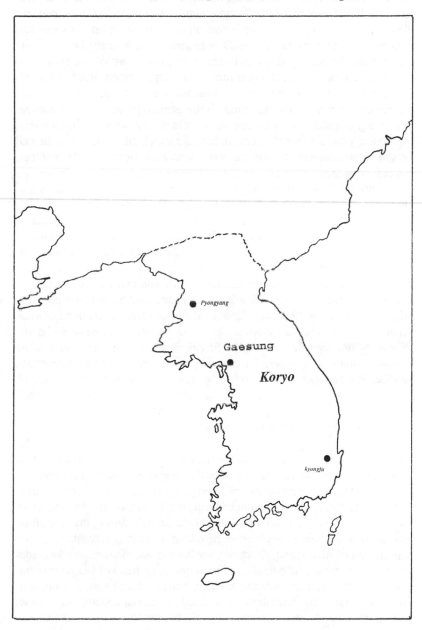

system and the civil service examinations. For the central administrative organs, Koryo adopted the Tang system of three ministries and six departments. Koryo's Chinese-style civil service examinations had succeeded in emphasizing academic regimens in the country. But by doing so, it ended up enlarging the powerful ruling class, which the court first battled to disband. This in turn meant more land allotments for the nation's nobility, who were exempt from taxation, thus increasing farmers' tax burdens. The Koryo court adopted Buddhism as the basis of the nation's spiritual guidance, a decision that was to affect every aspect of the society. Particularly during the early period of the dynasty, Buddhism was embraced by the royal families and the ruling class, who were instrumental in erecting several large temples. As Buddhism's popularity soared, the rivalry among adherents of its five sects and nine subsects again intensified, as it had during the Silla era. While Koryo embraced Buddhism as the kingdom's spiritual guide, it also adopted the teachings of Confucius as the mainstay of the nation's political philosophy. The systematic adoption of Chinese-style civil service examinations provided a powerful boost for the spread of the Confucian philosophy among Koryo's upper classes. The number of Confucian institutions of learning, both public and private, was soaring as they became the only avenue available for young men hoping to gain public offices. Korean Confucianism flourished so vigorously that during the late Koryo era it produced the scholar, Jung Mong Ju, respected as the "Eastern Confucius." Serving the needs and interests of the nation's wealthy and ruling classes, both Buddhism and Confucianism coexisted throughout the Koryo Dynasty.

2. Clashes with the Northern Tribes

During the early part of the tenth century China experienced another dynastic transition. After the collapse of Tang in 907, China entered the period of the Five Dynasties and Ten Kingdoms, a period of extreme political instability and squabbling. During the destructive internal struggles among the Han states, the nomadic Khitan tribe was gaining strength along the upper Liao River in southern Manchuria. Taking advantage of the diminished control Han China had over the region, the nomadic kingdom continued to expand its domain, finally dominating most of Manchuria and Mongolia. By 926 it extended its control to the northern Manchurian plain by subjugating the Kingdom of Balhae, a Korean state, and began encroaching on the northern region of China proper. In 946, the Khitan founded Liao, a Chinese-style state. Northeast Asia entered an era quite new to both Han China and Korea: the vast Manchurian and Mongolian plains were occupied by a nomadic power which not only geographically separated two traditional neighbors but exerted growing pressure on both nations. The rise of the nomadic powers in this strategic region eventually brought the new Korean state another critical test of survival and maintenance of its national identity.

The northern nomadic tribes, including the Khitan tribe, had very diverse ethnic backgrounds and life-styles. In general they were militant in their dealings with Han Chinese states, yet they exercised a great deal of flexibility in adopting Chinese culture to their advantage. Two groups were prominent. One group, consisting of the tribes of Khitan, Jurchen, and Tangut, founded heavily sinicized empires in the northern border regions of China by extensively embracing Chinese culture. The other group, including the Mongols, the successors of the Hsiung-nu, and the Turks, settled in the region south of Lake Baikal, farther away from China proper and its cultural influence, and maintained their migratory life-style for a longer period.

These northern tribes, commonly known to the Han Chinese as "barbarians," had been a serious threat to every Chinese empire from the early days of the Han nationhood. Chinese empires had resorted to periodic campaigns to subjugate them when feasible. Chin China built the Great Wall to protect its northern frontier from these barbarians.[2] When the nomads massed too strong a military power, Chinese empires often bought peace by offering lavish gifts and official titles to the leaders of the raiders. Yet the nomads never hesitated to raid China whenever an opportunity presented itself. At times they even penetrated to the central regions of China proper with destructive effects. In spite of Chinese efforts, sinicization of the nomads was slow, and colonization of the unstable northern border regions by transplanting Han Chinese(who were accustomed to a warmer climate and a sedentary culture) proved often to be quixotic. Having had no effective strategy program to suppress them, most Chinese empires learned to coexist with these unruly neighbors, who remained a basically manageable threat to China as well as Korea until the era of the Sung Dynasty.[3] But when they significantly improved their military capability by adopting China's advanced military tactics to their already formidable warrior traditions, the northern menace finally became real and dynasty-threatening. The Khitan, Jurchen, and Mongol warriors were much better organized and equipped than their predecessors of the Tang era.

The Korean states were only too familiar with the harassment of the nomads living along the edges of their northern frontier. Gohchosun and Koguryo, both militarily strong and aggressive in their territorial control, contained the nomads through periodic expeditions. Yet there were times when Korean kingdoms also appeased the raiders with generous gifts. In general, Korean courts successfully employed stern but flexible methods to contain the threats of the border tribes. Not until the tenth century did the northern nomads develop the military tactics and achieve the strength to threaten the Korean state. Border skirmishes waged by nomads primarily to acquire provisions and to secure warmer winter refuges now came to resemble wars intended for the systematic conquest of territory. Nevertheless, the Khitan's Liao posed no real threat to the Hahn nation in the early period of the Koryo Dynasty.

3. The Northern Tribes and Koryo's Northward Ambition

Koryo's fundamental China policy was to maintain a friendly relationship with its powerful neighbor, as evidenced by its close diplomatic ties to the Five Dynasties and Sung. Koryo resumed Silla's pro-China policy with little revision. It was a sensible and necessary approach, particularly when Han China was strong. But when the northern tribes gained strength and threatened the survival of Han China, the pro-China policy offered the court a painful dilemma. As the nomads succeeded in establishing a potent empire of their own in northern China, reducing the Sung Dynasty to a weak regional power controlling only southern China, Koryo's China policy faced a severe test. Yet when in 922 the Khitan demanded the establishment of diplomatic relations, Koryo summarily rejected its request.

During the early period of its dynasty, Koryo adopted militant policies toward the border tribes. It intensified its defenses along the northern frontier by adding garrisons. It also undertook the systematic buildup of the old Koguryo capital, Pyongyang, King Taejo's major initiative in his drive to defend the nation's border region and recover the Koguryo territory. This city on the Daedong River, which had been the northern boundary of Silla, commanded a region strategically important both for the protection of the frontier and as a base for the nation's northward expansion policy. During the period of 918 to 922 the king poured the nation's resources into Pyongyang to make it the nation's second city politically, culturally, and militarily. By the middle of the tenth century King Taejo's concerted efforts had paid off: Koryo had recovered a significant amount of territory north of the Daedong River, and Koryo's northward push had gained some momentum.

From the outset serious conflicts between sophisticated Koryo and the energetic Khitan kingdom were inevitable. Koryo, the most ambitious Hahn state after Koguryo, was eager to recover the old Hahn territory and regain the glory of Koguryo. The Khitan tribe, which had earlier conquered the Balhae kingdom and thus spoiled the Hahn nationals' dream of rebuilding the Koguryo glory, continued to expand its domain in northeast Asia. By occupying most of Koguryo's old territory, which remained beyond the control of the Hahn state, Khitan was the foremost obstacle to Koryo's northward thrust. In spite of Khitan's growing power, Taejo's militant policy was maintained toward the border tribes by his successors: King Jungjong created an army of 300,000 men, and King Gwangjong established a number of castles and defensive fortresses on the Chungchun River in the north to counter the growing threat of Khitan. In addition, Koryo maintained friendly relations with and rendered support to the Jungahn, a small kingdom founded by the subjects of the Balhae in the Yalu River basin.[4] By steadfastly maintaining a hard-line stand against the region's new power, Koryo could not long avoid a direct military confrontation.

In 986 the Khitan won a major military victory over the Sung Dynasty and was able to turn its attention to northeast Asia. It easily subjugated the kingdom of Jungahn, a small but significant Koryo ally, and also the Jurchen tribes in the lower Yalu region during the same period. In 989 it further expanded its control in the region. Having removed these minor obstacles, Khitan was ready to conquer its two major opponents: Sung, in southern China, and Koryo, in the Korean peninsula. The Khitan adopted a strategy of subduing first the smaller opponent, Koryo, which still maintained friendly relations with Sung, a Han Chinese state, even under the relentless pressure of the Khitan.

In 993 the Khitan invaded Koryo with a force of 800,000 men. Like its predecessor, Koryo was prepared to fight the imposing army and did so rather successfully, halting the invaders' advance along the Chongchon River, north of Pyongyang. Having faced the Koryo forces' adamant resistance, Khitan pursued a negotiated settlement and demanded that Koryo surrender its former Balhae territory and cease relations with Sung China, which had asked Koryo for military collaboration in repulsing Khitan from central China. Koryo did not yield much to the Khitan demands. It agreed to establish diplomatic relations with the invaders but managed to extract significant territorial concessions from them: six counties east of the Yalu River.[5] Khitan had to withdraw from northern Korea only with a symbolic gain but no territorial conquest.

Koryo's motivated military force and skillful diplomacy managed to defeat the Khitan's first attempt. The episode, however, did not alter the region's political landscape. Khitan remained the most intimating power of the region even after its failure in Korea. In spite of the military stalemate, the first Koryo-Khitan contest gave the invaders a serious geopolitical advantage: Khitan forced Koryo to agree not to attack its rear while it engaged Sung China in a contest for the hegemony of China. By gaining this concession, Khitan achieved the primary objective of its expedition- the neutralization of Koryo in its struggle with Sung, a Koryo ally. With its rear thus secured, Khitan finally concentrated its might against Sung and in 1004 drove out the Han state from northern China. A tentative peace returned to the Chinese continent, but at the cost of Sung's heavy annual tribute to Liao, the Khitan state.

Once its southern front was stabilized, Khitan again turned its attention to Koryo. It demanded from the Koryo court the return of the six counties in the Yalu region it had earlier yielded to Koryo. Koryo refused to comply with Khitan's demand and thereby risked bringing about another military confrontation with the greatest power of northeast Asia. In 1010, under the pretext of punishing an internal dissenter in the Koryo court, Khitan launched its second major expedition against Koryo. Unlike the first invasion, this time the Khitan forces quickly overran the Koryo capital, forcing the Koryo king to take refuge in the southern part of the peninsula. In spite of its failure to defend the capital, Koryo mounted stiff military resistance throughout the country and eventually forced Khitan to withdraw from the peninsula again with only a token prize, a promise to pay tribute to the Khitan court later.

Khitan's second invasion of Koryo clearly demonstrated its ultimate intention toward the Korean peninsula. The nomadic empire would be content with nothing but total subjugation of Koryo. In 1018, dissatisfied with the mediocre results of its earlier expeditions- concessions that Koryo never intended to implement- Khitan undertook its third campaign against Koryo. But this time Koryo forces were prepared; they destroyed the invading forces at Ghijoo, north of Pyongyang, thus successfully defending the nation from Khitan's third military attempt.

With the failure of the latest attempt to subjugate Koryo, Khitan realized that the best concession it could extract from the stubborn Hahn state was its agreement to "Hwa-Chin," a relationship based on peace and friendship. By this agreement the two countries restored peace along their common border. But for Koryo the peace was a short respite, a temporary arrangement that failed to secure long-term stability in the region. Peace in northeastern Asia remained essentially illusive and unpredictable. Koryo justifiably never felt safe from the northern nomadic powers. It continued to improve its defensive fortifications, erecting a defensive wall across northern Korea's rugged mountain ranges from the Amrok River to the east coast. The wall, with a total length of more than 1,000 ri, was designed to keep out not only the Khitan but the Jurchen tribes, which were gaining strength in northern Manchuria.[6]

The Jurchen tribes were formerly under Balhae's rule. After Balhae's fall the Jurchen remained under Koryo's influence and regarded Koryo as a parent state. Koryo in turn rewarded the tribes with some commercial dealings. The relationship, however, was not always peaceful; at times Jurchen raids on the Koryo frontier were serious enough to prompt Koryo's military campaign against them.

Early in the twelfth century a Jurchen group in northern Manchuria began to unify its tribes. Soon its strength reached a level enabling it to launch serious raids against both Khitan and Koryo. Alarmed by the growing Jurchen strength, Koryo sent a large expeditionary force to the north and in 1107 established nine defensive castles along its northern frontier. However, Koryo's military buildups in southern Manchuria provoked Jurchen's vehement protests, and two years later in an act of conciliation the Koryo court turned the castles over to the Jurchen. The loss of momentum in Koryo's northward thrust became evident in this period. By then the Koryo court was dominated by conservative officials who lacked the aggressive spirit so pervasive during King Taejo's reign.

Jurchen's strength continued to grow, eventually replacing Khitan as the rulers of southern Manchuria; the Jurchens established the Kin Kingdom in 1115 and destroyed the Khitan state of Liao the next year. The Kin soon controlled the entire Manchurian plain as well as northern China, reducing Sung China to a regional power in the south of the lower Yangtze River where Southern Sung, renamed after the relocation, was to remain for the period of 1127 to 1279. Like the Khitan, the Jurchen were aware of the strategic significance of the Korean peninsula. But unlike the Khitan, who resorted to futile military expeditions, immensely confident Kin demanded that Koryo accept a subordinate status, a humiliating king-subject relationship. Although there were strong objections, the weak Koryo court capitulated to Kin's ultimatum. The Koryo kingdom, whose sworn state policy was to regain the glory of old Koguryo and which had earlier courageously resisted the Khitan invasions, submitted to another northern nomadic power without offering serious resistance.

Like Koguryo, Koryo was unable to resist for long the unrelenting military pressure of the northern tribes. Like Gohchosun, which had suffered similar humiliation from the Han Dynasty thirteen centuries before, Koryo submitted not to military but psychological defeat. The court, dominated by officials of a defeatist attitude - the result of prolonged military confrontation- was not even able to rally military resistance. Repeated Khitan invasions could not conquer Koryo, but they managed to badly undermine the nation's spirit.

Koryo's ambivalent relationship to Sung China in this period showed its pervasive defeatism. Although the Koryo forces had managed to forestall the Khitan invasions, the court agreed to accommodate the aggressor's strategic demand, the downgrading of its relations with Sung China. Again, the defeatism shared by the court's influential officials was the primary reason for Koryo's crumbling submission, which deprived Sung of an opportunity to attack the Khitan from both fronts. The fact that Koryo chose to remain neutral in the Sung-Khitan contest indicated that Koryo had lost its will to challenge the Khitan militarily. Koryo's abrupt turnaround in its relations with Sung involved more than pressure by the Khitan, however. The remarkable thing was that the turnaround occurred while the pro-Sung faction was still influential in the Koryo court, where the Khitan and the Jurchen were held in contempt as barbarians. Koryo was intimidated by the nomadic powers; it was not that Sung lost the Koryo court's support, but that the northern nomads won new respect. Khitan's military power and its geographic propinquity to Koryo were so overwhelming that they effectively prohibited Koryo from forging a military alliance with Sung, a power that still commanded an emotional allegiance among the Koreans.

Koryo's reluctance to form a military alliance with Sung reflected another important factor. Sung, which had shown incompetence in its contest against the growing power of the Khitan, had little prospect of defeating its northern rival even with Koryo's full cooperation. On the other hand, Koryo's military cooperation was likely to provoke Khitan is retaliation. Koryo was aware that the Korean peninsula was so small that if a superior force invaded from the north, there was little room to maneuver. This was particularly true after the vast northern territory of Koguryo was lost. Koryo lacked Sung's uncommon advantage of a huge territory. Faced with a hostile, potent neighbor while its weak ally was far away, Koryo had to be either dominating or submissive. It could not afford to be a weak challenger.

Koryo's submission to the nomadic powers was not entirely a product of geopolitics. It was not rare in Korean history that a court was paralyzed by intense internal power struggles and thus unable to function even when the situation was critical. Many members of the nobility plunged into a destructive power struggle, oblivious of an approaching storm of foreign incursions. When the Jurchen gained strength in Manchuria, the Koryo court was so divided by power grabbers that rational deliberation of its foreign policy was virtually impossible. Thus Koryo's compliance with the Jurchen's ultimatum was the result of the court's inability to produce a coherent political consensus. It was neither the first nor the last time in Korean history that a partisan power struggle had undermined the nation's ability to formulate sound foreign policy decisions. The Koryo court's excessive political infighting was the direct result of a ruling structure dominated by factional nobilities, mainly the Confucian scholars, who had maintained a strong grip over the nation's politics since the Silla era.

From the beginning, the Koryo aristocracy became the main political obstacle, undermining the royal authority and resisting the capital relocation attempt that might have endangered its power in the court. The new dynasty, to which the Silla aristocratic families gave political support during the unification struggle, allowed the group to maintain its power base in order to secure a harmonious transition. However, the old ruling class did not intend to settle for their protected status, but to dominate the new court. It was this ruling class that had blocked King Taejo's attempt to move its capital to Pyongyang. In time Koryo's aristocracy encountered a strong challenge from the rural political leaders who had accumulated wealth and power in the political vacuum created by the lack of an effective central control. This group was later joined by younger officials appointed to powerful governmental positions through Koryo's universal civil service examinations. This odd coalition was more sympathetic to the court's drive for political reform.

Political clashes between the long-established aristocracy and the young, revolution-minded officials were vicious. The culmination of the political infighting was a rebellion led by Myochung, a Buddhist monk. In 1135, Myochung and his supporters proposed the relocation of the court to Pyongyang. They justified the relocation of the capital with the argument that Gaesung's geomantic strength that was needed to support the dynasty was now exhausted.[7] Naturally, the move to relocate the capital met strong objections from the ruling aristocracy, for which Gaesung was the base of power. At the end, the old guards managed to foil the rebellion, and the relocation envisioned by the founding monarch more than two hundred years before was forestalled again.

Myochung's rebellion reflected the growing nationalistic aspiration shared by his followers. In their drive to revitalize Koryo, they advocated not only the relocation of the capital but also two other highly symbolic reforms. One was the "Chingje Gunwon" proposal: "Chingje" was the adoption of the title "emperor" instead of the traditional title "king" for Koryo's monarch, and "Gunwon" was a royal reform requiring the Koryo court to use its own designation of the year independent of Chinese practice. Both proposals were highly symbolic, but in the Koryo society symbolism was often perceived as being as critical as substance. Conservative court officials regarded the unprecedented proposals as a revolt against Sung China, the nation of the "Son of Heaven." For these pro-Chinese court officials Myochung's bold nationalistic demands were nothing short of a capital offense.

It was an established practice in the Chinese Empire that the title "emperor," or "son of heaven" in literal interpretation, was to be used solely by the supreme ruler of the empire. The regional warlords were required to use the title "king," a title subordinate to "emperor." In Korea, however, the Chinese concept of "son of heaven" as a supreme ruler was foreign, and the title "king" connoted the nation's supreme ruler. The Chinese practice led to the interpretation that the Koryo court was subordinate to the Chinese court. In fact, Chinese courts, typically preoccupied with formalities, often meddled in the matter and insisted that the Koryo monarch use the title "king" rather than "emperor." The self-proclaimed "Middle Kingdom" pressed for Korean kings not call themselves "emperors," which would make them equal to Chinese rulers in international standing. Korean courts generally regarded the issue a nuisance which was not worth provoking the Chinese. Yet among more progressive Koreans the use of "king" instead of "emperor" was perceived as a symbol of submission forced upon Koryo by the "big nation." [8] Myochung and his followers reasoned that as the ruler of an independent state, Koryo's monarch should assume the same title as that used by Chinese monarchs and practice its own royal designation of the year, thus demonstrating the Koryo court's equality to that of Sung China. If the proposals were adopted, they would signal Koryo's refusal to submit to China, even in symbolic terms.

Myochung's other proposal was a military expedition against Kin. By that time Kin had become the ruler of northern China and the Manchurian plain. To Koryo's nationalists, who regarded the Jurchen as barbarians historically controlled by Hahn states of Koguryo and Balhae, Kin's ultimatum denoted the nation's undeserved humiliation. They saw an opportunity to regain the Koguryo territory by conquering Kin. For Koryo to take a more aggressive northward thrust and break the age-old subordinate relationship with China, however, it was necessary to relocate the court to Pyongyang, then known as the "western capital," where pro-monarch and anti-aristocratic groups had a powerful influence. Myochung's independence movement could not have been better timed: the Sung court was forced to flee to southern China under the pressure of Kin and was hardly in a position to hinder Koryo's initiative.

Koryo's aristocracy, however, mobilized its influence and blocked the initiative, preserving the status quo. Primarily to protect their own interests in the Koryo court, the conservative scholar-officials demonstrated their loyalty to the Chinese court. In doing so they ignored the interests of the nation as a whole. Unable to protect the court politics from corrupt officials willing to surrender national interests for individual or factional political fortunes, Koryo plunged into a dark era.

After Myochung's initiatives were forcibly rejected, Koryo's revolutionary zeal greatly subsided. The nation's mood markedly shifted toward the Confucian idea of rhetorical pacifism, and the influence of the scholar-officials grew further in the court.[9] The remaining obstacle to the total domination of the scholar-officials was the nation's military officers, many of whom were of rural origins. Eventually civilian politicians managed to drive the officers off the court's power structure and usurped the control of the nation's military itself. By suppressing Myochung's forces in Pyongyang and removing contentious military officers from the court, the aristocratic classes secured their total political domination. One prominent casualty of this development was the military; under the civilian control the military was dismantled, though the founding monarch's dream of recovering the Koguryo territory remained unfulfilled, and militant northern nomads continued to threaten the state.

Preoccupied with political infighting, the Koryo court failed to comprehend the serious shift in geopolitics of the region. The ruling Confucian scholar-officials still remained convinced that only a right relationship with Sung - that is, a subordinate relationship - would ensure the welfare of the kingdom. Even under extreme pressures from the northern states, their reverence for Sung China remained comically sincere even as they conveniently overlooked the fact that Chinese empires had been more exploiters and imperialists than benign benefactors to Korean kingdoms. Critics of blind loyalty to the Chinese were quickly swept from power by the overwhelming pro-China faction. Not only was the Koryo court unable to seriously assess its relationship with Sung China, but it also failed to recognize the implications of the rising power of the northern states, which shared a common heritage with Hahn nationals to a significant extent. Koryo's geopolitical reading of northeast Asia remained largely distorted by its preoccupation with Chinese empires. The Koryo society had exposed its early symptoms of emotional Sinicization. The failure of Myochung's uprising represented a lost opportunity to reverse that trend and bolster Korean nationalism.

In 1170, Koryo's worsening aristocratic rule incited a military coup. The kingdom's disgruntled military officials, supported by demoralized soldiers and peasants, seized political power and drove the scholar aristocracy from the court politics. For the next eighty-eight years Koryo was to suffer brutal oppression at the hands of military dictators.[10] Military dictatorship was arbitrary and oppressive, because it was motivated not by a revolutionary rationale but by continuing power struggles in the court. Regardless, the coup altered drastically the power structure of the Koryo court and simultaneously refuted the invincibility of the patrimonial nobility.

Under the military dictatorship the traditional urban nobility suffered a major political setback, for the ranks of the military ruling classes were drawn largely from the kingdom's common and slave classes in rural regions. Reflecting their own humble origins, the court's military leaders were reluctant to strictly enforce the nation's traditional class system, which consisted of nobility, the common people, and slaves. One result of such a political shift was the gradual disintegration of the nation's slave institution, although the erosion was still trifling and incidental rather than systematic.

Even under brutal military dictatorship, Koryo for over thirty years was swept by incessant rebellions of slaves and farmers. Most insurrections were against avaricious local authorities and landlords. Although the grievances were genuine, the resistance failed to evolve into a systematic movement powerful enough to challenge the central government. On the contrary, the uprisings remained sporadic and ill-organized. The impromptu leadership was ineffective for an organized, nationwide resistance against the military regime. Although the slave-peasant insurrections lasted for a prolonged period, they failed to secure able leadership from outside or to organize a credible military force. The movement persisted largely because the social maladies, which the incompetent, unstable court was unable to contain, were excessive and intolerable for the masses. In spite of good intentions the revolts of the oppressed never amounted to anything near a nationwide revolutionary movement.

Nevertheless, the revolts made significant contributions to the Koryo society. The court not only had to respond to public grievances but also realized the potent power of the masses. In addition, through the revolts the lower classes came to understand and express the spirit of social justice and class confrontation. They succeeded in airing their grievances, though they gained little in legal or practical terms. Furthermore, the revolts displayed the aggressive and forward character of the nation as a whole, in contrast to the ruling classes' timid defeatism. Such defiant spirit had a direct bearing on the nation's militant responses to another invasion that soon threatened the kingdom.

4. Koryo's Struggle against the Mongol Domination

By the end of the twelfth century, Sung China had been reduced to a regional power. Its effective rule was limited to the area south of the Yangtze River, leaving most of central and northern China to the Tartars' Hsia and the Jurchen's Kin. Sung, a Han Chinese state, was undergoing a fatal decline, and most of northeast Asia fell under the control of unruly leaders of nomadic traditions. It was under this unusual circumstance that the Mongols began to consolidate their power in the region between Lakes Balkash and Baikal, the area that now bears their name.

The Mongols were under the nominal control of the Jurchen's Kin empire. In the early period of the thirteenth century the Mongols created a unified state under the leadership of Genghis Khan. Capitalizing on a highly mobile fighting force known for its excellent horsemanship and devastating seizure tactics, the Mongols rapidly expanded their territory in all directions. In the end, the whole region, except Japan, suffered the Mongol rage.[11]

Genghis Khan rose to the supreme rulership of the Mongols in 1206, owing to his eminent leadership and exceptional fighting skills. With his small but highly mobile force he fervently pursued his grand ambition, the subjugation of the entire world known to him that extended well beyond the desolate central Asian steppe that he had inherited from his nomadic forefathers. Once his grand campaign to vanquish every nation in his path was under way, the ruthless advance of Genghis Khan and his sons was faithfully carried out by the Mongol military machine with peerless efficiency. Genghis Khan's force overran helpless foes almost at will: it subjugated the Hsia kingdom in 1209, invaded the Kin kingdom in 1211, and secured control of all the territory north of the Yellow River in 1215. In addition, his army conquered the Tarim Basin and half of Turkestan in 1217 and the remainder of west Turkestan, Afghanistan, and part of Persia in 1221. He also undertook a campaign against northern India in 1222 and Russia in 1223. Upon the death in 1227 of the greatest conqueror mankind has ever known, his son Ogodei became the Great Khan and continued to launch aggressive military campaigns.

The Mongol-Koryo confrontation began against this ominous backdrop of the Mongols' unrestrained militarism. Yet the early relations between the two neighbors were not only uneventful but even amiable; the Mongols even sent their forces to help Koryo expel the remnants of the Khitan from its northern frontier region. However, when the Mongol Empire had established itself as the undisputed ruler of vast central Asia, its relations with Koryo quickly deteriorated. The Mongols began to exert their dominance over the Koryo court. Their interference in domestic matters and demands for gifts and tributes became intolerable to the Koryo court, which was still ruled by military dictators. Military confrontation between the Mongols and defiant Koryo was inevitable.

In 1231, Ogodei Khan sent an invasion force to the Koryo kingdom. Koryo's military government deployed its forces to block the invaders but with only scattered successes. The Mongols were too powerful to be defeated by the hastily assembled Koryo defenders. When the military situation became desperate, the Koryo court pursued a negotiated settlement with the Mongols. Mongol peace terms included humiliating demands that were unacceptable to the Koryo court. Koryo abandoned negotiation and chose to continue military resistance. To avoid capture, the court was evacuated to Kanghwa, a small island at the mouth of the Han River on the west coast. There the Koryo court waged a long and costly resistance against the invaders. Although the court itself was safe, it was unable to prevent the Mongols from occupying most of the kingdom north of the Han River.

Koryo's stubborn resistance brought six separate Mongol invasions during the next thirty years. The Mongol attacks never threatened the Koryo court in exile, but they inflicted wanton destruction and excessive human suffering throughout the peninsula. All the major towns were repeatedly sacked; indiscriminate killings and willful destruction of temples and palaces were common. Even the nation's southern provinces, mostly rich agricultural regions, did not escape the Mongol rage. Still Koryo refused to surrender, and its exiled court remained safe from the invaders.

The Mongols began their final attack on Kin in 1232, and with support rendered by Southern Sung, conquered it in 1234. After the subjugation of Kin, the Mongols intensified their pressure on Koryo. Although they were still reluctant to undertake a naval expedition to capture Koryo's exiled court on Kanghwa, they continued to pillage the entire peninsula. In the protracted confrontation the masses suffered most from Mongol barbarism. In contrast to the superior quality of the invading army, Koryo's regular army existed only nominally; the remnants of its conscripted standing force had been further disassembled before the Mongol invasions. Furthermore the military dictators had turned the state forces into their own private armies, depriving the exiled court of a force with which it could mount effective military resistance against the Mongol army, the world's most experienced and successful raiding force of the time. The court in exile was hardly in a position to raise a new quality fighting force.

While the inept court was hiding on the island, the Koryo masses, exploited and ill-treated as they were, rose to wage sporadic but courageous battles against mighty Mongol invaders. All over the country slaves and peasants fought the Mongols with whatever weapons they could find. Although poorly organized, the people's war went on and often inflicted severe losses on the invaders.

In the end, however, the destruction became unbearable to the Koryo court. The allure of "Hwa-Chin" -peace and friendship- prevailed, and in 1258 the court formally ended its thirty-year resistance. It submitted to the Mongol court by accepting a subordinate status, but not before it had waged the longest, fiercest resistance to the Mongol Empire in history. The mobile and experienced Mongol army was far beyond what Koryo's pseudo military could match. The mountainous Korean terrain was no barrier to the Mongol army, which was at the peak of its strength during this period.

Koryo's long resistance to the Mongol invasion was by no means a total failure, however. It was a significant spiritual victory for the Hahn people; neither the mighty Kin nor the Southern Sung, nor any other state that happened to be in the way of the Mongol army, was able to withstand a single Mongol onslaught, much less repeated raids lasting for three decades. Koryo apparently won the respect of the invaders through its steadfast resistance; the Mongols excluded the Koryo territory from its new, Chinese-style empire built on the territory of China and Manchuria. If it had not been for Koryo's bloody resistance, the Mongols might have looted Koryo and made it a colony of the Mongol Empire. The Mongols allowed Koryo independence not accorded to any other state under their direct influence. Koryo became a "junior partner" to the Mongol Empire but not under its direct rule.

The Koryo court's submission to the Mongols was not without internal opposition. The most notable was the rebellion of the three special branches of the state military, the Sam-Bul-Cho. The group objected to the court's submission to the Mongols on any terms, and fought against both the Mongols and the Koryo forces, controlling for a while a large part of the peninsula's southern tip. Although they were objected by the court, which now favored "Hwa-Chin," their uprising was heartily supported by the masses nationwide. Until their annihilation by a combined force of Koryo and Mongol troops on Cheju Island, the Sam-Bul-Cho fought against the Mongols hardly, demonstrating the nation's sovereign spirit. Together with the slaves and peasants, who also fought gallant wars of resistance, the Sam-Bul-Cho's rebellion represented the true spirit of Hahn nationalism.

The Koryo court returned to the capital, Gaesung, in 1270, after forty years of exile in Kanghwa. Under the cover of peace and friendship the Hahn state was about to enter an era of humiliating foreign interference. The Yuan Dynasty, as the Mongol Empire was renamed in 1271, forced on the Koryo court systematic control through both direct and indirect interventions. Under the Yuan pressure Koryo was forced to adopt many Mongol customs, even though the Mongols were scorned in Koryo as unsophisticated both politically and culturally. The Yuan not only dominated Koryo politics but also periodically exploited Koryo in its military adventures.

After defeating the Southern Sung in 1276, the Yuan regime launched two major naval expeditions against Japan, which had signally ignored the presence of the Mongol power and remained beyond Mongol influence. Koryo was forced to participate in the expeditions, building warships and providing personnel.[12] The first Mongol expedition, launched in 1274 from Masan, a port in southern Korea, was a complete failure; it encountered strong Japanese resistance, and during their withdrawal the Mongol survivors were decimated by a severe storm. In 1281, the Mongols launched another invasion. Again Koryo was forced to build and provide the fleet. Yuan's second attempt turned out to be a repetition of the first. Again Japan resisted the invaders with great determination, and again a violent storm destroyed the invading fleet. After these two disastrous attempts, the Mongols made no more assaults on Japan. Unlike its peerless efficiency in land battles, the Mongol army was inept in naval operations. These unsuccessful naval invasions were the only significant campaigns the Mongol military had ever lost.[13]

Koryo's forced participation in the Mongol invasion of Japan was very costly to the kingdom in manpower and supplies. Although Koryo was a victim of the Mongol's long occupation, it had to accommodate Mongol demands; the Mongol exploitation caused a nationwide economic crisis. Material burdens were not all, however. Koryo soldiers were a part of the

Mongol invasion force though they had no motive to help the hated master to extend his power to the Japanese islands. If Koryo had been cooperative, it would have warned the expedition forces of the dangers of the kamikazes, the seasonal typhoons of the region, for Koryo's naval personnel should have been familiar with them. In spite of coercion, Koryo's collaboration with the Mongols was minimal and passive.

The Mongol's failure to conquer Japan was a crucial turning point in Yuan-Koryo relations. It was the Mongol intention to use Koryo as a stepping stone for the conquest of Japan. The Mongols had even set up their Eastern Expedition Command in Koryo to supervise the invasion operations. Had the Mongols been successful in invading Japan, Koryo's strategic importance in the Mongol Empire would undoubtedly have increased, resulting in much tighter Mongol control and domination. The nomadic empire's ineptness in naval operations saved the Koryo court and spared the nation from becoming the forward base for the Mongol rule of Japan.

When it finally decided to drop the plan to conquer Japan, the Yuan court removed its direct control from most of the Koryo territory. It retained a direct political overlordship over only three small regions, two in the northern part of the kingdom and one on Cheju Island. Two northern regions were returned to Koryo at its request in 1290 and 1301. The third, the Ssangsung Chongkwanbu, was held by the Mongols until the Koryo forces captured it in 1356.[14]

The Yuan court had employed various means of maintaining its political domination over the Koryo court. Some were of a symbolic nature, while others were rigid and substantive. The approach was designed to keep the Koryo court under its total domination, and it was essentially successful. By now the Yuan Dynasty was no longer a nomadic kingdom but a sophisticated, Chinese-style empire that had gone through a time of unprecedented cultural cross fertilization. The Yuan court's manipulation to dominate the Koryo court included many far-reaching measures; it demanded Koryo to reform its ruling and administrative organs, including the royal institution itself, so that it appeared inferior to its own. The Koryo court complied with the demand: the number of Koryo's administrative departments was reduced, and their names were changed to reflect an inferior status to the Mongols. The Yuan court's obsession with formality was not much different from that of earlier Han Chinese states. To a significant extent the Yuan court inherited the traditions of Sung China, a Han Chinese state destroyed by the Mongols. The Yuan court extensively employed the traditional Chinese practice of symbolism in its drive to put

Koryo under tight political control. The symbolism imposed on Koryo did not remain only symbolic, of course.

The Yuan court was particularly adamant in demanding that the Koryo court follows its system of royal intermarriage, a practice of political association through marriage which was a remnant of nomadic customs that the steppe tribes of central Asia practiced. Under the arrangement, Koryo's kings married Mongol princesses, and their offspring succeeded to the Koryo throne. To make Koryo monarchs thoroughly pro-Yuan, the child princes were taken to Beijing, the capital of the Yuan Dynasty, for education and rearing. A Mongolized prince was allowed to return to Koryo only when he was ready to succeed to the throne. Thus the Mongols installed their own people, at least in a cultural sense, as Koryo's monarchs, who were expected to serve primaily the interests of the Mongols. The damages of the royal intermarriage were serious; some Koryo kings were weak and confused, particularly during the latter part of the dynasty. Although these kings were mostly nationalistic and sought to gain independence from the Yuan court, the Mongol scheme was effective in holding the Koryo court in check.

In addition to the marriage system, the Yuan court liberally employed so-called "yiyi jeiyi," a political ploy of using opponents to defeat each other to keep the Koryo court weak and disunited. The Mongols made the Koryo court a living laboratory for its manipulative politics. Although the Yuan court's political interference was excessive, it was Yuan's incessant demands for material and personnel from which Koryo suffered most. Yuan's harsh economic exploitation of Koryo caused destitution in the small agrarian kingdom. The effects of the heavy burden imposed on Koryo during Mongol expeditions against Japan lingered for years. Notwithstanding, Yuan continued to press Koryo for huge quantities of precious metals and valuable local products such as ginseng and herb medicines.

Yuan's material demands were imperialistic, but its demand for Koryo's virgin girls was infamous. The Koryo court had to make herculean efforts to conscript enough females to meet Yuan's demand. The inhumane practice continued for a prolonged period; the official total number of conscripted girls was 10,000, but the actual number must have been much higher. Understandably there was a huge public outcry against this barbaric and humiliating practice. The reason for the Yuan court's inhumane demands for so many Koryo women was never clearly established. All in all, the cost of maintaining a semblance of independence from the mighty Mongols proved to be neither cheap nor honorable.

The forced emigration of Koryo people to Yuan extended Koryo customs into Yuan to some extent. But as the Mongol's domination of Koryo intensified, the propagation of its customs into Koryo was far more extensive. Some court officials and upper class citizens led the reluctant public in adopting Mongol customs of dress and hair style. In some instances an incoming monarch, after years of residence in Yuan before the assumption of the throne, brought the entire body of Mongol customs with him and encouraged court officials to adopt them.

Yuan's influence was not limited to imposition of its culture. Koryo also was forced to receive systematic transfusions of academic and philosophical knowledge from Yuan. Because of its unique heritage, Koryo had access to intellectual traditions of Chinese empires. Although Yuan extensively imitated Chinese culture, it never achieved the sophistication of Han China. Koryo scholars, many of whom were accomplished students of Confucianism, were generally contemptuous of Yuan's intellectual interference.

It was an embarrassing experience for the Hahn state to endure Yuan's blatant interference for so long. Nevertheless, Koryo's diplomacy of accommodation was not without some dividends. One of these was Yuan's appointment of the Koryo king as the ruler of southern Manchuria, where many Hahn nationals still lived. Yuan's delegation of power over the troublesome region to Koryo was an open acknowledgment that Manchuria was a legitimate concern of the Hahn nation. Ironically, for the first time since the downfall of Koguryo, a Hahn state gained some measure of control over most of the Korean peninsula and southern Manchuria, even though it was under the supervision of the Mongols.

Koryo's acceptance of the Mongols' terms and the subsequent return of its court to Gaesung meant the collapse of its military aristocracy. But the new authority of the monarch did not last long. As Yuan's domination was firmly established, a new power group emerged; court politics were increasingly controlled by officials who engaged in relations with Yuan. Those individuals involved with arranging the endless tribute payments quickly gained power and formed a new aristocratic group. They adopted the same corrupt practices of their predecessors, amassing huge landholding and large numbers of peasant slaves. The kingdom's commoners suffered excruciating tax burdens and forced labor, causing growing political instability.

Worsening abuses and corruption perpetrated by the pro-Yuan ruling class brought many reform movements among young scholar-officials. Although their attempts were repeatedly thwarted by Yuan's intervention, they were convinced that Koryo's economic, political, and military weakness could be cured only through extensive political reform. For its part the Yuan court was determined to maintain the status quo of a weak and divided Koryo. Two Koryo kings, Chungsun and Gongmin, attempted to end Yuan's political influence and to dismantle the corrupt pro-Yuan aristocracy, but their revolts against Yuan were piecemeal and ineffectual until the fortunes of the Mongol empire ebbed.[15] By the middle of the fourteenth century the Yuan dynasty had lost much of its political vitality. Its decline was evident when the Mongol Empire came under heavy attack from many insurgencies waged by the resentful Han Chinese. The court, besieged by internal struggles, was unable to subdue the growing opposition. In 1387 the Han Chinese finally toppled the Mongol dynasty and founded a new dynasty, the Ming. As the Han Chinese reestablished their rule in China, a new order prevailed in northeast Asia.

The downfall of the Yuan Dynasty had direct and profound effects on the Koryo court. Political factions with pro-Yuan inclination rapidly lost their influence as nationalist factions gained power. Finally, reform-minded officials prevailed over the pro-Yuan aristocracy and helped one of the nation's acclaimed generals to seize power. General Yi Sung Gye founded Chosun Dynasty in 1392. Again the Hahn state had survived adversity, enduring extraordinary sacrifices, but in the end outlasting Mongol domination.

4. Koryo and its Geopolitics

Koryo's resistance was waged against the Han Chinese and the northern tribes. Its other neighbor, Japan, had yet to become a major factor in the power politics of the region. The Hahn states' long, bloody struggles against their neighbors had clearly illustrated the critical role the nation's geography played in their foreign relations. The turbulent struggles of Gohchosun, the Three Kingdoms, the Unified Silla, and Koryo cannot be explained without taking account of the unique geographic characteristics of Manchuria and the Korean peninsula. The world has witnessed many nations whose histories were profoundly affected by their neighbors; a few even experienced the tragedy of loss of nationhood to stronger neighbors. Koryo's unusual predicament was a clear manifestation of geopolitics on the Korean peninsula.

The strategic importance of the Korean peninsula and the Manchurian plain had been known to the Han Chinese from the Gohchosun era. They expressed their interest in the region by repeatedly sending expedition armies, which had helped to reduce powerful Koguryo to a small kingdom based in the peninsula. Moreover, the Hahn nation had to surrender the control of Manchuria when Koguryo's successors were unable to recover lost territory. Not even Silla had managed to secure the entire Korean peninsula. Koryo managed to expand the nation's territory to roughly the present-day border, but only through humiliating submission to the Mongol empire. Except for Gohchosun and Koguryo, Korean states were weak and overly compromising to their northern neighbors.

No Chinese state founded by either the Han Chinese or the northern tribes was indifferent to Manchuria and Korea. Chinese empires, like the world's other great empires, were obsessed with the ambition to control their small neighbors. Often they attempted to establish direct control over strategic regions. The pre-Chosun Korean states were never free of heavy military pressure or political interference from the Han Chinese empires and the empires created in Han territory by the northern nomadic tribes. These empire builders were remarkably persistent in their attempts to subdue the equally defiant Korean states. The militant Hahn states, Gohchosun and Koguryo, provided the Chinese with justification not to wait for a strong Korean state, which would be a natural contender for leadership of the region. It was in China's strategic interest to launch preemptive strikes against the Korean states whenever they were capable of doing so. The Koreans responded to China's military ventures with equal hostility. In spite of vast numerical advantage, no Chinese kingdom ever managed to conquer a Korean state. Even under successive adversity, the Koreans learned to outlast the Chinese invaders. The Chinese states often dominated the Hahn nations, but they never conquered the Korean peninsula.

The fact that the Korean kingdoms managed to retain their nationhood, though at times precariously, indicates that Korea's early militancy had won the respect of the Chinese states. Unlike the more militant northern tribes, which China eventually absorbed, the Hahn states usually managed to forestall China's territorial ambitions and safeguarded their territorial integrity. The sole exception was the loss of Manchuria; no unified Hahn state gained strength enough to recover that vast territory.

In addition to periodic destruction and the human suffering inflicted by numerous invasions launched by the Chinese and the northern tribes, the Koreans paid an extraordinary price to protect their national integrity. Against the attempts of bigger and more powerful China, the kingdoms of Silla and Koryo employed various measures of resistance and appeasement. The Korean kingdoms never hesitated to resist the invaders with arms, but when they had exhausted their strength, they wisely chose to pursue the "Hwa-Chin" policy- peace and friendship. Even then the Hahn people had to tolerate their neighbor's tyranny from time to time: the Han and Yuan dynasties ruled parts of the Korean territory, and the Tang Dynasty briefly occupied the whole of Korea right after Koguryo's collapse.

In spite of persistent efforts China had never achieved the total subjugation of Korea. But it gradually succeeded in creating among the Koreans a passive and submissive psychology, replacing the proud militarism with which Gohchosun and Koguryo had commanded vast Manchuria. The Hahn states were more receptive to cultural Sinicization than to political domination. In the end, however, cultural Sinicization proved to be equally damaging to Korea, as the events of the Chosun Dynasty would show.

While the Hahn people were fighting for the survival of their nationhood, their other neighbor, Japan, remained isolated from the conflicts of northeast Asia. Separated from both Korea and China by a body of water, later named the Korea Strait, Japan did not play any significant role in shaping the political map of the region until the sixteenth century. The island nation, politically divided and militarily weak, had yet to gain the strength to project its influence onto the Korean peninsula or to China. Its presence was known only through the envoys it occasionally sent to the Chinese and Korean courts and through its infamous piracy, which often devastated the seacoast areas of its neighbors.[16] Moreover, the pirates, based on Tsushima, an island in the Korea Strait near present Pusan, were largely beyond the control of the Japanese government. Their raids did not diminish over time, and during the later part of the Koryo Dynasty they had become the court's major security concerns. Koryo repeatedly sent expeditions to the island base to eradicate the menace.[17] Except for the piracy, Japan remained little known to the Koryo court.

While the rise of China as a centralized empire often caused incursions onto its border regions, Chinese territorial ambitions never seriously threatened Japan. When its immense power and growing prestige proved incapable of subduing Japan, China rediscovered the strategic significance of the Korean peninsula. Korea was the most logical forward base for any Chinese attempt on the Japanese archipelago, and equally an ideal defensive buffer against any Japanese attempt on Chinese territory. Korea was a natural defensive front for China vis-a-vis Japan. The implications of Korea's strategic location became dramatically evident when the Mongol empire used the Korean peninsula as the springboard for its attempts on Japan. The reverse process was also obvious as later events demonstrated.

The complications of Korea's land-bridge geography were paramount; the peninsula was regarded as a natural extension for power by the world's most aggressive empire builders of modern times. Even after Yuan's domination of the Koryo court ended, the troublesome geopolitics of the Korean peninsula did not improve. If anything, regional geopolitics became even more complex and menacing. The new Korean state was about to enter an even more dangerous period in its history as predatory Japan and the West prepared to participate in the region's territorial and commercial lotteries.

Notes

1. Wang Ghun joined the faction that founded the Kingdom of Later Koguryo in 901 at Songak, present day Gaesung. He was an able and popular general and assumed the leadership when Kungye, the founder, was purged by his followers.
2. It was built about 300 B.C. and further extended in 220 B.C.
3. The Sung Dynasty managed to unify all the Han Chinese territories by 979.
4. Details of this kingdom are not known, yet the assumption is that it was founded by the people of Balhae. It received Koryo's political and economic assistance.
5. A county is a subordinate administrative unit to a province in Korea. But the exact size of these counties can not be determined.
6. A distance of 1,000 ri is equal to 400 kilometers, or about 250 miles. The ri is still used as a measure of distance in Korea.
7. Geomancy was imported from China during the late period of Silla. Under the system, known in Korea as Pungsujirisol or the theory of water, wind, and earth, every landscape was evaluated by four basic characteristics. It is believed that the land influences the destinies of persons, or in this case the court residing in that particular location.
8. The Koreans used the term "big nation" to refer to the Chinese state, the term referring not only to its physical size but also to its dominant relationship to Korea.
9. Confucian pacifism.
10. A number of military men ruled during the period. A series of coups and countercoups marred the early period of military rule. Only the Choe family, which ruled for the last sixty years of the period, managed to give the kingdom some stability.
11. Horse-mounted Mongol forces often used quick-encircling tactics to confuse and immobilize the enemy before they attacked it.
12. Koryo built a fleet of 900 ships using more than 35,000 workers. It also provided 5,000 troops for the Mongol adventure.
13. The Mongol naval failures included an aborted invasion of Java in 1293.

14. The Ssangsung Chongkwanbu was located in the northeastern border region of the nation.

15. King Chungsun reigned from 1308 to 1313, and King Gongmin from 1351 to 1374.

16. Japanese piracy was known to the region as early as the era of the Three Kingdoms, the period 57 B.C. to 935.

17. Koryo expeditions were generally limited to Tsushima, a midpoint between Japan and Korea.

Chapter 3

The Chosun Dynasty

1. The Rise of the Chosun Dynasty

Until the very end of its dynasty, Koryo was never completely free from the Yuan court's interference as Mongol's political dominance over the Koryo court remained firmly entrenched. Using its powerful military and effective royal marriage schemes, the Yuan regime continued to treat the Koryo court as a junior partner. By doing so the Mongols effectively derailed Koryo's aspiration to build a strong nation following the footsteps of Koguryo.

The Koryo court, which was often dominated by incompetent and corrupt pro-Yuan officials, became the subject of intense popular revolts during the later period of its reign. Encouraged by the bulging popular sentiment, the minority opposition initiated a series of reform measures only to find their attempts repeatedly unraveled by Mongol's intervention. The Yuan court was masterful in keeping the Koryo aristocracy divided among itself and alienated from the masses. Unable to unlock the Mongol shackles, Koryo's fate became too closely tied to Yuan's political fortune in the end.

The Mongol empire's political fortune took a rapid decline from the middle of the fourteenth century. Peasant revolts provoked by widespread famine quickly escalated into nationwide anti-Mongol insurrections. Among the most destructive were the Red Turban rebels, who swept many rural provinces and threatened the Mongol court itself. The disintegration of the Mongol empire was under way at a speed only its stunning rise could match. By 1355 most of China was free from Mongol control. Inevitably the rumble of Yuan's political upheavals was felt sharply in the Korean peninsula. The Koryo court's anti-Mongol factions gained strength as Yuan's political control progressively loosened, yet these factions failed to completely dislodge the pro-Yuan faction that managed to hold its power until the end of the dynasty.

In 1387 the downfall of the Yuan dynasty and the rise of the Ming Dynasty, a Han Chinese empire, brought much confusion as well as new hopes in Koryo. Many yearned for a new era away from the defaulting Koryo court, which was then besieged by a myriad of political problems: the chronic despotism of the aristocracy, extensive corruption among Buddhist ranks, the ruinous national economy, exacerbating conflicts between the ruling class and peasants, and the widening gap between small and large land holders. Internal problems were not all that the Koryo court was suffering from; Koryo was fighting against atrocious Japanese piracies along its long coastline in the south and raiding Chinese Red Turban Rebels in the north. Under these pressing circumstances the revival of Koryo was impractical, short of a total revolution. Yet the vintage Koryo court, still controlled by the pro-Yuan aristocracy, baffled popular aspirations by launching a series of belated, piecemeal reforms along with its new anti-China policy. The Koryo court's efforts to rejuvenate the Hahn nation by taking advantage of the power vacuum the collapse of the Yuan court created was, however, too late and too timid. By the time the Ming dynasty began to exert its pressure on the subsiding Koryo court, the Hahn nation had to face the dire consequences of squandering an opportunity to revamp its exhausted dynasty. Koryo became too weak to fend off Ming's pressure and the challenges of domestic opposition.

General Yi Sung Gae, the founder of the Chosun Dynasty, was a highly respected and knighted local warlord; he was one of the nation's most successful military leaders against Japanese piracies and the Red Turban Rebels. In 1392 the court appointed the general to lead an expedition of the Liaodong region in southern Manchuria, a Koguryo territory occupied by Ming. Instead of carrying out the Koryo dynasty's most ambitious military venture, however, he staged a coup by capturing the capital with his expedition forces. Subsequently dissolving the Koryo court, he installed himself as the founding monarch of the new Chosun dynasty, known as the Kingdom of Morning Calm. Although there was substantial resistance among high court officials, General Yi managed to overcome the loyalists' rejection with help of reform-minded officials.

The historical significance of the Chosun dynasty is hard to downplay. The fall of an old dynasty often means the passing of old ideology and thus the dissolution of an old order in favor of new spirit and new vision. The mere shift of the ruling monarch would, therefore, not be a sufficient condition for the opening of a new era. The Chosun court particularly in the early part of the dynasty displayed its ambition to open a new era, evidenced by the high level of energy and practical political philosophy badly lacking in the defunct Koryo court.

General Yi (posthumously called King Taejo) and his supporters pursued the revolutionary transformation of the Korean society by rejecting piecemeal reforms strongly advocated by the loyalists of the Koryo court. The founder of the new dynasty established clear political directions on two fronts: a close alignment with Ming China and a strong royal rule. Although the new regime was founded essentially through usurpation, General Yi emphasized strong, royal authority. He also displayed uncommon understanding of the kingdom's geopolitical limitations by pursuing pro-Ming foreign policy. The new court's directive was more conciliatory than overly ambitious.

The early period of the Chosun era turned out to be a precious respite for the Korean people. Not only was it free from characteristic external threats, but it was also replete with many nation-building programs. During this period the nation's education system was upgraded and a new tax system was adopted along with various social programs. Unfortunately most of these programs were narrow in their scope and slow in their implementation. In spite of good intentions, the Chosun court, like its Chinese counterpart, did not realize that it had barely enough time to upgrade its medieval society before the arrival of the threatening tide of Western imperialism. By the time the Western powers were advancing into the region, Chosun was still in its antiquated state, far from being able to effectively respond to critical international developments. Even under the leadership of the more knowledgeable Chosun court, Korea was not yet to mature fully to utilize the unique geopolitical properties of the Korean peninsula. Still, the region's patent geopolitical game was to be resumed regardless of Korea's poor preparation. This time, however, the problem had become even more compounded by the presence of a strong Japan, and the consequence was more dramatic.

General Yi's primary justification for his takeover of the Koryo court was that Korea should avoid any conflict with new Ming China. His view, although shared by many in the new, reform-minded ruling classes, was contradictory to the then aggressive Koryo court's view that it should take advantage of the situation that Ming was yet to consolidate its power. In this vacuum the Koryo court's ambition was to finally put southern Manchuria under its firm control. But General Yi and his supporters valued the recovery of domestic tranquillity more than the extension of its domain to the Manchurian plain at the risk of provoking Ming China.

Considering the fact that there was a realistic opportunity for Koryo to extend its political sphere to the southern Manchuria through military means, Yi's action was contradictory to the spirit of the aggressive Hahn leaders who ruled the vast northern territory during the era of Gohchosun and Koguryo. However, his maneuver to revert the expedition army to conquer the Koryo court may have been a reflection of the prevailing mentality of the Hahn nation at that particular period that it no longer desired to remain a contender for northeastern Asia. For more than seven hundred years Hahn was out of the Manchurian plain, and by the time the Chosun era opened, the Hahn nationals may have seen their proper role only as the defender of the Korean peninsula. Imperial Han China and militant northern tribes had effectively neutralized the Hahn people's traditional spirit of militant confrontation. The nation's deteriorating spiritual strength was best illustrated by the profoundly dissimilar philosophy of the founding monarchs of the Koryo and Chosun dynasties; Koryo's King TaeJo made it the national priority to recover the old Koguryo territory while Chosun's King TaeJo abandoned an opportunity to recapture some of the Koguryo territory just to assure Ming's friendship.

In spite of his military background, General Yi, like his many political allies, was a man of extensive pro-China sentiments. Following Koryo's heavily sinicized political practice, the Chosun court resumed seeking Chinese guidance in almost every aspect of their ruling without any sense of remorse or humiliation. For those Confucian scholar-officials so deeply accustomed to China sycophancy, an expedition on the Liaodong region was construed as an attack of simple disloyalty on Ming China, even though Ming was yet to make any attempt to take the territory between the Amrok River and the Great Wall held by the Jurchen tribes and offshoots of the Mongols. The Chosun founder and his followers chose not to risk the wrath of Ming even though it may not have looked upon a Korean expedition on this region as an act of bad faith.

Contemporary Koreans surely must wonder at how that gallant spirit of their forefathers had totally disappeared ever since the unification of the Three Kingdoms. They may be mystified by the fact that neither the unified Silla nor Koryo ever seriously attempted to regain the glory of Koguryo. Moreover, while the unified Silla was not able to extend its rule beyond the old Silla-Paekche territory, Koryo never even achieved moving its capital to Pyongyang putting its northward policy into effect, even though the recovery of the Koguryo territory was the founder's publicized desire. When the waning court of Koryo aspired to regain southern Manchuria by sending an expedition force to the Liaodong region, the commander of the expedition force sabotaged the rare Koryo courage and chose to conquer his own court in fear of provoking Ming China. The dream of resurrecting old Koguryo glory was again lost by Yi's pro-Ming coup. As if to make his intention to be the ruler of the Korean peninsula visible, King TaeJo, after consolidating his power, moved his capital to Seoul, south of the old Koryo capital. The Chosun court intended to be a peninsular power only.

Along with the defeatists' assertion that it was incorrect for a small country to attack a powerful country like Ming, the Chosun founder justified his refusal to carry out the expedition on the Liaodong region with another valid strategic argument, a Japanese factor. The general reasoned that it was unwise to drain off the kingdom's military resources when the Japanese raids were so common in the southern part of the nation.[1] This rationalization was based on some inevitable truth. The Japanese piracies, which in their wantonness and brutality were not unlike raids of the Vikings of the Western Europe, were particularly rampant during the middle of the fourteenth century. These raids were no longer confined to the seacoasts as the Japanese grew bold enough to advance even into Koryo's inland territory, occasionally threatening the safety of the throne itself. During the waning period of the Koryo Dynasty, the piracies had become one of the nation's primary security concerns; an extra defense wall was built about the capital, and all government granaries along the coast were moved far inland to protect them from the raids. The piracy was a legitimate security concern and a source of grave financial drain for the Koryo court.

While the Japanese piracy was inflicting severe property damage along Koryo's coastal regions, the Japanese kingdom was making great strides in forming an effective central government. Long shielded by sea from its potential rivals of the region, the island nation was on its way to rise for the first time in history as the region's major power, capable of projecting its military might onto the Asian mainland. Due to its geographic proximity, the Korean peninsula was the first to confront Japan's grand ambition that was slowly beginning to unfold.

In harnessing its extraordinary geographic property, a small peninsula attached to a continental power base, the Korean states had so far displayed only amateurish aptitude. Both the Koryo and Chosun dynasties were not only slow in developing an effective political strategy toward their predacious neighbors, but were also often too passive to engage in the region's peculiar power politics. This problem had become even more critical during the Chosun era; the court's inability to devise effective measures countering the peninsula's geoeconomic weakness was a fatal flaw that placed the nation again into an extreme predicament.

Japan took advantage of its island geography and achieved the state of a single national entity much earlier than Korea. Except for those ill-fated Mongol-Koryo expeditions and a few unsuccessful Korean expeditions directed against the piracies based in the island nation, Japan was left undisturbed by the chaotic political upheavals of the region. In a sense, General Yi was correct in anticipating the serious challenges the Japanese nation represented behind its infamous piracies. In spite of the keen awareness of the threat of Japanese piracies, however, the Chosun court understood only vaguely the growing power of Japan. Neither the founding monarch nor his successors expected that Japan would someday attempt their kingdom by challenging the power of the great middle kingdom, Ming.

While dark clouds approached from both directions, China and Japan, the Chosun court undertook a series of ambitious reforms that included farm policies, the ruling structure, administrative rules and regulations, and the education system. The court's primary objective was to dissolve the power of old aristocratic classes and to create a system to promote more equitable distribution of national wealth. In the process, however, the interests of the public were again severely compromised. The result was the creation of new ruling classes at the expense of the old aristocratic classes and the ever-suffering commoners.

Although the court's land reform produced a dismal result, its energetic reform movements in various other fields had helped the nation to improve its general state of well-being. The early period of the Chosun dynasty was blessed by unusually productive reigns of several visionary monarchs: King Taejong, King Sejong, and King Sejo. They were all radical reformers and worked a revolution in Korean life. Under the visionary leadership of these monarchs, the Chosun court was able to build a political foundation that supported the dynasty for some five hundred years. Particularly important historically was the invention of the Hahn Geul, the Korean alphabet, by King Sejong and his scholars.

King Sejong, the fourth monarch and one of the most brilliant in the history of the Chosun dynasty, sympathized with the inconvenience of his subjects not having their own alphabet. Contrary to the casual presumption that Korea may share the same language and alphabet with China or Japan, the Korean language is entirely unrelated to its powerful neighbors. Yet the language did not have its own alphabet; the first Korean alphabets were invented during the Silla dynasty, but their use was greatly restricted to a small number of commoners because of the popularity of the Chinese characters among the nation's ruling classes and scholar-officials. Until the Chosun era, the Hahn peoples were forced to learn the cumbersome Chinese ideogram if they intended ever to escape illiteracy. As a result, all learning institutions of the pre-Chosun society were in essence private tutorial places for Chinese literature open mainly to rich or ruling class children. For all practical purposes, a learning opportunity was closed to the common people and particularly among the poor and women.

The king appreciated the problem and led his able scholars to invent the Korean alphabet, the On Mun, a purely phonetic alphabet that scarcely has its equal in the world for simplicity and phonetic power. Although there were objections from the ruling-scholar community, who monopolized the nation's literary prerogatives, the use of the On Mun, later renamed as the Hahn Geul, gradually spread among underprivileged masses and then later to more resistant nobility groups. Today the Hahn Geul is Korea's only written language used by its nearly seventy million citizens, making it one of the major alphabets in the world. King Sejong thus achieved a most notable feat that has had an extensive and lasting effect upon the Hahn people.

King Taejo's single-minded pursuit of a strong royal rule continued throughout the early period of the dynasty. King Taejo was able to open his dynasty only with massive support of Koryo's powerful nobility groups, who intended to maintain their dominant power at the new court. Often accompanied by bloody purges, the power struggles went on between the monarch and courtiers of aristocratic leaning until the monarch's absolute direct rule power was clearly established. Yet the scholar-officials managed to retain considerable political power that was occasionally to threaten the royal power.

2. Chosun's Foreign Relations

When General Yi toppled the Koryo court and opened the new dynasty, Ming China was yet to recover from the disastrous Yuan rule. Most of the Manchurian plain was beyond Ming's control. Because of this power vacuum, Yi was able to found the new regime by abolishing the legitimate Koryo court. King Gongyang, the last monarch of the Koryo dynasty, was of the legitimate royalty, unlike his predecessor.[2] Thus, General Yi's usurpation was resisted by Koryo's loyal court officials as well as the Ming court. Under this adverse circumstance, King Taejo was forced to concentrate his considerable diplomatic talent in appeasing the Ming court. Not only did he declare that an attack on Ming would be wrong, but he also sought Ming's consent to the opening of the Chosun dynasty and his own elevation to the throne. He strived to stabilize his new regime by securing the weighty endorsement of the Ming court. As a result, deference to Ming became the Chosun court's official policy from the beginning. By pursuing a close affiliation with Ming, King Taejo sought the legitimation of his extraordinary political maneuver. He eventually succeeded in gaining the blessings of Ming for his throne. Yet the precedent was more than a flagrant display of the Chosun monarch's simple deference to Ming. It was a reflection of the nation's lack of self-confidence, which proved to be extremely harmful to the dynasty and to the Hahn state as a whole.

A close alliance with powerful Chinese states was a common practice shared by both the Koryo and Chosun courts. It is well known to the contemporary Korean public who openly despise such self-invited humiliation. Nonetheless, it is difficult accurately to define its nature or to measure the intensity of such an alliance. At times, the practice was forced by the overwhelming power of the Chinese states, and sometimes it was adopted by the Korean courts merely to neutralize the imminent Chinese hostility. In general, contrary to appearances, such alliances did not represent the Korean kingdoms' total submission to Chinese domination but was mostly political expediency born out of the nation's unique geopolitical circumstances. However undesirable that may have been, such political appeasement was practiced by the Chosun court primarily to prevent its total submission to the Chinese. The deference to the Chinese adopted by the Korean kingdoms was in essence a political dodge, not a submission. On the other hand, Korean kingdoms accepted the Chinese culture freely; they imported it with deliberation and selectivity in the early years but more randomly during the Koryo period under the Yuan pressure. The practice was intensified by King Taejo's pro-Ming policies in the early Chosun era.

The Chosun court expected that Ming's endorsement of the new regime would quiet the domestic opponents and render needed international recognition. Thus, the Chosun court's pro-Ming policy was more a tactical movement than a national submission. Chosun was not to accommodate Ming blindly; when Ming demanded excessive concessions from the Chosun court for its acquiescence on Yi's assumption of the throne, the court resisted with vigor. While it sought a peaceful resolution for conflicts between the two neighbors, the Chosun court was not captivated by undue illusion. On the contrary, King Taejo advocated a policy of maintaining an active plan for an expedition to the Liaodong region, which he had earlier abandoned to conquer the Koryo court, and he built a strong standing army in preparation for possible military confrontations against Ming China.

The new Chosun court moved quickly to establish its rule in the territory along its northern border. At this time most of the Manchurian plain was dominated by remnants of the Jurchen tribes. They made frequent raids on Chosun by crossing the Amrok and Tuman rivers to find food and other living commodities. The Chosun court undertook a successful military expedition to the region in the middle of the fifteenth century and established four counties and six armed garrisons along the rivers to protect the nation's northern territory from the Jurchen raids. In addition, the court moved thousands of people from southern regions to settle in this border region. The Chosun court maintained a hard-line policy particularly toward the Jurchens, although it did not neglect to offer a series of appeasement measures such as allowing the unruly warriors to marry Korean citizens and conferring the court's official titles to deserving Jurchen tribesmen in order to induce their good conduct in the border region.

Japanese piracy continued to be a security concern along the nation's seacoasts in spite of the elevation to the throne of General Yi, the military leader who was most successful in campaigns against Japanese piracy. The Chosun court, realizing the difficulty of eradicating pirates completely, adopted the policy of "Gyo Lin," a good neighbor relationship. When it was necessary to show its strength, the court chose to send expeditionary forces to Tsushima Island, the home base for the pirates. Also, the court sought a peaceful relationship with these highly destructive raiders; to appease the raiders, the court allowed the Japanese to purchase a fixed amount of rice and textiles in a year, and granted their access to three Korean ports. Nevertheless, this dual policy did not solve the lingering problems of Japanese piracy.

By the early sixteenth century, the relative tranquillity that prevailed in northeast Asia since the fourteenth century was profoundly disrupted. The decline of Ming China, the revival of the Jurchen, and the emergence of a unified Japan made the region undergo a transition toward a new military-political order.

3. Japanese Invasion

Japan had remained mostly an obscure power to the rest of the world until the sixteenth century. Japanese culture was developed largely in isolation, although it did receive significant cultural transplantation from both Chinese and Korean kingdoms. As a result, Japanese culture retained more home-grown flavor than those of the Korean kingdoms. By the fifteenth century Japan succeeded in building a quality civilization comparable to that of its two close neighbors in spite of its island location, thus displaying its uncommon capacity to harness its geography. For more than one thousand years Japan had been preoccupied by its destructive domestic infighting among highly divided regional warlords. Yet it was largely immune from foreign interference because of its insular geography. Under this favorable circumstance it gradually solved its domestic squabbles and was able to form a common emotional foundation necessary to build a single national entity.

Japan, a nation of chiefly Mongolian population, began its earlier history on a modest foundation. Although the Japanese myth holds that Jimmu, the legendary first emperor, established a centralized state in 660 B.C., the earliest Japanese society of verifiable historical knowledge existed only in the fifth century A.D. Japan's unique tradition of political decentralization characterized by inheritable political and military offices made the development of a fully centralized state difficult and meandering.

The early Japan experienced short periods of civilian rule before it entered a long period of military rule: the Nara period - 710 to 794 - known as the classic age of Chinese civilization, and the Heian period - 794 to 1185 - in which Emperor Kammu exercised the most potent political power in its history. During the late part of the Heian period some military leaders gained extraordinary political power by suppressing local rebellions and aborigines, and began to rule the country, initiating the military government known as shogunate. The Kamakura shogunate, the first shogunate, ruled Japan for the period from 1185 to 1333.

The shogunate was intensely interested in a central rule. For this end it created some effective administrative systems including one that required stationing its appointees in all of the provinces. As the rule of the shogunate grew firm, the role of the imperial emperor based in the Kyoto court was greatly diminished. The emperor was allowed to function only as a ceremonial figurehead. The failed Mongol invasions of 1274 and 1281 seriously weakened the power of the Kamakura government because it was forced to allow the local lords of Kyushu a degree of independence to fight back the invaders. Subsequently, an alliance of powerful local warlords overthrew the Kamakura shogunate in 1333. Replacing the old regime, the Ashikaga family assumed the shogunate and ruled the nation for the period from 1338 to 1573. Yet the Ashikaga shogunate remained weak and was never able to exercise a strong control over the country, allowing the decentralized country to slip further into feudal fragmentation and disorder.

By the middle of the fifteenth century the island nation plunged into the "warring state" in which military strength was the only means to ensure factional survival and to win power. As a result, successful warriors became provincial daimyos and feudal lords who exercised a virtually autonomous power over large territories. In the end, twenty to thirty large and powerful daimyos survived and controlled the greatest part of the country.

In the middle of the sixteenth century Nobunaga emerged as the conqueror of the central Japanese provinces and salvaged the nation from the anarchy. Although he pursued a grand ambition of unifying the whole nation, Japan's peripheral regions were still out of the central control when he died. Nobunaga's quest was resumed by his able lieutenant, Toyotomi Hideyoshi, whose campaign for national unification was both effective and skillful. He used military suppression of the defiant warlords in the central region but sought alliances from those in the more remote areas. Through his masterly maneuvers Hideyoshi finally achieved an effective central rule for the first time in nearly 200 years. Japan's drive toward a unified nation was greatly helped by its island geography, which sealed the fragmented nation from outsiders and allowed it time for reconciliation and accommodation.

As soon as the unification was achieved, ambitious Hideyoshi turned his energy to what later became the island nation's singular obsession, a territorial expansion abroad. Japan was to channel its militant energy into conquering its neighbors. It chose its closest neighbor, the Korean peninsula, as the first victim of its powerful war machine. What directly precipitated Hideyoshi's invasion of Korea remains somewhat controversial as the question whether he intended to conquer Korea only or eventually China cannot be answered unequivocally. Hideyoshi's government made known both to Riu Kiu islanders and Chosun envoys that its objective was China itself. Yet the size of his invasion force, known to be only 250,000 men, raises a question as to whether his threat was genuine or merely a bluff directed to put China off-balance and thus unable to assist Korea against his invading forces.

It is questionable if Hideyoshi, who would have been well informed about the Chinese military might through the Mongol invasions and perhaps through the notorious Japanese pirates, planned to launch the invasion of both China and Korea with such a meager force. His invasion force was not sufficiently large to be able to subjugate simultaneously both Korea, a significant military force by its own right, and mighty Ming China. The size of the initial invasion force and Japan's great reluctance to leave Korea at the end of the conflict left a strong impression that Hideyoshi's primary objective was to conquer Korea and not China.

Although Hideyoshi's first military venture out of his island territory was limited in scope, there is little doubt that Japan longed to subjugate Ming China, the nation of vast territory with resources that the island nation lacked. Moreover, Japan's Korean invasion would have been easily construed as an attack on China itself because of the special relationship existing between the two countries. Japan's military success against even Korea would have been a severe humiliation to the Middle Kingdom and would have helped Japan to gain international recognition.

The notion that Hideyoshi's invasion of Korea was motivated only by his desire to humiliate the Middle Kingdom is dubious, particularly in the light of the vehement territorial demands Japan made at the end of the war. In addition to the island nation's apparent territorial ambition, there were other probable motives more directly connected to Hideyoshi himself. Succeeding the popular Nobunaga Shogunate, Hideyoshi lacked a power base needed to effectively counter the strong discontent shared by defeated daimyos and samurai warriors. Under the circumstance he may have attempted to build his own political power base and simultaneously to quell the social unrest by initiating military operations abroad. The invasion was an ideal prescription for the new shogunate to pacify powerful domestic rivals as the war was expected to supply new land and trade routes.

Nevertheless, the most decisive single factor that prompted Hideyoshi's invasion of Korea was that there was utterly no meaningful defense preparation in Korea. In spite of repeated warnings of some far-sighted officials, the Chosun court failed to heed the appeals of some far-sighted leaders to undertake a national defense build-up to face the imminent danger.[3] Instead, the incompetent court was immersed in a fool's paradise, a disastrous ignorance created by the complacency of a long peacetime and a habitual demeaning of Japan as an inferior nation of "dwarfs." The leadership of the Chosun court was lacking both the energy and prescience of the early periods, but the factional power struggles made the courtiers overlook even critical matters such as national survival. The Chosun court's final invitation for the Japanese invasion was issued by its rejection of the proposition to build a 100,000 men standing army. The court was dominated by a short-sighted political faction whose only defense policy was to nurture a friendly relationship with Ming China. The court was in absolute dark over the nature and extent of the danger the nation of "dwarfs" was about to impose. It was unable to comprehend a situation that might endanger the very existence of the nation.

The introverted Chosun court naively assumed that the military might of its masterly neighbor, Ming China, would provide an adequate shield against any Japanese attempt. Ming remained Chosun's only ally, but Ming had entered a period of gradual political decline since the early sixteenth century; moreover, its inner court, heavily dominated by controversial eunuchs, was involved in a damaging power struggle among contending factions. Ming may have been neither willing nor readily able to commit a large military force on behalf of its tributary neighbor. Yet the Chosun court interpreted the deteriorating relationship between Ming China and Japan as a firm indication that Ming would resist any Japanese hostility in Korea. During the early part of the sixteenth century the Ming court adopted strict policies toward Japan as a response to ravages inflicted by its piracies.

The Japanese invasion force landed at the port city of Pusan in May 25, 1592, thus initiating the most needless, unprovoked, and cruel war that ever cursed Korea. In spite of desperate resistance of the local garrisons, Chosun's skeleton military was not prepared to fight against the highly motivated invading army. The defenders were hopelessly under-equipped and vastly outnumbered by the invaders; most early encounters proved to be tragic mismatches between Chosun's ancient military equipped with bows and arrows and Japanese warriors trained to use Western muskets. Japanese utilization of Western firearms during this period was limited but exceptionally effective against Chosun's antiquated force.

Japan's acquisition of Western firearms was a chance contribution made by its insular location. Japan learned the use of Western firearms and certain other military techniques from the Portuguese, whose stranded merchants visited the Japanese shore in 1542. Although Japan's attempt to purchase Portuguese warships failed, their new firearms, mostly pistols, proved to be devastating to Korean defenders, who were completely ignorant of such modern firearms. Facing the determined Japanese invasion, the Chosun court belatedly realized that its military force existed mostly on paper. The unscrupulous management of the nation's military, in which the court routinely collected money as a substitute for one's military service, had reduced the nation's standing army and lowered its quality. On its way to Seoul, the Japanese invasion force, led by Kato and Konishi, met little meaningful resistance. Even Chosun defenders' desperate stand at the bank of the Hahn River, the last strategic barrier in defense of the capital, was not effective in slowing the invading column.

The nation suffered a major defeat because of its grossly inadequate war preparation in terms of both competent military leaders and trained troops. In addition, the invasion army's employment of blitz tactics and new firearms devastated the unprepared defenders; the military prowess and martial spirit of the Japanese force, which took the defenders by great surprise, caused such universal panic that Korean forces were unable to offer any meaningful resistance during the first few weeks of the war.

The invasion force captured Seoul, the capital, within thirty days after its landing at Pusan. The fall of the capital turned out to be a great calamity and national humiliation for the Hahn nation. Paradoxically, however, the fall of Seoul helped to save Korea and perhaps Ming China from a total defeat. Instead of stopping at the capital, had the invasion force with its incredible impetuosity pushed straight to the Amrok River, a national boundary between Chosun and Ming, Hideyoshi's force would have been able to quite possibly threaten the Ming court itself without meeting any credible resistance. The invading army's prolonged stall at Seoul provided the Korean forces a precious respite to reorganize a counteroffensive and to prove their real strength. Although the invasion force's advance was resumed in northern Korea months later, by then the momentum of its blitz had been considerably weakened.

The northward drive of the invasion force continued for a while in spite of the Korean forces' rejuvenated resistance; the Korean defenders established two major defense lines at the Imjin River just north of Seoul and the Daedong River south of Pyongyang only to be overrun by the invaders. The futile defense efforts were a plain verification of the Chosun force's hopeless deficiency in both basic knowledge of modern warfare and, more importantly, an effective chain of command. Both engagements were lost in spite of the defenders' superior tactical positions because the Chosun forces could not employ effective counter measures. In addition, the Chosun forces' defense effort was hampered by the army's poor organization and its outdated leadership that was concerned more with individual reputation than a systematic organization of the war effort. Chosun's military leaders were in essence fighting personal but not national battles and thus were prone to the inexcusable blunder of risking the fate of the entire nation in pursuit of individual face-saving.

The court itself was able to provide neither effective leadership nor an overall war plan except for some impromptu responses motivated by rampant jealousy and suspicion of court politics. By squandering two strategic attempts to turn the tide of the war around, the court had no choice but to retreat further north near the Chinese border. By winter the whole nation except for small areas of the northern border region was under Japanese occupation. As Chosun's land-based defense force was unable to match the invaders, the fate of the Korean state depended upon the nationwide resistance of volunteer forces and Admiral Yi's navy.

Miraculously, however, this odd combination was turning the tide of the war in favor of Korea.

Despite the desperate wishes of the Chosun court, Ming China was slow to respond to Korean appeals for immediate military assistance. Only when the invaders advanced close to the Korea-China border, posing the danger that Hideyoshi's force could reach the strategic Liaodong region, did Ming China finally agree to send a small-sized force to help the exhausted Korean defenders.[4] By the time the Ming force entered the conflict, however, the war was already turned around by determined Korean defenders. If the Chosun court had been more analytical and far-sighted, it might not have asked the Ming force to participate in the war that was basically won by Korea's volunteer army and naval force.

When the fate of their nationhood was dramatically perilous under the siege of the invasion force, the Korean masses rose to defend their nation with their utmost bravery and sacrifice. Even though their grievances and disappointments over the nation's ruling classes remained severer than anytime before, the public rallied throughout the country to fight the invaders. They waged gallant guerrilla warfare all over the nation, which quickly added to the national resistance. The volunteer army, called "Eiy-Byung," or the soldiers of rightness, ranged from a few hundreds to thousands and was led by improvising leaders of farmers, scholars, former officials, socialites, and religious figures. They effectively harassed the invader's garrisons that were set up to guard long supply routes and helped to disrupt the advancement of Japanese frontline units. The voluntary forces' resistance was particularly vicious in the southern region so that the invaders were kept out from most of the Jolla provinces, the nation's richest agricultural region. The lightly-armed and untrained resistance army often suffered tragic losses but vividly persisted in portraying the undying spirit of the Korean people. As a result, the war produced many civilian heroes whom contemporary Koreans continue to revere greatly. In spite of the utter failure of the court and ruling classes, the spirit of the Hahn nation was splendidly displayed by the masses. They did not, in all fairness, win the war, but they were the backbone of the war effort the nation was finally able to muster.

Then there were the miracles of Korean naval forces commanded by the Nelson of Korea, Admiral Yi Soon Shin. While the early skirmishes on land were no more than repeated disasters for ill-prepared defenders, the situation at sea was entirely different. The admiral's control of the Korea Strait was such that it forced the invaders to retreat on land and finally to withdraw from the Korean peninsula. In reality, it was Admiral Yi who single-handedly salvaged the Hahn nation from the Japanese attempt. Admiral Yi, the most revered military man in the history of the Korean nation, assumed his post as the naval commander for the Jolla province only the year before the invasion. Nonetheless, the farsighted admiral quickly assembled a quality naval force and built the world's first iron-clad warships, named Goebuksuns or Turtle Ships. The ships had a curved deck of iron plates that completely sheltered the fighters and rowers inside, rendering the ship impervious to enemy fire arrows. In front was a crested head with wide open mouth through which arrows and other missiles could be discharged. The Goebuksuns were not only far more agile but profoundly more powerful than bulky Japanese warships.

Although the Goebuksuns were exceptional, the most decisive advantage the Korean navy had over the numerically superior Japanese navy was the presence of Admiral Yi, the resolutely loyal and outstanding leader. His single-minded loyalty and trenchant naval strategies greatly helped to salvage the nation from almost certain defeat and Japanese territorial ambition. He was the most brilliant military hero and unselfish patriot that the Korean nation ever produced in its long and battle-scarred history.

As soon as the war broke out Admiral Yi quickly established decisive control over the Korea Strait, a narrow body of international water that separated the two neighbors. Admiral Yi's highly disciplined navy, although it was disadvantaged both in number of ships and size, created instant havoc by effectively demolishing Japanese ships bringing reinforcements and supplies for the invading force. The Chosun navy turned out to be the kingdom's best kept secret and the last hope to defeat Hideyoshi. Admiral Yi's forces controlled the coastal seas of Korea so tightly that Japan's access to Korean ports soon became extremely hazardous. Doing so, the admiral denied the Japanese land army fresh replacement and reinforcement troops. Furthermore, Admiral Yi's spectacular success against the Japanese had motivated many civilian resistance fighters and the court to take a more positive attitude toward the war. The navy and voluntary forces soon imposed a war of great attrition upon the Japanese invaders. More importantly, the nation was gaining confidence that it could defeat the enemy.

Admiral Yi maintained a highly effective naval blockade throughout the war; his force not only frustrated Japan's repeated attempt to dispatch fresh troops but also trapped the invaders in southern Korea for many years. In the end, Japan's invasion army fell into a dread dilemma; they were fighting the war without any realistic hope of winning because of the growing strength of both Chosun and Ming forces, but they were not welcomed to return home while Hideyoshi's dream remained unfulfilled. Moreover, they were not allowed to leave the Korean shore alive by the watchful ruler of the Korea Strait, Admiral Yi. Gradually their northward marching army was forced to turn back and began to retreat to southern coastal areas. The Chosun court returned to Seoul in October 1593. The total eradication of the invading force was not accomplished for a while because the Japanese forces continued to resist the Chosun-Ming forces in the southern part of the peninsula. Nonetheless, as the conflict fell into a long stalemate, peace negotiation followed, which lasted for three years. The negotiation did not bear immediate results largely because of extensive Japanese demands, which included territorial concessions. As the negotiation remained bogged down, the bulk of the invading force continued to be trapped in the coastal areas of southern Korea while the sea was completely controlled by Admiral Yi's naval force.

Hideyoshi dispatched another invading force in 1596. This time his intention was clearly to punish Korea rather than to invade China. He was mindful that his great plan of humiliating China was scuttled by the Korean defenders. On the other hand, this time Korean defenders knew better how to deal with the invaders. That terrible glamour that surrounded the dreaded invaders' first appearance had worn off. Meanwhile, the Korean forces themselves had obtained some Western firearms and were trained to use them. The only Japanese advantage was the fact that Admiral Yi was removed from his command and now served elsewhere as a plain foot soldier, a victim of Chosun's notorious party strife, a prime cause of national weakness. No sooner did he arise as a war hero than he became the target for the hatred and jealousy of rivals, and no trickery was left untried to have him degraded and disgraced. Not until after Japan managed to destroy the Chosun navy, which Admiral Yi had painstakingly built, did the self-destructive Chosun court reinstate the nation's only naval hero to his old command post.

The admiral quickly regained control over Korean coasts. Under the most perilous circumstance the admiral did his supreme duty of defeating the Japanese invaders again with noble poise and unbending loyalty. He was killed during the last naval battle in which the Chosun navy inflicted the most crushing defeat on the Japanese navy. He managed to save the nation from the Japanese invasion by sacrificing himself.

The invading forces, trapped in southern coastal areas by the Chosun-Ming forces and cut off from their home island base by Admiral Yi's navy, were finally allowed to retreat to their homeland after Hideyoshi's death in 1598. In spite of the devastation, Chosun did not succumb to the ambition of its island neighbor. Ming's late, reluctant assistance did provide meaningful help, but the war was largely fought and won by the Koreans.

The Japanese invasion of Korea lasted for seven years. Hideyoshi neither achieved his proclaimed objective to open China to Japanese trade nor subjugated Chosun despite his early success. Instead, the war, the ominous portent of the island nation's yearning for a foothold on the Asian mainland, created nothing but excessive misery and destruction upon the masses of Korea. It did plant in Koreans long-lasting seeds of hatred and suspicion toward their island neighbor. The residents of the Korean peninsula had to realize the fatal dangers of having an extremely hostile and ambitious island neighbor in the south along with a predatory neighbor in the north. They also found the true nature of their meddlesome neighbor, Ming China, which had been intrusive in almost every aspect of their lives but proved to be reluctant to support them in time of dire need. Whether the Koreans learned enough from the ordeal of Hideyoshi's misfired venture was not that apparent.

The ramifications of the war were significant not only for Korea but also for both Japan and China. The Chosun court had to undertake massive rebuilding programs to heal the disastrous wounds of the war. Meanwhile, the war had accelerated the decline of Ming China. In Japan, Hideyoshi's death created room for a new shogunate, the Tokugawa regime. Ironically, it was the Chosun court that survived the war with the least political damage; docile Korean masses that showed such determined resistance to the Japanese invaders were yet to defy their incompetent court. Yet no participant came out as a victor.

Japan's first invasion of the Asian mainland was a categorical failure, and her ambition to be established as a mainland power was shattered. Moreover, the invasion force was not able to put a single fighter on Chinese soil despite the intention to attack and humiliate the great Middle Kingdom. The island nation suffered one of the most complete naval defeats ever at the hands of a nation supposedly with only a land army. For many years Japan's invasion force was not even allowed to retreat home by the Korean navy, a humiliation the Japanese navy had to long endure. The fiasco, however, produced no perceptible change in the region's political map; Ming China still remained a premier power although her prestige was damaged by inconclusive military operations in Korea. Chosun remained as close an ally to Ming as ever, and Japan returned to her customary isolation. It only proved that Hideyoshi's great ambition was much premature, although it plainly revealed for the first time the island nation's expansionist tendency.

Tokugawa Ieyasu, Hideyoshi's ally, prevailed on the remnants of the Hideyoshi shogunate and in 1600 emerged as the third unifier of Japan. Unlike dictatorial Hideyoshi, the new leader sought a legitimacy for his new national government by having the emperor confer on him the hereditary title of shogun. In contrast to Hideyoshi's costly Korean invasion, Japan under the stable rule of the Tokugawa shogunate was to experience a period of orderly domestic development: warfare was stilled, a cultural renaissance reached a height, education sponsored by academies of the Neo-Confucian persuasion broadened, and rulers of varying abilities made an orderly succession. Japan's traditional, self-imposed isolation continued until 1853 when the United States forced the island nation to end her seclusion.

Ming China, reluctantly at first but then desperately later, poured vast numbers of men and material into Chosun's war against Japan to protect its own territory and prestige. By so doing it impoverished the already declining fortune of the nation and left the Middle Kingdom vulnerable to the rising Manchu power. In many ways Ming China was the big loser of the war in spite of its superficial victory. For all its immense size, Ming revealed its military ineptitude against the island power. Moreover, its great reluctance to use its power to help the close ally left a distinctive impression of being an unreliable friend. The Ming court failed to reciprocate the Chosun court's loyalty to it; their traditional close relations prevented the Chosun court any cooperation with Japan.

4. The Rise of Ching

The rise of Ching China, the Manchu dynasty, began in the northeast Manchurian plain several decades before the end of the Ming dynasty. While the Ming court was absorbed in damaging factional infighting and suffered from the great financial drains through its military campaign against the Japanese invasion in Korea, a tribal leader of the Jurchen named Nurhachi began to consolidate his power by unifying tribes scattered in the Manchurian plain. By 1616 the Jurchen had grown to establish the Later Kin dynasty in the Liaodong area. The growing power of the Manchu regime threatened the waning Ming dynasty and naturally provoked its hostility. The Ming court attempted to eradicate the looming danger in its northeastern border region. Pursuing a strategy to attack the Manchu from two fronts, the Ming court sought Chosun's military cooperation. A concerted attack by a Ming-Chosun alliance would have been effective as the new Jurchen empire was yet to stabilize its power base in the region.

The Manchu regime also was conscious of the strategic importance of Korea in its confrontation with Ming. It requested Korea to maintain a neutrality in the conflict. For the Chosun court, sending a sizable force on behalf of withering Ming was an extremely ill-afforded venture as the nation was not yet fully recovered from the devastating war against Japan. Furthermore, the court, having experienced the Japanese invasion, grew more deliberate in its foreign relations. Nevertheless, its uniquely close relationship with Ming made it difficult for the Chosun court to reject Ming's overture. At the end, the court was compelled to respond to the Ming request favorably, although its military cooperation was only symbolic in nature; it sent a small force to join the Ming force against the Later Kin.

In spite of the vocal minority view that advocated its neutrality over the Ming-Manchu rivalry, the Chosun court maintained a loyalty to Ming. The Chosun court's pro-Ming policy was contradictory to its national interests, but its emotional tie to Ming was too great and deeply rooted. The Chosun court was swayed more by a highly sinicized notion of universal righteousness than by calculated national interests in conducting its state affairs. Such unsophisticated conduct was a distinctive shortcoming of the Chosun court. In this regard King Gwanghae's deliberate approach to remain loyal to Ming but neutral in the Ming-Manchu disputes was indeed a rare exercise of good judgment. The Chosun court's carefully maintained semi-neutrality in the Ming-Manchu conflict lasted only a short period as more deliberate and independent King Gwanghae was deposed. The successor, King Injo, discarded neutrality by cutting off the relationship with the Manchus and openly siding and collaborating with Ming to subjugate the Manchu regime. By strengthening its relations with fading Ming, the Chosun court committed a major strategic blunder.

To the rising Manchu power, Korea's defiant siding with its enemy was an intolerable provocation. Chosun's open challenge eventually drove the Manchu regime to undertake a military campaign against the Hahn nation. In 1627, the Kin of the Jurchen sent an invading force and quickly overran the Chosun defenders in the northern part of the peninsula. The Korean peninsula was again invaded by a neighbor less than thirty years after it suffered the Japanese invasion. Ming, suffering from nationwide military and peasant revolts, was hardly in a position to rescue Chosun from the Manchu assault. This first Ching invasion had two objectives: to eradicate the Ming forces from the Chosun territory in order to secure its rear, and to force the Chosun court to abandon its alliance with Ming. The mighty Ching force easily subdued the sporadic resistance of the Chosun force and extracted major concessions from the Chosun court. The invasion was terminated in fifty days with the signing of a protocol to establish a brotherly relationship between the two nations, Ching assuming the elder brother role.

Ching did not wait long before it demanded Chosun to rearrange their mutual relationship from a brotherly one to a sovereign-subjects relationship. The weak Chosun court succumbed to another internal turmoil as pacifist factions and hard-liners of justice collided over the Ching ultimatum. In the end, the hard-liners prevailed and the Chosun court rejected the Manchu regime's demand, risking another military confrontation. In 1636, Ching launched its second invasion of Chosun. Under the heavy pressure of a large invasion force, Chosun's defense effort quickly crumbled. Furthermore, the court's desperate attempt to survive the invasion on the Kanghwa island like the Koryo rulers did under the Mongol seizure failed. Facing total subjugation, the court had to accept the Manchu terms and recognize Ching as its masterly neighbor. The invasion lasted a short period, minimizing the war damages to the northwestern region. Yet in that region both human suffering and property damage were excessive, a result of Manchus' nomadic nature.

As Manchu's political influence grew, interfering in Chosun's domestic politics, the Korean people's hostility toward the Manchu regime also deepened. Chosun's animosity to its new dictator was greatly compounded by the feeling that the nation's latest humiliation was imposed by the culturally inferior tribes. Anti-Manchu emotions were to remain high and long in Korea. There were some strong sentiments to attack the Manchu in alliance with Ming. Even after Ming was destroyed by the Manchu, King Hyojong advocated an expedition to punish the new ruler of northeast Asia. None, however, was actually implemented. The Manchus captured Beijing in 1644 and proclaimed it the capital of a new Ching dynasty. More than anything its superior military power enabled the Manchus to conquer the declining Ming, an empire that had at least fifty times the conqueror's own population.

5. Chosun's Domestic Woes

One may deeply wonder how the repeated foreign invasions which took place on the Korean peninsula under similar circumstances always resulted in almost identical outcomes: inadequate defense measures and inept resistance. No one reason can be singled out as the sole cause, but there are some factors most responsible for the nation's uneasy and problematic foreign relations reviewed so far.

The geography of the Korean peninsula is unique and problematic in nature. However, it is not the exclusive cause for the nation's recurring failures and humiliations. Several additional factors provide some insights into the Korean kingdom's repeated failure to defend its territory and citizens. They were the peninsula's poor economic base, small population, mediocre political leadership, and the disconcerted spiritual make-up of the ruling class.

As in other nations in the pre-industrial era, agriculture was the backbone of the Korean economy from the early period of its history. The history of mankind testifies that a nation's ability to produce agricultural surplus is a prerequisite to progress in non-agricultural spheres. Theoretically, if every citizen is engaged in subsistence farming, there will be no extra manpower to be employed in other cultural or military activities. Korean agriculture up to the early part of the Chosun dynasty was not much beyond the subsistence level for most small plot farmers, who bore the majority of the nation's taxes. Because of the weak economic base, the Korean courts were not far from virtual financial collapse even in the best of times. The lack of financial resource, measured in the quantity of rice at government disposal, was the primary factor for the Chosun court's failure to build a strong standing army. The general conscription system was compromised most by the extensive practice of the in-lieu, cash equivalent for active military service, a method employed to supplement the regular tax collection. The military suffered both in size and quality as a result. The rampant corruption among the ruling class - which often abused its privileges in appropriating farmers' land and therefore further deprived the government of a source of tax revenue- exacerbated the nation's financial woes. The nation's numerous Buddhist temples, which were granted similar extraterritorial privileges, similarly damaged the nation's financial well-being. On the other hand, Chosun was slow to develop more productive farming methods; although the nation practiced sedentary farming from as early as the fifteenth century B.C., even rudimentary irrigation methods were not adopted in its rice farming until the last half of the Chosun dynasty. Adhering to old-fashioned farming methods, the nation's farmers suffered low yields and consequently higher tax burdens. The nation was never able to build an economy strong enough to compete against its much larger neighbors.

Korea's small population base was also a distinct disadvantage. Considering the size of China, Korea's human resources were pitifully limited; at the turn of the seventeenth century Korean population reached only five million compared to 120 million in China. Unable to maintain a strong standing army due to insufficient financial and human resources, Korean kingdoms were often defeated by even relatively small forces of determined invaders.[5] Various plans of strong defense and northern expeditions fizzled mostly because the nation could not afford the expense.

Korea's small land size, a poverty-stricken economy, and a hereditary ruling system all adversely affected the quality of Korean monarchs. Being a land of small size, the Korean peninsula was accustomed to house only one regime since the unification of the three kingdoms by Silla. Any political decentralization was not tolerated, unlike the case with Japan and China where a decentralized rivalry often produced rulers of better quality and intention. In Korea, the royal courts of each dynasty always prevailed over the entire nation and were responsible for providing a measure of political stability. By not having any political competition, however, the system allowed the rulers to fall into complacency and indifference. The intensive political pressures of powerful local warlords and administrators that motivated many Chinese emperors to govern better as supreme rulers did not develop in Korea.

Both the Koryo and Chosun dynasties' strict blood-line monarchy system did manage to produce a few outstanding monarchs. Unfortunately, their capable leadership was almost entirely consumed in laying a foundation for new dynasties. Except for several enlightened periods, both the Koryo and Chosun dynasties suffered greatly from stagnated political leadership. Even when Chosun was blessed with the ruling of some farsighted and unusually aggressive rulers, the nation's poor economy and incompetent ruling classes frustrated their ambition. The ruling aristocracy that was in a perpetual power struggle disproportionately harmed the nation. There is no doubt that Korea suffered more from its mediocre political leadership than anything else. It was the powerless masses, not the political leadership, that kept the nation alive from incessant foreign interventions.

The fourth important factor was the peculiar mental framework shared by many Korean rulers and the nation's ruling class. They had developed and clung to a flawed assumption that Han China was the power to be respected with loyalty and devotion. They believed that China was the center of the world, a father figure to Korea, and an entity not to compete against but to obey and to follow. The question of how Korean leadership managed to be so thoroughly sold to the Chinese dynasties only leads to provocative conjectures. Once China's image as the middle kingdom of the world was set in the mind of Korean ruling classes as early as the era of the unified Silla, Korea's political philosophy was hopelessly skewed and distorted. The Korean court's loyalty and devotion to Chinese states was often the very source of its own self-destruction. Yet the toady courtiers justified their shameful puppetry with the dubious notion of righteousness and justice, perhaps the correct assumption from the Chinese viewpoint. This self-defeating, pro-China stand was not necessarily a result of the successful sinification of the Korean peninsula. The pro-China ploy was brazenly employed by the Korean court officials as a convenient and mostly effective prop in their factional political infighting. Excessive power struggles that engulfed many Korean courts had a definite tendency to turn a blind eye to the nation's long term strategic interests. Some ruling monarchs conveniently showed their loyalty to Chinese emperors to save their sagging popularity and mediocre governing ability. A questionable succession in the Chosun court was often followed by urgent requests for Chinese consent, not recognition, for new ruler.

Pro-China politics was also a mainstay of Chosun's foreign policy; in exchange for the humiliating tributes and political subordination, they hoped that the kingdom's territorial integrity would remain intact and that their woes of foreign invasion would vanish. On the contrary, they often discovered the alliance with China was not an answer to the vicious hostilities of the northern tribes and Japan. Nevertheless, the Korean court's devotion and loyalty to Chinese empires was remarkably consistent even under the harsh treatment it had to endure from the non-Han Chinese dynasties.

Han China had failed to incorporate the Korean peninsula into its own territory, but it succeeded to some significant degree to sinicize Korean ideology partly through coercion and partly through the Korean people's genuine respect for Chinese culture. In reality, China's attempt to sinicize the Korean peninsula was quite successful during the Koryo dynasty, and a definite pro-China atmosphere settled into Korean society by the early part of the Chosun dynasty. In the end, the single directional political arrangement Korea had pursued under its Confucian tradition turned out to be extremely costly and harmful for the nation as testified to by further unfolding events.

6. Reforms Too Late and Too Little

After enduring the devastating invasions of both Japan and the Manchus, Chosun was given approximately two centuries of respite from foreign invasion. The nation had to utilize this rare tranquility to dismantle its medieval society and to prepare itself for the even more rapacious foreign challenges the modern age brought to the region. Even if the court had sufficient foresight to comprehend the momentousness of the impending Western imperialism, which it clearly did not, the time was pitifully short for the nation to recover from the war damages and to lay down foundations for an efficient and strong nation.

In spite of its almost deliberate ignorance of the outside world, the Chosun court was under gigantic pressure to undertake some major reforms. Such revolutionary reforms were necessary to appease the masses, whose livelihood had been disrupted so many years. Even before the Japanese invasion, Chosun was experiencing severe economic stresses. The invasions of Japan and the Manchus greatly exacerbated the problem, leading both the court and the nation's farmers into virtual financial collapse. The fact that Hideyoshi's invasion alone had reduced the size of the nation's cultivated land to two-thirds of the prewar level clearly illustrated the severity of the nation's economic woes. The result was extensive famine and socioeconomic chaos for which the court was obliged to provide ill-afforded relief. The nation's chronic food shortages and excessive tax burdens drove many small-plot farmers into the ranks of bandits and rebels.

The Chosun court responded to the kingdom's dire socioeconomic maladies with a series of tax reforms to lessen the financial burdens on small farmers and tenant farmers. It abolished a perennially corrupt practice of collecting local products for governmental use. Instead, it initiated a new tax for the government's procurement programs. This practice was responsible for the accumulation of the kingdom's infant commercial capital and the development of small manufacturing industries. In spite of some noticeable progress that the new tax procedures brought, the integrity of the nation's tax system continued to be marred by still widespread corruption.

Another heavy burden the nation's farmers had to bear was the inequitable military service. Under the law every non-gentry male from sixteen to sixty years old was obliged to serve military duties or to pay for the service instead. The result was that rich farmers were exempted from the service, leaving the nation's military services to poor farmers and slaves. This became such a controversial issue that in 1751 the court resorted to create another universal tax to equalize the burden of the military service. As usual, the new tax did not alleviate the extensive injustice but became only an additional burden to the non-gentry public. The Chosun society was still run by the aristocracy- the nation's political establishment and the rich gentry class-who exempted themselves from any tax obligations. This practice was to become totally self-defeating as the number of the nation's gentry kept growing.

In addition to the reform measures adopted by the court, there were some important initiatives taken by the nation's farmers. Chosun's impoverished farmers increasingly dared to adopt revolutionary farming methods notwithstanding the risk of a year's rice crop failure. It was a desperate move for farmers who confronted dismal prospects of a better life under the given situation. With an uncharacteristic enthusiasm, the farmers began to adopt seed-bed planting instead of the customary direct planting method in their rice farming. The seed-bed planting method was being practiced to some extent in the southern part of the nation but was being suppressed elsewhere by the government as the new method was more prone to crop failure by periodic droughts. The conservative court preferred the status quo while the hard-pressed farmers chose to gamble for their long-term welfare. In the end, the farmers prevailed and forced the government to commit itself to building extensive irrigation systems. The new method not only significantly improved the productivity of rice farming, but also allowed farmers to cultivate two crops a year. The farmers' initiative was generally responsible for the nation's two-fold increase in rice output that helped to lessen its chronic food shortages. This was one of the more farsighted moves Korean farmers were forced to take, a risky but imperative stand over the timid and often inept court.

The improved productivity in rice farming brought significant changes to the Chosun society; some able farmers began to expand their landholding, thus elevating themselves to commercial farmers. The coming of commercial farming that required fewer workers in spite of larger farm size, however, forced marginal farmers to leave farm work and to seek employment elsewhere. Many moved to urban areas and sought non-agricultural employment. Through this agricultural evolution, the Chosun society entered the era of a more diversified economy, although the process was slow and incomplete as non-agricultural sectors were to remain underdeveloped for a long period to come. The result was that prosperous farmers and affluent gentry landowners became more numerous at the expense of many small plot farmers who traditionally bore the bulk of the nation's revenue production. The evolution oddly managed to turn the kingdom's poor revenue base even more anemic while the nationwide problems of dislocated small-plot farmers worsened.

The Chosun court encouraged the development of commercialism through the court's new procurement methods. Under the new procedure, administrative agencies purchased their supplies from periodic markets in rural areas and permanent markets in urban areas in order to encourage the growth of competitive producers. Merchants that participated early in the market transactions sponsored by the court accumulated wealth by establishing monopolies. Other merchants entered the practice later and collaborated in building more autonomous commercial institutions nationwide. Some progressive merchants gradually expanded their activities to new but closely related sectors such as banking, warehousing, transportation, and manufacturing. By the middle of the eighteenth century some merchants had amassed such a wealth that they gained status high enough to exercise substantial political influence.

The development of the manufacturing industry followed a route much similar to the commercial sector. As the nation's economy continued to expand, progressive merchants who filled governmental orders gradually abandoned their monopolistic practice and began to participate in the market system. Industrial production of mainly household items and weaponry grew as the public's purchasing power increased and trade with neighboring countries expanded. The expanding manufacturing sector and a readily available labor force made the mining industry also grow at a rapid rate at this time. One interesting aspect of Chosun's manufacturing in this early period is that the industry was extensively oriented to handicraft areas. Somehow Korea was extremely slow to develop machine industries, an obvious victim of Korea's long devotion to the Confucian tradition in which scientists and skilled technicians and their works were relegated to near the bottom of the social hierarchy, while the literary-officialdom was at the highest.

The evolution that was reshaping Korea's medieval economic structure brought profound changes to its traditional social hierarchy. The traditional caste system that divided the society into gentry, ordinary citizens, and slaves was markedly undermined by the rise of affluent farmers, powerful merchants, and industrialists. As the gentry class's influence was being undermined by the wealthy, the society began to lose class rigidity. In the end, the gentry status itself could be bought by anyone who could afford the price. The degradation of the gentry class reached the point that some poor and unemployed gentry became tenant farmers.

The general devaluation of the gentry class in the Chosun society was a symptom of a deeper flaw that the society was suffering. Through the wars against Japan, known as the "Dwarf's War in the Yimjin Year," and the conflicts with the Manchus, known as the "Barbarian War of the Byungja Year," the number of the gentry class was inflated tremendously as the court was compelled to sell public offices to finance the campaigns.

Moreover, during the Yimjin War a gentry status was liberally conferred to soldiers with distinguished service. The sale of public offices continued even after the wars to supplement the court's insufficient revenue collections. The inflated gentry classes created a vicious cycle; more commoners and slaves wanted to obtain a gentry status to avoid the exacerbating tax burdens and compulsory military service. Tax burdens for ever smaller numbers of farmers had progressively worsened as rich farmers were exempted from the duties due to their elevation to the gentry classes. For ordinary citizens, gaining a gentry status remained the only alternative to escape the intolerable exploitation; thus non-gentry citizens resorted to various methods in this endeavor, including buying or stealing family-tree books of gentry, or simply forging certificates. Between 1700 and 1850, the number of the nation's gentry class increased by more than sixty percent. By the middle of the nineteenth century the number of the nation's gentry class in one major city reached 70.3 percent of the total households.[6]

The inflation of the gentry classes also greatly affected the nation's slave population; increasingly, a large number of slaves attempted to obtain their freedom and a better status through buying-out or simple desertion. The runaway slaves became so common that the court in 1778 was forced to repeal a law which allowed owners an authority to recapture deserted slaves. The court set free all publicly held slaves in 1801. Even in the private sector where the ownership of slaves continued to be lawful, the strict master-slave relationship was rapidly disappearing as the fateful nineteenth century arrived.

In the transformation of the backward Chosun society, the role of the nation's intellectuals, particularly the groups that were identified as the "realism" school of Confucianism, was eminent. These scholars emphasized more practical approaches and values by rightfully criticizing the traditional Confucian scholars for their advocacy of empty theories. As this group mostly consisted of gentry scholars who had no government appointments but actively involved themselves with Confucian studies in rural areas, they were in a position to better appreciate the problems the masses were experiencing. As a result they took more liberal stands than the conservative aristocracy. Although their criticism of government policies was often affected by personal grudges, they generally reflected the dire living conditions of the nation's farmers and commoners.

The progressive scholars advocated more agricultural programs, such as farmland regulations in rural areas, and were concerned with foreign trade, private financing, and transportation methods in urban areas. The realists also strongly promoted the importation of Ching China's Western technologies into various areas. Their stand on the technology issue was particularly noteworthy because the Chosun court harbored heavy anti-Ching sentiments since its humiliating defeat in the war against the Manchus. In spite of widespread anti-Ching emotion, the realists appealed to the court to adopt the more practical approaches employed by the Ching court. Their interests included every aspect of Western technology available in Ching, acknowledging the extreme backwardness of the Chosun society in modern technologies. Notwithstanding the timely proposals, the court was reluctant to import Western technologies, leaving only piecemeal introduction through private sources.

During this period the Chosun society experienced a strong surge in the study of its own history and geography. After a long and painful assimilation process that lasted throughout the Koryo dynasty, Hahn nationalism was finally beginning to appear. In spite of repulsive toadying to China that was epidemic among selfish courtiers, the national pride was nurtured by the realists through their extensive writings. The fervor of Hahn nationalism in this period proved to be the most critical factor for the survival of the ancient kingdom, which was about to be engulfed by the imperial power politics of the region.

While the Chosun society was undergoing a profound transformation in its economic and social life, the political life of the dynasty was not making a comparable progress. The peace that had prevailed after the court's acceptance of the Manchu terms resulted in an intensified power struggle between political rivals in the court, resulting in more of Chosun's notorious party strife. Political factions headed by a few high level court officials and their followers both in and out of the government initially engaged in competition over policy matters. Subsequently, however, the factional rivalry broadened and sharpened as the need to secure court appointed positions for a now swelling gentry of followers intensified. The practice in which the extensive privileges of a gentry family were to be taken away if it did not occupy a government position within the span of four generations exacerbated the competition for the limited government posts. The political power to appoint all important government positions was quintessential in preserving the factional strength. In the process, the rivalry that was at first merely policy-oriented had turned into a struggle for the total domination of the government. Factional political infighting among high level courtiers was not a mere power struggle but a merciless contest for survival.

The Chosun cast system did not allow gentry to engage in farming, commerce, or manufacturing, leaving government appointment the only available avenue. Yet Chosun Korea, a small nation of simple administrative functions and modest means even in times of peace, supplied only a limited number of government positions. The competition for a few available government positions had inevitably intensified as the size of the nation's gentry continued to grow. Hopefuls for a government appointment were attracted to powerful political factions as only the strongest were capable of arranging government positions for followers. Consequently, the strongest faction was to dominate the nation's governing structure. When the prolonged factional political fighting ended with the rise of one party dictatorship, many political losers returned to scholarly lives in rural villages and opened private academies that became the nation's foremost learning institutions with a long lasting legacy.

As the nation's official posts were allocated according to candidates' political affiliation, the traditional civil service examinations lost universal appeal. An increasing number of young scholars spurned the exam, opting instead to concentrate on the scholarly works at academies and to practice exemplary personal conduct. These scholars, seclusionists in rural areas called San Lim, grew in influence and later exercised considerable political power. Their presumably untainted opinions soon became the political norms and standards as their political participation was eagerly sought by contending political parties. However, when they joined mundane politics, their scholastic background provided no immunization from corrupt political practices. On the contrary, some of these Confucian scholars emerged as willing and major participants in the factional political infighting.

The Chosun court's chronic political infighting, which had subsided for a short while, resumed as soon as its Ching relationship was stabilized. These conflicts were so intensified that the court was almost paralyzed by the middle of the eighteenth century. This recurring national malady compelled King Youngjo to adopt a series of measures to lessen party strife by assuring an equal influence for all major political factions. With this extraordinary measure the Chosun court was able to maintain relative calm and harmony for a while. Yet the roots of the severe political infighting were not eradicated by any means but were merely covered by a thin blanket of royal maneuvering. The number of gentry whose whole lives were directed to obtaining a government appointment kept growing. On the other hand, the nation's governing system was hardly expanding to absorb even a fraction of those ardent office seekers. Soon the precarious political equilibrium collapsed and another dictatorial power emerged. This time a family related to royalty, the queen's family, grabbed power over contending political factions.

The Chosun court entered the fateful nineteenth century with an eleven-year-old monarch amid renewed factional infighting. As the established procedure dictated, the young monarch was assisted by many relatives, one of whom was the queen's father, Kim of Ahndong. The Kim family took advantage of the minor monarch by quickly maneuvering to dominate court politics and to monopolize most high level appointments for their family members. Finally the factional political parties were effectively removed from court politics. The dictatorship of the royal relatives that was to last until the middle of the century was exceptionally effective in suppressing opponents and in practicing wanton corruption. Yet there was no credible opposition to the dictatorship.

The corrupted dictatorship of the royal relatives caused equally severe harm to the nation's socio-political development. The factional strife had originated from differing political views, regardless of however inconsequential they may have been. Thus, the party struggle that paralyzed court politics for so long and gave rise to the dictatorship by the Kims was in a sense an aggravated political competition between political factions. Although it is generally thought that policy issues were merely used to justify selfish power struggles, party strife did represent some aspects of policy competition, a normal development in any political organization. On the other hand, the dictatorship by the royal relatives was in a sense an extension of the royal power that was authorized and protected by the monarch. It served little useful purpose as the court under its guardianship was marred by the worst cases of political corruption.

The dictatorship of the Kim family represented a reactionary movement to the fragile socioeconomic reforms being pursued by the common people. The old social structure was undergoing a rapid transformation because of the introduction of more productive farming methods, growing commercial-industrial activities, and the general degradation of the nation's unproductive gentry classes. The socioeconomic reforms were expected to accelerate even more because of growing Western influences signified by scientific knowledge and the Catholic church doctrines that began to penetrate the nation through Ching China. Although a few progressive scholars of Confucian learning joined the attempt to curb the dictatorial power, their effort was ineffectual. The outdated and futile dictatorship was adamant to strengthen the feudal system while the masses preferred to disband the old exploitative and backward-governing structure. Chosun's medieval feudal system was exposing its most damaging dimension by clinging to power against the masses. The Chosun court's profound failure to heed the masses was to haunt the entire Hahn nation for a long time. The pitifully incapable monarchs and beastly factional courtiers managed to waste the precious time allocated to the nation.

Korea had its opportunity to refurbish its medieval nation with new economic systems and social structures. The masses favored such a profound reform, which was forcibly blocked by reactionary court officials. Chosun Korea was still in a dark age by default when vastly modernized Western nations of strong imperial inclination arrived at the shores of Northeast Asia.

Notes

1. The Koryo court in its final stage often sent forces to southern regions to battle against the Japanese pirates.
2. There is considerable disagreement over who was legitimate ruler of Koryo during the last moment of the dynasty. Some of King Gongyang's predecessors were speculated to be unrelated to the royal family.
3. High officials of the Chosun court such as Yi Yee openly campaigned to build up the nation's depleted defense force but were rejected by the opponents.
4. Ming initially sent a force of 5,000 men. When the Japanese defeated this token force, Ming sent an additional 40,000 men.
5. Chosun's conscription law required that every male serve active military duty until he reached 60 years of age, indicating the nation's insufficient human resources.
6. The town in question was Taegu in Kyongsang-Do province. Such high percentages may not have been common in other parts of the nation.

Chapter 4

Chosun Society and the Confucian Heritage

1. Evolution of Confucianism

The period from the late seventeenth to the early nineteenth century offered a rare respite for the Chosun court to reorganize its old-fashioned political structure and correct its muddled national priorities. Yet tragically it failed to do so. Widespread and chronic corruption in public life, the nation's zealous attachment to the past, and the anti-reform reactionary factions in the court were some prominent contributors to the failure.The failure, however, was more than the court's political failure; in a sense it represented a general default of the Chosun society itself, particularly of the kingdom's political and intellectual traditions. The failed traditions that had retarded the society as a whole had diverse contributors. Still the most eminent may have been the influence of the Confucian tradition, which served as the Chosun society's paramount moral and ethical basis as well as its foremost political philosophy.

The Chu philosophy (Yuhak in Korean), known in Western literature as Confucianism or the teachings of Confucius(551-479 B.C.), dominated the conceptual framework of Chosun ideology. The Chu philosophy was, in pre-modern Chinese history, nearly comparable to a religion in other countries in the sense that it so overwhelmingly contributed to the formation of the nation's unique mentality and outlook of life.[1] However, most contemporary observers are reluctant to accord Confucianism the status of a major religion. Instead, they typically consider it as a moral and ethical code.[2] Regardless of its status as a religion, Confucianism is an ideology that has left lasting legacies in the Far East.

Confucianism started essentially as a philosophy based on a system of social and political ethics. It originated, along with other major systems of early Chinese philosophy - Taoism, Mohism, and Legalism, between the sixth and third centuries B.C. The period was one of the most chaotic in Chinese history, as old institutions and social orders in general had lost their influence while new ones were yet to be firmly established.[3] Confucius, a historically-minded humanist by nature, undertook his lifelong crusade to arrest the current political and social instability by teaching a rigid humanitarian-ethical system, one based on his quintessential doctrine of *Jen*, or human-heartiness. The mainstays of his teaching were a wide variety of normative social-political values extracted from the experience of ancient sage kings and orthodox feudal concepts of the Chou period.[4]

Confucianism remained relatively obscured throughout the Springs and Autumns era, its inception period.[5] At the time, Legalism, the concept of universal equality before the law, was the dominant ideology for the much compartmentalized, unstable society. Yearning for law and order, the Chinese society sought answers from the Legalists, who advocated that rules be public and be implemented without any divergent interpretation.[6] Still, under the shadow of Legalist domination, humanistic Confucian teachings offered the society a new dimension. Attracting the followers from mostly learned classes, Confucianism had grown to replace Legalism as the primary doctrine of the court by the early period of the Han dynasty.[7] In spite of its vastly elevated status, Confucianism failed to convince Han's ruling bureaucracy to accept it as a state religion. It had to compete against the growing popularity of Buddhism that newly imported from India in the first century A.D., had quickly established itself as one of the main Chinese religious traditions. By the second half of the Han period it had grown to compete against other indigenous doctrines for influence and was particularly strong in intellectual-political areas.[8] Buddhism and Taoism never were able to dislodge Confucianism's domination from the court.

The foremost objective of the Confucian moral and ethical code was to achieve loyalty, hierarchy, and harmony within the family and society. To reach these lofty ideals in ethics, politics, and life, Confucius employed the concept of *Jen* as the foundation.[9] He maintained that human relations should be based on the moral element of *Jen* in the individual, which is the natural compassion of the human heart, a trait to be found in the virtues of filial piety and fraternal love. In the greater realm of Confucian ideology, human compassion, expressed through filial piety and fraternal love, was to lead to the bond of social solidarity and the connection between succeeding generations. Filial piety is to signify the eternity of time, fraternal love, and the infinity of space.[10] Thus, Confucianism recognized the family unit as the basis for all human morality. Only after it instituted a family unit as the most fundamental of human morality did Confucianism embrace the doctrine of service to society. This pattern of priority was both the essence and significance of Confucian ideology.

Li, or ritualism, was another important concept in the Confucian ethical system. Confucius transformed the concept of ancient *Li*, originally a code of sacrificial and religious ritual for feudal lords, into one of basic virtues in his expanded ethical system. He insisted that the proper observance of *Li* be in its principle and sincerity rather than in its appearance; such practice was essential to the development of goodness in an individual as well as in a society. Confucius understood *Li* as a source vital in avoiding extremes and in reaching perfect harmony among individuals. Yet *Li* was not separated from the concept of *Jen*, his central theme. Rather, he argued that the observance of *Li* was required to complete the ideology of *Jen*. Thus in the world of perfect Confucian ethics, man must achieve *Jen*, which was believed to be within the reach of every individual, and act according to *Li*. *Jen* and *Li* represent Confucian substance and formality.

Confucius believed that the early Chou period, around 1000 B.C., was an exemplary age of peace and prosperity that his contemporaries needed to recreate. Therefore, he attached capital importance to the revival of the Chou era as a means of resolving the social and political chaos of his time. His crusade for having everyone recognize and fulfill individual morality was an attempt to recreate the unprecedented peace and prosperity the Chou feudal system had been known to have achieved. Even in political ideology Confucius did not depart from the fundamentals of Chou's autocratic rules; by defining the foremost responsibility of the government as maintaining social order and political stability, he steadfastly defended the Chou practice. At the same time, to justify an autocratic rule, Confucius demanded that the ruler maintain the highest degree of moral responsibility. In political systems he recognized and approved a need to strengthen central control and to maintain a rigid political hierarchy. In the Confucian world the ideal political process was an autocratic leadership in which the ruler lead wisely and the people followed, much like the grass bends to the direction of the wind.[11]

In the seventh century Confucianism was transformed into neo-Confucianism, which became the dominant state ideology during the Sung (960-1278) and Ming (1368-1644) periods. The conceptual framework of neo-Confucianism, or Chuism, was formulated mainly through Chu Hsi's extended interpretations of Confucian teachings. Chu Hsi's version did not alter the fundamental tenets of Confucian teachings; the virtues of filial piety and loyalty remained paramount, and the importance of harmonious social and personal relationships was emphasized as before. Neo-Confucian scholars, the most prominent being Chu Hsi himself, however, had expanded the traditional Confucian ethical concept by incorporating elements of Buddhist cosmology and Taoist metaphysics. As a result, neo-Confucian features were more speculative and metaphysical than the old version but did not compromise any of the basic Confucian principles regarded as orthodox Confucianism.[12]

Just as with Confucianism, neo-Confucianism stressed the cultivation of the self and the exemplary management of the family as the foremost requirements for reaching man's maturity. It also assumed that one could obtain worldly wisdom and human virtues only through the study of the teachings of both Confucius and Chu Hsi. Inevitably, this approach led the followers to engage in extensive conceptual discussions over the interpretation of these two ideological giants. As a result, by the late Ming period most neo-Confucian scholars were captivated by endless abstract discourse and metaphysical argumentation. The movement was so preoccupied with such elaborate metaphysical speculations that the practical applications of Confucius's teachings became increasingly remote and difficult.

Eventually the scholars' excessive fixation upon textual interpretation of Confucian teachings prompted the birth of a reform movement, which advocated intellectual responsibility and morality. The reformers sought to shift the Confucian scholars' preoccupation away from abstract disputes into practical applications, from individual introspection to commitment toward public affairs.[13] Scholars continued reform efforts initiated during the Ching era. Having harbored less inclination in abstract thinking than did their Ming counterparts and placing more emphasis on practical values in general, they launched an attack on speculative neo-Confucian disputes. They realized the extensive socio-political impairment that the abstract speculations of the neo-Confucian tradition had caused to the nation, and thus attempted to steer the neo-Confucian tradition to more practical, constructive ideology.

Progressive Ching scholars were particularly critical of the exclusionist mentality for which neo-Confucian tradition was largely responsible. They viewed that such a myopic approach had blocked Ching from adopting new ideas and knowledge from the West, thus jeopardizing the nation's reform and progress. In spite of this provocation, Chinese society's ideology had so ossified that it lacked a national will to free itself from the grip of entrenched old traditions. The similar New Culture Movement of the 1920s was equally ineffectual in reforming the doctrine that became increasingly detrimental to the nation's welfare.[14] By this time Neo-Confucian ethical-moral principles had been firmly implanted in the mentality and temperament of the Chinese.

Neo-Confucianism was the most powerful doctrine ever conceived in feudal China. For more than twelve centuries it gripped Chinese society so tenaciously that it eventually became "something of a prison, from which the Chinese intellect was able only with difficulty to escape."[15] The Ching court's monumental difficulties in dealing with the Western powers in the late nineteenth century were a telling indication of the spiritual and political decay brought about by entrenched Confucian ideology.

2. Legacies of Chosun's Confucianism

Korea's experience with the Confucian tradition is generally in line with that of China, though Korea's exposure to the philosophy had been shorter. Confucianism entered Korea as the early representative of Chinese culture and had remained in the nation as its foremost intellectual tradition among the ruling elites. For the most part, the public both in the Three Kingdoms period and the unified Silla era maintained a distance from Confucian ideology largely because it was written and taught by cumbersome Chinese ideograms. A long period of germination was needed for the nonliterary public to accept it. At the same time, the Korean states acknowledged that Confucianism was the primary carrier of China's sophisticated academic and cultural tradition. They had to adopt it but little envisioned that it would leave Korea with long and painful legacies.

Confucianism entered the Korean peninsula as early as the fourth century. Koguryo, located in the northern part of the peninsula, was the first to be exposed to the doctrine and founded its first national Confucian academy in 372 A.D., adopting a code of administrative law the next year. The southern kingdom of Peckche followed suit shortly. However, it was during the unified Silla era that Confucianism found its most enthusiastic Korean clients. Seeking a measure of centralization in a patriotic code of conduct for its ruling warrior classes in peace and war, unified Silla embraced the Confucian doctrine. It founded its royal Confucian academy in 682 A.D. and commenced its Confucianism-oriented meritocracy in 788

A.D.

With its rigid moral doctrine Confucianism easily met the needs of Silla's ruling class. Silla's autocratic court also did not overlook the positive role Confucianism performed as the main medium through which Chinese culture was transferred. The masses, however, did not have means to understand or practice Confucian routines. Only the kingdom's ruling class possessed the knowledge of the Chinese characters with which the complex ideology of Confucianism was written. As a result, Confucianism remained for long merely a domain of the ruling class. The masses still practiced various indigenous religions.

In spite of its growing popularity among the ruling elites, Confucianism was overshadowed by Buddhism at the Silla court. As the religion of national prosperity and security, Buddhism was the heart and soul of Silla's ruling class and the public. Its influence grew so extensively that Buddhist monks came to dominate court politics. Naturally, Silla's royal families remained the most ardent Buddhist followers.

It was during the early Koryo period when Confucianism, transformed into Chuism of the Sung tradition, emerged as the nation's predominant political ideology. Pressing for a Confucianism-oriented administrative style, the court of King Kwangjong (949-975 A.D.) adopted the Chinese-style civil examination system, which helped to formally inaugurate a long-lasting legacy of Confucian teachings in Korea. Along with the adoption of civil service examinations, the court's systematic acceptance of neo-Confucianism as the basis for the nation's political-social doctrine gave the old Chinese philosophy an increasingly powerful mandate over Koryo's political ideology. Still, throughout the first half of the Koryo period Buddhism lost little ground as the national religion; Buddhist monks were routinely appointed to positions as the nation's highest royal scholar-advisors. The overwhelming influence of Buddhism as the nation's spiritual guide was yet to be seriously challenged by Neo-Confucianism, although it was gaining strength throughout the Koryo period.

Though it failed to replace the dominating influence of Buddhism in the court, Koryo's Confucian scholars began to monopolize the Gwageo system, the nation's civil service examinations. The Chinese-style examinations required extensive academic training in Yuhack classics, mostly Confucian teachings. As the Gwageo system was firmly established as the nation's primary institution in recruiting government officials, Confucian learning became progressively more important to the nation's ruling scholar-gentry classes, who strived for the perpetuation of their privileged status. Following Confucian belief that literary accomplishment was the only valid indication of one's qualification for administrative duties, the Koryo court conveniently overlooked an intrinsic shortcoming of the examination system: the Yuhack-oriented training was obstructively narrow in scope and speculative in nature. The court accepted with little critical assessment the Chinese practice in which all public appointments were based on high literary qualifications, the essence of which was expertise in the Chou period and teachings of Confucius and other Chinese philosophers. The system's other prominent shortcoming was also overlooked: it hindered rather than encouraged creative leadership due to seniority-oriented bureaucratic career patterns and a consensus-building tendency.[16] Nevertheless, by the late Koryo period Neo-Confucianism gained sufficient strength to threaten Buddhism, the perennial influence in the court. This development coincided with the outstanding progress the Koryo Confucian scholars had achieved in their pursuit of mastering Chu Hsi's Neo-Confucian doctrine.[17]

The founder of the Chosun dynasty, King Taejo, had extensively collaborated in his coup against the Koryo court with Koryo's Confucian scholar-officials. In the new dynasty Taejo rewarded his Confucian collaborators by appointing them to influential public positions. Taejo's policy to rebuke the Buddhist influence in favor of Confucian scholar-officials in the court was deliberate and consistent. When the founder adopted a pro-Ming foreign policy as the new dynasty's foremost political doctrine, Confucianism naturally became its ideological guide.

From the beginning of the new dynasty Taejo was resolute in installing the Ming-style ruling system and laying down the foundation for the policy of Ukbul-Sungyu, or suppression of Buddhism and promotion of Yuhak. This represented his profound respect for the Ming court. In addition, Neo-Confucian tenets such as acceptance of authority and an interest in harmony may have appealed strongly to the new regime. Adopting the Ming political system, the new regime sought the advice of Chosun's leading Chuism followers and thus allowed them to wield extensive political influence in the court. Having being convinced that Confucianism was the sole source for the universal truth applicable to all civilized societies, the Chosun court made it the top priority to establish a Confucian polity and society in Korea.[18] Various programs and institutions created by King Taejo were intended to expedite this transition; he thus established public Confucian institutions throughout the country. The founder's vigorous pro-Ming, pro-Confucian pursuit was emulated by his successors; most prominent was Chosun's fourth monarch, King Saejong, who organized a royal institution of Jiphyunjun as the kingdom's highest academic organ, to which young and capable Confucian scholars were appointed.[19]

Following the Koryo practice, the Chosun court continued to hold Gwageo civil service examinations as a formal avenue through which scholars were elevated to government positions. The examinations, usually held twice a year, were intended to select quality public servants from the nation's upper-class or the Yangban society. The nation's ordinary citizens and slaves were allowed to take examinations on non-literary subjects, such as medicine, military skills, and arts.   Although it originated in China, Chosun's Gwageo system, like its predecessor in the Silla and Koryo period, lacked the prominent merit of the Chinese system, the egalitarian tradition in which the ladder of success was available to everyone, regardless of family status.[20] In contrast, in highly autocratic Chosun society where upward mobility among lower social groups was virtually nonexistent, the practice did not promote the egalitarian causes but greatly contributed to social stratification by reinforcing the class barrier. This further helped to perpetuate another damaging Chosun tradition, discrimination against all those employed in menial work. In practice, the examinations were used to provide a legal ground for the Yangban class's political grip on the nation's ruling bureaucracy.

By limiting the scope of the examinations to contestants' literary merits, the Gwageo examinations continued to single out the study of the Chinese classics, of which Confucian teachings remained the most prominent, as the essential qualification for political appointment. In the heated pursuit to master the teachings of the old sages, Chosun's Confucian learning became entangled in the minutiae of textual research on the meaning of often abstract concepts. When court politics indulged in partisan competition, speculative academic strife among the nation's Yuhak scholar-officials inevitably intensified.

By rejecting the Chinese egalitarian tradition, Chosun's Gwageo system failed to promote national unity by assuring the convergence in government of educated, capable men from all walks of life. By law the Chosun system was subject to only limited restrictions; barred from the contest were individuals of criminal background, sons of remarried or unfaithful mothers, sons of disgraced officials, and illegitimate sons. In practice, however, only sons of the gentry or the Yangban class were allowed to compete for the national scholarly examination. The fact that examinations for military officers were more open, with only sons of most humble origins barred, indicated further that the court was sold to scholar-official practice. The Chosun method not only failed in giving men of superior intelligence and common sense an opportunity for public service, but also increased the chance for nepotism and other forms of favoritism by making the social status rather than individual merit an essential qualification for public service positions.

The Gwageo system remained Chosun's primary method for civil service examinations until the very end of the dynasty, never deviating from its profound devotion to mastering Chinese historical facts and teachings of great Chinese philosophers. Deprived of other means of entering public service, the nation's young gentry immersed themselves in the textual research of the Chinese classics. Preoccupied with writing exegeses and commentaries of a mostly abstract nature, these upper class scholars further lost contact with the reality of society. Chosun's Gwageo system was the thing that sealed the supremacy of Confucian values in the nation's educated population.

By the mid-sixteenth century the Confucian political ethos came to prevail in every aspect of the Chosun society; all political and social judgments and decisions had to be justified by Confucian rhetoric. Inevitably Chosun's intellectual tradition became hopelessly skewed as it lacked any utilitarianism and conceptual flexibility. Moreover, the large cadre of Confucian scholar-officials failed to provide the court with realistic and flexible leadership against mounting external threats. Chosun's Confucian tradition and its primary accomplice, the Gwageo system, were most accountable for the nation's unique moral and spiritual disposition. Although it is beyond any practical solution to quantify the nature of national impairment caused by dogmatic Confucianism, the Silhak (practical learning) scholars' insistent outcry for the realignment of the nation's intellectual tradition toward practical application, away from the abstract Confucian speculation, should serve as a prominent reference.

By the nineteenth century Chosun had acquired a national mentality of passivity and abstraction, derived from the consistent emphasis on the cumbersome observation of Confucian rituals and on the scholastic tradition of empty linguistic studies and textual criticism. As the nation's prolonged exposure to the ideological tradition of speculative and abstract persuasion led to the acquisition of such damaging national mannerism, Chosun society suffered many symptoms of this acquired malady.

Ritualism and Sadaeism, two prominent socio-political practices that characterized the Chosun period, are commonly cited as the direct legacies of the long, dedicated acceptance of the Confucian tradition.[21] The two phenomena were not, however, a separate development; they had evolved closely intertwined as the Confucianism-oriented court maintained a pro-China policy as its fundamental political doctrine. The combined effects of these two damaging mannerisms were deep and extensive; the most notable was the pervasive mentality of submission and passivity that had transformed the once highly spirited nation into what was almost a cultural imitating, political dependency of China.

Sadaeism, or serving the powerful, was Chosun's most humiliating political tradition. Blind and uncritical acquiescence to the Chinese courts was a natural byproduct of its long cultural submission to China. Uncritical reverence for Confucian philosophy and for more sophisticated Chinese civilization as a whole, in turn, begat political submission- Sadaeism- which was most responsible for the Chosun court's becoming a political hostage of the Chinese courts for so long. In a sense, it was a cultural conquest spearheaded by the entrenched domination of the Confucian ideology over Chosun's ruling class. Although Chosun's practice of Sadaeism amounted, in essence, to no more than a convenient political appeasement of a very powerful neighbor, it resulted in prolonged political impotence; this proved to be particularly devastating during the period when the nation was under Western pressure. The court's customary practice of servile accommodation to Chinese wishes often led to a toleration of blatant interference. Such political submission inevitably eroded the court's ability to formulate and execute dynamic national policies.

Cultural-political dependence on China was so deeply ingrained that even in the fateful nineteenth century Chosun's political agenda remained closely aligned to that of the Ching court, which had already displayed its ineptness in dealing with the West.[22] The petrified Chosun court relied more on Ching's political tutelage than on its own initiative to formulate a timely, constructive response to external threats. Nor had it the spiritual strength to resist openly Ching's political interference. Furthermore, Chosun's political leaders, most accomplished Confucian scholars who devoted their lives to the teachings of the old sages, scarcely had any curiosity to comprehend either the world beyond Ching or the nature of Western culture, which was already based on advanced science and technology. Even when the havoc the West had fomented loomed to endanger the nation's survival, the Chosun court was still hoping that its Confucian wisdom would provide a noble answer.

As the nation's leadership remained willing prisoners of Chinese ideological dogma, the Chosun society suffered most from the lack of progressive spirit. The ideological rigidity and political-cultural Sadaeism led to the general ossification of the regime's spiritual vitality, effectively suffocating the spirit of Koguryo's daring militarism and Silla's Hwa-Rang-Do nationalism. Confucian ideology taught Koreans no universal solution but bequeathed a cultural legacy rampant with pernicious elements: veneration of China, factionalism, classism, class conflict, literary effeminacy, discouragement of commerce, reverence for titles, and excessive reverence for the past.[23] As a whole, these legacies sewed seeds of spiritual poison, greatly undermining the traditional vigor of the Hahn people.

In spite of its elaborate rituals designed to build a perfect person, the Confucian doctrine made no provisions for opposing points of view. This rigidity inevitably encouraged narrow theoretical disputes in which the notion of a single absolute truth dominated. Because of this narrow view, the Confucian doctrine allows no room for intellectual pluralism or for an alternative of amicable compromise or for a dualistic solution. Instead, the universal truth was vigorously sought, and any deviation from the established norm was harshly criticized. Under this rigid theoretical framework, sound policy competition was seldom possible as the court was too preoccupied in unproductive debates over issues of often impractical universal truth. The winner of this purely speculative competition prevailed over court politics, and the opposition was reduced to that of a wrongdoer, a socio-political heretic.

The Chosun court's notorious factional infighting, which mostly originated from personal animosity and desires for power, was often carried out under the convenient pretext of the poorly defined disagreement over Confucian teachings. Swamped by empty formalities and factional political interests that often prevailed over substance and public interest, the court remained largely unable to undertake rational policy deliberation. The court's political squabbles were seldom free of theoretical disputes over Confucian teachings.

Confucianism places special emphasis on a proper relationship between ruler and subjects, father and son, and husband and wife. Yet it recognized correct personal conduct in a family setting to be the supreme achievement of an individual.[24] The result is that an individual's moral obligation to his own family supersedes those civic and national obligations. The Chosun society's adherence to the individual-family morality doctrine was amply manifested throughout the period; many Chosun scholar-officials chose to sacrifice their lives to prove their moral character and save individual and family honor. Only after one secured the maintenance of individual and family esteem could he exercise his public obligations to the court. Many voluntary resistance movements that fought gallant wars against Japanese invaders were motivated primarily by the desire to defend their own families and villages, not nationhood itself; this serves as ample illustration of the Chosun society's fatal infection with Confucian morality of individual-family orientation.

Chosun's adoption of Confucianism as state orthodoxy was largely responsible for hampering the development of a strong national identity. This phenomenon was pervasive not only among the court officials but also within the masses, who had never developed strong loyalty to the court. As a result, national unity, an indispensable element in safeguarding a nation's territorial and cultural integrity, was long to remain elusive in Korea. It is not that Confucianism overlooked the importance of loyalty to the court; on the contrary, it emphasized one's loyalty to the monarch as one of the supreme virtues that citizens must practice. But by placing the overwhelming emphasis on one's obligation to the family and on the individual's self-cultivation, the Confucian doctrine managed to undermine the public's devotion to the national cause. It was Chosun's Confucian intoxication that made citizens and political leaders unable to fully comprehend the fact that one's family obligation could be fulfilled only when the nation's territorial and political integrity were secure. Chosun's Yuhak scholars singularly failed to distinguish the external threats of feudal origins in the time of Confucius from more poignant contemporary ones that endangered the very existence of the nation itself.

Confucian teachings also emphasize the importance of legitimate royal succession. The doctrine helped the Korean courts to adhere to legitimate successions most of the time, thereby promoting the stability of the Chosun dynasty. The legitimate succession doctrine had made revolution or usurpation of power much more difficult, for illegitimate succession was extremely difficult to be accepted by both the masses and powerful courtiers. In spite of some beneficial effects, Chosun's primogeniture rule was not without serious disadvantages; under the practice the public rejected even an otherwise justifiable but illegitimate succession.[25] The court's Confucian officials supported the royal legitimacy even at the price of unstable and poor leadership.

Confucian teachings advocated enlightenment that was not contaminated by material possessions. Following this antiquated tradition of agrarian China, Chosun's upper classes came to disdain any economic activities other than farming as a source of living, although the farmers, not the gentry, did the actual farm work. The gentry spurned any activities related to commerce for profit and service activities. The ruling classes' anachronistic prejudice against a non-farming economy brought about the public suppression of trade and deprived the Chosun court of revenues from this potentially rich source of wealth. Chosun's merchant class remained the lowest social strata among the non-slave population, below even farmers and industrialists.

The Chosun court not only demeaned but placed a tight control over commercial activities to discourage their proliferation. The court's Confucian attitude greatly hampered the growth of the nation's commercial sector. Consequently it remained backward, based on an archaic barter system with rice and textiles serving as the principal media of exchange. Complete dependency on a traditional but impoverished agricultural economy not only deprived the court of a natural avenue of remedy for its incessant financial difficulties but also stripped the nation of invaluable opportunities to make contact through trade with the Western powers.

3. Confucianism and Political Leadership

Korea's last two dynasties were founded and ruled by two families: the Wang family for the Koryo dynasty, and the Yi family for the Chosun dynasty. Throughout both dynasties the political monopoly of the ruling family was strictly observed and jealously protected. In the small kingdom where a systematic feudalism had never developed, the ruling monarchs were seldom challenged, except for a few occasions where leading court officials overshadowed the ruler. The monopoly of power by these families was further assured through the primogeniture rule, which was more prominent in the Chosun era.

The result of Chosun's rigid succession scheme was an abundance of mediocre rulers. The Chosun dynasty was ruled mostly by undistinguished monarchs except for two highly productive and enlightened periods: 1400 to 1468, and 1724 to 1800. During the first half of the fifteenth century, the period in which the Chosun dynasty was founded, dynamic monarchs successfully laid down a foundation that sustained the kingdom for more than five hundred years. These energetic and imaginative rulers were followed by weak and mediocre ones, who often assumed a role of mere spectators rather than leaders. The Chosun dynasty was again blessed by the revitalizing energies of quality rulers in the eighteenth century; during the period it not only reached a rare political stability but inspired vigorous national progress in many areas. Unfortunately, except for these two short periods, the kingdom was led by mediocre rulers besieged by perpetual factional fighting or foreign invasions.

Though the Chosun court was often in the hands of incompetent or minor monarchs, the Korean masses exercised remarkable restraint in not resorting to rebellious challenges, regardless of a monarch's ability to govern and the quality of the court he led. This public acquiescence was perhaps the most tangible and persistent reward the Korean courts received from their loyalty to the Confucian doctrine. When the fateful nineteenth century dawned, the Chosun dynasty was again under the leadership of a minor monarch whose power was exercised by the exclusionist regent.

The modest leadership ability of the Chosun kings was not the sole cause for the monarchy's so frequently displayed political ineptitude, particularly during the last half of the dynasty. The court system was designed so that royal leadership was advised and supplemented by the court's able officials. In particular, under Chosun's strict succession system the exceptional quality of the court officials was quintessential to the stability and progress of the kingdom, and the Chosun dynasty indeed produced many quality court officials. Yet their prominent expertise in Chuist Confucianism had made them more suitable to be loyal followers rather than innovative policy advisers. The court's scholar-officials, concerned primarily with perfecting their individual conduct or with theoretical competition in Confucian teachings, were content to be role models for individual virtuous conduct rather than worthy political advisers. They were unusually effective in brutally suppressing opponents, but were extremely uneasy with the essential advisory task of reaching a compromise; flexibility was a quality most of the Chosun court officials singularly failed to demonstrate. Rather, Chosun's court officials were too often immersed in disastrous political infighting, often generated by conflicting political interests of diverse factions, creations of fierce Confucian disputes.

Time after time, the kingdom's critical reform movements were thwarted by the court officials' factional disputes. In a frenzied political atmosphere where the most profound concern was a faction's political survival, national interest became inevitably remote and abstract. Furthermore, to protect their own political interests, many narrow-minded courtiers practiced disguised loyalty to the throne, further eroding the judgment of rulers.

The Chosun court's lack of quality political leadership became painfully obvious during national emergencies. Not only was the court unable to provide a rallying point for the masses, but it often panicked first. Rarely did the court muster resources and political leadership to formulate and implement appropriate policies against major events. The Japanese invasion was deadly not because the masses were unpatriotic, but because of poor military and political leadership. The Chosun court's poor leadership in times of national emergencies was a national scandal as was its corruption and factional politics. Its collective behavior was largely responsible for the nation's perennial failure adequately to prepare for foreign invasions by building national consensus and unity. Rather, the court, divided by hard-liners and peace proponents who typically rushed to submit, was often forced to surrender or retreat even before offering any meaningful resistance. It was one of the most unfortunate legacies of Confucianism in Chosun that the concept of individual and family honor had not evolved into the greater cause of national welfare.

The pedestrian quality of Chosun officialdom reflected the inadequacy of the whole governing system. The court's scholar-officials were recruited solely from the nation's gentry class. Moreover, the ones with strong factional backing dominated the cabinet or advisory positions. Consequently, appointees were often equipped with only superficial knowledge or complex historical facts about ancient China. The fact that an expertise in Chinese literature, including Confucian teachings or ancient China, could hardly be a sufficient qualification for the nation's high offices was customarily overlooked under the commanding influence of Confucianism. The pronounced tendency to regard contemporary problems in the same light as vaguely understood historical facts about ancient China was an inevitable outcome of intellectual and spiritual Sinification.

At the dawn of the nineteenth century the Chosun court remained totally oblivious of the West, choosing to pay no attention to the world beyond Ching. Chosun's inward isolation was even firmer than that of Ching itself; when Ching undertook desperate reforms under the encroaching threat of the West, the Chosun court simply ignored them. Furthermore, it took every precaution to isolate the hermit kingdom from Western influence, contradicting Ching's active pursuit of a limited open-door policy toward the West. Chosun's single-minded reliance on Confucian doctrine and Sadaeism resulted in the nearly complete ossification of spiritual vigor and the fatal lack of political dexterity to venture into the unknown world. Its addiction to Confucian ritualism and abstraction had become so firm and pervasive that an escape from the old tradition was virtually impossible, barring some kind of rude awakening.

Nevertheless, Chosun did attempt to unshackle itself from burdensome Confucian tradition. As early as the middle of the seventeenth century, progressive intellectuals critical of Chu Hsi's Confucian doctrine formed a faction known as Realistic Learning, or Silhak in Korean. Silhak followers demanded that traditionalists discard Neo-Confucian formalism and ritual triviality in favor of more practical and progressive approaches. Not only did they demand a departure from Neo-Confucian stagnation, but they also proposed liberal policies such as breaking class barriers to ensure equal opportunities for all in public service and education. Their proposals were timely and revolutionary. But the conservative Chosun court was still dominated by officials who regarded any criticism of Confucian doctrines as treason. Nevertheless, they rightfully challenged the Confucian assumption that the history of ancient China held the solution to the nation's contemporary problems. Attesting to the overwhelming grip of Confucian mentality on Chosun society, even the Silhak reformers were not totally free from the damaging tradition. In spite of their progressive stands on many issues, Silhak scholars still ended up embracing a purely agricultural economy for the kingdom; they preferred to keep commercial activities to a minimum, much as more traditional Confucian scholars had advocated. Predictably, the court did not accept the enlightened Silhak movement, though it did help the nation achieve significant improvements in agriculture, medicine, and manufacturing. Despite the failure of the bold challenge, the Silhak movement was vital to dealing effectively with the kingdom's socioeconomic problems. It was a remarkably fresh idea for the nation's minority intellectuals to publicly insist on breaking away from the entrenched traditions of Confucian teachings. The Silhak movement was the first manifestation of Korea's advancing intellectual maturity, but it was not quite powerful and persistent enough to derail the nation's long Confucian tradition overnight.

Initially, the Koreans embraced Confucianism as a tool to transform their backward society into one more cultured. When the nation experienced its share of political upheavals, Confucianism provided the rulers with a sophisticated political philosophy that offered a measure of political centralization and a sophisticated code of conduct. The rulers and the ruling class became devoted Confucian followers. As time went by, it formed the intellectual cornerstone of the nation. Only slowly was this cumbersome foreign doctrine introduced to the public, whose emotional and spiritual devotion was focused on Buddhism and a variety of local religious practices. The doctrine of legitimate royal authority, the leadership role of virtuous men, and selection of officials based on literary merits were particularly strong attractions to the nation's highly politicized ruling class.

It is a troublesome proposition to blame the Chosun dynasty's political impotence solely on the flaws of Confucianism. Nevertheless, the fact that it had been the nation's foremost political doctrine and intellectual foundation for so long makes the Confucian tradition a prime suspect. There were other plausible elements, such as indigenous political and social patterns, that may have contributed to the making of a uniquely Korean circumstance. At a minimum, Koreans should share the responsibility of not being selective in adopting Confucian teachings or formulating their own philosophical basis using Confucian building blocks. Had they been able to do so, Confucianism could have been a blessing to Korea's cultural and political development with drastically different results.

Notes

1. Chu Chai and Winberg Chai, *Confucianism,* New York: Barron's Educational Series, Inc., 1973, p. 1.
2. Kaji Nobuyuki, "Confucianism, the Forgotten Religion," *Japan Quarterly,* January-March 1991.
3. This refers to the Springs and Autumns period(722-481 B.C.) that followed the period of Shang, China's earliest known state, founded around 1700 B.C. The Springs and Autumns period is known for Chou's weak central control that caused incessant warfare among numerous feudal states.
4. Western Chou was established circa 1025 B.C., and its successor, Eastern Chou, lasted until 255 B.C.
5. The Springs and Autumns (Chun-Chiu period) lasted from 722 B.C. to 481 B.C.
6. Jacques Gernet, *A History of Chinese Civilization,* translated by J.R. Foster. New York: Cambridge University Press, 1982, p. 91.
7. Liu Pang proclaimed himself the emperor of the Han dynasty in 202 B.C.
8. Taoists, led by Mo-tzu, emphasized that salvation of everyone does not lie in collective action but in retirement and in the practice of procedures which permit one to withdraw from the world and to master it. Chuang-tzu, who lived c. 370-300, is the best known Taoist.
9. Jacques Gernet, p.35.
10. Ibid., p. 35.
11. Ibid., p. 46.
12. Ibid. p.113.
13. Immanuel C. Y. Hsu, *The Rise of Modern China.* New York: Oxford Press, 1970, p. 108.
14. Chai and Chai, p.7.
15. Immanuel C.Y. Hsu, p.119.
16. Gilbert Rozman, ed., *The East Asian Region: Confucian Heritage and its Modern Adaptation.* New Jersey: Princeton University Press, 1991, p. 37.
17. During this period, Koryo Confucian scholars reached an academic eminence in their interpretation of Chu Hsi's teachings. Some of them were heralded to have surpassed the level of great Ming scholars.
18. Jahyun Kim Haboush, "The Confucianization of Korean Society," in Rozman, ed., *The East Asian Region.* p.94.

19. Jiphyunjun was first established during the Koryo period but remained obscure. King Sejong reestablished it as a royal institution and appointed the nation's most promising Confucian scholars to its staff. Jiphyunjun scholars engaged in research, publication, and royal counseling. Its most prominent contribution was the invention of Korean alphabets under the direction of the king.

20. Immanuel C. Y. Hsu, p. 91.

21. Sang Baek Lee, *Korean History,* book 4, pp, 476-479.

22. The East India Company started to import opium into China in 1816, and by 1820 China began to experience serious problems in its balance of trade.

23. Hyon San Yun, *Chosun Yuhaksa(A History of Korean Confucianism).* Seoul: Mingjung Sogwan, 1949, PP. 15-37.

24. Chosun's family concept was an extended one, unlike today's nuclear concept. In this sense it had more similarity with a clan rather than a single family.

25. King Sejo usurped the power from the minor monarch in 1455. The king proved to be one of the most capable rulers of the dynasty but was rejected by the nation's Confucian officials because of the illegitimacy of his succession.

Chapter 5

Western Incursion

1. Western Adventures in the East Asia

By the middle of the eighteenth century the Western maritime powers had made their presence felt throughout East Asia. In their initial thrust into the region, the primary focus was on China, an old-fashioned kingdom of largely untapped natural resources. The Europeans projected the nation of over three hundred million potential consumers to become the largest virgin market for their industrial products. In addition, European traders were aware of the fact that China was the world's premier producer of popular trade items such as jewelry, silk, and ceramic wares, which were much desired by their affluent clients.

That the Western powers' arrival at the Chinese shores coincided with the Ming dynasty's fatal dynastic decline was history's worst irony. In spite of its long, consummated cultural heritage, Ming had failed to escape from the entanglement of its old-fashioned system in time. When the West arrived demanding open relations, the middle-kingdom was not only unprepared for the encroachment of the *barbarian* Western powers but was unable to fully comprehend the gravity of the development. The Ming court was yet to realize the fact that the touted intruders were centuries ahead of itself in science and technology.

The Western powers rushed to East Asia with the spirit of adventure, fed primarily by the mercantile search for lucrative trade. To a lesser extent they were also motivated by the evangelical zeal to spread Christianity to the heathen world.[1] Thus the West was often able to utilize its evangelical cover in concealing its true intention of commercial gains.[2] Because of its complexity and international dimension, the West's commercial and evangelical pursuit became an ultimate political test for both the Ming and the Ching courts.

The West's intrusion into China was spearheaded by Portugal, a major maritime power of the time; in 1535 it extracted from the Ming court a legal sanction to reside and trade in Macao. Spain quickly emulated the Portuguese venture by winning in 1575 a Ming concession to trade along the southern Chinese coast. Shortly other Western powers followed suit. The Dutch, who established a limited trading operation with Japan in the late sixteenth century, organized a China post by 1656. With its extensive commercial interests in India laid down in the early seventeenth century, England was the most aggressive European power in Asia during the period. Naturally, it was eager to expand trade with China following other maritime powers' East Asian ventures by establishing a Chinese commercial outpost in 1690. France did the same in 1728. By the first half of the eighteenth century, most major European powers had managed to establish commercial outposts in China.

Soon after securing the court's legal sanction to trade, the Western powers pursued systematic exploitation of China by employing their seasoned mercantile techniques. They hardly concealed their imperial ambition from the outset, fully taking advantage of the dying empire's political futility. On the other hand, Ming's mediocre political leadership and cumbersome bureaucracy proved to be grossly inadequate in responding to the West's concerted exploitation maneuvers. Ching, which succeeded Ming in 1616, inherited Ming's shortcomings; its countermeasures to the West's calculated ploy were equally ineffective. The West's early commercial activities did not overly disturb the giant middle kingdom. The Ming court remained contemptuous of Western commercialism but did not regard the West's token presence on its soil a major risk; it was more of an unpleasant irritation for the court and the society as a whole that still harbored strong sentiment for the Confucian anti-commercial doctrine. The court was not alarmed as there was only a negligible effect on the giant empire. Nor had the Christian religion the Western powers brought in impressed the court.

Soon the Western traders realized that their China dream was quite premature. Ming's essentially agrarian, self-sufficient economy proved to be far from reaching a state capable of furnishing sustained consumer markets for European industrial products. The impoverished Chinese farmers could ill-afford what the West was eager to sell, relatively high priced industrial items. On the other hand, as the West had expected, China possessed ample non-industrial commodities highly sought after by wealthy European consumers. Contrary to the expectations of the European industrialists, it turned out that China was more of an enormously profitable exporter of its own non-industrial products than an importer of Europe's sophisticated industrial products. This trade pattern quickly forced the European powers to incur a huge payment imbalance in favor of China. For the Western mercantile powers such development was highly intolerable.

The West's systematic attempt to establish its mercantile control of China was closely followed by its Christian evangelism. St. Francis Xavier of the Society of Jesus, who managed to introduce Catholicism to Japan earlier, came to China in 1552 with the same intention. However, in a society dominated by long established Confucian tradition his efforts quickly fizzled. In spite of the initial setback, other Italian Jesuits came in 1577 to continue Xavier's evangelical work. Their efforts bore fruit slowly as they skillfully avoided conflicts with Chinese sensibilities and customs within the limits of basic doctrine that the church set.[3] Some missionaries even managed to establish good personal rapport with the higher officials of the Ming court. By 1651 their deliberate proselytizing efforts had won 150,000 Chinese converts, a notable but modest achievement in populous China.

The Ching court took realistic views toward missionaries but more reserved attitudes toward Christianity, treating the Western missionaries more as intellectuals than bearers of new religious ideals. Thus missionaries were quite well accepted; some even won high government positions.[4] On the other hand, the court was uncommitted to Christianity. It anticipated that fundamental and irreconcilable conflicts would eventually develop between Confucian doctrines and monotheistic Christianity, and remained skeptical of the constructive role of Christianity in Confucian China. In spite of its apparent willingness to maintain contacts with some missionaries, the court was vigilant about Christian evangelical work.

While remaining ambivalent toward Christianity itself, the court's interest in the Western technologies that the missionaries brought continued to be high. Recognizing that the missionaries were couriers of Europe's scientific knowledge, the court actively sought their cooperation. As a result, many missionaries became the Ching court's window in adopting the West's scientific and technological knowledge and were the most important source of modern Western knowledge for Ching, but as a whole churchmen's knowledge was more general than specific. Yet their contributions- significant and more noticeable in some technical areas such as cannon casting, calendar making, and cartography- were far from being the catalysts for the modernization of Ching.

The Ching court's moderately tolerant disposition toward Christianity drastically shifted around the 1770s when the West's exacerbating commercial exploitation had prompted the court to take an antagonistic approach toward the West in general, enforcing its anti-Christianity laws more strictly. Ironically, because of the presence of the West's growing commercial and political clout in China, fledgling Chinese Catholicism encountered a major setback from which it did not recover until the nineteenth century.

While the West's attention was primarily focused on India and China, other Asian regions such as Japan and Southeast Asia attracted only secondary interest. The Hermit Kingdom of Chosun was even out of the Western powers' customary commercial interests. Its remote location and Chinese-oriented foreign relations had effectively deterred the small kingdom from establishing contacts with nations beyond its immediate neighbors. There had been no direct trade or diplomatic relations between Korea and the Western nations prior to the dawn of the nineteenth century. Chosun Korea, still known in the West as a Chinese dependency, remained hidden from the views of the Western powers even when their Chinese adventure had much progressed.

As the Western powers made their presence in China known, the Chosun court had become, although vaguely, aware of the nature of the highly advanced Western world. The knowledge brought home by court officials who made contacts with European missionaries in Beijing included some fragmentary information on Western science and the world outside China in general. Although far from comprehensive, this trickling of details was enough to shake some court officials' long-standing conviction that the Middle Kingdom was the only civilized society in the world.

2. Western Efforts To Open Korea

The Ching court's intractable policy toward Catholicism, or the Western religion as it was known in Korea, was closely scrutinized in the Chosun court. Nevertheless, the Chosun court did not imitate the Ching court in its overwhelming reservations against the Western religion. Nor did the Ching court advise the Korean court regarding Catholicism. In spite of its close alliance with China, the Chosun court remained independent in making its own policies in both domestic and foreign spheres. The Chosun court, however, paid close attention to the Western powers' intrusive activities in China, which later became the foremost reference in Chosun's anti-Christian policies.

Christianity could have been the most appropriate messenger of advanced Western culture which the old-fashioned Chosun society could have eagerly embraced. Nevertheless, the Chosun court had been receiving only unfavorable notices on the West and the Western religion from its trusted neighbor, Ching. It was the unfortunate experience of Ching that had effectively precluded the Chosun court from viewing the Western church objectively.

Officially, Christianity landed in Korea in 1784. However, an unofficial date goes back further; some publications of Matteo Ricci, the leading missionary of the late Ming period, were introduced into Korea in the early seventeenth century. Unlike the Chinese, Koreans had to import the new religion piece by piece from the Chinese source and recreate it through a long self-study process. As reflected by the time-consuming transfer process that went on undetected for a long time, the Chosun court was little concerned with Christianity during its infancy.

The early couriers of Korean Catholicism were a few lower-level court officials whose visits to Beijing led to initial contacts with the new religion. Even with the limited introduction, the new Western doctrine of philanthropism and salvation found receptive converts in Chosun, mostly among commoners and the oppressed. The nation's unstable social order and economic hardship that were worsening during the later part of the eighteenth century provided an ideal environment for the new religion. By 1794 the new church's followers reached 10,000, a significant enough success in a land traditionally Confucian and Buddhist.

A growing number of Christian converts, who later included some intellectuals of the gentry class, eventually alarmed the introverted Chosun court. Catholicism not only contradicted basic rituals of Confucian doctrines practiced and protected in Korea even more jealously than in China, but also threatened the very foundation of the nation's spiritual tradition. To restrain the spread of the scarcely known foreign religion, the court decreed in 1785 a prohibition against the "wrong religion and wrong doctrine." This was followed by the first crackdown against the Korean Catholic church; in 1791 the court inflicted upon the church its first serious setback with persecution of some three hundred Korean converts. The court's hostile oppression forced the germinating Korean Catholic community to go underground temporarily, thus freezing the church's energetic expansion.

The Chosun court's anti-Catholic stand remained firm. But the enforcement of the prohibition was often inconsistent due to fluctuating political stability. Repression was loosened when the court was plunged into another round of political instability and factional power struggle during the early part of the nineteenth century. Benefiting from the court's ineffective enforcement of the law, the resilient Korean Catholic community gained strength again. The Seoul diocese was separated from the Beijing diocese in 1831, signifying the Vatican's recognition of the strength of the Korean Catholic community. When Father Pierre Philibert Maubant managed to enter Korea covertly to assume the post of Bishop of Seoul in 1836, the Korean Catholic community had grown to some 9,000 followers.

A. France's Gunboat Evangelism

The church's rapid expansion again touched off the court's intensified enforcement of the prohibition edict. Amid the renewed government crackdowns there occurred a small episode that was to have a profound implication in Korea's foreign relations for years to follow. The incident was touched off by the authority's discovery of a letter written by a Korean convert requesting the French mission in Beijing to arrange a French naval intervention on behalf of the pressed Korean Catholic community. The letter became timely and justifiable evidence for the suspicious court to intensify its anti-Catholic campaign. In 1839 the court ordered the persecution of more than seventy Korean converts and three French missionaries. The fact that French missionaries were persecuted along with Korean converts was a drastic departure from the Chosun court's conservative attitude toward the West. The court, which had until then shown unusual tolerance and goodwill toward the Westerners, mostly shipwreck victims, had begun to single out the Catholic church as a dire national threat. It decided to apply the most extreme measures in dealing with the Western religion and the Western powers in general.

Chosun's radical shift was greatly influenced by the infamous "Opium War" of Ching.[5] The court received detailed information about the West's evil opium trade that had triggered extensive socio-economic calamity in China. The military defeat Ching suffered when it resisted the British for its opium trade was also known to the Koreans. Ching's Western- caused predicament convinced the court that the very objective of the Western powers' eagerness to open the region was no more than destructive economic exploitation.   Having observed the West's immoral and injurious business practices in China, the Chosun court was compelled to take all precautions to frustrate Western advances in Korea, whether it be

Christianity or naval squadrons. The Chosun court was convinced that the Western missionaries were merely playing a lead in the profound Western conspiracy to exploit the kingdom; thus it determined not to allow itself to be drawn into the same predicament as Ching. Whatever the true intentions the Western powers might have had, the developments in China provided Koreans with solid warning that the West had less than noble intentions in the region.

In 1846, France dispatched three warships to Korea and demanded an explanation for the court's persecution of three French missionaries. The Chosun court was at loss in dealing with this scarcely known foreign power because it had no prior experience to deal with any foreign power. Facing the first-ever encounter with a Western power, the court adopted its non-response stand. Such an unorthodox policy, not out of deliberate defiance but rather for lack of alternative, was, however, effective; the French gunboats shortly had to withdraw. Despite this failure, France again sent two warships to Korea for the same mission the next year. In spite of the French naval intimidation, the Chosun court maintained its no-response stand. France did not resort to the use of military means against the determined Korean court, and the incident was resolved without resorting to actual hostility.

The French incidents greatly intensified the Chosun court's suspicion about missionaries and the intentions of the Western powers in general. By threatening the use of its military power against the Hermit Kingdom, France overlooked the fact that Korea was an independent nation whose sovereignty must be respected. However, France had a legitimate concern over the court's persecution of its missionaries in Korea. France also should have realized the fact that those unfortunate missionaries had entered Korea without the court's permission to work, having been prohibited by a royal edict. Nevertheless, France opted to intimidate the kingdom by show of its naval power, an act which did not resolve the matter but helped deepen the Chosun court's suspicion and prejudice against Western religion in particular and Western powers in general.

France's gunboat diplomacy, a poorly conceived move for the self-proclaimed protector of the church, was an inauspicious omen for nineteenth century Korea. Although it helped to demonstrate France's determination to support Korea's Catholic converts and to pursue the propagation of Christianity in Korea, the gunboat diplomacy also created social unrest for the invasion-detesting kingdom. The direct consequence of French gunboat diplomacy was not the Chosun court's submission but its initiation of another round of harsh Catholic persecution, which included the sacrifice of the Korean nation's first ordained priest.[6]

The successive persecutions did not, however, muffle the growing popularity of the Christian church in Korea. On the contrary, the church experienced another strong growth period when the court was preoccupied with its recurring political infighting after the death of King Choljong in 1864. The lack of strict enforcement of the prohibition encouraged more French missionaries to enter the country clandestinely, and allowed the Korean Catholic community to continue a slow but steady growth. Under the pastorship of twelve French missionaries, the number of Korean Catholics increased from around 11,000 in 1850 to some 23,000 in 1865. The church had taken full advantage of the totally relaxed political suppression.

The Korean Catholic church was in its most robust growing period when Taewongoon, the most colorful leader of the late Chosun period, assumed political power in the ruling regency. During the early period of his rule, Taewongoon's stand toward the Christian religion was uncertain and even neutral in contrast to the hostile distrust of the earlier leadership. The regent was aware of the controversies of the religion; the foremost was potential contradictions to the nation's Confucian tradition to which he was strongly attached, as were most of the nation's ruling class. The temporary halt of Catholic persecution during the early period of the Taewongoon regency did not result from his tolerance of the Western culture. Rather it was caused by the regent's insufficient reading of the church's growing strength at the time. His brief tolerance of the church also may have suggested that he was measuring the utility of the new religion for national interests.[7] In any event, the regent allowed the Western religion to maintain a stable growth and imposed little restraint until 1865.

After the brief period of indecision, the regent apparently concluded that the Western religion and the Western doctrine were incompatible with the kingdom's traditional way of life. His government was to oppose the church by strictly enforcing the prohibition decree. The Anglo-French expedition of Beijing in 1860 and then frequent appearances of Russians along the nation's northern border region reinforced his suspicion about Western motives. Once his policy on the subject was clearly formulated, its implementation was characteristically drastic and thorough.

The regent's Catholic persecution commenced in 1866 and lasted for almost three years. During the period the Korean Catholic church was effectively decimated; approximately 8,000 converts were executed, including most major Korean Catholic figures and nine French missionaries. Only three French missionaries managed to survive the purge. The regent clearly intended to totally eliminate the church from the peninsula.

The regent's bloody persecution of the Catholic church should not be construed as a mere religious persecution, however. Although the Western church contradicted the nation's cherished Confucian tradition, the severity of the regent's abuse showed that he and the court were strongly influenced by the anti-Western frenzy. What the court so violently opposed was not the matter of a choice of religion or religious doctrine, but the perceived and speculated fear of Western imperialism, which was widely believed to be hidden behind the Western religion. The deleterious developments in China led the nationalistic regent to take preemptive measures against the church.

In 1866 France responded militarily to the Chosun court's second persecution of its missionaries by sending seven warships to Korea. Unlike its first quest that was more of an exploration than a military confrontation, the new campaign was a serious undertaking. The French expeditionary force, which included six hundred marines, quickly captured the lightly defended town of Kanghwa on Kanghwa Island, a strategic isle at the mouth of the Han River that flows around the kingdom's capital city, Seoul. It is ironic that the island was the first to fall to Western invaders after it had served as a the traditional refuge for the Korean court in times of the Chinese and the northern tribes' invasions. In a way it symbolized the coming of a new era in which Korea's adversary was a faraway naval power. Finally, Chosun was drawn into world politics, although reluctantly.

The Chosun defense force, which had been for some time a symbolic presence instead of a fighting force in this highly literary-biased society, was not prepared to wage any effective resistance to the French invasion. Nevertheless, the regent confronted his first international crisis with his categorical rejection of any compromise. Offering no hint of retreating from his seclusion policy, he made clear his desire for peaceful coexistence with the faraway nation, offering the idea of non-intervention and non-diplomatic discourse. Still preoccupied by the nation's long seclusion principle, the regent regarded his foremost responsibility as maintaining the nation's isolation from the non-Chinese world at any cost. Beyond his comprehension was the likelihood that his court's diplomatic accommodation of the French grievance might lead to the Hermit Kingdom's access to the West's far-advanced, industrial-scientific culture. On the contrary, the regent decided to repulse the French expedition militarily and ordered a national mobilization. The invasion-fearing public was solidly behind the court's quixotic militancy.

The Chosun court's response to French occupation of Kanghwa was a stern reprimand. Focusing on the intruder's violation of its territorial integrity, the court flatly rejected all French requests, including the establishment of diplomatic relations between the two countries. Instead it advanced a justification that the kingdom had always been generous to the Westerners-mostly shipwreck victims-even without the benefits of formal diplomatic relations. Furthermore, it correctly pointed out that humanitarian acts did not require a diplomatic channel to be effective. By doing so, however, it plainly demonstrated the fact that it did not grasp the nature of modern international relations.

The court further rationalized the persecution of the French missionaries by claiming a sovereign nation's right to administer established law. It also spurned the French request for a more tolerable atmosphere for evangelical work in Korea on the ground that it reserved, like any other nation, the right to protect its own religious preference. In spite of the intimidating presence of its naval force, France had failed to impress the Chosun court. The Chosun court's obstinate seclusion doctrine must have been a great enigma to maritime France. On the other hand, the French demand to open the door and accept Christianity, which was neither solicited nor deemed necessary to the Confucian society, had equally perplexed the regent. As a result, the French endeavor did not contribute to the resolution of the crisis. On the contrary, it deepened the Chosun court's suspicion that France was perpetrating a grand conspiracy against the kingdom. As the standoff continued, the French expeditionary force realized that it would extract no concession from the regent unless it defeated him by force.

The regent's uncompromising stand had left the French with two alternatives: a withdrawal or an expanded military offense. France opted for a military solution by vastly escalating its military pressure on the court. Its initial objective was to cut off the civilian supplies to Seoul by blockading the Han River, the lifeline of the capital. As the French had expected, the blockade proved to be quite effective in isolating the capital from the nation's agricultural hinterland. But its daring wish that the court would have no alternative but to surrender did not materialize. First of all, Taewongoon's besieged court resisted the French blockade with resourcefulness and perseverance; it adopted various successful measures to pacify the disturbed public and managed to keep the capital city operational without undue difficulties. In addition, the regent's single-minded resistance efforts had won public support.   As the blockade produced no tangible result but the hardening of Korean resistance, the invaders shifted their tactics to even more belligerent provocation by attacking Korea's coastal areas with their naval guns. In spite of the French desperation, the tide of this small war was turning in favor of Korea as the court was increasingly successful in enlisting a large number of voluntary defenders. The nation was fully mobilizing its resources to repel the invasion under the regent's leadership as it recovered from the initial shock. Finally, a decisive battle took place at a strategic mountain in Kanghwa island, where the Korean defenders soundly defeated the small French marine detachment. The expeditionary force sustained prohibitively high casualties, which forced their withdrawal from Korean waters. The old-fashioned but resolute regent had overcome the nation's first military crisis provoked by a Western power.

The French expedition was of little military significance. After all, the military strength France had committed to the adventure was hardly large enough to subdue even small, outmoded Chosun. The symbolism and psychological implications of the outcome, however, were extraordinary. The regent and his court were more than ever convinced that Christian followers were the cause of the French invasion. The court's escalated Catholic persecution was inevitable. Contrary to its intention, the French military adventure had further complicated the West's evangelical efforts in Korea.

An even more far-reaching consequence of the episode was that it drove the regent into an extreme anti-Western mentality. He then pursued categorical rejection of any relations with the West or anything related to the West, virtually eliminating any chance for the nation to join the contemporary world community. The misfired French adventure had failed to impress the anachronistic regent but instead reinforced his belief that Korea was still strong enough to repel Western invaders. It might have become a small, forgotten episode for imperial France, but the French gunboat evangelism greatly altered the course Korea had to travel during the climactic nineteenth century.

The French expedition had not been authorized by Paris but was initiated by the French minister in China. At the time, France under Napoleon III was heavily involved with the political games of Bismarck; Napoleon had gambled with the shrewd Bismarck only to find a much stronger Prussia opposing him. Under the circumstances, Napoleon had hardly any room to contemplate the conquest of the little known kingdom in the Far East while German power politics were under full swing in the central Europe. Had Napoleon been allowed to dispatch his mighty naval force to conquer the Hermit Kingdom, the outcome of the skirmish would have been drastically different. If Napoleon had managed to subdue Korea, it would have been most likely that the kingdom would have become

France's second foothold in Asia after French Indo-China.

The victorious regent did not comprehend the macro-geopolitics of Europe that had saved Korean independence from the French expedition. On the contrary, the little war gave him a false confidence that his antiquated kingdom could stand against Western powers, a tragic misjudgment even for the anachronistic Chosun court. However, the Chosun court's illusion about the nation's military might did not discourage other Western powers' interest in opening the little known kingdom.

B. America's Gunboat Diplomacy

After the French episode the Taewongoon regime had every reason to avoid similar encounters with others. It was eager to return to anonymous seclusion, maintaining its normal diplomatic discourse only with Ching China. Ever-treacherous waves of the intensifying Western advances in the region had failed to awaken the court. Nevertheless, the West was hardly in a mood to grant the befuddled Chosun Court the tranquility it so eagerly sought. On the contrary, America, of which the Chosun court did not have even rudimentary knowledge at the time, was to apply its renowned "Perry Tradition" on the Chosun court even before the jolt of the French adventure had subsided.[8]

To the Chosun court, America was even more remote than Europe. Unlike the Europeans who had provided the Koreans a glimpse of acquaintance through its shipwrecked sailors and missionaries stationed in Beijing, America was virtually unknown to the Hermit Kingdom. The diplomatic contacts between this emerging Western power and faraway Chosun remained nonexistent until they encountered an unexpected need for a dialogue to settle an incident created by an American merchant ship.

The American schooner General Sherman entered Korean waters on August 16, 1866, allegedly to exchange goods. This first Western commercial venture proceeded against the Chosun court's strict seclusion policy. Naturally the Korean authorities had made repeated attempts to turn back the ship as the nation's seclusion policy dictated. The ship, however, sailed up to the bank of Pyongyang, the nation's second largest city. There the crew of the General Sherman managed to provoke the local authority and citizens. In the ensuing confrontation, the enraged public burned the ship with the entire crew on board.

The local authority and the court, even after the incident, did not clearly comprehend the nationality of the General Sherman or the nature of her visit.[9] The authority in Pyongyang had simply been executing the nation's seclusion policy by refusing the ship's crew to land. In the process both sides engaged in unspecified hostility that no record can verify. Nevertheless, it seemed certain that the incident was most probably spontaneous with no pre-meditation involved. The fact that the crew provoked such a violent response from the Korean public that had been almost without exception generous to foreign visitors regardless of their nationality implied that the sailors had engaged in some activities that were highly unacceptable and unforgivable. The Chosun court's official position was that the General Sherman was on a mission of piracy punishable by law. Moreover, the ship's Chinese crew commanded by two American officers seemed to have committed undetermined offenses against the local authorities and onlookers.

Upon the disappearance of the merchant ship, America attempted through its Chinese contacts to extract an explanation of its fate. To the American inquiry the Chosun court conveyed a largely vague and defensive response, which may have been all the court could afford due to lack of more detailed information. Yet the unsatisfactory response prompted Washington to dispatch a naval squadron to Chosun. Although its immediate excuse was the fate of the ship and her crew, America was interested in using the occasion to sign a formal treaty with Korea, justifying the undertaking in order to establish a formal diplomatic relationship that would protect shipwrecked American seamen in Korean waters. The maritime excuse was a simple pretext used to conceal its germinating commercial-political interests in the region, because there would have been only a remote chance for such an accident to occur in Korean waters. America's true intention was to negotiate with the Chosun court a treaty of amity and commerce similar to one that it had earlier concluded with China and Japan. In case there was a need for stronger persuasion, America was ready to apply the "Perry Tradition," the gunboat demonstration through which it succeeded in opening secluded Japan in 1854.

America's first Korean expedition force was comprised of five warships carrying eighty-five pieces of artillery and 1,230 marines and sailors. Entering Korean waters on May 21, 1871, the American expedition demanded of the Chosun court a peaceful resolution of the conflict. Even under the threat of the naval squadron that was significantly more powerful than the French expedition, the regent was not to alter his once-successful, no-negotiation doctrine. The regent's court undertook measures to strengthen its defenses around Kanghwa Island and brought a formal charge against America's unlawful intrusion into Korean waters. The regent took the same uncompromising stand with which he succeeded in turning back the French force and was quite willing to endure another military confrontation unless the American force withdrew. He was confident that his stubborn defenders would defeat another "barbarian conspiracy."

The American intentions were not much different from that of France except that they were fully authorized by their government. Nonetheless, the Taewongoon court was not ready to abolish its cherished seclusion policy no matter who was demanding an open relation. Characteristically the court rejected American demands outright; it reasoned that the kingdom's poor domestic economic situation did not allow any meaningful foreign trade, and if there were any outflow of domestic products, the nation would not be able to feed itself. The Chosun court's narrow view on international trade clearly illustrated its total lack of understanding modern trade relationships, but its apprehension was based on its genuine concern over the nation's chronic economy. Encountering the Chosun court's outright rejection, the American expedition realized that its objectives were obtainable only through a successful demonstration of its military might.

The standoff led to a military confrontation in which the modern American military inflicted a severe blow on the Chosun defenders. But overcoming the initial setbacks, the Chosun defenders again persisted against well-equipped invaders. The ensuing stalemate eventually left the American expedition with two equally painful alternatives: the voluntary termination of its gunboat demonstration, or escalation of the standoff with active military engagement. It chose a peaceful solution, and shortly the naval force left the area, aborting America's "little war" on Korea. America's impulsive mission gave the Hermit Kingdom its second victory against the Western powers, however insignificant and deceptive that may have been.

The repulsion of the American expedition was the crown of the Taewongoon regency's seclusion doctrine. But the ramifications of the episode were far-reaching for the seclusive Chosun court; the regent was completely captivated by his lucky play of fate and became convinced more than ever that his antiquated seclusion policy was fully exonerated. The grave consequences of the nation's missed opportunity to open its door to the West at the expense of America's modest demands completely escaped the attention of the victorious regent and his court. At the outburst of the anti-West hysteria, the court overlooked the fact that America's mostly benign demands may have led to an opportunity to adopt Western industrial-scientific culture and to upgrade its outdated economy and administrative structure. It lacked the foresight to recognize that massive cultural cross-exchange may have been the only avenue open to the nation's aspiration to elevate itself to a position where it could compete against its more populous and refined neighbors on more equal footing. Pursuing the largely meaningless victory, the Chosun court committed one of the nation's truly historical blunders: it lost the opportunity to open its door with dignity and to dodge the penalty of anonymous seclusion likely to be imposed upon the nation. Unaware of this historic fallacy, the regent celebrated his puerile victory by erecting stone tablets known as Chuckhwa Bi throughout the country with the following engraved declaration: "Western barbarians are attacking us; should we not fight, an accommodation must be made. To accommodate the enemies is to betray the country."

The West's desire to open the Hermit Kingdom for trade and Christian evangelism was benign in nature. But as both expeditions had demonstrated, their approach was unnecessarily heavy-handed. Both France and America had the military capability to defeat the Korean kingdom if they had chosen to press the cause with their might. Their attempts to coerce the Chosun court were more impulsive than deliberate. They believed that a simple show of force would impress the small nation enough to accept a negotiated settlement. Their optimistic and hopelessly naive expectation represented complete disregard of the desire and apprehension of this small but historic kingdom. The Chosun court lacked adequate understanding of the faraway Western world. But it did have time to observe carefully what the extensive Western interference had done to China. For the kingdom that had become so anxious to avoid a similar fate, it was a rational policy option to resist all Western encroachments. The Western powers' impatient demand for open-door discourse failed to calm but rather intensified the court's suspicion of their motives.

It was a grave misfortune for Korea not to utilize the occasion for its own advantage as Meiji Japan had done earlier. Yet the court's determination not to yield to Western pressure at any cost was an amicable pursuit of its own nationalistic concerns. The regent's intention was noble and considerate, even though in retrospect it proved not to be a prudent move for the nation. On the other hand, it is difficult to speculate today what might have been the ultimate consequences if the Chosun court had given in to either French imperialism or American commercialism at the time.

3. The Rise of Korean Nationalism

A. *The Rise of Dong-Hak (Eastern Learning) Doctrine*

The founding father of the Chosun dynasty adopted Confucianism as the nation's basic ideology and acquiescenced to the Ming court by practicing Sadaeism, or serving the great. The kingdom's early monarchs had followed the footsteps of the founder by making unbending loyalty to the Chinese court the nation's basic political practice. As a result, the kingdom's public as well as private spheres were carefully tailored so as not to contradict established Chinese practices.

The court's persistent efforts to appease the Chinese court by playing Mo-Hwa, or adoration of China, inevitably led to worsening spiritual deterioration. Particularly the nation's ruling class had become too dogmatic to escape from the age-old Confucian tradition, thus alienating themselves from the kingdom's aggravating socio-economic realities. Inevitably conflicts between the ruling classes and the masses became deeper and wider. The resumption of factional political infighting in the early nineteenth century had further weakened the coherence of the kingdom's social fabric and diminished the public confidence in the court and the ruling class as a whole. As the kingdom's political leadership remained incapable of establishing a clear national focus, the despondent masses were increasingly turning to Western religion for their salvation. During the late nineteenth century Chosun's deteriorating socio-economic amenities further escalated the spread of rebellious sentiments among commoners. While some resorted to the foreign religion to escape from an unbearable life, others rose against the corrupt local governments. Their revolts, in general, lacked systematic organization to become a nationwide movement that could challenge the central government. Yet these spontaneous uprisings represented growing public discontent. To make the situation even worse, the kingdom was suffering from widespread natural disasters and epidemics. Frequent appearances of the unfamiliar Western naval ships and their military activities along the coasts also greatly disturbed the already fragile Chosun society.

Because of its foreign origin and many contradictions to the nation's Confucian traditions, the Catholic church was a spiritual answer only for some venturesome citizens. To the vast majority of citizens, Catholicism was just another religion with foreign dogma and questionable motives. Still, they continued to lose confidence in the traditional religions such as Confucianism and Buddhism.

The movement of Dong-Hak, or Eastern Learning, as opposed to Suh-Hak, or Western Learning (i.e., Catholicism), was formally launched around 1860 by Choe Jae Woo, who represented the masses that had lost faith in both the Western and traditional religions. Seeking a religion that could rejuvenate the nation's spiritual vigor, he formulated a new religion based on the doctrine whose elements were extracted mostly from three religions widely practiced in Korea: Buddhism, Confucianism, and Taoism. In addition, the founder had studied Western religion extensively for his synthesized version of the Eastern doctrine. The Dong-Hak movement adopted discipline and righteous personal relationship from Confucianism, compassion and equity from Buddhism, and nihilistic naturalism from Taoism. The founder succeeded in forging the new doctrine using eclectic virtues extracted from the major Eastern religions known to the kingdom. Only through his extensive study of each religion was he able to achieve such a difficult undertaking.

The basic philosophy of the Dong-Hak doctrine was also heavily influenced by Korea's long indigenous tradition, Hwa-Rang-Do, which had flourished during the Silla period as the nation's most prominent educational doctrine. Following the Hwa-Rang-Do tradition, the Dong-Hak emphasized the supreme importance of nationhood and the welfare of the public, thus giving the new movement a strong political dimension. The founder sought an ideological harmony in which Eastern religious doctrine and the secular doctrine of nationalism could be complementary to each other.

The Dong-Hak movement was the kingdom's first serious attempt to regain its religious and ideological independence in history. It rejected the encroachment of the Western religion by embracing native ideologies and traditional values through its creative, practical, doctrinal formulation. In addition, unlike Confucianism's abstract, literate tradition, it emphasized the militaristic discipline of the Hwa-Rang-Do tradition and thus later was able to produce prominent national leaders. In this sense it was the first public manifestation of budding Korean nationalism, which had been suppressed for more than ten centuries under the Chinese domination.

The movement was also notable for its conceptual liberalization. It espoused the revolutionary concept of "the people are the divine," distancing itself from the religions of a monolithic god. By conferring supreme importance to secular living, it placed the plight of the common people on center stage; it strongly reprimanded abuses committed by the oppressive gentry, and proposed egalitarianism and democracy for a new society and a new order. The Dong-Hak was for the salvation of the living, not the dead; it was for the common people, not for the nation's ruling class. It was for the Hahn nation, not its imposing neighbors. It was more than a simple new religious movement, but a national awakening. In the era of extreme conservatism and Sadaeism that prevailed among the court officials and the gentry classes, the Dong-Hak, the first comprehensive religious doctrine developed by the Hahn people, represented a fresh, new wind.

The Dong-Hak doctrine and its religious arm, the Chun-Do-Gyo, or the religion of Heavenly Way, were widely accepted, particularly in the agricultural south. Within three years after its inception Dong-Hak followers reached more than three thousand. Having established its strongholds in the south-central region, the Chun-Do-Gyo concentrated its evangelical efforts upon farmers and the oppressed. The masses were receptive to the enlightening movement and followed its teachings with vigor.

The extraordinary growth of the movement inevitably caught the attention of the court, which had suspected the Dong-Hak to be a pseudo Catholicism. The court that already had shown its extreme revulsion to any Western ideology or practice through its bloody persecutions felt again threatened by this domestic movement. It was unable to comprehend the significance of the Dong-Hak's noble ideology. Instead, it reacted with vehement oppression; in its first crackdown against the movement in 1864 the court executed most of the higher leadership of the movement, including the founder. Nevertheless, the movement that reflected popular desires for a new order and an equitable society above everything else survived the initial setback.

B. Taewongoon's Nationalism

The Dong-Hak's political-religious crusade was the Hahn nation's fresh awakening. It represented the nation's rising consciousness that could no longer tolerate the plight of the exploited farmers and the oppressed. It was a grassroots movement organized and supported by common people. Almost simultaneously Korea witnessed the rise of another national movement, one led by the court. With bold, energetic drive, Taewongoon attempted to recreate the old glory. It was a seclusion-oriented approach with little realistic potential to succeed. Both phenomena were much motivated by the dangers exposed by the Western encroachments and exacerbating domestic problems. Although they were disparate in their direction and nature, both epitomized the Hahn nation's dual character: tenderness and rigidity.

Taewongoon, who took over the government in 1864 as a ruling regent and exercised an absolute political power for the ensuing decade, proved to be one of the most dynamic political personalities in the history of the Chosun dynasty. Yet he was old-fashioned in political ideology and highly inflexible in his dogmatic rule. His powerful idealism and uncompromising rigidity were, however, a double-edged sword for the kingdom, which desperately needed a strong but highly flexible and far-sighted leader.

The regent prominently possessed many of the cherished virtues typically found among accomplished practitioners of Confucianism: perseverance, honesty, and dedication to the monarchy. He was also a man devoted to upholding the rigid Confucian tradition, the commitment known generally detrimental to progressive politics. Inevitably his political legacy was full of extreme self-righteousness, ideological rigidity, resistance to change, and anachronistic dogmatism.

Having long been shunned by his royal clan, Taewongoon had accumulated an unusually thorough understanding of the kingdom's domestic problems. His experience was valuable as shown by his early domestic policies, which reflected his desire to rectify the worsening living conditions of the common people. On the other hand, both his knowledge and experience in international matters were almost non-existent, except for some understanding of the nation's traditional relationship with the Chinese. The kingdom's misfortune was that this powerful figure was totally oriented to domestic policies when equal or even more attention should have been paid to the rapidly evolving regional politics. While maintaining the antiquated system basically intact, the new ruler set out to keep the kingdom's isolation from the non-Chinese world complete. By so doing, the near-sighted regent unwittingly managed to squander the precious little time allotted to Korea to prepare itself for the approaching Japanese menace.

Unlike his obsolete foreign policy, the regent's domestic policy consisted of some bold reform measures for the kingdom's corrupt and ineffectual system. His brutal drive to break the abused power of royal clans and to terminate the suffocating factional political infighting in the court was an undertaking no one but he could attempt. Only his unyielding conviction and the absolute political power he exercised enabled the regime to carry out such bold domestic policies, which helped revamp to some extent the kingdom's impoverished political institution. The nation's profound misfortune was that his outstanding leadership had contributed more than anything to the hardening of its immensely harmful seclusion policy.

Taewongoon was the first Chosun ruler who advocated an equal opportunity principle in hiring public officials; he insisted that the hiring criterion should be one's ability, not factional affiliation or social status. He encouraged hiring people of the non-gentry class if their quality was exceptional, a revolutionary departure from the court's long-established hiring practice. Through such shrewd symbolism, the regent pursued becoming the champion of the nation's oppressed non-gentry public. He was more popular and powerful than any political leader of his time.

The regent waged a difficult assault on the nation's deeply established gentry class by abolishing most of its historic sanctuaries, the private Confucian academies, which were ubiquitous throughout the country as preparatory schools for civil service examinations. Over time, they became a major source of factional fighting and political power as most quality academies belonged to the nation's contending political factions. Some renowned academies exercised considerable political influence over local governments while enjoying exemption from all taxation. Taewongoon was well aware of the extensive harm these institutions inflicted and dissolved most of them. His bold charge on the established order of the powerful scholar-gentry class encountered formidable resistance, but through his determination and shrewd political manipulation he succeeded to an extent that no other leader might have been able to repeat under such pressing circumstances.

Taewongoon's great political skill was also evident in his ability to read public sentiments and to appreciate the value of symbolic gestures in the political process. One of his notable achievements was the rebuilding of the old palace, Kyongbukgoong, which was burned down during the Japanese invasion in 1595. For more than two centuries the palace was left untended because no ruling monarch found enough financial means to rebuild it. The time of the Taewongoon regime was no better than any other period to commit to such expensive construction work, yet unlike preceding rulers, he appreciated the symbolic value of the rebuilt palace in reestablishing the authority of the monarch. The splendid new palace would become the focal point of rallying the depressed public and of projecting the national confidence and prosperity to the world. In spite of great financial difficulties and public outcry against the involuntary labor to be donated, the regent undertook the project and succeeded in rebuilding the palace.

Taewongoon's other major accomplishments included a large-scale modification of the nation's strained financial and tax system. He pursued a dual objective of increasing revenue sources and preventing waste and corruption, particularly among the upper class and government officials. The fact that by the end of the regency the kingdom's financial state was much improved was a solid indication that the revisions were effective. In spite of his seclusion policy, the regent was well aware of the peril of a weak defense and of an urgent need to revamp the impoverished national defense apparatus. The appearance of Russian soldiers in the northern border area obviously compelled the regent to pay greater attention to national defense. His military reform included the separation of the nation's defense command from civilian control and strengthening coastal defense, which played a preeminent role during the Western invasions years later. The regent also displayed his foresight by encouraging the development of new weaponry. Yet the state of the nation's industrial technology was so far behind the West's that the regent's desire to invent new weaponry was no more than farfetched dreams at the time. Nevertheless, his directives demonstrated his profound concern for the kingdom's precarious security problems. On the other hand, he maintained his characteristic unwillingness to admit the shortcomings of the kingdom or to seek assistance from its neighbors, not to mention the West.

Although the regent's rule was effective and fresh in the domestic sphere, it was his belligerent stand against Western powers that created his most profound legacy to Korean history. The irony was that the fiery anti-Western disposition the regent maintained throughout his rule originated from his intense nationalism. A careful review of his anti-Western stand leads to a conclusion that the seclusion policy was his deliberate choice to protect the antiquated kingdom. His view of the West was not firmly established when he came to power through the regency. The events that were mostly initiated by the Western powers from his very first year of rule, however, gradually drove him to extreme anti-Western seclusion. Contrary to the general characterization that he was a natural anti-Western leader, to a great extent he was forced to take such an extreme foreign policy in order to safeguard the kingdom. Of course, it is most unfortunate for the nation that he was not able to seize the opportunity and take advantage of Western industrial culture by establishing normal relations with the Western powers. The regent was not a man of broad knowledge in international political developments. For a man of profound nationalistic pride but of little practical knowledge of the non-Chinese world, the hostile and short-sighted reaction to Western incursion was even predictable under the confusing circumstances of the time.

The regent's persecution of Korean Catholics and French missionaries rightly remains one of the most infamous atrocities in the history of Korean Christianity. It was also a costly strategic error committed by a xenophobic regent at a time when modern commercialism and technologies of the West could have transformed the old-fashioned kingdom. However, his harsh oppression of Catholics transpired partly because of his apprehensive reading of the church's influence in the region. For the ruler whose self-appointed mission was to restore the authority and glory of the Chosun court, the church's posture looked extremely dangerous as demonstrated in China. The Taping revolt almost toppled the Ching court, and the Western powers, the promoters of the church, were exploiting China openly and destructively.[10] The predicament of Ching China, which was suffering terminal blows under Western domination, was the foremost cause of Taewongoon's anti-Western policy. His intense desire to safeguard the kingdom from Western aggression so overwhelmed the court politics that it deprived the nation of an opportunity to formulate a rational approach to the Western religion, the lead carrier of Western culture in the region.

The remarkable thing about the regent's uncompromising resistance to the West was that he chose to fight against the invasions, knowing that the West had already extracted extensive concessions from mighty Ching. Despite this fact, Taewongoon confronted the Western expeditions with his antiquated armed forces and defeated them. Against a highly confident French force, Taewongoon skillfully rallied the public and offered stiff resistance that the small foreign expeditionary force could not long resist. He won the first contest against the West with his stubborn resistance. It was the triumph of Taewongoon's nationalism but a short-lived glory of the Hahn nation, the ruler of the vast Manchurian plain in its heyday.

France's Korean expedition left the regent with a tragically distorted view of the nature and strength of the contemporary West. His perception of the West, regardless of its inaccuracy, made him rush to defend the kingdom from the ploy of another "Western barbarian" with every means available when the American force demanded an open Korean door. In a sense, he was forced to declare the Korean Monroe Doctrine, backed not by modern arms but by the unequivocal determination not to open his kingdom to Western imperialism. The Perry tradition that opened Japan to the West earlier was not applicable to this profoundly proud ruler, the determined defender of the nation's territorial integrity and a five-hundred-year-old monarchy.

Taewongoon's war against France and America was the most clear signal that he did not intend to follow the steps taken by his neighbors, China and Japan. Developments, particularly in China, convinced him there would never be any possible advantage in associating with any Western powers. Moreover, his victories, regardless of the aggressor's partial default, vindicated his judgment and seclusion policy. The arrogant gunboat evangelism and diplomacy were, however, exactly what prompted the regent to press his seclusion policy to the extreme and kept the kingdom away from the West much longer than necessary.

Taewongoon's nationalistic intentions were beyond doubt. His profound suspicion about Western ambitions in the region was well found. Yet his xenophobic reactions to the Western advance proved to be severely detrimental for the nation's entry into the contemporary world community led by those very powers that had made unsuccessful overtures to his country. It was both the nation's severe misfortune and proud legacy that the regent successfully frustrated attempts of two of the world's premier powers.

4. Neighbors Undergoing Transition

A. China Under Western Domination

The Chinese tolerated only a token presence of the Western commercial interests until the middle of the nineteenth century. When the maritime powers of the West requested trade relationships, the Ming court tolerated them and placed no serious obstacles in the way of foreign trade along the nation's southern coast, although the early Western traders were suspected of being more interested in looting than in practicing legitimate trade. The Ching court was more careful about the Western religion. In spite of the West's persistent pressure, the Ching court put Catholicism under its tight control until the ban was lifted in 1844. The West's initial attempts to establish bilateral relationships with China got mostly unfavorable responses from the Ching court, which did not see merit in establishing a formal relation with the "barbarian" world.

By the time the West determined to open East Asia for systematic commercial exploitation, Ching China was merely an old dynasty undergoing a rapid decline of power. Regardless of its traditional over-confidence and patience with its periodic invaders, Ching was too outdated and disorganized to defeat the determined West. In the end, Ching had to accommodate Western commercial advances. The treaty of Nanking, signed in 1842 with England, was followed by the treaty with America in 1844. Under these unequal treaties Ching was forced to grant the Western powers two major concessions that significantly reduced its sovereign power: the tariff exemption on Western products, and a judicial autonomy to the Western communities within their enclaves. Still, the West's relentless drive for commercial exploitation was pushing for a total domination of the old empire. In 1858, a combined force of English and French occupied Beijing and forced the Ching court to sign the Treaty of Tientsin. With the new treaty China's door was now much more widely open to the West; its initial concessions to any Western power were automatically applied to other Western powers under the provision of the most-favored-nation clause.

Ching's growing woe was not limited to the Western maritime powers, however. Russia, first posing as an ally during the Anglo-French expedition of Beijing, extracted from the dispirited Ching court a territorial cession of a vast region between the Ussuri and the Pacific. With this controversial acquisition of Far Eastern real estate, European Russia brought itself into territorial contact with Korea and northeast China.

While Western imperialism intensified, the Middle Kingdom kept its eyes fixed on the glorious past and was unable to adjust itself to evolving international political realities. Even if Ching were to brave the harsh reality with foresight and determination, the West would not have allowed it to succeed. None of the four major Western powers would have risked jeopardizing its profitable position by opposing the other's advance on the decaying Ching empire. The West's pressures, applied severely and rapidly, were major contributors to the Manchu Empire's final disintegration in the middle of the nineteenth century.

Chinese rulers were to exercise their supreme political power only under the "mandate of Heaven." The Heavenly grant was considered withdrawn when a ruler was unable to preserve the domestic tranquillity and to protect the empire from foreign powers. There were growing signs that the Ching court severely compromised its ability to govern and thus was about to lose the quintessential mandate of Heaven as the West's Chinese venture continued to be successful. To make the situation even worse, minor emperors were in power for thirty years in this pivotal period of the late nineteenth century. Particularly, the regency of Tzu Hsi, a woman of eminent quality otherwise, proved to be profoundly inept in leading China at this time of trial.

Public dissatisfaction over the Manchu court spread rapidly. The most serious threat to the throne came from the Taiping rebellion, a movement based on dubious religious doctrine which contained elements of Christianity. This powerful revolt, lasting fifteen years, dramatically revealed the court's inability to maintain civic order and almost succeeded in ending the Ching dynasty. Although it collapsed because of its own weakness, the revolt was the harbinger of the end of the Ching dynasty. Along with the numerous rebellions came catastrophic natural calamities of flood and drought that made the survival of the Manchu empire a virtual impossibility.

At the time of opening its door to the West, the Chinese territory consisted of China proper, Manchuria, and a number of dependencies including Tibet, Mongolia, and Sinkiang. In addition, China exercised much political influence on the two independent states of Korea and Vietnam. The Ching-Korea relation was close and historical, but not one of sovereign-subject formality. A more accurate description of the China-Korea status would be as a close tributary relationship. Chosun tolerated such a relationship as an alternative to the Chinese kingdom's territorial ambitions over the Korean peninsula. Thus, the characterization of Korea and Vietnam as Chinese vassal states is inaccurate, although an atypical historical relationship did exist between China and its two neighbors.

The Western advance in East Asia brought a drastic change in the relations between China and its two close allies. China was no longer able to extend its help to Vietnam when that country fell into French control in the 1860s, although both sides made known the existence of a special relationship between them. In 1884, the Ching court was forced to waive its claim to a suzerainty over Vietnam, thus effectively handing over its controlling influence on Cochin-China to France. While the inevitable change was taking place putting Ching's status as the region's prime power in great jeopardy, both Vietnam and Korea were still hoping for the Middle Kingdom to exercise its traditional role as the leader of their world. They were yet to accept the emerging reality that Ching was experiencing extreme difficulty in defending itself from Western imperialism and pacifying domestic turbulence.

Ching had adopted some tentative steps to modernize its antiquated nation during this period. An educational mission was sent to the United States, and some initial steps to build up a modern navy began. In 1881, its first railway was opened, and the next year a telegraph line was operational. Although China was not quite ready openly to recognize the superiority of the West's industrial culture, it conceded to it by selectively adopting Western practices. In spite of some small and tentative attempts taken to adopt Western ideas and practices, there was no widespread interest by China in moving toward a major institutional reform or reorganization as was so prominent in Japan during the same period. Until the late part of the nineteenth century the Middle Kingdom as a whole still remained outmoded, little touched by the Western industrial-commercial culture.

B. Japan Becomes the West's Best Pupil

From as early as the end of the twelfth century, Japan's governance resembled a military system. Warring feudal chiefs exercised the real political power while the emperor was a mere titular head. The island nation remained more of a vacillating amalgamation of small feuding military states than a unified nation until 1603, when the Tokugawa Shogunate emerged as the central authority. The rule of the Tokugawa Shogunate lasted for over 250 years until the imperial authority was restored in 1867. During this period Japan's feudal culture added a flavor of aggressive and venturesome nationalism, a unique characteristic that set Japan apart from its more literati-oriented neighbors.

Like its continental neighbors, Japan operated as a "rice economy" at the outset of the Tokugawa period. Although farming remained profoundly important to feudal rulers, farmers themselves were not highly regarded much as in Korea and China. Japan was a member of East Asia's Confucian society, but unlike its two neighbors, Japan was an overwhelmingly warrior-ruler society.

Ever since introduced by Koreans, Confucianism and Buddhism played a major role in Japan. Buddhism was popular among commoners while more literate Confucianism was embraced by the nation's ruling class as a foundation for its intellectual realm. As profound as both religions were, they neither displaced the native Shintoism nor dominated the cultural world of the island nation. As a result, Japan was able to maintain most of its unique insular culture in spite of the strong cultural influences of both China and Korea.

Unlike its two neighbors where a literati class dominated national politics, Japan was ruled by powerful warlords and their followers, the Samurai, or warrior class. The Samurai, who played a crucial role not only in the warring period but also in more pacific times, remained the cornerstone of Japan's strong military character. The Samurai institution, a Japanese invention, had sustained its political leverage until the late Tokugawa period when the Shogun's declining interest in Samurai-oriented armies and the long peace had deprived it of its usual utility. Even with waning interest in its service, the Samurai class harbored the spirit of traditional martial ardor. When its traditional role was no longer in demand, many former Samurai willingly became students of Confucian classics as well as the nation's history, thus successfully transforming themselves into a learned and sophisticated middle class. As a learned, motivated pressure group, the defunct Samurai class made a significant contribution to the birth of modern Japan.

Since the eighteenth century the West's interests in opening Japan to commercial ventures were expressed under various pretexts. Like its two neighbors, however, Japan was not interested in a trade relationship and refused to consider the requests made by both Russia and England. It was America that made more resolute attempts to open the secluded nation to the world; Washington justified its request with the pretense that it needed a coaling station in Japan to develop a direct sea line with China.

When it was apparent that the Japanese would not consent to the request peacefully, Washington dispatched a naval squadron. The expedition force, commanded by Commodore Perry, entered Yokohama Bay in 1853 and demanded of the Tokugawa government an immediate acceptance of its open-door request. Under the imposing naval intimidation, the Shogunate quickly submitted by agreeing to enter a treaty relationship. Under the Perry treaty, as it was popularly known, Japan granted America open ports, the right to appoint a consul, the protection of shipwrecked sailors, and most-favored-nation treatment. Other Western powers quickly took advantage of the success of the Perry mission and extracted similar concessions from Japan: England in 1854, Russia in 1885, and Holland in 1857.

In 1858 America upgraded its relations with Japan by signing a comprehensive treaty for regular diplomatic and consular relations. By this treaty Japan not only was obliged to open additional ports to American traders, but more importantly had to surrender its sovereign right to regulate tariffs on imports from America and to confer extraterritoriality on American diplomatic posts. In the end, Perry's rather benign treaty had turned into a costly and unequal treaty for Japan. Yet the Land of the Rising Sun, with the central authority weak and signs of the downfall of Tokugawa rule beginning to show, could not mount any resistance against it.

The opening of its door to the Western powers accentuated Japan's internal turmoil. Powerful feudal lords began to defy the Shogunate rule when the signing of treaties with the West shattered the nation's old order, which was the foundation for its long-standing seclusion policy. Overlooked was the fact that the Tokugawa government chose to accommodate Western demands by realizing that it could not resist militarily if the West launched an invasion. In any event, with the signing of the treaty, the Tokugawa Shogunate voluntarily relinquished its 250 year-old political domination in favor of the Emperor Meiji, who had long remained a figurehead. The court quickly consolidated political power in the nation's central authority and was in firm control by 1869. The era of the remarkable Meiji Restoration was begun.

Meiji Japan accomplished a truly remarkable feat in laying down a sound foundation for a modern industrial nation. However, its chief achievement was not the extensiveness of its reform but the rapidity of its implementation. Discarding a feudal seclusion policy, it aggressively sought Western ideas and practices for its own benefit. Its priority went entirely to revamping the old-fashioned governing structure. It adopted the representative assembly system and the Prussian government form as the model for its new government. The Meiji government promulgated a new constitution in 1889 that embraced a mixture of the Restoration idea and the feudal idea. Under its provisions, the emperor was both sole source and dispenser of all power, but the power was to be exercised through governmental bodies such as the council of ministers. The judiciary was modeled upon that of France and Prussia. Japan's new, Western-style government was fully operational in 1890 with the convocation of its first Diet.

The abolition of the feudal system was problematic even for the highly motivated post-Tokugawa regime. In order to reinstate the imperial authority, it was most urgent to neutralize the feudal authority throughout the country. By 1871 the new regime obtained major clan members' consent for total abolition of the feudal system. Even with effective persuasions and generous offers, the undertaking caused some serious aftereffects. Nevertheless, the ending of feudalism was an auspicious beginning for the new government.

Japan's social and educational development during the Meiji Restoration period was equally impressive. A large number of students were sent to America and Europe to study Western ideas, practices, and institutions in various fields. The nation promptly experimented with selected Western practices, and errors were freely corrected. A number of Western nationals were hired into government service until the foreign-trained Japanese experts were able to replace them. While the Westernization of its governing system was clearly intended, the Meiji government was also careful not to become too dependent upon one system. Instead, it was highly selective: the American system for primary and secondary education, the French system for universities, and the German system for vocational education are examples. Under the new system, public education was particularly emphasized from the beginning.

Equally systematic efforts were directed to economic development. The Meiji court's priority went to building the nation's commercial infrastructure; railroads and improved roads in which the reform-minded government had heavily invested became responsible for the early blossoming of commerce. Moreover, by emphasizing the respectability of business vocations, the government encouraged the energies of the Samurai and former feudal ruling class to be used in commercial and industrial undertakings. In most areas Japan was actively seeking a radical departure from Confucian culture by adapting itself to the West's industrial-commercial culture.

Along with its wholesale structural transformation in the civilian sector, Japan also rebuilt its backward military. It was natural for the nation with a long military tradition to emphasize strong armed forces. The importation of Western military hardware was not new for Japan; it had obtained some advanced firearms from the Dutch as early as the sixteenth century and used them with devastating impact against the Koreans during the Hideyoshi's Korean invasion. This time Japan also adopted the Western military system, departing from its clan-oriented feudal tradition. Its first national army was organized under a system of universal service in 1873. The new military was not only armed with modern weapons but also trained in Western tactics. More importantly, Japan rebuilt its navy, still a vastly inferior force to that of the West, with the help of England, the world's mightiest naval power at the time. By adopting Western practices and weaponry, Japan was rapidly establishing itself as the premier military power of the region.

The successful transformation of the whole society modeled after Western practices gave the Japanese a new sense of national pride and confidence. Moreover, the rise of modernized armed forces caused the birth of powerful military bureaucrats who came to wield increasing leverage over domestic as well as foreign policies. Advocated early on the agenda of hard-liners both in and out of the government was the nation's territorial expansion onto the continent of Asia; they insisted on occupying Korea, Manchuria, a large portion of China, and Siberia.[11] For a while the reemerging imperialism was blocked by the nation's more conservative faction, the civil bureaucrats, who, though they endorsed the imperial expansion, insisted that any campaign not be launched until the completion of national reorganization. Both ends of Japan's political spectrum were in agreement over territorial expansion and differed only in time and method. As imperial sentiment rose high among military bureaucrats and former Samurai, Japan was becoming the region's first imperial power.

In a remarkably short period Japan became the accomplished pupil of Western culture, including its imperial tendency. By 1894 it had successfully implemented Western style reorganization; its feudal system was dismantled and new Western-style government structures were in place in spite of earlier difficulties. Industry and commerce were in a state of vigorous growth benefiting from new respectability and an expanding communication-transportation systems. Western-style educational systems were established, and systematic efforts to acquire the West's advanced knowledge and skill had been launched. More importantly, the land of the rising sun obtained an army and navy modeled after the best of the West. In a period of some twenty years Japan had managed to transform its feudal society into a major, growing power of the region.

As the eventful nineteenth century was winding down, Japan achieved its most ambitious wish and was anxious to confirm its new status in the world community. It was not only ready to claim its newly earned international prestige but anxious to play the territorial games the West had monopolized. The island nation had become confident enough to challenge the Middle Kingdom, an ancient but continental power, for the leadership of the region.

The fact that it took Japan merely twenty years to achieve such total national reorganization was simply remarkable. More than anything, Japan was blessed with many far-sighted and brave political leaders at this critical period, perhaps the most profound difference that set her apart from less fortunate neighbors. The progressive leadership and the national unity only insular Japan could have mustered contributed to this outstanding accomplishment.

Notes

1. Immanuel C.Y. Hsu, *The Rise of Modern China*, p. 122.
2. France's later efforts to convert the Chosun Dynasty, for example, was accompanied by no commercial interests, unlike its earlier contacts with Korea.
3. An Italian missionary named Matteo Ricci was particularly well known for his close rapport with the Ming Emperor and his judicious Christian work.
4. Adam Schall von Bell was appointed as the court's official astronomer. His friendship with the court's high officials was prominent.
5. The conflict lasted for the period 1840-1842.
6. Father Kim Tae-gon(Andrew Kim) and other lay converts were persecuted in 1846. He was ordained as the first Korean priest in 1845.
7. The Regent was known to have some first-hand knowledge about the religion through his relative, who was a convert.
8. Refer to Commodore Perry's naval intimidation that persuaded Japan to open its door to America.
9. There is no clear record to show the Chosun court was involved with the incident. The only record available is about incidents which followed the *General Sherman* episode.
10. The Taiping rebellion started in 1850, lasting for 15 years. The French and British forces sacked Beijing in 1860.
11. As early as 1871 the militant faction of the Japanese government pushed for an expedition to both Formosa and Korea. The idea was blocked by the opposition.

Chapter 6

Chosun at the Crossroads

---

1. The Downfall of the Taewongoon Regency

Just as its sudden rise, the fall of the Taewongoon regency was an epochal development for the Chosun dynasty. Throughout his brief reign, the regent Taewongoon, a man of unquestionable integrity and equally impressive strong-will, strived to transform the ancient kingdom into a nation of prestige and prosperity. Various initiatives, conceived and carried out with his single-minded devotion, exemplified his uncompromising loyalty to the tradition-rich monarchy. Yet in spite of his noble intentions, his rule was more contradictory than effective. His domestic policy, which included some surprisingly liberal elements, was largely overshadowed by his anachronistic foreign policies, characterized by a narrow world vision that was effectively limited to the traditional Korean-Chinese relationship. As a result, the lasting legacy of his rule was not the national rebuilding program he had intended, but a quixotic anti-West stand. He failed to guide the kingdom toward much needed modernization and enlightenment. It was Korea's profound misfortune that his overflowing energy and strong leadership were consumed by such an old-fashioned foreign policy.

Even when Chosun's more powerful neighbors were forced to accommodate the emerging new world order, the regent's court steadfastly refused to compromise with the trend. Instead, it shunned the establishment of diplomatic relations with the West and spurned the progressive measures critical in transforming its outmoded nation into a strong, modern state. The regent, relying on his intense personality and lofty nationalistic aspiration, resolved to keep the antiquated kingdom totally isolated from pervasive international intercourse. He was not only contemptuous of the West but rejected anything connected to the West's flourishing commercial and scientific culture. By doing so, his leadership singularly failed to reverse the kingdom's declining political fortunes; and, more importantly, he failed to prepare the nation to face the imperial storms that were about to overwhelm the kingdom. Notwithstanding his intense nationalism, he proved to be an unfit leader for the Hermit Kingdom during the perilous period of the late nineteenth century.

The fall of the Taewongoon regency was not an ordinary political succession but a grave juncture that triggered the Chosun dynasty's terminal disintegration process. Ostensibly, the regency was abolished when the ruling monarch reached his majority. In reality, however, the event was hastened by the court's relapsing into factional infighting and the growing unpopularity of the regent's often harsh dictatorship. Despite noble intentions, his anti-West, autarchic rebuilding policies caused grave social uneasiness and economic hardship to the nation and ultimately drove him out of power as the kingdom's paramount leader.

Taewongoon's downfall caused the rise of political fortunes of his chief political opponent, Queen Min. The extensive political power previously monopolized by the regent was then transferred to the queen, his young daughter-in-law, and her powerful Min clan, while the young king, generally apolitical and soft-willed, remained still the titular ruler. The bitter political succession inevitably intensified infighting between the two opposing factions, which put the entire nation into another lengthy political turmoil. As in most of the Chosun court's political disputes, the political rivalry between the regent and his daughter-in-law was rooted in strong personal animosity rather than political disagreement. There were few outstanding differences in political philosophy between the two competing political camps. Nevertheless, during its rise, the queen's faction provided the regent's followers with a serious opportunity for personal revenge; it regarded the queen's forcible ejection of the regent as a flagrant violation of traditional filial piety, one of the most sacred ethical principles in the Confucian doctrine. Queen Min's purge of her father-in-law was the only known such case in the long history of the Korean monarchy.

Given the region's already volatile political current, the resumption of factional infighting was something the Chosun court could hardly afford. Yet, characteristically, Chosun's political leaders, being unaware of Japan's mushrooming imperial designs in which the Korean peninsula was the primary target, were not able to unite the country for the greater good in the national interest. The fact that modernized Japan had become an increasingly serious threat to the kingdom's national security was yet to emerge as a major political consideration in the Chosun court.

2. Forced Open-Door

Meiji Japan did not overlook the opportunity created by the Chosun court's political instability. More than anything, the controversial leadership change in the Chosun court presented the Japanese with a vastly altered challenge; Japan now had to face Queen Min, a political neophyte, not the regent, who was a seasoned politician whose unbending seclusion policy had centered on his disdain of not only the West but also much-Westernized Japan. Japan-Chosun relations had deteriorated beyond repair since the regent had summarily repudiated the Japanese request to upgrade their already strained relations in 1868. In the aftermath of the regent's deliberate rebuke to Japan's diplomatic overture, Japanese-Korean relations remained chilly but uneventful. In spite of the widespread discontent among Japan's restless hard-liners, who had unsuccessfully proposed to organize a punitive expedition against Korea as a retaliation to the regent's open contempt, the Meiji court maintained a policy of careful observation toward Korea.[1] Inevitably, recurring political turmoil in the Chosun court encouraged the Japanese hard-liners, who renewed their effort to persuade the more circumspect Meiji leadership to take an aggressive approach to Korea, thus taking advantage of political developments in the Chosun court.

By then it was apparent to even Japan's more conservative leadership that a Korea controlled by imperial Japan would serve many purposes. Foremost, it would provide an outlet for a large number of unemployed and thus dissatisfied samurai warriors. This would divert the public attention from simmering domestic problems, residual of various reform programs implemented by the revolutionary Meiji Restoration.[2] In regional power politics, Japanese supremacy in Korea would mean that Japan could overshadow China's political domination in East Asia. In addition, Japan's militarists had anticipated another immediate benefit; their supremacy in Korea might help to forestall much feared British and Russian interests from securing a foothold in the region. Thus, Japan's renewed ambition over Korea was not only an indemnity for the failed Hideyoshi campaign, but, more importantly, a drive toward securing an advanced base needed in furthering its germinating imperialism.

While the Japanese leadership was decisively shifting toward a militant approach in its Korean policy, the Chosun court, partly due to its traditional contempt for its island neighbor and its non-existent intelligence-gathering apparatus within Japan, remained largely ignorant of these critical political developments in Japan. Not only its inability to sense the gravity of shifting regional geopolitics persisted, but its knowledge of rapidly modernized Japan and her intentions for the use of a vastly modernized military force continued to be meager. Even a development as ominous as Japan's expedition to Formosa in 1865 was not known to the Hermit Kingdom until later when it was informed by the Ching court.[3] Preoccupied by the internal political turmoil, the Chosun court was unable to pay even modest attention to the nation's precarious security problems.

Contrary to the obtuse Chosun court, Meiji Japan's Westernized government was gathering accurate information on the nature of the Chosun court's political instability. Sensing the arrival of an opportune moment, the Meiji court formally endorsed a militant Korean policy long advocated by the nation's hard-liners and expansion-oriented military bureaucrats. As a result, in 1875, Japan dispatched armed vessels to Korea's coastal waters on the pretext of surveying the area, concealing its real purpose of provoking the Chosun court into a military confrontation. The Japanese leaders were all too well aware of the fact that the old-fashioned Chosun force would be no competition for their Westernized military.

As the Japanese ships made unauthorized entry into the Korean waters, Korean coastal defenders responded with benign but established measures designed to block the intrusion. Yet Korean defenders failed to discourage the intrusion but instead provided the Japanese the very excuse they were seeking. The intruders reacted with force, and shortly a military engagement followed. Although the encounter occurred on the Korean coast, the Chosun defenders were at a dire disadvantage; against Japan's sophisticated Western weaponry, Korean defenders were armed with mostly ineffective, antiquated weapons. They neither possessed weapons capable to counter Japanese naval bombardments on the coastal areas nor commanded a naval force capable of thwarting the Japanese from getting replacement materiel and forces through the narrow Korea Strait. Three centuries earlier, Hideyoshi's invasion had repulsed largely by the Korean naval force's ability to control the sea; now, however, there was neither Admiral Lee, the hero of Hideyoshi's Imjin War, nor a highly motivated Korean naval force. This time Korea did not even have a single steamship that could challenge the modern Japanese navy, a product of Meiji Japan's single-minded modernization drive. Moreover, unlike the previous Western expeditions that were greatly hampered by their limited knowledge of the Taewongoon regime and its defense capability, the Japanese court was exceptionally knowledgeable of the Chosun court's domestic politics as well as of the kingdom's limited military capability.

Another factor pernicious to the Koreans this time was the defeatist disposition of the Ching court. Reflecting rapidly transforming regional power dynamics, China, the only backer that the Chosun court had relied upon in times of national emergency, was succumbing to the Japanese pressure by issuing a timid disclaimer of responsibility. The Middle Kingdom, the self-claimed overlord of Korea for centuries, revealed its utter inability to help its traditional ally. The Ching court's submissive response to the Japanese aggression in Korea signaled the drastic relapse of Ching China's political prestige that had long commanded unparalleled influence in the region. Furthermore, this relapse foretold the arrival of a new era in which Northeast Asia was the stage for an unprecedented power struggle between the two competing imperial powers.

Taewongoon had survived the Western expeditions not by winning battles but by protracting the conflict with no compromise offered, a strategy which proved to be effective against distant Western nations. The situation was entirely different when the invader was a power that could draw logistical support from a nearby home base. The resistance offered to such a superior adversary by the Chosun court's poorly equipped coastal force was quite limited, and fallacious confidence that had prevailed among court officials after their illusive triumphs over the Western expeditions quickly shattered. In the end, the court was compelled to submit to Japanese military superiority, thus suffering for the first time in its military history a defeat from a power neither based in nor originating from China.

Even after Meiji Japan displayed its renewed territorial ambition and newly-acquired military might, the Hermit Kingdom was in disarray over its policy toward Japan. Its still-powerful gentry class continued to oppose the forced abolition of the long-standing seclusion doctrine. On the other hand, the ruling queen-faction found that normal diplomatic relations with the non-Chinese world would be ideologically appealing. Its drastic transformation toward a more progressive stand was naturally motivated by the need to distinguish its own rule from that of the Taewongoon regency, the champion of steadfast anti-West, anti-Japan campaigns. The young monarch, King Gojong, was sympathetic to such liberal causes.

Although it was unable to defend its traditional ally from the Japanese aggression, the Ching court chose to play a pivotal role in the Chosun court's drastic policy shift, the opening of its door to Japan and the West. Overlooking Ching's receding prestige and power, the Chosun court sought the counsel of the Ching court, which encouraged the Koreans to enter negotiations with Japan for diplomatic relations.[4] It was a difficult undertaking for the Chosun court to agree to a momentous political initiative such as signing a treaty with Japan, even under military intimidation, unless there was an unequivocal consent from its traditional backer.

In 1876, Korea and Japan signed the Treaty of Kanghwa, the first international treaty entered into by the Hermit Kingdom in its history. With the treaty, Chosun officially abandoned its anachronistic seclusion policy and opened its door to Japan, the first non-Chinese nation that established such formal diplomatic relations with the Chosun court. Regardless of the fact that the treaty was coerced, the diplomatic tie to Japan provided Korea a historic beginning in interacting with the world community beyond its immediate environs traditionally dominated by the Chinese. The West was, however reluctantly, willing to wait for Korea to come to its senses in recognizing the evolving world order, but Japan, obsessed by its budding imperial ambitions, was not agreeable to exercising such patience. Squandering favorable opportunities to pursue an orderly transition away from the self-imposed isolation, the distracted Chosun court put itself into a predicament of being forced to open its door to the nation that the Koreans habitually held in contempt.

In appearance, the Treaty of Kanghwa was an ordinary diplomatic treaty, containing provisions typical of the time: exchange of envoys, opening of ports, and extraterritoriality. But in reality the agreement exemplified Imperial Japan's profound geopolitical plot to further its political ambition in the Far East. However, the Japanese negotiators deftly concealed their premeditated, sinister ploy with a seemingly innocent and justifiable manner by embracing an unconditional recognition of Chosun Korea as an independent state. Notwithstanding the Japanese intention, it was in direct contradiction to the Chinese claim that there was a unique, established relationship between Korea and China, a relationship resembling that of a vassal-sovereign. In an attempt to publicly deny the Chinese claim, the Japanese negotiators managed to place, at the head of the treaty document, a paragraph that declared Korea's independent status. The statement was correct and valid, but it was motivated by Japan's diplomatic ploy which had enormous consequences.

By encouraging the Chosun court to negotiate with Japan, the Ching court unwittingly put its long standing privilege in Chosun into great jeopardy. Even worse, the Tsungli Yamen, the Ching court's foreign affairs ministry, did not realize in time the implications of the clause, which, invalidating the existence of a unique China-Chosun relationship, created legal grounds for Japan to deny China's inordinate influence in Korea. Nor were the Korean negotiators fully aware of the real motive of the Japanese enthusiasm to declare Korea's free, independent status to the world. It was not yet evident to both the Chinese and Koreans that the real motive for Imperial Japan's being so anxious to secure international recognition for a free-standing Korea was a cynical diplomatic maneuver rather than a democratic political ideal.

Once the treaty was signed, Japan's aggressive Korean policy emerged in a systematic manner. Not only did Japan actively seek political influence but it also solicited admirers and followers in the Chosun court; within months a group of Korean officials were invited to visit Japan. As the Japanese might have expected, modernized Japan easily impressed the Chosun court's provincial scholar-officials, whose knowledge of the non-Chinese world remained paltry. This visit and extensive Japanese courtship helped the Chosun court's perception of Japan undergo a marked improvement. Soon some progressive intellectuals acquired a strong sentiment for transforming Korea after the Japanese model. Thus, Chosun's progressive political faction was born. But its aspirations were to remain in the shade years to come as the court was still under the domination of conservative officials.

The Chosun court's favorable inclination toward the Japanese prodding and the subsequent birth of progressive political ideology caused a drastic rise of Japanese influence in Korea; Japan's ambassador to Seoul quickly emerged as the most influential figure in Korean politics. Japan's initial objective, replacing Ching's political influence in the Chosun court, was within an easy reach. Against escalating Japanese political manipulation, the Chosun court merely waged sporadic protests in vain. To block the well-designed Japanese advances while maintaining interest in the Western culture Japan represented was nearly an unattainable task for the antiquated Chosun court.

Japan's imperial aggressions in Korea, which followed its annexation of the Ryukyu Island in 1879, had alarmed the Ching court. By then, however, Ching's deteriorated prestige and power were no match to the growing power of Japan. Still unwilling to concede to the Japanese advance in Korea, the Ching court countered the Japanese move by urging the Chosun court to open the nation to the Western powers as well. In order to countermand the growing Japanese prestige in Korea, Ching sought the Western powers as a counterbalance. With its renewed vigor to contain the Japanese advance in Korea, the Ching court put in charge of its Korean affairs Li Hung-Chang, its most eminent political figure. These desperate arrangements reflected, more than anything, the urgency and gravity of the situation that the Chinese had realized as Japan's advance proceeded unopposed in Korea.

As the Ching court's belated countermeasures were being placed to check the Japanese advance in Korea, the Chosun court was drawn into progressively more complex international power politics. Although it had neither experience nor strength to cope with the multi-directional pressure directed against it, the Chosun court singularly lacked leadership to pursue an innovative geopolitical solution as the dire situation dictated. The court, still dominated by the nation's scholar-official leadership, became paralyzed and unable to establish a clear political agenda.

Contrary to the Chosun court's nearly total lack of understanding the ever-shifting regional geopolitics, some foreign observers noticed broad ramifications of evolving regional politics over the Korean peninsula. A Whang Jon-Hun, a Chinese diplomat stationed in Tokyo, forwarded a most interesting analysis of such apprehension.[5] In his book titled *Korean Strategy*, Whang insisted that the Chosun court should pay closer attention to Russia's imperial ambition in the region. Based on his apprehension of alleged Russian intentions in the region, in 1880 he further proposed that the Koreans form a de facto alliance with China, Japan, and America to counter such dangerous prospects. Although Whang's idea caused no immediate response in the still intensely domestic-oriented Chosun court, it was a glaring indication that the world community had become aware of the Korean peninsula's unique geopolitical property, which had potential to affect not only regional but also world politics.

Aside from its diplomatic relations with Japan, the Chosun court's indoctrination into the international community was slow and fragmented. Still, through greatly liberalized contacts of its own and the Chinese sources, Chosun's political leaders were gaining some valuable insight into the nature of the Western powers. Their attitude toward the West continued to be tentative, but they had become more tolerant and positive about Western culture as a whole. As the court all but abandoned its anti-Christian crusade, contacts with Western missionaries became free and frequent. To some significant extent, the court, being dominated by the liberal queen faction and progressive young officials, was undergoing a major transformation; it was increasingly willing to experiment with various Western practices in order to achieve the nation's modernization. Yet the Confucian scholars, who were alienated from the ruling party but still exercised significant political influence, remained resolutely opposed to an open-door policy.

3. Expanding Diplomatic Ties

Japan's success in opening Korea prompted the United States to reassess its policy toward the Hermit Kingdom. In 1878, the United State Senate passed a resolution authorizing the administration to seek a treaty of normal relations with the Kingdom of Corea [Korea]. Reflecting the vastly altered political atmosphere in the region, America's new attempt was received with much favorable attention in both Korea and China. By then the Chosun court had developed a strong inclination to enter multiple treaty relationships with the non-Chinese world. It was a revolutionary departure from Taewongoon's categorical rejection of Western overtures, but it was also a belated political awakening.

The Ching court was understandably disturbed when Commodore Shufeldt, a Washington envoy, attempted to establish a dialogue with the Chosun court through Japan. However, Shufeldt, who had expected Japanese assistance in his endeavor, produced no tangible progress. It turned out that Japan was reluctant to risk its dominant position in Korea by assisting Washington in arranging a treaty relationship with Korea. The lukewarm collaboration of Japan made the Americans feel that it was manipulating the negotiations to serve its own interests. Disappointed by the lack of progress, Shufeldt then turned to the Chinese and accepted the offer of Viceroy Li Hung-Chang's help in negotiating diplomatic and trade relations with Korea.

Li Hung Chang's timely intervention and the growing awareness among officials of the virtues and advantages in securing the friendship of the Americans helped the Chosun court agree to a negotiation with the American envoy. Still, the Chosun court was by no means confident in opening its door to the Western world despite its established diplomatic ties with Japan. Furthermore, it was unsure of the public support of the negotiation, so the court kept the talks in extreme secrecy. Notwithstanding much improved perception of the West in general, the Chosun society's knowledge of the faraway Western nations remained greatly inadequate.

The Chosun court established formal diplomatic relations with America in 1882. The Korea-United States treaty, negotiated at Tientsin, China, where Li Hung-Chang served as an arbitrator, was typical of the time; two countries agreed to exchange diplomats, to establish consulates at trading ports, and to treat each other based on equality. Following the Japanese precedent, the United States recognized the government of Korea as that of a fully independent state. To achieve this, however, American negotiators had to foil Li's persistent attempt to portray the China-Korea relationship as a suzerainty-subject relationship, the very relationship the Korea-Japan Treaty had earlier refused to acknowledge. Americans declined to include in the treaty document a phrase that might be interpreted that Chosun was a dependent state of the Chinese empire. After all, the Chinese ploy was contradictory to America's democratic tradition of pursuing freedom and independence for all nations. Even the Hermit Kingdom of Korea could not be an exception.

The Korea-United States relation, which had to overcome an earlier military confrontation and the complete lack of any appreciable knowledge of each other, was destined to experience many successes and difficulties for decades to come. It was ironic that Korea's most cherished international relations set out with such an inauspicious beginning. Nevertheless, when the treaty was signed, the United States, a faraway nation of entirely dissimilar culture, made its presence felt in Korea. The spirit of America, called Meeguk, or Beautiful Nation in Korean, was prominently introduced by the humanistic gesture of Dr. Allen, who saved the life of a high Korean official during a domestic revolt.[6] Largely due to his heroics, Koreans quickly learned to accept the Americans with the highest esteem. The court, once the citadel of the anti-West emotion under the Taewongoon regency, was also showing its favorable leaning toward its new diplomatic partner by granting extensive leniency for its missionaries and their propagation of the Western religion. As a result, Protestantism brought by the American missionaries grew more vigorously than Catholicism, which was much earlier introduced to the nation by French missionaries.

American missionaries earned their good reputation by undertaking many social projects that were beyond typical evangelical efforts; they set up many Western-style educational and medical services that became the cornerstone of modern Korea's social infrastructure. Even under the shadow of Japan's deepening imperial ambition, American missionaries were quietly working on their nation's cherished commitment: teaching and fostering the spirit of freedom, democracy, equality, and love.   Their unselfish contributions were duly acknowledged by the Korean public.

The Korea-United States treaty had become a good precedent for other Western powers interested in establishing similar treaty relationships with Korea. In 1883, England followed the American precedent, concluding a pact with Korea which largely imitated the Korea-U.S. treaty except for additional provisions intended to secure its commercial interests in Korea. Unlike Japan and the United States, however, the British agreed to station in Seoul only a consulate-general instead of a minister plenipotentiary. This irregular but convenient avenue was to appease the Ching court by not openly contradicting the Chinese claim that Korea was its dependent state. Germany also adopted this handy diplomatic practice when it opened diplomatic channels with the Korean kingdom the same year.

Russia was far more troublesome a neighbor for the Koreans even before the nation opened its door to the West. Soon after Russia extracted from Ching its Far-Eastern territory that shared a common border with Korea, it made to the Chosun court repeated demands for the establishment of trade relations.[7] It did not persuade the reluctant Chosun court, but its demands were construed as another Western plot against the kingdom. Being unsure of Russia's political intention in the region, the court ignored periodic Russian overtures for closer ties and maintained a distance from its northern neighbor. However, occasional Korea-Russia communications, mostly unofficial contacts, took place to discuss the illegal immigration of Korean nationals to neighboring Russian territories, a trend that began in the early 1860s and continued during the 1870s.[8] Naturally, it was the seclusion-oriented Chosun court that objected more to the unauthorized border crossings.

The Chosun court's already unfavorable perception of Russia was greatly fortified when China and the Western powers warned the Koreans of the possible Russian ambition for warm-water ports in Korea. Korea's two neighbors as well as most Western powers were naturally concerned about the intentions of European Russia in the region and earnestly opposed its rumored ambition to secure a foothold in Korea. Alerted by its recent experience of costly territorial concessions to Russia, the Ching court discouraged the Koreans from establishing diplomatic relations with the Russians, whose influence it was anxious to contain in the region.

Facing widespread objection and obstruction, Russia was equally resolute in establishing diplomatic relations with its small Far Eastern neighbor. Unable to obtain Li Hung-Chang's help, which was freely extended to most other Western powers, Russia used various initiatives to win diplomatic ties with the Chosun court. In 1885, with the help of the Chosun court's powerful German advisor, Mulendolf, Russia finally managed to sign a treaty with Korea. Once diplomatic relations were established, however, Russia made itself one of the most visible foreign powers in Korea. Its able envoy, Carl Waeber, quickly rose to a hidden political power and exercised significant influence in the Chosun court during the pivotal period of the late nineteenth century.

France was the last major Western power that signed a treaty with Korea. Ironically, France was the first that had attempted to open Korea during the Taewongoon administration. Although the court had relaxed its restrictions over activities of French missionaries since the opening of its door to other Western nations, its lingering ill-feeling, a result of the French expedition and suspected activities of French missionaries, prevented the early consummation of a treaty with France. But as the Chosun court's attitude toward Christianity shifted from harsh persecution to "toleration," it found no legitimate cause to refuse diplomatic relations with the French. France's primary interests in Korea for some time remained the missionary works, even after the two nations signed a treaty in 1887. Most other major Western countries had established their diplomatic ties with Korea by 1902.

By the dawn of the twentieth century, Korea had emerged as a full and free member of the world community as far as diplomatic recognitions were concerned. Yet the issue of an independent nationhood was not completely resolved. Most European powers evaded the thorny dilemma of the Chinese claim that Korea was its dependent state by assigning their envoys to Beijing to also serve as their representatives to Seoul. Only the Americans followed the Japanese precedent in recognizing the government of Korea as that of a sovereign state with no conditions attached. The United States not only commissioned an envoy to Korea, independent of the legations at Beijing and Tokyo, but also insisted on dealing with a Korean envoy directly as the representative of an independent state in Washington. The American approach thus inadvertently helped the Japanese objective, the establishment of international recognition for Korea's independent standing. Yet there is no indication that the Americans had been aware of the real Japanese motive in their insisting for Korea's independent status.

4. Mounting Domestic Discontent

While Korea's foreign contacts were widening with establishment of diplomatic ties to Japan and the West, the nation's still powerful conservative faction remained opposed to the kingdom's new international posture. The Chosun court's forced treaty relationship with Japan was a source of great apprehension for the majority of Korean reactionary scholar-officials, but it was the treaty relationships with the dreaded Western powers that sparked the reactionary faction's categorical rejection of the new policy. Amid growing resistance to the open-door policy, the court's alleged participation in an international alliance, a China-Japan-Korea-U.S. pact, had become an explosive issue in the nation. The rumor that the Chosun court was about to join the alliance prompted the nation's Confucian scholars to shift their opposition to the open-door policy to a categorical rejection of the court's entire foreign overtures.

The opposition staged by the nation's conservative scholar-officials was poorly organized but lacked no courage. Decrying the impropriety of engaging in any exchange with the Western powers, they pointed out that Ching China's fatal predicament had been caused by the negative influences of the predatory Western powers and Westernized Japan. For them, seclusion remained the only sensible policy for the nation to follow until it grew strong enough to deal with the West on an equal footing; this was the same logic that nationalistic Taewongoon had invoked when he resisted Western demands for diplomatic relations. Intensely nationalistic as they were, the reclusive Confucian followers could not comprehend the political proclivity of the time: neither the West nor Japan was amenable to leaving the kingdom alone so that it could pursue modernization at a leisurely pace. The nation's conservative activists waged violent nationwide protests, clamoring for a reversal of the open-door policy and a return to strict Confucian principles. Their fervent dissension was eventually directed to the reigning monarch himself, a rare instance in the history of the Chosun dynasty. Nevertheless, the court, controlled by the Queen Min faction, was in no position to make a compromise to the anti-open door faction without risking its own political survival. The court suppressed the protests with brutal purges and persecutions.

The conservative faction's protest against the open-door policy was but one problem the reform-minded Chosun court encountered. The court was also the subject of worsening public discontent, partly caused by its scandalous financial mismanagement and corruption. The nation's treasury, which had been extensively mended by Taewongoon's painstaking efforts, was quickly pushed to a state of virtual bankruptcy under the new regime's irresponsible management and widespread corruption. Wasteful spending was common practice among the court officials, most of whom belonged to the ruling Queen Min faction. Suffering from exacerbating tax burdens and eroded social services, the nation's farmers rapidly lost faith in the court's leadership.

The Chosun court's outdated financial practices stood in salient contrast to those of Japan, which had already entered the era of modern management. Given the fact that Chosun society's political development was much behind that of the West and Japan, the court's chaotic situation in financial affairs was not entirely unexpected. Although the ruling faction had forged a close alliance with Japan by then and had carried out some reorganization of the nation's administrative structure primarily after the Japanese model, the court was equipped with neither the political leadership nor the resources to undertake systematic nationwide reform as the Meiji government had done for Japan.

Reorganization of the obsolete Korean government, though only partial, had created many disenchanted groups in the Chosun society; notable among these was the military. The reform-minded court had created the so-called "new military," which was fashioned after the Western model. While the new military was being formed and trained by Japanese instructors, the "old military," the court's antiquated defense force, was not yet formally dissolved but remained out of service. The court's predilection for the new military force inevitably caused discontent among the soldiers of the now ill-treated old military.

In 1882, Chosun's castaway members of the old military rose against the court. The disillusioned soldiers escalated a small incident, sparked by a dispute over their long overdue salary, into a full scale revolt; they quickly overran the barracks of the new military and occupied a large part of the palace. Under the fury of the rebel force, the court's authority crumbled, and the queen, who as head of the ruling faction was the real target of the revolt, was driven out of the palace. After they had effectively decommissioned the nation's foremost political institutions, the court and the monarch, the rebels ushered Taewongoon back to power. The king, under siege, was obliged again to bestow upon the regent the full authority to govern.

Thus, Taewongoon, the champion of the anti-West and anti-Japan seclusion policy, resurfaced as the nation's supreme political leader. He might have been the only person capable of pacifying the volatile situation, but his return to power mainly reflected the monarch's uncertain leadership. Taewongoon's restoration as a supreme ruler meant the dismantling of those reform programs the queen faction had adopted under the open-door and national development drive. Naturally, the regent replaced the officials of the progressive faction with conservative scholar-officials. By undertaking wholesale measures to countermand the queen faction's reform programs, Taewongoon intended to steer the kingdom back to its old seclusion era and to retreat from the nation's infant open-door doctrine.

The rebels also directed their wrath toward the Japanese influence in the kingdom. They were understandably resentful of the Japanese, who had, after all, encouraged and supported the court's undertaking of modernization programs for the military, which in turn caused their losing the court's favor. Identifying the Japanese influence as the cause of their predicament, the revolters attacked the Japanese diplomatic post in Seoul and killed their most hated enemy, the head of Japanese military instructors. However, the diplomatic mission was allowed a safe retreat to Japan.

The revolt was spontaneously staged by a group of dismissed soldiers full of personal animosity toward the Japanese influence in the court. Nevertheless, their attack on the Japanese diplomatic mission was an ominous mistake, even though it could not be expected that the outraged soldiers, in reality a mob rather than an organized military force, would exercise rational judgment. It would have been beyond the revolting soldiers' comprehension that their attack, which had inflicted personal and material damage to the legation of audacious Japan, could, however unintentional it might have been, furnished the Japanese imperialists a remarkable opportunity to further their political ambition in Korea. They tragically overlooked the fact that Japan was the foremost foreign power in Korea.

5. Ching's Reasserting Influence

The Ching court often lost its bid to surpass the Meiji government's opportunism in Korea. Nevertheless, when the Chosun court was rocked by new political upheaval, the Ching court was most anxious to take advantage of the situation. The Chinese had interpreted the current political turmoil in the Chosun court as presenting them an unusual opportunity to regain their lost influence. Ching's favorable reading of the situation was greatly affected by its expectation that the Chosun court's pro-monarch faction would at least temporarily be inclined to side with the Chinese instead of the Japanese, fearing Japan's hostile reactions for the incident. The Ching court was confident that, under the circumstances, the reinstalled Taewongoon would have to provide the Chinese the political support needed to supersede battered Japanese prestige. Ching was convinced that it was time to put its full weight into regaining its political influence in Korea.

The Ching court promptly dispatched a large military contingent to Korea under the pretext that it was needed to restore order in Seoul. Although it cited King Gojong's request, the Ching court's speedy reaction was motivated by its attempt to preempt the probable Japanese response. Doing so, Li Hung-Chang intended to use the occasion to completely eliminate Japan's political influence in the Chosun court. In spite of its bitter and humiliating submission to the Western powers, the Ching court was unwilling to accept Japan's supremacy in Korea. Thus it took bold steps intended to reverse the tide by replacing Japan as the dominant political power in Korea.

The Ching court had some valid reasons in employing such an aggressive approach. Japan's open imperial ambition had made the declining empire better appreciate the value of the Korean peninsula as its buffer zone. China needed a friendly Korea more than ever to protect its eastern flank. Militarily, China was, it was believed, capable of defeating Japan at the time, though a large-scale military confrontation would have been difficult due to domestic instability. With this backdrop, the Ching court put the so-called "Li Hung-Chang diplomacy" into motion. Along with troop deployment, the Ching court punctually informed Japan that its diplomats would be in charge of the Korean situation, including protection of Japanese interests in Korea. It made clear to Meiji Japan that it intended to be the authority in Korea. Li's preemptive maneuver, designed to obstruct the recovery of the Japanese political influence in Korea, was brilliant.

The Ching court's latest attempt to reassert its influence in Korea was a notable departure from its traditional Korean policy. Historically, the Chinese had played the role of distant political guardian in their Korean relations. They maintained with the Chosun court a close rapport not through political intimidation or coercion but through frequent cultural exchanges and political collaboration. Such tender dealings had proved most effective in sustaining its long-standing prestige in the Chosun court. It was the signing of the Korea-Japan treaty and the subsequent rise of Japanese influence in the Chosun court that brought a major setback to the carefully managed Chinese policy in Korea. Following the treaty, the Ching court's desperate efforts to recover its drastically tarnished prestige in Korea was ineffective; its attempt to reverse the Japanese advance by winning an international recognition for its unique influence in Korea proved a categorical failure. Yet it was increasingly evident that whoever controlled the Korean peninsula was likely to earn a decisive advantage over the other in the competition for the regional leadership. The Ching court was thus to wage a last challenge before conceding the Korean peninsula to the Japanese. Chosun's revolting soldiers had unwittingly created such an opportunity for the Ching court.

Through its lightning dispatch of troops, the Chinese plotted to deny the Japanese an opportunity to undertake a similar movement. Barring the Japanese response, the Ching court was confident that it could secure the Chosun court's alliance using the leverage its overwhelming military strength might provide. Yet the plot was based on the erroneous calculation of Japan's counter move. Contrary to the Chinese assumption, the Japanese had their own design, which was equally imperial and aggressive.

Notwithstanding the Chinese move, Japan also acted quickly in dispatching forces to Korea; naval detachments of both countries arrived on the western coast of Korea nearly simultaneously. The Japanese delegation was the first to enter the kingdom's beleaguered capital and quickly extracted a major concession from Taewongoon. By this agreement, the Korean government was obliged to pay a severe indemnity and to prosecute soldiers who had attacked the Japanese mission. Moreover, the besieged Chosun court was forced to accept an unspecified number of Japanese soldiers to be stationed in Seoul under the pretext of protecting their diplomatic post. The court, which lost both old and new branches of its military due to the revolt, was unable to resist the Japanese coercion, which was backed by a newly arrived force. Japan had succeeded, through the concession, in recovering most of its political influence. Nevertheless, the Japanese leverage over the Chosun court was now significantly compromised due to a vastly strengthened Chinese presence bolstered by a force that transcended the Japanese both in number and tactical deployment.

Ching's military detachment in Korea enjoyed a numerical advantage over the Japanese. More importantly, the Chinese force was deployed around the outskirts of Seoul. By surrounding the city under the pretext of maintaining order, the Chinese quickly transformed themselves into a de facto occupation army capable of applying unbearable pressure against the court and the citizens of the capital city. Primarily through these seizure tactics, China was soon able to regain its political preeminence in the court, eclipsing Japan. The Chinese intention in Korea was more than mere political domination; it was seeking total subjugation of the kingdom, a feat no Chinese empire had ever achieved. Yet Ching's self-imposed occupation force spared no efforts to control the kingdom. For this end, it even employed an act of international political piracy; collaborating with the anti-Taewongoon faction, it abducted Taewongoon, the father of the ruling monarch and the foremost political leader of an independent state. The regent, who was interrogated by Chinese officials as the perpetrator of the revolt much like a common criminal from one of Chinese provinces, was detained in China for more than four years.

By forcefully removing Taewongoon, the Ching court pretended to support the badly shaken King Gojong and his followers, but, in reality, openly began to usurp the Chosun court's sovereign power through intimidation. By means of reckless and flagrant aggression that followed the abduction, the Chinese solidified their overwhelming political influence in the Chosun court, successfully overshadowing the Japanese. In spite of the obvious setback, however, Japan was by no means eliminated from the two-way Korean competition; she simply conceded to the reality created by Li Hung-Chang's preemptive maneuvers.

The Ching court's attempt to restore Korea as its political dependency, a situation that had never existed in reality, was manifested by its unprecedented interference in Korea's military-political matters. Ching's blatant political interference was indicative of its unrealistic fancy. Nevertheless, the coarse pressure forced the Chosun court to reverse the pro-Japan stand which the Queen Min faction had adopted to oppose seclusion-oriented Taewongoon. Consequently, Pro-Ching politics became again the mainstay in the court. The nation's progressive political faction - primarily eager, young, pro-Japan intellectuals favoring national modernization - lost its political base in the government. The reform drive that sought national development through drastic restructuring and Western-style modernization suffered a severe blow.

While the Chosun court remained unable to rebuild its own force, six Chinese battalions stationed in Seoul exercised virtually unlimited political influence. In addition, the Japanese force stationed in the nation's west coast region not far from Seoul remained a force to be reckoned with. Unable to contain the competing forces, let alone force their withdrawal, the Chosun court was inevitably preoccupied with the task of appeasing both powers. It did not matter that Japan had dispatched its forces to the kingdom under a pretext of a treaty provision or that Ching had almost invited itself in as the high commissioner of the nation. The ultimate tragedy was, even under this extraordinary circumstance of perilous multiple aggression, that the Chosun court had failed to marshal a national unity sufficient to challenge the two intruders' political piracy.

The nation's progressive political faction, which had not only suffered a severe political setback but had also witnessed its reform programs deserted by the Chinese-dominated court, was increasingly frustrated by the nation's political wandering. Shunned by the reactionary court officials, the members of the faction sought the counsel and aid of the Japanese ambassador, still a source of significant political influence in Seoul. This development further aggravated the nation's already clouded political climate; the court was supported by the Chinese, and its primary critics, the progressive party, were being protected by the Japanese. The standoff between the court and the progressive party sharpened as the Japan-Ching rivalry intensified.

In 1884 the progressive party's frustration over the stalled reform programs ignited a coup. Assisted by a small contingent of Japanese stationed in Seoul, the liberal activists broke into the palace and took custody of the monarch. The coup, which looked promising when it scored a major triumph in overpowering the palace guards, quickly crumbled, however, when the Chinese mobilized their superior force stationed in Seoul. Unlike the halfhearted support provided by the Japanese legation, the Chinese force, under the command of Yuan Shih-Kai, rushed to the palace and overwhelmed the coup activists and the small Japanese force.[9] Moreover, the coup suffered from poor planning and lack of popular support. The plot collapsed in three days, but it was a courageous challenge directed against the old-fashioned court and its anachronistic politics.

The motive of the progressive party's coup attempt was refreshing. The young liberals demanded reforms that were not only necessary but far-sighted; their proposals included establishment of a just relationship with the Chinese by abolishing tributary practices to the Ching court as well as a demand for equal opportunities in government employment. Pursuing a drastic departure from the submissive foreign policy and the corrupt domestic politics dominated by clan interests, the liberals sought sweeping reforms in every aspect of the government, following the Japanese model. The nation's misfortune was not that the coup failed, but that Chosun continued to be governed by a submissive court controlled by the corrupt Min clan, whose old-fashioned politics had repeatedly frustrated the spirit of progress and independence championed by these pioneers of awakening Korean conscience.

The public, yet to be liberated from the xenophobic backwardness that was still pervasive across the social strata, failed to support the progressive party's revolutionary move and sided with the court. Failing to win the support of both the court officials and the masses, the coup had little chance to succeed unless Japan provided the military force capable of defeating the Chinese. Nevertheless, Japan was not yet willing to challenge the Chinese, who were numerically superior.[10]

When the Chinese force easily suppressed the coup attempt, the Ching court's political domination over the Chosun court was much strengthened. Inevitably, Japan's political influence in Seoul further eroded. The Chosun court, which survived one of its most dire challenges with the Chinese assistance, continued to be controlled by the Queen Min faction, which was supported by Yuan Shih-Kai, Li Hung-Chang's personal representative to Seoul. Japan's limited support for the coup attempt, stemming from its unwillingness to challenge the Chinese militarily, had caused the collapse of Japan's ideological ally, the progressive party. The setback, however, did not lead Japan to surrender its ambitions in Korea; it simply shifted its tactics by assuming a lower profile in Seoul.

After the Chinese had regained their political predominance in the Chosun court by actively suppressing the coup, the Japanese concentrated their efforts on diplomatic maneuvers. These persistent efforts bore results when the Chinese, suffering from the increasingly destructive domestic turmoil caused partly by the hostile confrontation with France, agreed to negotiations to demarcate each other's sphere in Korea. In 1885, representatives of China and Japan met at Tientsin, China, and worked out a temporary political truce. It was, however, the Chinese, through the Tientsin Treaty, who made most of the concessions. The treaty stipulated (a) withdrawal of both Chinese and Japanese troops from Korea within four months; (b) replacement of both Chinese and Japanese instructors for the Korean military with a third nationality; and (c) mutual notification in case either country's troops were dispatched to Korea in the future. In spite of the agreed-upon troop withdrawal, the treaty in reality had put Korea under the joint custody of China and Japan, a clear indication that both powers, using whatever methods, intended to maintain their influence in the Chosun court.

The troops were withdrawn according to the treaty provisions. But the Chinese continued to exercise overwhelming influence over the Chosun court through Yuan Shih-Kai, who stayed on in Seoul. Li and the Ching court were unwilling to surrender their hard-won supremacy in Korea regardless of the treaty concessions. Although the Tientsin Treaty revealed that Japan was not yet ready to offer a military challenge to the Chinese, at least while its modernization was under way, the accord also demonstrated the fact that Li and the Ching court had come to accommodate Japan's growing international prestige. The Chinese thus sought a compromise rather than a confrontation with the growing power of the Japanese.

6. Fragile Balance of Power

By 1885, the Japanese managed to recover their influence and achieve a rough balance of power with China in Korea. Japan's diplomatic success was effected largely through its crafty diplomatic maneuvers engineered by its two able ministers, Ito and Inoye.[11] Once a balance of power had been formally arranged, the Japanese concentrated on economic exploitation of Korea. For this end, they were even willing to acquiesce to China's domination over the kingdom's political-military matters. Division of the sphere of influence was a clever compromise that allowed both powers to pursue aggression against Korea but to avoid a direct confrontation between each other. Nevertheless, indirect and undeclared rivalry became increasingly fierce as both intruders were in no position either to eliminate the other by force or to yield the peninsula.

The two Asian imperial powers for a short period maintained a superficial status quo in the Korean peninsula, underscoring Korea's increasingly pivotal role in the regional politics. For the disintegrating Ching empire, the Korean peninsula was its only eastern buffer against the now menacing power of Japan. Korea was even more critical as a bridgehead for Japan in its attempt to conquer continental Asia. Just as Ming China had been forced to help the Chosun Dynasty divert the advance of the Japanese forces during Hideyoshi's venture, the Chinese again faced a grim prospect of another potential Japanese attempt. This time Ching chose to wage a defensive war against the Japanese by keeping Korea under its tight control.

The geopolitical game pursued by China and Japan in Korea was a prelude to Japan's imperial aggression that engulfed the whole region in the twentieth century. Each nation's moves might have been justified from its own imperial standpoint. In the process, however, the woeful Korean state, whose strategic sense had yet to be fully developed, was to become an innocent but tragic victim of regional power politics. Yet Korea had squandered a critical opportunity, a decade of time, a period during which the precarious balance of power between the two aggressors had been sustained.

While the two Asian imperialists languished in a momentary truce on the small Korean peninsula, one European imperialist, Russia, entered the contest, making the geopolitical game over the Korean peninsula even more complex. Sensing an unusual opportunity to further its political influence, Russia doubled its efforts to win over Korean court officials, who had already been offended by the heavy-handed interferences of both the Chinese and Japanese. Russian diplomats' concerted pursuit produced swift dividends; their standing in the court improved noticeably, provoking serious rumors that a secret agreement for an alliance was being reached between the two countries.

Growing concerns of both the Chinese and Japanese notwithstanding, it was the British who manifested the first serious reaction to Russia's alleged grand design in Korea. In 1885, the British navy occupied Port Hamilton, a small but strategically located anchorage in a group of islets off the southern coast of Korea.[12] The British justified the "temporary occupation" of the islet as a move necessary to correct the disturbance of the Asiatic equilibrium, which was feared to benefit the Russians, Britain's principal rival in Asia. The incident was sparked by the Chosun court's rumored concession to the Russians of Port Lazareff, located in northeastern Korea on the East Sea.[13] The British attempted to establish their base on the anchorage so that they could closely monitor the naval movements of Russia, not only those activities originating from Port Lazareff but also from the Russian Far East. This British move, underscoring a concern over the growing Russian influence in Korea, was a profound strategic maneuver designed to safeguard Britain's trade interests in the region and, furthermore, to extend their influence to the Pacific hinterland. More importantly, however, British naval forces stationed at Port Hamilton would be a significant factor in regional politics and thus might be better able to check the advance of France into Japan as well as Japan's advance into Korea and China.

The British navy's illegal occupation of the port was universally disapproved, and the Korean government maintained its steadfast demand for the immediate withdrawal of the force from the port. As added pressure, the Russians responded to the British move by threatening to occupy a part of the Korean peninsula in case the occupation continued. In 1887, the British withdrew their forces from the port after the Russians made a pledge not to carry out their threats. The unlawful British occupation of Port Hamilton was a blatant violation of Korean sovereignty. Yet, as contended by a British observer, it did serve some useful purposes; for the first time in history the British occupation helped to focus international attention on the geopolitical significance of the Korean peninsula.[14] Britain, an experienced and dominant naval power of the time, would not have taken such an action unless it was dictated by some serious strategic considerations. In any event, Britain's publicized determination to counter the Russian influence in the Far East would not have been totally negative to Korea's growing security concerns.

The four-way competition over the Korean peninsula, staged by Russia and Britain in addition to China and Japan, made the Hermit Kingdom a focal point of Far Eastern power politics. Here the contemporary strategic interests of the two Western powers and those of the two Asian powers converged. For purely geopolitical reasons alone, this impoverished kingdom had become of strategic concern to the major world powers. As potentially explosive circumstances persisted, some nations, notably Germany, England, and Japan, had entertained at times the idea of Korea's assuming perpetual neutrality. The suggestion would have been worthy of consideration, for it might have been Korea's most practical alternative to offset the mounting geopolitical pressure that it had no means to repel. Nevertheless, there is no indication that the Chosun court ever considered the idea seriously, and if it did, the likelihood would have been that it was too weak to pursue such a lofty international undertaking. In spite of the growing international interests on its unique geopolitical property, this remote kingdom remained a political neophyte, much less a power that might exploit the international attention to its advantage.

7. The Disintegrating Chosun dynasty

The rumored Korea-Russia alliance was a serious threat to both the Chinese and Japanese. The alliance, if it did materialize, would have the potential to seriously hamper Japan's territorial ambition over continental Asia by denying the island nation the use of the Korean peninsula as a stepping stone. For the Chinese, it meant that their eastern flank would be exposed to another powerful adversary. Moreover, China's self-claimed tutelary duties over Korea obviously conflicted with the growing Russian influence in the Chosun court. A deepening suspicion over Russian political influence in the Chosun court made the Chinese even more committed to strengthening their political influence in Seoul. Regardless of its precarious position at home, the Ching court and Li Hung-Chang were determined to cling to Korea. The Ching court's intensified Korean policy included not only indiscriminate interference in Korean politics but also systematic efforts to penetrate the kingdom's economic affairs, a sphere where the Japanese over the years had built a dominant position. This deliberate encroachment into the Japanese sphere inevitably led the two Asian imperialists into a direct collision. Yet the Japanese maintained calculated restraint and countered the Chinese challenge only with opportunistic diplomacy.

Growing Russian influence in the Chosun court was another troublesome concern for the Japanese, who still strove for an uneasy collaboration with the Chinese. Yet even the three-way political race and the intensifying scrutiny of the international community over its intentions in Korea did not deter Japan's imperial ambitions. On the contrary, amid the stalemate with the Chinese, the Japanese achieved another major diplomatic triumph. Again, instead of directly challenging the Chinese, Japan enlisted the Chinese as the co-sponsor of its policy in Korea by extracting a Chinese endorsement for a Korean political reform package. The two self-imposed overlords, the Japanese claimed, needed to take an orchestrated approach to their disoriented neighbor. The Ching court, its power progressively impaired at home, might have had few alternatives except a passive collaboration with the Japanese. The new Chinese-Japanese agreement caused Korea to lose most of its sovereign power; with Chinese consent, Japanese diplomats took over the office of Korea's foreign affairs. They further strangled the Chosun court by requiring it to seek their approval for high-level appointments. The Japanese had finally succeeded in systematically stripping away from the Korean court its most sovereign governing functions.

The arrangement Japanese negotiators extracted from distracted Li was a well-disguised scheme. They managed effectively to lessen Chinese suspicion over the Japanese ambition in Korea, and thus prompted the Chinese to agree to elevate the Japanese to be their de facto equal-partner, if not a superior, in Korean affairs. By dexterously feigning collaboration with the Chinese, the Japanese had secured a critical strategic advantage that even the determined efforts of the Chinese would not be able to overcome. Nevertheless, on the surface, the Ching court and Li Hung-Chang, through Yuan Shih-Kai, continued to dominate the Korean kingdom. Japan was willing to support symbolic Chinese domination, being content with its more substantial gains.

Oblivious of Japan's systematic drive, Yuan Shih-Kai was still obsessed with his total control of the Chosun court. He maintained close scrutiny on the monarch and the ruling Min clan faction to discourage their alleged pro-Russian, anti-Ching sentiment. His brash meddling, however, drove more Korean officials away from the pro-Ching ranks. Notwithstanding the growing number of high court officials who preferred Russian protection as opposed to both Chinese and Japanese interference, Yuan's absolute power over the Korean court remained intact. So did the Koreans' disdain of his meddling.

Ching's incessant political interference in the Chosun court was motivated by a desire to salvage China's disappearing international prestige. To a great extent, the Ching court was a prisoner of Confucian symbolism from which it was not able to free itself in spite of a mounting need to do so in order to avert the imminent disintegration of its dynasty. The Ching court was suffering from a lack of both political foresight and courage to face reality and rearrange priorities accordingly, a problem the Japanese had successfully handled through the Meiji Restoration. Instead, China pursued an unrealistic obsession - through Yuan's often irrational and childish interference - to attach Korea to the disintegrating Middle Kingdom. The Ching court's desperate attempts to gain an international recognition for its dominating influence in Korea were not much different from its traditional preoccupation to dominate Korea. Even with thousands years of intercourse, the Chinese had utterly failed to understand the Korean reality; a Korean state could be dominated, but it could never be subjugated.

Nevertheless, Ching was not the only power that attempted to obtain such a strategic advantage in the kingdom. The Japanese had come to harbor an even more sinister ambition for the Korean peninsula. The difference between these two imperial powers was that Japan was capable and willing to exploit, to the maximum extent, the temporary partnership with China to achieve its ultimate objectives. It was a well-conceived strategic game for Japan to maintain the truce, often tolerating a role that required it to remain under the shadow of the competition. When a political conflict arose, the Japanese graciously exercised a spirit of magnanimity along with generous compromises and, at times, even a submission to the Ching court and Li Hung-Chang's prestige.

Yet in commerce and trade, the Japanese did not willingly yield their dominant position to the Chinese. But as the competition between the two further intensified, still operating under mutual accommodation, their sphere of rivalry extended to the Kingdom's trade and commerce. When the Chinese entered to exploit their political leverage in Korea's lucrative commercial and trade interests, Japan's response was fierce. Ever since it forced Korea to abandon the seclusion policy, Japan had dominated Korean trade. During this period Korea's major import items were both Japanese and European manufactured goods, while raw materials were the mainstay of its exports. Although poor public purchasing power led to the kingdom's exports outweighing its imports, profits generated by the monopolizing interests over the nation's trade should have been significant enough for the Japanese to strongly resist the Chinese encroachment. After Korea's treaty relationship was expanded to other Western countries, Japanese dominance in Korean trade declined. Yet, as in other spheres of influence, the Chinese remained Japan's only serious competition in Korean trade. By 1893, in spite of Japanese resistance, the Chinese improved their influence in Korean trade by greatly undermining the Japanese position; the Chinese that year handled forty percent of the total Korean trade volume, a marked improvement from mere fifteen percent in 1885. As a result, Japan lost its dominant trade position at the nation's two major ports, Wonsan and Inchon, and managed to maintain its premier position only at Pusan, a port nearest to the Japanese islands. The Chinese had not only unraveled the Japanese monopoly in Korean trade, but threatened Japan's standing as Korea's prime trading partner.

The Ching court's successful challenge to Japanese domination in Korean trade was possible only through Yuan's aggressive political support in the Chosun court. Yuan, young and ambitious, had spared no efforts to advance Chinese trade interests in Korea. While Chinese merchants in Korea were supported by Yuan, Japanese traders were buttressed by their government's comprehensive trade policies, which included sophisticated financial support. Unlike the Ching court's antiquated practices and political meddling, Westernized Japan had already adopted government-sponsored trade practices.

The ever-intensifying Ching-Japan rivalry in Korea was not restricted to trade interests; it also extended to most commercial areas, including fishery, communications, transportation, and urban commercial activities. Systematic commercial aggression was soon evident when transplanted Chinese and Japanese merchants managed to drive off most Korean merchants from Seoul's commercial districts. China and Japan had become excellent students of Western imperialism; the two Asian imperialists practiced in Korea every Western exploitation method from which they had suffered in their own countries earlier. They had been even more inventive, for they were familiar with Korean culture.

The worsening Ching-Japan rivalry often endangered their uneasy partnership; the early division of spheres, in which China was more interested in political-military control while Japan exercised the dominant influence in economics, increasingly blurred. Yet there remained some fundamental differences between the two: Chinese intrusion was primarily motivated by the prestige factor and more tactical needs, while the Japanese were more motivated by practical benefits of commercialism and strategic considerations. In any event, their imperial rivalry was being staged in Korea, and the Korean people were forced to carry the aggravating burdens.

By the waning moments of the nineteenth century, Chosun was reduced, in reality, to an imperial laboratory for two Asian giants. Yuan was the de facto high commissioner in charge of Korea's political and military affairs, while the Japanese legation in Seoul was the powerhouse of the nation's economic and diplomatic affairs. The court, still under the control of Queen Min and her clan, showed an increasing anti-Chinese and anti-Japanese sentiment. Yet its contacts with the Russians had not produced any tangible benefit in protecting the kingdom from the rampaging predators. The United States, for which the Chosun court had developed such unusual affection and reverence ever since a diplomatic tie was established, was reluctant to side with this troubled small kingdom against the rising prestige of the Japanese. America remained committed to the policy of maintaining a close tie with Japan, the nation it regarded the leader of East Asia.

The Chosun court's mounting political difficulty made the tending of public welfare arduous. Furthermore, the court's incompetence in the management of the nation's economy was striking; the results were worsening bureaucratic exploitation and corruption. The court was financially insolvent most of the time, for most tax collections fell into the hands of corrupt local officials. Farmers, forced to surrender almost their entire harvests to meet excessive tax levies, left the villages disillusioned. Yet the ruling faction, monopolizing most high government positions, was totally preoccupied in persecuting the opposition with an almost inhumane cruelty. The nation's political leadership as a whole was losing its credibility to rule.

The Chosun court's aimless drift continued. The chaotic social order and the foreign political seizures were now strangling not only the inept court but the dynasty itself. The kingdom was approaching, as the dynastic degeneration process continued, a state of fatal exhaustion. Only revolutionary reforms and a miraculous international tranquillity, an unlikely prospect but critical for fostering such a radical change, could offer a chance to salvage the old dynasty.

Notes

1. Taewongoon rejected the Japanese request to upgrade the Korea-Japan relations on the ground that their state letter was improperly written.
2. Hilary Conroy, *The Japanese Seizure of Korea: 1860-1910*. Philadelphia: University of Pennsylvania Press, 1960, p. 35.
3. Japan's militarists insisted on including the Korean peninsula in its Formosa(Taiwan) campaign, which was launched in 1865.
4 The Ching court's affirmative advice was conveyed to the Chosun court through Viceroy Li Hung-chang's letter.
Hereafter, Ching's Korean policy was known as the "Li Hung-chang affair."
5. Whang Jon-Hun was attached to the Chinese embassy in Tokyo. His exact official position at the embassy was not known.
6. Dr. Horace Newton Allen, a Presbyterian missionary who came to Korea in 1884, exercised a great deal of influence on the nation's early modernization drive in areas of religion, education, economics, and politics until his departure in 1905. For details, refer to Kim, Won Mo, *Diplomatic Chronicle of Modern Korea.* Seoul: Dankook University Press, 1984.
7. During the 1858-1864 period, Russia coerced Ching to surrender a huge territory, which included the Siberian territory south of the Amur River and the Maritime Province. It founded there Vladivostok, Russia's foremost outpost in the Far East, in 1860.

8. Those who settled in the Soviet far East through the unauthorized border crossings, reaching 10,000 persons by 1882, were the forefathers of the present-day Korean - Russian community in the central Asian republics. Most of the Korean settles were sent to the region far from the Korea-Russia border during the Second World war.

9. Yuan Shih-kai was a political and military strongman of the late Ching period and the early period of the republic of china. He became provisional president of the Republic of china i 1912.

10. The Chinese had 1,500 solders to about 200 Japanese soldiers in Seoul at the time. The Japanese guards posted at the Palace were defeated with heavy casualties by the Chinese force.

11. Both men were Japan's political giants during the late nineteenth and the early twentieth century. Its Hirobumi was Japan's most influential elder statesman who later became Japan's first Governor-general to Korea. Inouye served as Imperial Japan's foreign minister.

12. The island is known in Korea as komun Island, about twenty miles off the southern tips of the peninsula. It has two small sister island nearby. All islands are sparsely populated.

13. Wonsan was the largest port on the northeastern shore of the Korean peninsula. How it acquired the name of lazareff cannot be verified.

14. Lee Sun-Kun, *hankusa*, Book, 5,pp.774-781.

Chapter 7

Japan's Quest for Domination

1. The Dong-Hak Insurrection

As the Chosun court remained unable to undertake systematic reforms badly needed to modernize the antiquated nation, the nation's ability to tend the welfare of the public suffered progressive deterioration. Becoming disdainful of the incumbent political leadership, the nation's common people increasingly turned to religious movements for salvation from pressing socioeconomic hardships. In spite of the strength of traditional religions, Buddhism and Confucianism, a growing number of Chosun's hard pressed farmers was attracted to the Dong-Hak movement. For them the home-grown religion represented their values and tradition best.

The Dong-Hak movement had been outlawed in the kingdom since 1864. Nevertheless, it survived underground and continued to appeal to the nation's oppressed in the rural areas. By 1893, it had grown to become the nation's most vigorous religious movement. Confident in its newly-earned strength, it sought the court's blessing. As the first step, it initiated a petition to reverse the court's decree which had earlier branded the Dong-Hak leaders as sorcerers and heretics. In addition, the movement's present leaders demanded the court to grant Dong-Hak the same religious freedom and privileges accorded to the Christian religion. Regardless of the question of just cause, the reactionary court rejected the petition and responded with renewed persecution.

Spurned by the court and blaming the influence of foreign powers, the Dong-Hak leaders quickly escalated their simple petition drive to a series of decidedly anti-Japan, anti-West political protests. In addition to political reforms, they demanded the expulsion of all foreign nationals and abolition of the nation's diplomatic ties to foreign powers. The movement had in essence been transformed into the nation's first public protest against foreign political-economic domination. This rapid transformation was possible because the Dong-Hak doctrine did not distinguish political from religious pursuit. Moreover, as reflected in the name of the movement, the Eastern Learning, Dong-Hak was resolutely nationalistic from its inception and opposed to all Western influence. Following the kingdom's long tradition, the Dong-Hak leaders clearly identified the foreign powers as the source of the nation's overwhelming woes. Also, they demanded that the court purge the nation's corrupt and exploitive ruling class, which, after all, had failed to safeguard the nation from the escalating domination of the foreign powers. Dong-Hak was not willing to confront the nation's royal institution but directed its anger and frustration to the ruling class. Thus, Dong-Hak became the first national movement to declare a war against the nation's ruling class, a revolutionary development by itself.

The inauguration of the Dong-Hak insurrection followed a well established but timid national tradition: revolts against tyrannical local officials.[1] In 1893 General Jeon Bong Joon, the insurrection's military leader, led his combined force of Dong-Hak followers and sympathetic farmers against town officials in the Jeolla province, a region of rich agricultural tradition where the tyranny of corrupt officials had been particularly rampant. The Dong-Hak force quickly overwhelmed not only the town of Goboo but most major towns in the region. Local garrisons and forces dispatched by the court did not offer any meaningful resistance to the motivated rebel force of more than 10,000 men. After exceptionally successful initial campaigns in rural towns, the Dong-Hak forces proceeded to occupy Jeonjoo, the administrative center of the region.

The Dong-Hak insurrection quickly became a movement powerful enough to challenge the debilitated court. It attacked local garrisons at will and it was fearfully thought to be capable even of toppling the central government. Yet the Dong-Hak leaders were reluctant in transforming the movement into the court's political opposition. They were more comfortable with being a religious movement mainly intending to send the court a message and to purge the region's corrupt officials. The Dong-Hak's military campaign had limited scope; it lacked the zeal of extensive sociopolitical agenda that would have reflected the movement's deep concerns over the plight of the nation's ordinary citizens. The Dong-Hak movement was yet to adopt the platform that was suitable to its rapidly expanding strength.

2. The Sino-Japanese War

Although the Chosun court categorically rejected the Dong-Hak's demands, it possessed no effective military means to put down the powerful insurrection. Still, the court was too adamant to accommodate even the legitimate demands of the movement. Out of desperation the court turned to the Ching court and requested its meddlesome neighbor to send troops to subdue the insurrection. China, which had already offered to help and even urged the Chosun court to make the request, readily complied and sent a detachment of 1,500 men to Korea. Observing the provisions of the Tientsin Treaty, China duly notified Japan of its action and noted that the troops would be withdrawn when order was restored in Korea.

Ching's enthusiasm shown in sending troops to Korea was motivated by the long-standing desire to strengthen its political influence over the Chosun court. However, it apparently failed to predict the probable Japanese reaction. Japan's domestic political instability, which was caused in part by the absence of foreign distractions, may have misled the Chinese to assume that Japan was not able to challenge the Middle Kingdom at this time. On the contrary, Japan countered the Chinese move by sending a larger detachment of its own troops to Seoul. Yuan's frantic efforts to prevent a Japanese landing in Korea was a failure. As the two nations placed their troops in the Seoul region, a military confrontation between these two Asian great powers became a likely prospect. In the meantime, the Dong-Hak force had withdrawn from Jeonjoo voluntarily when its campaign provoked the foreign powers' military intervention. By freeing the occupied city, the Dong-Hak leaders intended to end the political crisis. This not only removed any justification for the landing of foreign forces in Korea but required their withdrawal.

Although the Dong-Hak's preemptive maneuver calmed the situation, China was insisting on maintaining its force until Japan recalled its force from Korea. Like China, Japan apparently had followed its own grand design when it sent its military contingent to Korea and now was unwilling to recall its force. As both sides adamantly refused to give the other a decisive advantage, a stalemate set in. Japan then proposed to China that the two countries maintain their forces in Korea and pursue the reorganization of the Korean government. The Chinese, preferring a simultaneous withdrawal of both forces, rejected the Japanese proposal, choosing to leave the task of reorganization to the Koreans. This meant that China would resume its extraordinary political-military influence over Korea as before. Upon the Chinese rejection, Japan was forced to make a choice: it could either accept the Chinese position and concede the Chinese political overlordship in Korea, or challenge the Middle Kingdom with force.

This time Japan chose military confrontation. It should have been expected that the rising power of Japan would eventually challenge waning Ching in Korea. The uneasy partnership had been possible only because Japan needed time to build its national strength to confront the Middle Kingdom. Nevertheless, the two powers resorted to perfunctory talk that, not surprisingly, produced no results and was quickly terminated. In 1895, Japan's war- ships fired upon a Chinese troopship and thus commenced the first Sino-Japanese war.

There was abundant indication that the war was not an accident but a part of Japan's premeditated strategic game. Japan may have concluded that only through the war could it drive out its traditional adversary from the Korean peninsula. The war could have served two strategic purposes for Japan: first, by defeating the Chinese, Japan could secure its long-sought political domination over Korea, the "dagger pointed at the heart of Japan," which, if aggressively inclined toward or under control of such a hostile power as Ching, would be able to threaten seriously Japan's security. Secondly, Japan's undisputed overlordship of Korea would secure the peninsula as the gateway to its continental expansion.[2] Japan's other strategic consideration may have been the Russian factor: Many Japanese leaders felt that it was imperative for Japan to establish itself firmly in Korea in order to discourage Russia's manifested imperial interests in the Pacific region.

Contrary to Japan's ostensible claim, the war was intended neither to buttress Korean independence nor to assure the reform movements. Korea was simply the first strategic target for Japan's grand imperial ambition. In addition, Japan's growing economic interests over Korea's natural resources and its consumer market were contributing factors.[3]

Although Japan had significant strategic advantages over China, the Middle Kingdom was not exactly in a position to acquiesce to the Japanese challenge. China had opposed Japan's advance in Korea with every means at its disposal. After expending considerable energy and resources to establish itself as the dominant influence in Korea, China could ill afford to relinquish its hard-won domination. Domestically, Li Hung-Chang's Korean policy was under severe criticism from his conservative opponents, who sought to curb his extensive political power by attacking his Korean policy. Moreover, Li was considered by then to have completed his extensive modernization programs for the Chinese Northern Fleet, which was under his personal control. Any move that could be construed as submission to the island nation, a power still generally believed to be inferior to China in every aspect, was no less than a personal political disaster for Li. Neither China nor Li had any justifiable excuse to evade the Japanese challenge.

The war started at sea with a Japanese preemptive attack on Chinese transportation ships, forcing the Chinese to respond. Simultaneously, Japan was busy manufacturing justifications for attacking the Chinese forces stationed in Korea. To instigate plausible causes, it first seized the Korean palace by force and coerced the King to reorganize his court with pro-Japanese officials. Once this process was completed, Japan demanded that the Korean court abolish its official relations with China. Under the intimidation of Japanese forces, the Chosun court complied with the demands and unilaterally revoked its relations with China. Then the court requested China, again under Japanese intimidation, to withdraw its forces. To no one's great surprise, China refused to accede to the Korean request. As if following a well-rehearsed plan, Japan then quickly coaxed the Korean court into asking for help in expelling the Chinese. Through these cumbersome maneuvers, Japan finally succeeded in fabricating a plausible pretext for launching a military action against the Chinese forces in Korea.

Ominously, China's first major military confrontation with Japan in three hundred years was led not by the central government but by a regional leader, thus illustrating the Ching court's diminishing political leadership. It was fought primarily between Japanese forces and forces under Li Hung-Chang's personal control. This peculiar circumstance reflected China's highly divisive domestic politics; the majority of southern and central forces did not wish to participate in the war, which was generally regarded as the private affair of Li Hung-Chang or that of the north. In spite of Japan's all-out efforts, the war was a distant affair to most Chinese governors whose territories were unaffected by the conflict.

The war was a contest between Japan's thoroughly reorganized and modernized forces and Li Hung-Chang's numerically superior but poorly trained and equipped forces. The result was plain: Li's soldiers and sailors were decisively defeated both on land and sea by the highly motivated Japanese forces. Easily defeating the Chinese in Korea, the Japanese quickly pushed on into Manchuria and threatened China proper itself. When Li's private war turned into an all-out skirmish threatening the regime itself, the Ching court panicked and sought a settlement. Japan agreed to a negotiated conclusion but continued its military campaigns, consolidating its gains before the negotiations opened. In 1895 the belligerents agreed to terminate the war by signing the Treaty of Shimonoseki.

Although the war had been limited in scope, the ramifications of its outcome were extraordinary. Overnight it gave the region a new political order which was bound to have direct and profound implications for Korea's political fate. By signing the treaty, China was forced to drop its claim of political dominion over Korea and to recognize Korea's status as a fully independent state, thus giving the recognition Japan had sought so persistently since 1876. China finally, under duress, publicly acknowledged the inevitable truth - Korea was a sovereign state entitled to manage its domestic as well as external affairs as it pleased.

The defeat for China was costly; in addition to its painful concessions in Korea, China had to make other humiliating accommodations to the victor. It was forced to cede part of Manchuria, Formosa, and the Pescadores to Japan. Among the forced concessions China had to suffer, the cession of the Liaodong peninsula of Manchuria was domestically and internationally controversial. The world powers duly noticed the fact that the Japanese presence in the strategic Liaodong peninsula could mean the extension of Japanese power to the region from which it could easily make an attempt on Beijing itself. The West was anxious not to allow the land-hungry island nation to establish a strategic outpost that could dominate the resource-rich Manchurian plain and eventually threaten northern China.

Formidable opposition to Japan's expected permanent occupation of the Liaodong peninsula quickly formed among most of the world's leading powers. Russia had well-founded reasons to fear a Japanese advance into Manchuria; the Japanese presence there would be detrimental to Russia's ambitions in the Pacific and to its desire to secure ice-free ports in the region. France, which was tied to Russia by a treaty, took a similar stand, fearing the Liaodong peninsula might become a Japanese prelude for an advance into Southeast Asia. Citing its commercial interests in China as a justification, Germany also collaborated with Russia and France in urging Japan not to occupy the Liaodong peninsula. Only the United States maintained neutral in this international tug-of-war. The West's concerted pressures eventually persuaded Japan. With predictable reluctance, it surrendered the war's prime catch by abandoning its occupation of the Liaodong peninsula. In so doing, it exposed its weakness, an indication that Japan had not yet reached a power plateau where it could withstand such international pressure.

Although Japan had to yield to the West in the Liaodong question, it was determined to retain its gains in Korea. Unlike the Liaodong incursion, the West was silent over Japan's profound advance in Korea; Korea was alone in its feeble resistance to the leading military power of the region. When the Chinese were expelled from Korea, Japan took steps to reorganize the whole of the Chosun society; overnight, under Japanese direction, the newly created National Affairs Council issued decrees aimed at reorganizing the nation's governmental, social, and economic life. Politically, the kingdom was forced to adopt a new, Western-style cabinet system closely imitating the Japanese model. Social reform measures were carried out in order to abolish the nation's traditional customs. There was little doubt that some of these forced reforms included measures that were needed to modernize the nation. Yet rushed, wholesale reform was hardly practical, regardless of the virtue of the program. Furthermore, most of the reform programs were too drastic for a nation of the Confucian tradition and, as a result, were largely ineffectual. Korea was not willing to undertake such forced modernization programs overnight. Overlooked by Japan were vast dissimilarities that existed between itself and Korea. Having a continental temperament, a product of its geography, the Koreans were far more deliberate and reserved than were the Japanese.

Regardless of the Korean people's refusal, Japan was adamant in pushing reorganization programs, coercing the hardly functional government to issue hundreds of hasty decrees ranging from the abolishment of old but desirable customs to the adoption of a money economy. As a result, often ill-considered and impractical reform policies were met by determined public opposition. In addition, the fact that the Japanese envoy to Seoul was the principal executor and supervisor of the Korean reform policies made the drive even more unacceptable to the public. In spite of Japan's extraordinary pressures, the forced reforms achieved only symbolic results in this initial stage.

While its hasty endeavor to reform the antiquated kingdom was anything but successful, Japan's political domination of Korea had become almost complete. Japan's Seoul legation, usually manned by an envoy of considerable political weight, effectively replaced the influence of Yuan, the powerful Chinese envoy to the Korean court. The Korean court was then under the supervision of the arrogant Japanese ambassador, who, acting as a self-appointed royal advisor, perversely interfered in the court's political process. Japan, which allegedly fought the Chinese to protect Korea's independence, now discarded its cumbersome mask and shamelessly and systematically manipulated Korea's political process to undermine the sovereign power of the kingdom. Shortly, Japanese political domination reached a new height, totally suffocating the Chosun court's political functions. The court vainly sought help from an indifferent world community. In spite of Korea's appeal, the world community remained unwilling to side with the Hermit Kingdom, though the deepening Japanese plot should have been evident. China, Korea's meddlesome neighbor but frequent ally against Japan, had been reduced to a disabled giant no longer able to provide support.

Japan's renewed domination over the Korean court prompted a renewal of the Dong-Hak's military campaigns against the Japanese and the pro-Japanese government. This time the insurgency clearly focused on the new intruders, making this the nation's first organized resistance movement against the Japanese.[4] As the insurgents continued to gain popular support throughout the nation's rural south, the court and its Japanese supporters intensified their attempt to put down the rebellion. Highly motivated Dong-Hak forces scored early victories against government troops, prompting a confrontation between nationalistic Dong-Hak forces and the government forces, who were buttressed by Japanese troops. Seeking a decisive victory against the government, Dong-Hak prepared for a battle with the best resources they could muster.

The final showdown took place at the town of Gongjoo in central Korea; the Dong-Hak force of about 30,000 men battled against a Japanese-Korean army of about 10,000 men.[5] Though they were gravely ill-equipped and under-trained, the Dong-Hak troops fought heroic battles against the modern Japanese force but lost the contest. With the defeat, not only the noble cause of the Dong-Hak movement but the Korean nation's aspiration to remain sovereign had suffered a major loss. Nevertheless, by waging daring campaigns against the region's premier military power, the Dong-Haks fully displayed the Hahn people's unending fighting spirit. By the end of 1895 the Dong-Haks terminated their military campaigns and underwent a drastic transformation, channelling the movement's energy to ideological pursuits. The major thrust of the movement shifted to non-political, religious activities as Chundogyo, the religion of Heavenly Way, was established. Like the Dong-Hak movement, Chundogyo was well received by the nation's rural population and quickly became one of its leading religious movements. It remains Korea's most popular native religion today.

The Dong-Hak insurrection was a conspicuous demonstration of maturing Korean nationalism. It had roots in the nation's cherished tradition of resisting foreign invaders regardless of unfavorable odds. While the perpetually timid court readily sought refuges and accommodations, the exploited and oppressed public always fought the invaders as it did against the Chinese, Mongols, Manchus, and Japanese. The nation had been endowed with pitifully few outstanding political leaders, particularly at the time of national emergencies, but the public was always willing to risk their lives to protect their country from invasion. In spite of its military defeat, the Dong-Hak movement was not the end but an auspicious beginning of Korea's earnest national movement to secure its just sovereignty.

The Dong-Hak movement failed because it did not possess the military means to fight against a modernized and trained Japanese army. The spontaneous public insurgency failed to find and enlist quality military leaders with strategic as well as tactical expertise in modern warfare. Furthermore, the large number of untrained farmers that made up the bulk of the Dong-Hak force often had been more of a hindrance than an advantage in the war against a highly organized, modern military force. In addition, the movement willingly committed a strategic mistake. In spite of its spontaneous nature, the Dong-Hak had mustered a force of sufficient strength to topple the inept government in the early period of the campaign. Had the rebels rushed to Seoul, they might have captured the court before any foreign intervention was feasible. Their failure to do so was a fatal mistake but a chosen course that reflected a deep loyalty to the monarchy, for they intended only to punish and cleanse the corrupt government system without destroying the nation's tradition-rich royal institution. Their sense of priority was characteristic even though the operation proved to be a military disaster.

3. Growing Japanese-Russian Rivalry

Japan's imposition of overlordship was met by the Korean people's growing resentment. Yet the Chosun court was too weak and old-fashioned to challenge Japan's growing power and prestige alone. Yet the West had shown every indication that it would not risk its own interests for this scarcely known country. China had been effectively neutralized and driven out of the country by the Japanese. The Chosun court's only hope was Russia, which was considered capable of exercising some restraining influence over Japan. Not surprisingly, being greatly interested in wrecking Japanese ambitions in the region, Russia had become Japan's last competition in Korea.

The upsurge of Russian influence in the Chosun court was quite spectacular. Japan's reckless imposition of radical reforms, its rash attempt to monopolize power at the Korean court, and its yielding to the Western powers in the Liaodong question all helped turn many Korean officials toward Russia. Russia reciprocated the favor by making its envoy to Seoul readily available to Korean officials. As the court became sure of Russian political support for its attempt to lessen Japan's domination, it undertook a major cabinet restructuring. Consequently, the pro-Russia faction rose to compete against the pro-Japanese faction for political domination. Overnight, the close political collaboration between the Korean court and the Russian legation threatened Japan's hard-won political influence. Rampant were rumors that a secret Russo-Korean treaty was imminent. The collapse of Japan's political control over the Korean court was progressing so fast that even the disbandment of the Japanese-trained army was contemplated. Tension between Japan and Russia was bound to rise.

The swift collapse of its Korean policy forced Japan to reassess the situation. Unable to reverse the overwhelming tide orchestrated by the Russians, Japan resorted to a political truce by openly stating that it had no intention of interfering in Korean politics. For a brief period it appeared that the Russians had successfully checked Japanese political schemes in Korea. The Russians and their Korean supporters did not fully appreciate the critical importance the Japanese had attached to their Korean adventure. Japan by no means intended, on the eve of the twentieth century, to surrender the strategic Korean peninsula to its rival. In spite of its superficial assent to Russian participation, it was unwilling to accept Russian domination of the Korean court without trying every available political maneuver. At this point in time Japan's Korean policy was in reality its Russian policy.

In a desperate attempt to counter the growing Russian influence in Korea, Tokyo dispatched a new envoy to Seoul. Ambassador Miura, known for his militant view, quickly surveyed the deteriorating situation and chose to pursue a most sinister path in regaining Japanese political influence over the Chosun court. Presumably on behalf of his government, he decided physically to eliminate Queen Min, leader of the powerful pro-Russian Min faction. On October 8, 1895 Japanese hoodlums led by none other than Miura himself invaded the palace and killed the queen. By murdering the "mother of the Korean nation" Japan had perpetrated a crime unthinkable in a land of Confucian doctrine. It was obvious that Japan was willing to do anything to advance its imperial ambition in Korea.

It is difficult even today, with the benefit of history, to comprehend this particular act of wanton barbarism. There was no direct evidence that the Japanese government had ordered the envoy to carry out this inhumane crime against a sovereign state. Nevertheless, it was assumed that Miura had felt the action was warranted and compatible with the policy adopted by his government. Moreover, it is difficult to believe that such a conspiracy, even if it was a purely individual action of the envoy, was executed undetected by any of the many Japanese government agencies functioning in Seoul at the time. Nevertheless, the Japanese government should have assumed the responsibility for the crime its envoy had perpetrated. On the contrary, the evidence was quickly buried by the Japanese government; Miura and some forty others were shortly freed on grounds of insufficient evidence. The Japanese government had refused any responsibility for the barbarous act committed by its own minister.

Queen Min had been a woman of uncommon political instincts, yet by acting not so much as the mother of the nation but as the leader of the powerful but largely power-hungry Min clan, she had come to be despised. This queen, the first and only woman to exercise such strong political power during the entire Chosun period, was more concerned with safeguarding her clan interests and her young son than in managing national affairs. Her incessant political interventions had often disrupted the political fabric of the fragile monarchy, inadvertently causing the kingdom more harm than benefit. Nonetheless, she did not commit any wrongdoing against the state of Japan deserving of such a tragic death by foreign hoodlums in her own palace.

The murder of Queen Min alarmed the community of foreign envoys in Seoul and temporarily diminished the power of the Japanese ambassador, who was implicated in the incident. The Western envoys assumed a collective responsibility in advising the Chosun court to replace the discredited Japanese. Again it seemed that Japan's standing in Korea would suffer a fatal blow. The gravity of the crime should have brought down upon Japan major condemnation from the world community. However, its damaged political influence in the Korean court aside, Japan suffered no lasting punishment. Even the withdrawal of its forces from Seoul was not actualized amid the conflicting interests of the Western powers. The West's highly ambiguous treatment of the incident was an indisputable reminder that Japan's prestige and power had grown to command significant international respect. Moreover, Korea's inability to extract an appropriate punitive response from the world community amply illustrated its minor status in international politics.

Though the court might be immobilized, the public was now again aroused. In spontaneous nationwide demonstrations, the people protested the unpopular reforms and demanded revenge for the murder of Queen Min. The court was forced to respond with force; the chaotic disorder worsened when the court unwisely decided to dispatch most of its meager military force to local areas to subdue the uprisings. The widespread unrest created yet another political drama; in 1897 the king secretly moved his residence to the Russian legation. By escaping from virtual imprisonment in his own palace, King Gojong, usually a passive man, staged a sort of coup against the Japanese overlords. The Korean monarch's unorthodox political maneuver placed him beyond the Japanese reach. The King then took measures to unravel Japan's Korean scheme; he dissolved the pro-Japanese government and replaced it with a new, pro-Russian, pro-American government. Reform measures that had been adopted under Japan's coercion were abrogated, and a few pro-Japanese politicians were executed in public. The sudden turn of events thwarted Japan's Korean scheme.

Despite being superbly manipulative, Japan had few options now. Shortly, proving its uncanny sense of the political reality, Japan took steps to defuse the situation by openly acknowledging Russia's superior position in Korea. Suddenly, with the reining Korean king under its protection, Russia had become the powerful political force in Seoul. For a while, with a greatly strengthened influence corresponding to its new status as the primary protector of the Korean kingdom, Russia was to enjoy its heyday in Korea. Still, the balance of power was not entirely favorable to Russia as Japan's overwhelming influence in military-economic areas remained intact.

With Russia's political influence reaching new heights after the "Ah Guan Pa Chon," or the royal refuge in the Russian legation, Japan sought a negotiated co-existence with its new rival. In 1896 the two powers signed a memorandum in which Japan reaffirmed the autonomy of the Korean kingdom and accepted Korea's new pro-Russian government, a tacit acceptance of Russian domination in the Chosun court. In return, Japan was allowed to station a military force of limited size to protect its interests in Korea. Russia reserved the right to do the same if it deemed necessary. Thus, Japan and Russia managed to establish a rough balance of power in Korea.

Neither Japan nor Russia considered it necessary to consult with the Korean government even when they engaged in negotiations that pertained to Korea. Notwithstanding its long civilization and cultural history, Korea remained no more than a tempting pie to be cut. It now only remained to distribute the slices among the imperial powers, which had to include not only Russia and Japan but other Western nations.

When Japan and Russia established an uneasy co-existence in Korea, the world powers rushed to claim a share. The nation's remaining commercial interests were quickly taken away. Russia extracted interests in mining, forestry, banking, and military instruction; the United States in railroad construction, gold mining, and street car rail construction; England in banking and mining; France in railroad construction; Germany in mining. By 1898 Korea's major commercial interests were almost completely expropriated by the world's leading imperialists. Even Japan, which had already accumulated most of the commercial interests in Korea, continued to augment its share by purchasing those interests obtained by the Western powers.

The Chosun dynasty's fatal decline into a dark age of expropriated sovereignty was not unnoticed by its young intellectuals. Among them, Dr. Philip Jaison, a native Korean educated in the United States, was most prominent. In 1896 he began to publish a newspaper titled The Independence both in the Korean language and in English. His primary objective was to educate the Korean people in nationalism and the democratic process he had observed in the United States. Through his persuasive editorials he spread democratic principles and also admonished the confused court for its lack of political direction. Soon his newspaper became an integral part of his prescient campaign for the independence and modernization of Korea.

The surge of independence sentiment led to the birth of the nation's first organized political entity, the Independent Council. The council, which consisted of thirty or so progressive intellectuals, played a powerful role as a political watchdog and undertook many symbolic projects designed to promote the nation's independent spirit. It maintained a steadfast opposition to the court's vacillating stand toward imperial foreign powers and urged the king to return to his own palace from the Russian legation, the place where he earlier had moved his residence.

In spite of the nation's burgeoning independence sentiments, Korea's political fortunes remained clouded. Its exercise of sovereign power had been increasingly hampered by Japanese interference, while its efforts to escape Japanese domination were ill organized. Still, the nation was becoming more aware of the danger posed by the Japanese overlordship; many young intellectuals urged the court to take the necessary steps to recover political integrity. By this time even the inept court felt such an undertaking warranted, and in 1897 it attempted a political revival by adopting a new title for the nation. The Hahn state, under political seizure by a foreign power, renamed itself the Daehahn Empire, the Empire of the Great Hahn. Thus it formally abolished the mismanaged and exhausted Chosun dynasty. Yet its new title provided no immediate dividend for the Hahn state, which was still managed by the same incompetent officials. The court, suffering from the foreign powers' worsening political interference, could hardly be effective for the multitude of woes the nation faced. The nation was too seriously ill to be saved by symbolic gestures, however noble they might have been.

The Korean court's ineptitude had become an increasingly volatile issue among young intellectuals. They openly voiced their disapproval for the nation's grossly inadequate political process, although the court was yet to adopt a political system through which public desires were channelled into the political decision-making process. These young intellectuals organized a massive forum, under the leadership of the Independent Council and the Independent Newspaper, not heeding the fact that the court was hardly in a position to accede to their highly nationalistic demands. The public's growing political awareness, however, did not even persuade the archaic Chosun court to adopt measures imperative for the nation's modernization and political independence.

On the contrary, the citizens' open defiance provoked the neophobic Korean government to take hostile measures against the civic forum itself. It not only expelled Dr. Jaison but also severely restricted the activities of the Independent Council and created a new pro-government organization to oppose the cause of national salvation. The court's political oppression of independence aspirations was an unfortunate but characteristic behavior for the nation. One of its more prominent political shortcomings had been an inability to recognize the opposition's just cause or to accommodate it in a conciliatory manner.

In the end, the court outlawed the Independent Council and thus proceeded to suppress the voice of national awakening. It was most ironic that a government that was virtually powerless against foreign powers became so adamant in cracking down on its domestic opposition. An equally grave irony was that a government that was willing to accept reforms dictated by foreign powers was summarily opposed to less drastic reforms proposed by the domestic opposition. Such a fatal political relapse was a characteristic of the government that was being dominated by old-fashioned factional interests. The court, grossly inadequate to lead the Daehahn Empire in this time of high political drama, was the most prominent accomplice for the eventual demise of the kingdom.

During this treacherous period of national development Korea was not without prescient patriots and pioneers. To its misfortune, however, it lacked a collective political leadership capable of wisely leading a nation of troublesome geopolitics through the turbulent waters of high imperialism. Although the political circumstances of the late nineteenth century had been particularly formidable, Korea could have achieved, with national unity and prudent utilization of its unique geography, national rejuvenation such as Japan had accomplished through its Meiji Restoration. In spite of the unusual suffering it had caused, the Koreans failed to transform their most cherished tradition, Confucian individualism and righteousness, into a national oneness, or nationalism. Unable to achieve a high degree of social cohesion and collaboration, the nation squandered its opportunities to achieve the modernization that might have averted the ultimate geopolitical penalty. By 1904, Japan managed to put Korea under its full control. Any hope of avoiding a grave national catastrophe had by then vanished.

4. The Russo-Japanese War

The roots of the Russo-Japanese war trace back to the Sino-Japanese war of 1895. Under the intense pressure of the Dreubund, the West's three-power partnership, Japan was forced to surrender its prime war gain, the strategic Liaodong peninsula. Russia, as the leader of the triple intervention, had argued vigorously against Japanese occupation of the peninsula, a significant strategic location from which Japan could have easily controlled Port Arthur, the home port of the Chinese Northern Fleet. Inevitably, Japan had come to harbor strong sentiment against the Russian intervention; the fact Russia had became Japan's chief rival in Korea did not help the situation. Still, Japan maintained a conciliatory stand toward Russia and concentrated on improving its position in Korea through diplomatic maneuvers while undertaking an extensive military buildup.[6] A major setback for Japan's Korean scheme came when King Gojong took refuge at the Russian legation. While Russia had not overwhelmed the deeply entrenched Japanese interests in Korea, initially neither side was anxious in the intensifying competition to resort to military prowess. Instead, yielding to the ascending Russian political fortune in Korea, Japan attempted to settle for a co-existence with Russia through a series of imperial settlements.

Japan proposed to Russia the division of Korea into two spheres of influence: a Russian sphere would occupy the part north of the thirty-eighth parallel, while the remainder would be the Japanese sphere. Rejecting the Japanese ploy, known as the Yamagata proposal, Russia claimed to support and to recognize the independence and territorial integrity of Korea. The Russians justified their refusal to collaborate with Japan's cynical conspiracy by citing essentially the same excuse invariably employed by the Japanese to protect their dominant interests in Korea from other powers.

Contrary to its public claim, Russia's rejection of Japan's division ploy was motivated primarily by its political interests. Russia feared that the division of Korea into two spheres of influence would create complications with the United States, which still favored Korean independence. Moreover, Russia knew that southern Korea was more developed and far more richly endowed with agricultural resources than the northern part, which the Japanese proposed as the Russian sphere of influence. From Russia's strategic and naval standpoint, yielding southern Korea to Japan was even more disturbing because of Japan's strong interests, notably among naval officers, in ports on the southern coastline. In addition to these more immediate concerns, Russia may have had a long range strategic consideration, perhaps preferring an eventual takeover of the whole peninsula than a premature agreement to divide the catch with a power generally believed to be far inferior to itself.[7]

Although Russia spoiled the Japanese conspiracy to divide Korea into two parts, it granted Japan some important concessions through the Yamagata-Lobanov protocol. The new agreement allowed Japan to exercise over the Korean government an influence basically equal to that of Russia. While this appeased Japan's discontent by making it a co-overlord of Korea, Russia by no means abandoned its ambition to be the sole influence in Korea. Russia actively sought an ice-free port in the south and also in the northeast corner of the Bay of Korea. Russian naval commanders strongly preferred Korea's largest port, located at Pusan in the southeast corner of the peninsula. This desire to secure warm Korean ports was not unnoticed by Japan, which considered Russian control of the southern Korean ports to be a grave security threat. Japan vigorously objected to the Russian move, and, in the end, the Russian government, which was heavily dominated by the proponents of Manchuria and railway interests rather than naval interests, abandoned the provocative idea. As a result, Russia never secured a Korean port.

While it reached a calculated stalemate in Korea, Russia was highly active in Manchuria. In 1898 it extracted from China a major concession in the form of a 25-year lease for the harbors of Port Arthur and Talienwan with a neutral zone along the frontier of the leased territory. Having earlier frustrated the Japanese plot to occupy the Liaodong peninsula, Russia had established its own imperial bridgehead there. To counter the expected Japanese objection to this move, the Russians made further concessions to Japan in Korea. The strategy of using its influence in Korea as a bargaining chip for its venture in Manchuria was quite effective; Russia's conciliatory gesture in Korea prevented the Japanese from taking other countermeasures.[8]   Japan's moderate protest over its rival's Liaodong advance was also affected by the more accommodating diplomacy under the leadership of Ito, who was known to have greater respect for Russia than most Japanese leaders did.[9]

As Russia's strategic interests in the region were becoming more oriented to Manchuria, Japan's Russian policy also shifted significantly. Japan's early scheme for the division of Korea was now transformed into the even more cynical settlement of "Man-Kan Kokan," or an exchange of Manchuria for Korea. Japan justified the proposal on the ground that its territorial propinquity and extensive commercial interests in Korea mandated its close control of the kingdom. The imperial swapping scheme would have put the Korean peninsula under Japan's sole control, while Russia would have a free hand in Manchuria. Japan was willing to disown the claim to Manchuria, a claim having no basis in reality, for its absolute overlordship in Korea. The Man-Kan Kokan was not well received by the Russians, who were content to have control of Manchuria but balked at the price - the surrender of the Korean peninsula in entirety. Despite the Russian rejection of the cynical plot, some factions of the Japanese government, including the elder statesman Marquis Ito, did not give up the land-swapping scheme until the last moment in the failing negotiation.

The Russo-Japanese conflict worsened after the Russians undertook a major imperial move in Manchuria after China's Boxer Rebellion, a peasant uprising of 1900 that exploded because of the nation's exasperating food shortages. The Ching court, much abused by the West and exhausted by domestic political squabbles, had sided with the rebels by not intervening in the Boxers' bloody seizure of foreign quarters in Beijing. The Boxers' offense against missionaries and foreign nationals quickly invited military intervention by allied forces of the maritime powers and by neighboring Japan and Russia. Poorly organized, the rebellion was swiftly crushed by the armies of the world's most advanced industrial powers.[10]   After the Boxers were subdued in Beijing, the allied forces were withdrawn. However, the Russian troops that pulled out of China proper remained in Manchuria and became a de facto occupation force in the region. Suspicious of Russia's intentions, Japan protested the occupation, justifying its objection on the ground that the presence of a Russian force in Manchuria would weaken the Japanese security perimeter. In spite of St. Petersburg's repeated claim that it did not intend to annex the strategic Chinese territory to its expanding empire, the Russian stand on Manchuria was unanimously criticized by the world's leading powers.

Japan, England, and the United States registered strong objections to

Russia's forceful domination of Manchuria. England opposed the Russian move although it had already reached an accommodation with Russia by securing railway concessions in the Yangtze basin for Russia's similar interest in the region north of the Great Wall. The United States, by insisting on the Open Door policy that mandated the world powers an equal access to Manchuria both in terms of leases and spheres of political influence, also objected to the presence of Russian troops in Manchuria. However, the most vocal and hostile opposition came from Japan, which acted as a de facto leader of these maritime powers. Public protest aside, most of the Western powers were yet unwilling to dislodge the Russians by force.[11] Steadfastly refusing to submit to international pressure, Russia insisted that its occupation of Manchuria was a subject to be discussed between China and Russia, not by other world powers. Yet, in an unambiguous attempt to placate Japan's vocal protest, Russia offered to reopen the Korean question with Japan. Again, Russia was willing to make concessions in Korea to salvage its profound interests in Manchuria.

During this period of hectic Russo-Japanese struggle, Russia's disposition toward its two regional interests, Manchuria and Korea, was undergoing a rapid transformation, largely reflecting its relations with Japan and China. As Japan's strength in the region grew, Russia became more convinced of the need to secure control over Manchuria. Russia still enjoyed a leverage over the weak Ching government, which was dominated by such pro-Russian leaders as Li Hung-Chang.[12] The Russians chose to overlook the fact that the Chinese no longer viewed them as friends and would not hesitate to apply the traditional tactic of setting one enemy against another. On the other hand, Russia started to apply marked restraint toward the growing power of Japan, a policy which had continued to strengthen its position in Korea since the Nishi-Rosen protocol was signed in 1898.[13]

As an alternative, Russia proposed the neutralization of the Korean peninsula, which was to be supervised by both Russia and Japan. The Russian scheme, devised mainly as a measure to protect its eastern frontier from hostile Japan, did not fool the Japanese, who instead demanded that the Korean issue be linked to the Russian evacuation from Manchuria. The neutralization initiative, quickly discarded by the Japanese rejection, caught the attention of some Korean officials at the time, although there is no indication that they seriously considered the idea. It was also coolly received by the American minister to Seoul, who did not even take the trouble to convey it to Washington. The proposal, which may have been an idea worthy of deliberation, failed to be considered a viable political solution to Korea's predicament amid the international power struggle.

As the neutralization proposal showed, Russia was extremely reluctant to allow Japan an unrestricted political domination over Korea. While Russia maintained its unwillingness to surrender its hard-won influence in Korea, Japan's position over the Manchuria-Korean question had hardened as its military buildup progressed as planned. Japan no longer regarded the Man-Kan Kokan as an acceptable option. It would not grant the overlordship of Manchuria to Russia even in a trade for the sole domination of Korea, for it had grown to feel comfortable with the prospect of directly challenging the Russians.

Japan was gaining momentum; the nation had completed its military buildup, and the public was solidly behind the government. Japanese officials were well aware of Russia's political-financial difficulties and its chronically ineffective political system. In addition, Japan had scored a major diplomatic success with the signing of the Anglo-Japanese treaty in 1902. It further strengthened its international standing by establishing a cordial relationship with the United States. As Japan had succeeded in systematically isolating it from major world powers, Russia was without a major ally in its adventure in East Asia. France remained only a reluctant partner in spite of the binding French-Russian alliance.[14]

In 1902, Russia submitted to international pressure orchestrated by Japan and signed an agreement to evacuate its army from Manchuria. Although the agreement was a Russian compromise under the maritime powers' pressure, it was also the manifestation of the Russian government's inability to develop a coherent policy in its Manchurian venture. During this period the Russian government was divided between the faction favoring a militant pro-annexation policy and the opposition that supported railway and commercial interests but did not actively support the annexation of Manchuria. The Russian government was unable to formulate a sensible, coherent policy for both Manchuria and Japan.

Amid the lingering controversy, Russia defaulted on its promise to withdraw its troops from Manchuria.[15] The three Open Door powers renewed their demand for immediate withdrawal and pressured the Chinese government to engage in more vigorous protests for it. Japan was fully exploiting Russia's unwillingness to execute the withdrawal agreement and the illegal occupation of Yongampo to its advantage in the dispute against Russia.[16] Along with its diplomatic maneuvers, Japan was pushing forward a contingent military plan to fight a war against Russia. Conversely, Russia neither expected Japan to resort to a war nor properly appreciated the quality of the Japanese army. Russia committed a grave error in underrating the Japanese fighting machine, as did the world community as a whole at the time.

In 1903, Japan and Russia exchanged new proposals to resolve the impasse over the predatory domination of Manchuria-Korea. Russia proposed that it would recognize Japan's supreme position in southern Korea if the northern part above the thirty-ninth parallel were recognized as a neutral zone. Russia still pursued the establishment of a buffer zone between Manchuria and Japan's political sphere at the expense of Korea. Rejecting the proposal, Japan countered with an offer to set up a fifty-kilometer neutral zone on both sides of the Amrok River along the Korea-China border. Japan obviously saw benefits in installing a buffer zone between its sphere of interest and that of Russia's, but not at the expense of surrendering the northern half of Korea. Both imperial powers no longer took trouble to justify their overbearing ambitions with the pretext of protecting Korean independence and territorial integrity. Each simply behaved as a sovereign power tending a domestic dispute, acting like two hungry beasts over a tempting catch. Neither China nor Korea was allowed to voice its views, although the struggle was over their own territory and their own fate.

By the end of 1903 Japan's negotiation with the dilatory Russian government produced no major breakthrough. The faint hope of negotiated settlement vanished, and the two powers exhausted their search for a mutually acceptable imperial scheme in the region. To militant Japan the only viable solution left was a military contest. Its decision to resort to an early military campaign was greatly affected by the ongoing construction of the Trans-Siberia Railway. When completed, it would give the Russians a significant strategic advantage by connecting European Russia with its East Asian frontier. Japan saw the benefits of engaging the Russians before the completion of the railroad. Domestically, Japan had already completed its war mobilization, an effort bolstered by strong public support. Even before the negotiation was officially terminated, Japan all but announced a war against Russia. On the other hand, Russia remained blinded to Japanese intentions and grossly misjudged the military capabilities and determination of its smaller adversary. The Russians were still entertaining the erroneous assumption that a negotiated settlement was the only path open to the small, insular nation.

In February 1904, Japan initiated its military campaign against Russia. Characteristically, the immediate victim of this geopolitical confrontation was none other than Korea. At the beginning, the Korean peninsula became a major operational field for the Japanese army, which successfully coerced the Korean court into signing an alliance treaty. By doing so, Japan finally succeeded in formally subjugating the peninsula some three hundred years after its first invasion was crushed by Admiral Li. The Korean government's feeble call for international intervention moved no major world powers. The question of Korean sovereignty was effectively buried under the thick gun smoke of the Japanese forces and was conveniently ignored by the world community until the end of the Second World War. No world power was willing to challenge victorious Japan on behalf of the Hermit Kingdom.

Korea's best hope was the United States. The Korean court, under the control of the pro-Russian faction during the years of Russo-Japanese rivalry, maintained a friendly relationship with the United States. Many progressive young intellectuals were fond of the nation that had distinguished itself as the protector of freedom and democracy. Yet the United States was more of an ally of Japan than of Korea; it stood by Japan in the Sino-Japanese war, and it declined to intervene on behalf of Korea after the assassination of Queen Min - instead, recalling its minister to Seoul, who opposed Japanese aggression. The United States pursued a common front with Japan in preventing Russia from monopolizing Manchuria.[17] Although America was little interested in Korea politically and commercially at the time, its support for Korea's independence and territorial integrity could have been most effective in checking Japan's imperial ambition. Instead, America and Japan practiced a certain amount of reciprocal imperialism; America's silence over the Japanese advance in Korea was rewarded by Japan's restraint when the United States annexed Hawaii.[18] Reflecting the global collaboration, American bankers supplied the external credit for Japan. As a whole, the people and the government of the United States remained sympathetic to the Japanese.[19] Other Western powers did nothing on behalf of Korea; France remained "a neutral benevolent to Russia," and England "a neutral benevolent to Japan."

The Russo-Japanese war was fought over the political control of Manchuria. Yet the battlefields were confined mostly to the Korean peninsula, which did not belong to either participant. Although the object was the control of Chinese Manchuria, the Ching court remained largely neutral, and China proper was little affected by the military operations. From the beginning the Japanese forces scored uninterrupted successes both on the sea and land. With the fall of Port Arthur and the Russian defeats at the Amrok and Mukden, the war's outcome was shortly quite clear; the poorly led and ill-disciplined Russian forces had to withdraw from southern Manchuria. The Russo-Japanese conflict was one of the great surprises in the history of modern warfare. For the first time in history, a well-prepared dwarf conferred a decisive defeat upon an overwhelmingly favored but totally unprepared giant. The result illustrated the fact that just as China had done during its earlier encounter with the island nation, so did Russia fail to mobilize its great resources in time.

By the spring of 1905 Japan's victory had become an established fact. The war was formally terminated by the Portsmouth Treaty in September. With the defeat, Russia's long ambition toward East Asia crumbled; it surrendered its exclusive influence over Manchuria. In addition it had to recognize Japan's "paramount political, military and economic interests" in Korea. More importantly, by defeating its two larger foes, Japan paved a way to claim itself the overlord of the region. There remained no power capable of restraining Japan's ambition in the region.

After the war Japan aspired to solidify its gains in the region by gaining international approval. It easily extracted recognition of its ascendant position in Korea from its maritime co-conspirators, the United States and England. Under the 1905 Taft-Katsura Agreement, the United States recognized Japan's special interests in Korea in return for a Japanese promise not to object to American rule in the Philippines. Japan and England signed a similar agreement that included a Japanese pledge to be supportive of English ambition in India. In order to preserve their own imperial ambitions, the Western nations became willing supporters of Japanese aggression in Korea, although that nation's right to be independent and to preserve its territorial integrity was well understood and preached by those same Western powers. Nevertheless, the self-serving exchange of political support and acquiescence was more a common practice than an exception for most world powers during this era of rampant imperialism.

Notes

1. Koreans tend to use two definitions for the Dong-Hak uprising; some use "revolution" and others use "insurrection." There is no consensus. But this writer prefers to use "insurrection" because of its limited scope and inconclusive outcome.
2. Harold M. Vinacke, *A History of the Far East in Modern Times.* p.137.
3. Ibid., p.140.
4. Lee Sun-Kun, *Hahnkuksa.* Book, 5, p.357.
5. Only a fraction of the 30,000-man Dong-Hak force was believed to have been worthy of being called soldiers. Most were farmers and civilian followers of the movement, more hindrance than help to its military operation.
6. Ian Nish, *The Origins of the Russo-Japanese War.* p.28.

7. William L. Langer, *The Diplomacy of Imperialism: 1868-1910.* p.406.
8. Nish, p.45.
9. Ibid., p.44
10. The Boxer indemnity reached 450 million U.S. dollars.
11. Nish, p.93.
12. Li died in 1901.
13. The protocol was used to define mostly economic interests of Russia and Japan in Korea. Through the protocol Japan recovered its paramount commercial interests in Korea.
14. Nish, p.132.
15. Ibid., p.174
16. Russia occupied this small strip of land on the bank of the Amrok (Yalu) River in 1903 by putting up buildings without the Korean government's sanction.
17. Tyler Dennett, *Americans in Eastern Asia.* p. 645.
18. Ibid., p.645.
19. Vinacke, p. 182.

Chapter 8

Japan's Colonial Rule

1. Pre-annexation Period

After defeating its two regional rivals, Japan concentrated on extracting international recognition for its dominant position in Korea. When it finally collected varying degrees of acquiescence from the Western powers, Japan was ready to push its long-delayed scheme to colonize Korea at full speed. After all, Japan had not fought the wars against China and Russia only to remain merely a dominant influence in Korea.

Japan's systematic domination of Korea began with the signing of the Portsmouth Treaty. Next, Japan coerced and usurped many sovereign powers from the then totally helpless Korean court; the most blatant was the Japanese foreign ministry's takeover of the court's function in foreign affairs. Under this arrangement the Korean government was forbidden to enter any new international agreement independently. In addition, Japan was to station in Seoul its Resident-General, who was empowered to exercise the exclusive right to intervene in the court's political affairs. Overnight, with an array of forced agreements, the Japanese had all but transformed the sovereign state into a colonial subject. Despite ample, transparent evidence that the Korean court's surrender agreement was coerced under Japanese military threats, the Western powers chose to remain silent.

In early 1906, Ito Hirobumi, a leading Japanese elder statesman, arrived in Seoul to assume the office of the Resident-General, thus initiating Japan's notorious rule of Korea. The beginning of Japanese overlordship meant the end of the independent Korean state; shortly all the foreign legations except the Japanese had deserted Seoul. The West had given its formal approval for Japanese takeover of Korea. Ito's primary task at this time was to lay down a foundation for a permanent Japanese colonial administration. He carried out the task of dissolving the Korean government with ruthless suppression and unabashed intervention over Korea's political process. Quite contrary to his publicized restraint toward Russia during the pre-war period, he proved to be an aggressive political operative, a man of merciless drive destroying weaker competition.

Ito's systematic crusade of dismantling Daehahn's political infrastructure began with the disbanding of Korea's military. His coarse aggression reached the point of political piracy when he seized the Korean palace to force the sovereign emperor to resign on the ground that he had plotted the independence of his own kingdom. Far from being the benevolent protector, an image it had tried hard to project to the world, Japan finally abandoned its pretensions. It revealed its true nature as a brutal aggressor determined to dismantle the five-hundred-year-old Korean monarchy by using most inhumane schemes. More importantly, Japan had taken its initial steps toward its fateful venture to build an empire that would comprise the greater part of the Far East.

Japanese leaders, including Ito, well understood the Korean people's poor aptitude for waging a concerted resistance, but they foolishly misjudged the resilience of the Korean people. Because of their more deliberate temper, Koreans in the past had waged resistance that was more passive than either explosive or direct. Nevertheless, Japan should have known the fact that Koreans were fully capable of waging long, hard opposition to foreign aggression. The Hahns had never before surrendered their land for very long to foreign invaders no matter how powerful the adversaries were.

From the beginning Japan was attempting to extort not only political control but total control of Korea. Along with political consolidation, Japan appropriated a variety of economic interests with no less passion. Under the Resident-General's full protection, Japanese residents of Korea totally monopolized Korean commercial and industrial interests. Economic exploitation was spearheaded by growing Japanese land ownership in Korea as colonists from crowded Japan were allowed to purchase farm land in Korea. Ito's office, which had effectively replaced the Korean government, was taking extensive measures to promote the interests of fellow citizens at the expense of the Korean public. Still, the heavy financial burden to support these high-salaried Japanese employees was, of course, placed on the shoulders of the exploited nation.

Early in its Korean domination the Japanese government had encouraged its citizens to move to Korea to alleviate overcrowding in its home island. This open attempt to colonize must have caught the fancy of many Japanese citizens, as indicated by an explosive increase then in the number of Japanese residents in Korea. Increasing from only 20,000 in 1897 to 170,000 in 1910, Japanese who chose to move from their overcrowded homeland to Korea included all strata of society, including a large number of unemployed. Korea had become Japan's new frontier, greatly exciting both the imperialist government as well as the claustrophobic public.

Although it was left alone to face the fatal reality of the most predatory imperialism of the time, Korea was not going to accept a tragic fate without offering a desperate fight. Emperor Gojong, whose power and prestige were rapidly fading under Ito's overlordship, had made attempts to inform the world community about his nation's usurped sovereignty in order to enlist international pressure against Japanese aggression. Royal envoys were secretly sent to the second World Peace Conference held in the Netherlands and to President Roosevelt.[1] His appeal, however, failed to bring an intervention of any major world power. By then the rising power of Japan was respected enough worldwide to spoil such Korean attempts to stir world opinion.

While the Korean government's diplomatic endeavor to appeal to the world community produced no immediate results, the nation's anti-Japanese struggle was gaining momentum among diverse citizen groups. For the second time in its long and difficult history Korea faced a foreign aggressor whose intention was not just to establish a symbolic political domination over Korean kingdoms, as many Chinese empires had done before, but to liquidate the independent Hahn state. By then the conspiratorial intention of Japan was well understood by most citizens of the kingdom, and they expressed their anger and frustration in a traditional Confucian manner; many Confucian officials protested the Japanese intervention by committing suicide. Others organized military resistance, with varying degrees of success. The protest spread quickly from the court to farmers as the country finally realized that a nationwide mobilization was in order. Japan had become Korea's most hated enemy, one that had to be resisted with whatever means available.

In July 1907, Japan coerced Emperor Gojong to abdicate the throne in favor of the crown prince, Emperor Soonjong, a retaliation for his sending secret envoys to the second World Peace Conference. The court's high ranking officials who opposed Japan's political piracy were also forcibly removed from government service. Then Japan proceeded to extract from the rubber-stamp Korean government a new agreement which gave the Japanese Resident-General power to appoint all government positions. Furthermore, the vice ministry of each cabinet was to be filled by a Japanese national. At the same time, all other foreigners were forbidden to hold a government post in Korea. In reality, Japan had initiated a premeditated plot to control the Korean administrative system by filling all managerial and technical posts of the Korean government with Japanese citizens. By 1909 the number of Japanese occupying senior positions in the Korean government reached two thousand.

The anti-Japanese campaigns waged by Koreans at this early stage of the aggression were sporadic but inevitably bloody. The resistance took various forms, including direct attacks on Japanese forces and attacks on pro-Japanese officials and Japanese institutions. Nor was the campaign restricted to the Korean territory; an American employed by the Japanese government was gunned down in San Francisco, and Ito, the first Japanese Resident-General and the foremost architect of the Japanese takeover of Korea, was assassinated in Manchuria by a young Korean patriot named Ahn Joong-Geun.

The disbanded Korean military forces also waged spirited campaigns against the Japanese force.[2] Later they established bases in the nation's eastern mountain regions and continued to harass the Japanese with raids on installations. However, facing well-armed Japanese forces that never hesitated to respond to the Korean resistance with indiscriminate brutality, Korean resistance fighters quickly adopted a more suitable guerrilla warfare. Yet Korea was poorly endowed with the geography suitable for a long guerrilla war. As their operational freedom became increasingly restricted under the systematic attacks of a vastly reinforced Japanese force, many guerrilla fighters were forced cross the border to Manchuria, where they continued to engage in military raids on the Japanese.

The nation's young cultural institutions, mostly established during the 1880-1905 period, turned to critics of the Japanese aggression. Newspapers championed the independence movement by stirring public sentiments. The Independence Association continued to spearhead civil rights campaigns and encouraged a spirit of national unity through mass meetings. A number of political organizations initially established to foster civic education also became important forums for anti-Japanese intellectuals. Characteristically, the Japanese rulers in Seoul were not disposed to tolerate the Korean people's growing anti-Japanese sentiment; they employed harsh measures to suppress freedom of speech and assembly. Thus began Japan's long and infamous oppression of Korean intellectuals.

One institution that had been particularly prominent for the cause of the Korean independence movement was the Western missionaries. They generally opposed the Japanese aggression and supported Korean people's resistance movements. Particularly, Western-style schools set up by American missionaries became the backbone of Korea's modern educational system and in a variety of ways instilled a spirit of democratic independence in progressive-minded students. Naturally, many graduates of such schools later played a leading role in the nation's struggle against colonial rule. Encouraged by the constructive role of the schools founded by the missionaries, many Korean leaders turned to education as a means of building the foundation for national independence. By 1910 there were more than three hundred private schools in Korea, a clear indication that the nation's resistance against the Japanese was proceeding both by force of arms and by education of the nation's young citizens. The movement to propagate a spirit of independence and nationalism through education, however, met stiff Japanese resistance. By assigning their own teachers to all public schools, the Japanese authority strictly controlled the curricula of even private schools. Japan intended to block all avenues that might help strengthen the Koreans' nationalistic spirit against their foreign rulers.

Japanese aggression inevitably expanded to include suppression of Korean religious movements that were now more politically vocal and staunchly anti-Japanese. Chundogyo, a religious successor of the Dong-Hak movement, was a little tainted by the collaboration of one of its leaders with the Japanese, but as a whole remained a resolutely anti-Japanese movement. Grown to three hundred thousand followers by 1910, it developed several important social-educational institutions through which it later made significant contributions to the nation's anti-Japanese campaigns. Christian churches founded by American Protestant missionaries were, because of their dedication to freedom and equality, natural breeding grounds for leaders of the resistance movement. For religious protection and intellectual freedom, a large number of young Koreans turned to the Protestant churches and the mission schools. The American Presbyterian Mission-North and the American Methodist Episcopal Mission-North were the most prominent contributors to this cause at the time.[3] The YMCA, founded in 1903 in Seoul, was another outstanding Christian organization that made positive contributions to the cause of Korean independence. Although the Protestant groups were well known for their generally anti-Japanese attitude and sympathy with the Korean resistance groups, during the early period of its Korean domination the Japanese did not actively repress them for fear of offending the West.

As the formal annexation of Korea approached, Japan's oppression intensified throughout the nation, forcing a large number of the Korean resistance groups to flee abroad. The bordering states of Chinese Manchuria and Russian Siberia provided easy sanctuaries for most Korean resistance groups.[4] Along with the stream of political refugees, an increasing number of farmers who had lost their land under the Japanese rule crossed the border and later provided indispensable shelters for the resistance fighters. Some Koreans found their safe political refuge in the West; the United States provided an important forum, although limited and tentative, for the Korean independence movement. Such well-known figures as Syngman Rhee, the first president of the Korean republic some four decades later, were waging a diplomatic battle in Washington for the cause of Korean independence. By 1910 Korean independence organizations were also established in numerous other foreign locations including Mexico City, Vladivostok, Shanghai, Harbin, and many American cities. While Japan was getting ready to annex the kingdom, the Korean resistance groups were establishing political sanctuaries throughout the world to engage in the longest and most exhausting battle the Hermit Kingdom would ever fight in its long history.

On August 22, 1910, the day of the nation's ultimate humiliation, the rubber-stamp Korean government was forced to sign the Korean-Japanese Annexation Draft in a ceremony guarded by Japanese military force. After more than two millennia of constant resistance against the territorial attempts of its predatory neighbors, Korea finally succumbed to the determined plots of imperial Japan. The Hahn state, which had presided over the Korean peninsula with the proud spirit of Koguryo fighters, had to close its reign. Korea had become part of the rising sun.

The Koreans could have avoided the dark age of Japan's colonial rule by effectively managing the problematic properties of their unique geopolitics. More than anything, the Koreans had suffered from an overwhelming dependency on their powerful neighbors. Their passive adjustments to regional power shifts had been far from effective even in the most favorable circumstances. Korea had never been able to free itself from the constraint of being a weaker neighbor of two world-class powers. The nation's Confucian idealism, which had long blinded court officials to the reality of modern international power politics, had greatly contributed to the court's extreme inward-looking politics. Extensively experienced in exploitive   Chinese politics, but unprepared to deal with the utter ruthlessness of predatory Japan, the Koreans had to pay the ultimate penalty, the surrender of their sovereignty.

2. The Annexation

Japan's annexation of Korea was an inexcusable international aggression, regardless of its feeble justification. Although colonial expansion was a common relic of the nineteenth century and by no means limited to Japan, the forced expropriation of a sovereign state was inhumane and counterproductive. Japan might have argued that it was an alternative to chaos in Korea. But Japan's Korean aggression was really a premeditated political drive and part of its greater territorial ambition in the region. It was hardly an accidental result of unique circumstances of that particular era, as Japan contended. The nature of Japanese colonialism betrays any such fabricated excuse.

The historical records plainly verify the fact that Japan's territorial ambition over Korea was the island nation's enduring obsession. The evidence is too strong to even attempt manufacturing a plausible excuse. Japan's territorial attempt on Korea goes back to the Hideyoshi invasion in the sixteenth century. After Korea managed to repulse its rash ambition, Japan had resumed its historical stand as a remote bystander. In the late nineteenth century Japan's territorial interest in Korea resurfaced in the so-called Conquer Korea (Seikan) movement. It became highly popular in the early 1870's, particularly among those Japanese political leaders of strong samurai heritage. The pro-Conquer Korea party lost the argument to the more cautious faction in 1873. However, the disagreement was not over the basic scheme but the timing of such an undertaking. The question was not whether the conquest of its forever naive and myopic neighbor should be launched, but when the attempt should be made. Neither Japanese faction was bothered by the feeble excuse they had manufactured that the Chosun court had insulted the new Meiji government when Korea rejected Japan's request for an upgraded relationship. The fact that the Korean court had some legitimate concerns about the new Japanese government when it rejected the Japanese request had never been fully considered by the Japanese government.[5] Instead of further consultation that a normal international intercourse might have followed, Japan was eager to use the development as an excuse to launch a military strike.

Although the proponents of Korean conquest had accumulated formidable support under the pretext of avenging the Korean court's insult, pro-conquest and pro-expansion politics were derailed by opponents, who preferred more long-range but by no means a less imperial strategy. Notwithstanding the temporary setback imposed by the realists' persuasion that the Conquer Korea idea was premature (due to the lack of internal preparations to take on such a costly venture and the generally unfavorable international political climate of the time), many militant Japanese leaders never abandoned resolute territorial ambitions over Korea.[6] While the Korean conquest stalled, Japan undertook equally expansion-oriented moves, but over signally less costly objectives; it absorbed the Ryukyu Islands in 1872 and conquered Formosa in 1874. Korea, a much bigger and more strategic target, was left in its nominal state of independence while Japan pursued more discreet commercial, political domination. Yet being unable to comprehend the ever deepening ploys of methodical Japanese imperialism, the incoherent Korea court was unable to undertake the revolutionary reforms that might have foiled the Japanese scheme.

Although Japan had pursued its advance into Korea with relentless passion, it displayed some remarkable inconsistency at times. Largely reflecting its fluctuating strength, Japan's position in Korea was strong in the 1894-1895 period, which was followed by the weaker period in 1896. Then it gradually grew strong again after 1897. In addition to its political strength in Korea, other factors such as domestic economy, internal political situations, and particularly, international power relationships affected Japan's Korean drive. Japan drove to achieve basically two objectives before its final move to annex the peninsula in 1910: the dominating political influence over the faltering Korean court, and an international carte blanche for its activities in Korea. It achieved them through wars, shrewd politics, tradeoffs, and plain manipulation.

It was customary for Japan to claim that it did not have any territorial ambition other than commercial interests in Korea, even though its aggression was widely acknowledged to be conjured up as a pure imperial ambition and to have foreshadowed Hitler's imposition of the German protectorate over Bohemia and Moravia in 1939.[7] To conceal its cynical intention from the world community, Japan had fully utilized every opportunity to portray itself as a champion of Korean independence and as a benevolent neighbor anxious only to lead a backward kingdom into the light of modern civilization. Contrary to its diplomatic disguise, what Japan had pursued was simple approval, or more accurately, acquiescence of the world's leading powers for its total domination of Korea, which, it quibbled, would remedy Korea's deplorable conditions.

In 1905 Japan signed the Taft-Katsura memorandum with America and renewed its alliance with Britain. It had managed to obtain an international carte blanche for its freedom to exploit Korea. International acquiescence served two purposes for Japan: (1) in Japanese aggression the world powers were expected not to intervene on behalf of Korea, a distant and minor state, and (2) an international silence would be understood as a sufficient admission that Korea was a legitimate security concern for Japan.[8] Japan had never ceased to emphasize its security concerns in Korea and often succeeded in so convincing the world powers.

After its victory over China, Japan's foremost security concerns were the probable Russian advance into the region and an overriding interest in keeping the Russians from seizing a predominant position in Korea.[9] When Russia was defeated, Japan manufactured another excuse to justify its aggressive stand in Korea. It then claimed that its position was closely linked to the future of Manchuria. The open display of such strategic interests could not be interpreted as a mere speculation but a definite policy statement. Japan had contemplated its future actions in the region based on its militant view that the island nation's immediate expansion could be obtained only in Manchuria and Korea.[10] As history bespeaks, Japanese ambition was not confined to Korea. Japan needed Korea as a convenient stepping stone to its advance into continental Asia. Yet it had been Korea, the perpetual victim of its unique geography, which provided the first leg for Japanese imperialism. Japan continued to manufacture covetous justifications at the expense of Korea, and the world powers were inclined to buy them for their own short-term self-interests.

At the conclusion of the Russo-Japanese war, Japan deployed another highly deceptive excuse that its intervention in Korea was needed lest Korea revert to its old habit of imprudently entering treaties with foreign countries.[11] By portraying itself as a considerate neighbor, Japan persuaded a mostly indifferent world community that Korea, the hopeless Hermit Kingdom that could not handle its own affairs, needed guidance. In spite of its thin disguise, Japan's meddling in Korean politics became progressively bolder and imperial as its international status was ascending, the direct result of its impressive military victories over powerful rivals.

Japan was doing everything, including spreading false propaganda about Korea to the West, to justify its ensuing action in Korea. Under an intense Japanese public relations campaign, the West had become more inclined to believe that Japan would provide Korea some desperately needed guidance and advice of a benevolent nature. There is no question that Korea did need fresh currents of ideas from the outside. Nevertheless, the West overlooked two pivotal questions when it threw its tragic though tacit support to Japan's aggression. First, the West chose to ignore the moral justification of imposed reforms over the nation, despite the reigning Korean emperor's efforts to inform the West about the coercive nature of the Japanese advance into his country. Most Western powers would have had little difficulty comprehending the overwhelming evidence that Korea was capable of tending its own national affairs if the predatory interference of outsiders ceased. Second, the West failed to scrutinize Japan's public claim that it intended only to provide some friendly advice to Korea, a statement that was contradictory in the light of its uncanny territorial ambition over Manchuria. If the Western powers had been more objective and critical of Japanese intentions in the region, they could have drawn a conclusion entirely different from the Japanese version.

Just as the European states did in their Asian and African colonies, Japan advanced a greatly exaggerated notion that Korea was a backward kingdom wandering around outside of the civilized world. Japan was anxious to prove to the world that the declining Korean dynasty did not share interests and values acceptable to the civilized world. In spite of its elaborate public relations efforts, what Japan was really apprehensive of was that the Korean court's independent conduct of international relations could become detrimental to the island nation's political-economic interests. Having already established itself as the foremost power in Korea, imperial Japan had no problem inventing its exaggerated role as the self-appointed Korean regency.

Japan no doubt understood the extensive implications of colonizing the Korean peninsula. When Japan considered its ambitious imperialistic options, the annexation of Korea could have been the most tempting avenue to pursue. In all fairness, Japan had a right to put the interests of its own nation first in international relations, however revolting it might be. Whether that had to include such a flagrant violation of another nation's sovereignty is an entirely different matter.

Japan's imperial ambition was obviously encouraged by the defective but pervasive notion that a weak and troubled country of strategic importance had to be controlled by a stable power even with oppressive measures, if necessary. The clumsy justification for the purely imperial, self-serving sophistry was that the peace and progress of the world are more important than the sovereignty of any individual nation - obviously referring to small and powerless ones rather than powerful nations. The world's major imperial powers conveniently chose to ignore the fact that most disturbances associated with weaker nations were being stirred not by themselves but by other rapacious world powers.

Contrary to their feeble justification, the Japanese annexation of Korea was a premeditated, unprovoked aggression. The ambivalence shown in some Japanese political and ideological circles and the enigmatic behavior of Ito Hirobumi, the first Japanese Resident-General in Seoul, were nothing but the results of evasive tactical maneuvers used to portray the aggression as a benevolent act. It is true that Japan's liberal party had initially opposed the expansionist attempt to conquer Korea and instead supported the efforts of the Korean progressive party to let Koreans modernize the kingdom by themselves. Nevertheless, the voice of the opposition had been weak and short lived; the minority subsequently supported the powerful Ito-led oligarchy that favored militant expansion but with a more gradual advance than the outright conquest demanded by the reactionaries. In the end, the liberals became advocates of Japanese leadership in Eastern Asia, supporting the nation's militarism. Like their reactionary counterparts, they were more interested in the island nation's glory than in Korea's sovereign right and followed the ideological line of oligarchy, which had long contended that Korea had no prospect of establishing democracy itself.[12] When the annexation decision was reached, Japanese liberals gave emphatic support and became willing collaborators with the aggressive oligarchy.

Ito's policy in Korea did not furnish any credible argument against the consensus that Japan had premeditated the annexation scheme. His systematic appropriation of diplomatic and later many domestic powers from the Korean court - the forced abdication of the emperor, the disbandment of the Korean army, and the brutal repression of the Korean resistance - were hardly considered the best examples of his anti-Conquer Korea credentials. Ito's credentials for being not only a pro-Conquer proponent but the leader of the cynical ploy were impeccable. The records of the Ito administration in Korea plainly contradict the claim that Japan intended to achieve the reform of Korea without annexing or resorting to brutality; they also defeat the moral responsibility concept of imperialism, the notion that advanced peoples had obligations to those less advanced to offer guidance and advice. Ito may not have been a hypocrite, but he was a man of vast international experience and political savvy who exerted his best efforts to advance Japan's imperial interests, even if it meant the sacrifice of a sovereign state. From the very beginning Japan intended to take Korea by any means, including military force, and keep it for long, if not in perpetuity.

In the annexation scheme, Japan's interests were thoroughly considered, while Korea's interests or basic rights were summarily ignored. Ironically, Japan's profound Korean conspiracy was supported by some naive Korean officials who had hoped that the Japanese courtship would bring a new and promising beginning for the Korean nation. They were kept misinformed by the Japanese officials about the nature of annexation. Consequently, the demise of the Korean state was greatly facilitated by none other than these misguided Korean officials.

To the Korean court the threat of Japanese invasion was not new. Ever since Hideyoshi's invasion in the 1590s Japan remained a serious security threat to the kingdom. Under the Tokugawa Shogunate such direct hostility ceased, but the threat of Japanese piracy remained more than a casual nuisance to the court. At times the court was under dire pressure from the pirates. The Conquer-Korea movement under the Meiji government was also known to the court. Yet it was able to build neither the national strength nor the political unity to stave off the Japanese ambition to conquer the kingdom. It took thirty-seven years for Japan's Conquer Korean faction to achieve its objective. During this lengthy period the Korean court should have been able to take appropriate measures to counter the aggression if the kingdom's creative energy had been united under a truly capable leader. Unfortunately, the court was not endowed with outstanding politicians. Ching was served by remarkably capable and worldly Li Hung-Chang, and Japan was fortunate to have Ito Hirobumi and his capable political allies. Tragically, Korea did not have a single leader of comparable stature in this period of great upheaval.

The last two monarchs of the Chosun dynasty served particularly poorly, although the serious effects of hostile foreign interventions should not be discounted. The Chosun court under the stewardship of Emperor Gojong was particularly in disarray until the last moment of its tragic mandate. The vacillating monarch, in spite of his good intentions and tender disposition, was politically naive. Moreover, his reign was dominated by his father in the early period and his queen and her faction later, a rare and unfortunate phenomenon for the kingdom where male domination had been long accepted. Emperor Gojong's harsh suppression of the Dong-Hak and of the reform movements led by the kingdom's progressive intellectuals was self-defeating and in the end brought the military intervention of both China and Japan. Gojong's internal exile to the Russian legation was not only unorthodox but a poorly conceived maneuver. Considering the fact that the court's inconsistent, amateurish foreign relations had done the greatest harm to the nation's aspiration to remain free and independent, the nation's political leadership should have accepted most of the blame for the historic humiliation of the Hahn state.

In view of history, it is evident that the United States should have been able to check the Japanese ambition in Korea. Instead, it gave the Japanese the most sought-after international backing for its aggressive advance in Korea through the Taft-Katsura memorandum. Washington took a position equating American interests in the Philippines with Japanese interests in Korea, and thus indirectly endorsed Japan's ambition to establish suzerainty over Korea. In reality, two imperial powers had agreed, in effect, that Korea was unfit to maintain its sovereign status in a world where the law of survival of the fittest prevailed. America's unwillingness to intervene on its behalf was most unfortunate for Korea, yet it represented the political power equation in the Pacific at the time. America was a new and rapidly growing power, but its sphere of domination had reached only the Philippines in Eastern Asia. America was not yet a power that could overcome the ambitious Asiatic power and reach the remote Hermit Kingdom. America needed the next forty years to build the power that eventually reached almost every corner of the world.

By formally annexing Korea, Japan had achieved its long-standing objectives; by securing the peninsula as its legal domain, regardless of the overwhelming disapproval shown by the Korean public and the monarch, it now possessed a convenient bridgehead for its more ambitious drive on the Asian mainland. It also meant that Russophobiac Japan had successfully denied Russia a strategic base to threaten the island nation across the Korea Strait. Commercially, the peninsula was to serve as a consumer market for Japanese products while providing raw materials for the now expanding Japanese industrial machine. Annexation was not merely the "better-safe-than-sorry" approach but the culmination of Japan's long premeditated territorial expansion, a drive engineered by the unity and determination only the single-minded island nation could have provided. On the other hand, Korea managed to squander the precious opportunities to safeguard its precarious independence by remaining blind to rapidly evolving international politics and indulging in exhausting political infighting. In all fairness, the foremost blame should be placed upon Korea itself. Consequently, Korea was to be punished for its failure to protect its territorial integrity with the humiliating loss of its sovereignty.

3. Abusive Colonial Rule

The bitter experience of Japanese colonial rule remains too emotional an issue for contemporary Koreans. Nevertheless, Japan's colonial occupation was a most epochal event for Korea, an event to which the nation's current successes as well as its difficulties can be traced to a certain degree, directly or indirectly. The colonial rule that was abolished at the end of World War II was sufficiently long to leave a lasting legacy for the nation, although contemporary Koreans tend to view the period with only highly emotional indignation. Nevertheless, it is incorrect to dismiss the colonial period as a total loss for the nation because during the time Korea underwent significant societal transition, even though the change was brutally and indiscriminately pushed by the colonial administration. Although motivated by its own selfish reasons, imperial Japan did help Korea in laying some limited social infrastructures valuable to modern Korea: the nation's education system and transportation networks are prominent examples. No doubt the human and economic sufferings Korea sustained during the period were far greater than the limited benefits the colonial administration managed to generate. In spite of deep emotion, it is necessary for Koreans to accord to the colonial administration some deserved credit while reproaching it for the damages and harms inflicted on Koreans to such an unforgivable magnitude. To the present day, however, a systematic evaluation of the Japanese colonial rule in Korea has not been made.

From the beginning Japan's colonial administration in Korea was sustained by its large scale military-police force. Imperial Japan intended to use this force to check the Korean independent fighters in Manchuria and Siberia, to apply military pressure to Chinese Manchuria, and to provide support to the colonial administration in Seoul. The Japanese army directed campaigns against Korean resistance fighters based in the border regions, while its military police, who were given control of the civilian police, became the principal means for the colonial administration's suppression of anti-Japanese activities in Korea. The Japanese military police had become the most dreaded enforcers of the colonial directives, and their brutal oppression became the most conspicuous grievance of the Korean public throughout Japanese colonial rule.

Even before the annexation agreement was formally signed, Japan had been exceptionally successful in accumulating vast commercial interests in Korea, including fishing rights, railroad concessions, communication rights, and timber and mining rights. After annexation, the Japanese economic domination of Korea became virtually complete. Japan's encroachment was most villainous in its systematic efforts to control Korea's agricultural land. In no time the colonial rulers had adopted laws that allowed the Japanese to own land in Korea. With the colonial administration's open political support, a large number of Japanese residents in Korea readily became owners of choice farm lands. The organized pillage of Korean farm land was not limited to Japanese individuals, however. Japan established the infamous Oriental Development Company in Korea with the purpose of seizing Korean land; as a consequence, it quickly became the largest landholder in Korea. As the systematic seizure of farm land by the Oriental Development Company and Japanese individuals continued, farm land owned by the Koreans was progressively reduced. The farmers who were forced to surrender their farms to the Japanese became tenants for subsistence earnings or homeless wanderers. Many landless farmers emigrated to Manchuria or Siberia for land and freedom.

Japanese infringement in the areas of commerce and finance was equally methodical. Japanese capital was not only allowed to enter Korea but also encouraged to overwhelm the backward Korean economy. Colonial laws adopted by the Resident-General singularly favored the Japanese but made it virtually impossible for native Koreans to set up new businesses. As a result, the overwhelming majority of large firms in Korea were owned and operated by the Japanese. Many of Japan's major banks, utility companies, and industrial giants established their Korean operations, securely protected by the colonial administration. Japan was methodically successful in its endeavor to colonize Korea commercially, as its ventures were well organized and implemented with harsh determination.

One of imperial Japan's difficult tasks in Korea was public education, an area that proved to be even more important than the commercial activities. In order to justify its colonial rule, Japan was obliged to provide Koreans limited opportunities for modern education, although it plainly realized the risks of having a large number of educated Koreans. In spite of their great reluctance, the colonial masters proceeded with dual systems; both traditional and modern educational systems were adopted. Traditional Korean learning institutions such as Hyanggyo and Sudang of Confucian learning were left operational. In addition, a few modern schools were established. As might be expected, Japan's efforts to provide learning opportunities to Korean children were by no means strenuous; on the contrary, the learning opportunities for Koreans, particularly in higher education, were prohibitively limited. All but a selected few were denied education at post-elementary schools, making basic education at elementary schools terminal for most Korean children. Even elementary schools were so limited in number that many children were unable to attend any school at all. By 1916, Korea had 447 elementary schools, seventy-four vocational schools, three high schools, and four colleges. For a nation of more than twenty million subjects, the colonial administration's entire school system was pitifully inadequate.

While it tentatively supported limited public education for its colonial subjects, imperial Japan was most anxious to keep Korean youths from developing aspirations for national independence. A strict control on instructional content was enforced in every school regardless of grade. Nonetheless, as apprehended by the Japanese colonial administration, the nation's school system became the bastion of the aspiring Korean independence movement. In spite of the colonial rulers' extensive surveillance, Korean teachers never gave up their self-appointed responsibility to instill a spirit of national independence and anti-Japanese sentiment into their receptive students. The nation's vocal student movement was sprouting under the watchful eyes of the Japanese colonial police.

To imperial Japan, the public education system in Korea was no more than another colonial tool devised to teach Japanese values and morals, a first step toward molding the children into the Emperor's subjects, although they were to remain second class subjects. Still, the colonial administration's dilemma over public education continued unresolved; Japanese officials understood the need to expand public education to build strong public support for their colonial policies, yet the more educated turned into anti-colonial activists. In the end, the Japanese resorted to a tightly controlled public education along with intensified efforts to assimilate Koreans into Japanese culture. Their attempt produced only dismal results; their infamous colonial oppression failed to destroy the Koreans' budding aspirations for independence. Although Korea's colonial education system was grossly inadequate and artificially regulated by its colonial rulers, it became the foundation for the nation's long delayed and circuitous journey toward modernization.

Korea's anti-Japanese movement was harshly suppressed from its inception. As a result, its armed resistance against Japan's colonial administration was vigorous but brief. The early independence fighters were quickly overwhelmed by Japan's harsh, large scale military assaults nationwide. The poorly equipped and inexperienced Korean resistance fighters did not stand a chance against Japan's well-equipped, modern military force. Shortly after formal annexation the Japanese army had largely subdued the small Korean resistance force by denying it meaningful sanctuaries in the country. As Japan's military assaults on the resistance continued in the country, the majority of Korean independence fighters gradually shifted their operational bases to Manchuria and Siberia. Others were forced to go underground in Korea.

Throughout colonial rule most Korean independence fighters were constrained to remain in foreign territories and never gained a military strength powerful enough to offer the colonial ruler a credible armed contest. Most armed clashes between Japanese forces and Korean independence fighters took place in regions along the nation's northern border. Here the resistance movement established its operational bases, supported by the growing number of Korean residents in the region.

In the territorial scheme of greater imperial Japan, Korea was not only an important conquest but also a critical linkage to Japan's even greater objectives, Manchuria, and eventually China itself. As long as its megalomaniac territorial ambition remained as the engine of its political drive, it was imperative for colonial Japan to keep Korea under its firm control. Japan could not relinquish its colonial rule in Korea unless it abandoned its ambition to control Manchuria and northern China. It did not display any such intentions, even though its China scheme had experienced a setback when the British rejected its plot to intervene in the affairs of the disintegrating Middle Kingdom right after the Ching dynasty was overthrown by the Chinese revolutionary forces in 1911.

Japan's China scheme was greatly facilitated by opportunistic Japanese manipulation at the outbreak of World War I. In the very beginning Japan quickly declared war against Germany, using the pretext of the Anglo-Japanese alliance. Along with this expeditious political move, Japan proceeded to capture jiaozhou Bay, the territory that Germany had leased from China. Japan made the war an extraordinary opportunity to advance its China ambition.

In 1915, Japan presented the Chinese government with the infamous "twenty-one demands." These demands were followed by an arrogant ultimatum that threatened an unspecified retaliatory action in case the Chinese government did not accede to Japanese wishes. Japan, grown to feel confident of its ability to coerce the world's most populous nation, demanded an extension of its lease on the Guangdong territory, the South Manchurian Railway, and the Andong-Mukudan Railway. In addition, it also demanded in the twenty-one demands extensive commercial concessions in Shandong, south Manchuria, eastern Inner Mongolia, Central China, and various diplomatic and political concessions. For all practical purposes, what Japan had sought at the time was complete economic as well as significant political domination of China. The fact that Japan insisted upon unrestricted freedom in south Manchuria and eastern Inner Mongolia for reasons of national security was indicative of its extensive territorial ambition in East Asia.

Japan's aggressive exploitation of China was met with generally negative reactions from the world powers. Japan regarded Britain's concern with its "twenty-one demands" to be friendly. Yet it perceived Washington's disapproval of these demands to be distinctively hostile. The United States objected to Japanese aggression on the ground that it impaired the political and territorial integrity of the Republic of China. Although the American protest did not reverse the Japanese advance in China, it markedly cooled the two nations' cordial relationship and eventually became a significant restraint to Japanese imperial ambition in the region.

America's firm stand against Japanese aggression in China provided the Korean resistance movement with a powerful lift. The Koreans were hopeful that the American reaction would help educate the world community about the true nature of Japan's reckless imperialism. Furthermore, President Wilson's progressive Fourteen Points proposal, which was advanced as a basis for the treaties of peace at the Paris Peace Conference, excited the hard-pressed Korean independent movement. What particularly caught the attention of the Korean people was Wilson's principle of self-determination, which declared that every person has a right to choose his own government freely and not to be governed against his will. Wilson had given a potent emotional and political boost to the Korean people's struggle against their colonial masters. Koreans celebrated Wilson's self-determination doctrine with spontaneous anti-Japanese campaigns nationwide.

Against the backdrop of the encouraging international developments, Koreans staged daring multidimensional protests against Japanese colonial rule. Intended to indict Japan's unjustified imprisonment of Korea to the world community, various diplomatic initiatives were taken by the Korean resistance movement based in China. In 1917 it sent a representative to the World Socialist Conference in Stockholm and another to the Conference of Small Nations in New York. In 1919 it sent a delegation to the Paris Peace Conference to plead the nation's just cause. Contacts were also made with Russia to seek her political support. Korean residents of Siberia, Japan, and the United States also were taking measures to solidify their resistance movements. In spite of the Korean people's renewed attempts to enlist the political support of the world community, the Western powers were not quite ready for confrontation with one of the premier powers on behalf of the faraway country. Consequently the Korean people's just appeals to the world's conscience failed to receive significant political support.

Their vain efforts to rally world opinion against imperial Japan had convinced the Korean activists that a nationwide protest would be needed to enunciate their grievances and to bring international pressure on Japan.

Subsequently, the nation's resistance movement organized a massive nationwide protest under the watchful eyes of the Japanese military police. Considering the draconian circumstance, the clandestine preparation went remarkably well, and the execution was even more impressive. On March 1, 1919, Koreans, who were ridiculed as not having any concept of nationhood or patriotic spirit, simultaneously staged thousands of unarmed protest rallies nationwide. More than two million Koreans participated in about 1,500 rallies.[13] These peaceful protests were a truly remarkable landmark in the nation's resistance history. Predictably, the colonial masters, renowned for their harsh and single-minded suppression, responded to the protests with indiscriminate slaughter. Japanese forces killed more than 7,500 unarmed Korean citizens. This protest, called the March First Movement, is still being celebrated as the Korean nation's most cherished patriotic uprising.

The spirit of the March First Movement was well reflected in the "declaration of independence" signed by the nation's thirty-three leading citizens and read in public at every rally throughout the nation. In it the protesters declared that the nation had its sovereign right to be free and independent and decried Japanese aggression. The protesters demanded that Japan be a neighbor that would contribute to both regional and world peace. While reflecting on the manipulations and intrusions committed by Japan, they eloquently stated their willingness to forego the past mistakes and forgotten promises of the Japanese for the new era and new order in the region. Koreans made abundantly clear that the nation demanded independence but not revenge. Yet, demonstrating their civilized manner, the protesters solemnly declared that the rallies would proceed in a peaceful fashion and without resorting to violence. The protest participants, armed only with the unquenchable desire for freedom and independence, kept their promise and faced the Japanese force with no resistance. It was more than a decade before Mahatma Gandhi utilized similar tactics against India's British colonial masters.

Notwithstanding a moral victory, the March First protests failed to break the iron grip of Japan's colonial rule of Korea. The protests were fully justifiable and spectacular in displaying the Korean people's moral anger and political maturity, yet they did not possess corresponding political strength to force the colonial rulers to yield to Koreans' demands. On the contrary, in the aftermath of the protests Japan not only intensified its drive to indoctrinate the Korean people but pursued its China ambition even more vigorously. By then, with steady encroachment and manipulation, Japan was on the verge of achieving its grand dream of colonizing the Middle

Kingdom.

Although the world community as a whole was not quite ready to extend its support to the Koreans, the March First Movement, with blood and sacrifice, successfully indicted the Japanese oppression in the court of world opinion. Notwithstanding a postponed final verdict, the cause of the Korean people's sufferings and aspirations had become common knowledge within the world community. Even imperial Japan's characteristically ruthless and single-minded aggression could not long silence the Hahn people's resilient spirit.

4. Birth of the Provisional Government

Although the March First protests were far from effective in extracting direct political concessions from the Japanese, they were nevertheless a glorious success for the Korean nation. More than anything the nationwide protests helped achieve a sense of national unity. Through their brave confrontation with colonial brutality, Koreans shared a sense of common fate and of shared destiny. The movement brought about a national awakening that was to haunt the colonial masters thereafter.

The March First Movement was carried out by people of all ages, classes, and regions. It was the nation's first experience in which the public willingly participated in organized protests demanding national independence and freedom from foreign tyranny. Ironically, under the burden of colonial oppression Korea's modern nationalism surfaced with conviction and harmony, which had been rare in its history. This would be profoundly more important in the future than some cosmetic concessions Japan could have made to appease the situation.

Destroying once and for all the fabricated excuses for Japan's colonial annexation of Korea, the protests rejected the oppressive colonial rule so flatly that never again were the Japanese able to pretend that annexation had been invited by Koreans. For imperial Japan it was a rude awakening from the fantasy that Korea, ignorant and soft as it might have been in the oppressor's eyes, could be controlled by force. It was a courageous display of national character that again convinced some Japanese leaders that they could not coerce the Hahn nation indefinitely, no matter what tactics they might employ. Yet imperial Japan was still too deeply immersed in its grandiose colonial dream to comprehend the grave consequences of the fatal course it was pursuing.

The protests helped resurrect in the mind of the Korean people a profound confidence about their ability to stand against the overwhelming enemy. Through the massive nationwide protests, a new and fresh experience for the docile Confucian nation, Korea had finally displayed its maturity in transforming cherished individualism-oriented values and morals into civic responsibility and nationalism. Under the most trying circumstances Korea took a giant step toward building modern nationhood.

Despite the protests, Japan intensified its merciless economic exploitation, disregarding the worsening economic hardships suffered by Korean farmers. In 1933 more than half of Korea's total rice production was expropriated by the colonial administration to feed the expanding Japanese population. On the other hand, the woeful plight of exploited, increasingly landless farmers remained untended and ignored by the colonial rulers. Under the mounting exploitation, Korea's impoverished agriculture had become its most convenient sacrifice. Japan's systematic exploitation of Korean resources was, however, not limited to agriculture; various mineral resources were also heavily exploited to feed the burgeoning Japanese industrial machine.

After the conclusion of World War I, the Japanese government took calculated measures to encourage its industries to set up factories in Korea. Japan did not overlook Korea's advantageous location for producing a large quantity of war materials for the probable Sino-Japanese war. Shortly, government-sponsored industrial transplantation had turned Korea into a logistical base for Japan's impending conquest of Manchuria and China. Korea was called upon to produce Japan's war materials, feed its population, and provide raw materials for its industries. As the strategic importance of the peninsula became even more critical with the gradual progress of its China ambition, Japan further tightened its oppressive rule of Korea.

One significant by-product of the enlightening March First Movement was the formation of the Korean Provisional Government in Shanghai, China, which became the symbol of the Korean people's aspiration for their independence. It was not only the symbol of Korea's defiance of Japanese colonialism but also of its clear intention to open a new era once colonial rule was repulsed. In designing the structure of their new government-in-exile, the Korean leaders conveyed the nation's yearning for a modern democratic state. They were unanimous in wanting a clean departure from the humiliating past by replacing the Chosun dynasty's antiquated monarchy with a modern democratic system. The new republic, envisioned to have a freely elected president, legislators, and an independent judiciary branch, was to guarantee freedom of speech, press, religion, and assembly. Korea's political leaders adopted a governmental form for their new nation akin to the American political system, thus demonstrating their admiration of America and its governing philosophy. Summarily abolished was the Korean state's two-thousand-year-old political institutions, the monarchy and the nobility. The fact that this radical political departure, though it was a provisional-government-in-exile, was accomplished without any serious ideological squabbling was indicative of how the Korean intellectuals and independent activists felt about the old system of the Chosun dynasty. The nation had matured enough to comprehend the need to adopt a modern political system. Korean leaders had realized the fact that the old-fashioned, submissive system had brought the nation to its ultimate humiliation.

In reality, the Chosun dynasty was destroyed by Japanese imperialism even before the annexation. Yet the adoption of a republican system for the provisional government served as the nation's formal declaration that the antiquated monarchy was over. With its typical manner of calm, Korea had finally buried its perpetually oppressive, corrupt, and ineffectual royalty. Along with the monarchy, its heinous accomplice, the nobility was also officially abolished by the leaders of the new republic. Thus, Korea's modern political structure was born as a Provisional-Government-in-Exile.

The erection of the Provisional Government was an immensely important political milestone for modern Korea. It was a clear and open expression of the Korean people's immediate aspiration and distant dream for their political future. It also provided a rallying point for the nation's political leadership and its resistance fighters who were scattered all over Manchuria and Siberia. Nevertheless, it had never fulfilled the people's ardent expectation of becoming a political organization capable of consolidating the nation's diverse anti-Japanese energies. The exiled government remained largely a symbolic institution until the nation recovered its sovereignty.

Notwithstanding the Korean people's awakened aspiration to be an independent nation, Japan persisted in pushing its ultimate dream, a total absorption of Korea into the island nation. Under the cynical scheme the citizens of the Hahn nation, renamed as the "special territory" of Japan, were prohibited from using their own language and were forced to Japanize their names. Frenetic cultural assimilation campaigns prohibited the Koreans from engaging in anything even remotely related to traditional Korean values and sentiments. The so-called "Naesun Ilche," the unification of the inland (the Japanese version of its home island) and Chosun, was under forced implementation. As the third decade of the twentieth century dawned, Japan's colonial grip over Korea remained firm and resolute. The heroic March First Movement managed to inflict only a small dent in the determined Japanese colonial scheme. The sad reality was that in spite of its growing awareness and aspiration for independent nationhood, occupied Korea simply did not have resources to confront unilaterally the military and industrial might of imperial Japan.

The victimization of Korea by Japanese colonialism was, of course, an outgrowth of Japanese imperialism. Demonstrating its well-conceived premeditation, Japan's advance was undertaken with full international collaboration. Thus, when Korea was unable to untie the Japanese colonial shackle by itself, the world powers had a moral obligation to share the burden of punishing Japan's colonialism. However, the existing international power structure of the 1920s could not promise such an intervention. Koreans could only endure the colonial master's exacerbating oppression, the multidimensional pressure ranging from cultural assimilation to outright economic exploitation. The end of Japan's oppression seemed as remote as ever.

Although the prospect of defeating Japan militarily was fading, Korean independence fighters continued to wage hopeless battles against the Japanese. With whatever means at their disposal they confronted the enemy on the windswept Manchurian plain, in Siberia, in Shanghai, and even in unsympathetic Washington. Many intellectuals undertook highly effective passive resistance in Korea. The Korean people's determination to drive out the colonial master grew in proportion to the ruler's resolution to annihilate the nation forever. It was a lonely but spirited struggle and a trying time for Korean survival instincts.

During this period the fledgling international communist movement found a receptive audience among the hard-pressed Korean resistance movements. The appeal of Marxism-Leninism was strong for intellectuals, whose own country was occupied by an imperial power backed by the capitalist West. Following the footsteps of the Chinese Communist Party, founded in 1921, Koreans founded their own communist party in 1925, which was to serve as the ideological backbone of the Korean socialist movement. Korea's new socialists readily accepted the communist ideology, believing their nation a victim of a ruthless capitalist system. The ideology held that capitalism is bound over the course of time to grow to the point that industrialized capitalists would need overseas markets in which to sell surplus products and from which to acquire raw materials. Korean socialists regarded the communist theory as an accurate description of the behavior of imperial capitalists, one of which was certainly Japan. Koreans adopted communism primarily as an avenue to defeat Japanese imperialism.

To liberal Korean independent activists, the communists' interpretation of the destructive nature of capitalism and its claim of the impending destruction of capitalistic imperialism were powerful attractions. In addition, the success of the Bolshevik Revolution and Russia's friendly overtures had convinced those despondent Korean resistance fighters that communism was an ideology capable of salvaging their nation from Japanese occupation. Because communism was adopted by the Korean activists as essentially a political and ideological weapon against the Japanese, there was no immediate cleavage between Korean communists and their non-communists confederates. For a while communists remained cooperative with other Korean independence movements. However, the inevitable conflicts later developed between the two groups. In the late 1920s communists broke all relations with non-communist groups when Comintern, the international communist organization, abandoned the policy of a united front. By this division Korea's anti-Japanese resistance suffered a major setback; after that time communists remained a separate resistance movement until the end of the colonial occupation. The Japanese did not overlook this ominous development, and Korea's germinating communism was forcibly suppressed.   In 1930 the central structure of Korea's communist movement was crushed by the Japanese authorities while its activities in China and Japan were absorbed by the communist party of each respective country. Although the socialist idealism eagerly accepted by the Korean intellectual community was temporarily frozen out, the movement was by no means totally eradicated. The spirit of socialism remained strong; going underground, it often surfaced in frequent labor disputes between oppressive colonial industrialists and exploited Korean workers.[14]

5. The Pacific War and Liberation

As colonial rule entered its third decade, imperial Japan did not relax its rule nor did occupied Korea resign from its determined struggle against oppression. Yet Korea's resistance abroad had reached a stalemate; its guerrilla warfare in Manchuria remained the backbone of the military resistance but became only a gesture with no military significance against the mighty Japanese military. The desperate diplomatic endeavors waged by the exiled Provisional Government in Shanghai and others in Washington had produced no breakthrough.

Contrary to the impasse abroad, resistance within the nation escalated; a growing number of Korean citizens came to participate in anti-Japanese activities, often expressing their defiance by boycotting Japanese goods. However, it was students who ignited another round of explosive, nationwide anti-Japan protests during the period, the most significant being the student revolt of 1929, which started in the southern city of Kwangju and spread throughout the nation. For more than four months 54,000 students participated in anti-Japanese protests and openly confronted the brutal Japanese occupation forces. This made it clear again that the nation would not accept Japanese rule regardless of whatever appeasement and oppressive measures were tried. Japan's ability to exploit Korea remained solid, yet it became increasingly clear that the colonial ruler signally failed to gain the support of the Korean people's mind and soul. The Japanese entered the peninsula as a hostile conqueror and remained as a hated occupation force. Imperial Japan had never been able to elevate its rule of Korea to that of a constructive imperialist administration giving the ruled what they could not otherwise enjoy; Japan never conferred even a superficial improvement of socioeconomic well-being nor a sense of partnership in pursuing human aspirations and dignity.[15] In the midst of defiant rejection and equally determined oppression, the public suffered cruel hardship both for lack of political freedom and basic commodities.

Undeterred by its inability to persuade the Korean public to accept colonial rule, Japan was ready to try its grand scheme of subjugating the Middle Kingdom; in 1932, she managed to set up a puppet regime, Manchukuo, in Chinese Manchuria. With this aggression Japan removed Chinese sovereignty from Manchuria and finally became the master of this resource-rich and strategic region. By taking the region of former Koguryo territory and a strategic outpost from which it could be able to exert direct military pressure on both China and Russia, Japan drastically altered the political map of East Asia. The new Chinese Republic, too feeble and divided to challenge Japan's growing power, nevertheless did not surrender the region without offering military resistance. The second Sino-Japanese military conflict was soon to become a reality.

By 1937 armed clashes between the Japanese and the Chinese had escalated into all-out war. Japan's imperial attempt to turn North China into a second Manchukuo, a Japanese puppet regime, led to the full scale military confrontation between these two Asiatic giants. Unlike the first Sino-Japanese war, however, the second one was a long struggle of attrition that ended only by Japan's unconditional surrender to the Allies in 1945. Japan's territorial ambition on the Asian mainland was thwarted not by an Asian power but by the Western powers. Japan suffered an ultimate defeat and had to relinquish its long, hard-fought ambition to become a nation of the Asian mainland. Yet its megalomaniac craving inflicted serious political upheaval on its neighbors; by thoroughly exhausting the Chinese Nationalists, Japan's long and harsh occupation helped the Chinese communists conquer mainland China. In 1949 the Chinese communists drove out their rival to Taiwan and seized total control of the Middle Kingdom. The legacy of Japan's colonial occupation was no less tragic in Korea; it provided a direct cause for the nation's division even before it recovered its lost sovereignty.

As expected, Japan's full-scale China campaign imposed murderous burdens on the Koreans. By then Korea had already lost its mostly superficial freedoms permitted under the so-called "Civilized Rule," the appeasement initiated after the March First Movement protests. When imperial Japan added America to its enemies with the commencement of the Pacific War, its desperate efforts to keep Korea as its primary logistical base and the producer of raw materials and manpower caused even harsher colonial oppression and exploitation. No Korean identity and tradition was left unmolested by the colonial administration; all Korean newspapers and magazines were abolished. As its struggle against China and later against the Allies faltered, Japan's oppressive rule in Korea became even more unbearable. In 1938 Japan issued the national mobilization order to use Korean men and women in its imperial war. Under this most inhumane order more than 3.5 million men and women of Korean nationality were forced to serve the Japanese war efforts, some as fighters and others as laborers in war-related industries. Until the very last moment Japan continued to manufacture many edicts to put Korean nationals into its war activities. Many lost their lives for the cause they despised so intensely, and some significant numbers were detained in Sakhalin and have to date not yet been able to return home.

In 1945 Korea was liberated, or rather one may say that Korea found its nation vacated by defeated Japan. The Japanese defeat was imposed by the United States; it was not imposed by Koreans. In reality, Koreans lost their nation by their own default and found it by Japan's default. In spite of those inspiring anti-Japanese protests such as the March First Movement and the Kwangju Student Revolt, the Korean people's efforts to defeat militarist Japan had never been a major factor. Even the brilliant guerrilla warfare waged by the Korean resistance fighters around the Korea-Manchurian border were not enough to inflict any critical blows to the Japanese military machine. Although the Korean resistance movement's ineffectiveness could be attributed to many factors, a divided leadership was by no means the least responsible one.

The Korean Provisional Government should have been the nation's central political institution in directing various anti-Japanese campaigns. Yet the organization had remained nominal because of its weak leadership and often suffered from divided resistance ideologies and tactics. Its leadership generally preferred more moderate approaches than direct military confrontation. It was only in the waning moments of the Pacific War that the provisional government organized its own "liberation army" in China. This force did cooperate with the British in Southeast Asia to a limited extent but never made any significant contribution in fighting against Japanese forces inside Korea. While the provisional government was mainly preoccupied with relations with its host, the Nationalist Chinese Government, Dr. Rhee was conducting his one-man diplomacy in Washington. His long and arduous effort, however, yielded no tangible results and never gained American recognition of the Korean government in exile. He was long unable to make official contacts with the American government as the representative of the Korean nation, although he was clearly performing such a role. The divided leadership of the Korean resistance movement and its inability to wage a sustained anti-Japanese offense may have made the American administration question the logic of recognizing the Korean government-in-exile. Nonetheless, it was Dr. Rhee's signal failure not to be able to convince the Americans of the rationale and necessity of recognizing the government-in-exile. The Korean resistance movement's diplomatic maneuver was almost a total failure.

Considering its sanctuary in the border region, Korea's resistance fighters should have been able to bring some serious military pressure on the Japanese forces both in Manchuria and in northern Korea. The region was particularly suitable for guerrilla operations for the Koreans because of its rugged mountain ranges and generally supportive local population. As a result, some guerrilla groups did score significant victories in the region. Nevertheless, the prominent failure of the nation's military resistance was its inability to sustain the pressure and to escalate the border skirmishes and sporadic guerrilla attacks into a full-scale liberation war. The Korean resistance's armed struggle, which emphasized more politicized military activities from the early period by carrying out some spectacular attacks on eminent Japanese figures, was unable to evolve into an organized liberation movement.

The difficulties that Korea's guerrilla groups encountered in the border region were directly related to Japan's military activities there. By the time Japan launched its final assault on China, it had amassed an army of some 600,000 men. The powerful Kwangtung Army totally dominated the region and effectively deprived the Koreans of any significant room to maneuver militarily. By the middle of the 1930s, under intensified Japanese military pressure, Korea's independence fighters had largely retreated to China proper or Siberia. Some still carried out independent military campaigns, but other units operated along with Chinese forces. The movement's socialist factions maintained close contacts with the Communist forces of China and Russia. By the late 1930s the border region was effectively controlled by the Japanese force, and the Korean independent force lost most of its sanctuary in the region.

Japan's colonial rule of Korea lasted for thirty-six years. Throughout the harsh colonial rule Koreans jealously guarded their heritage and resisted Japanization with their lives. They effectively frustrated Japan's concerted attempts for cultural assimilation. By enduring long and cruel mistreatment, Koreans rejected Japan's overtures to make them second class citizens. They remained resolutely nationalistic until the end of the ordeal.

The most confusing enigma of the colonial rule was the fact that the Koreans proved to be highly ineffective in organizing and supporting their liberation armies. The nation of long, enlightened civilization and of more than twenty million souls should have been able to do otherwise. In spite of many factors that might have intervened to disrupt such an attempt, it is an immensely difficult proposition to explain such a pronounced shortcoming adequately. However, Korea's incompletely developed nationalism had to bear some significant blame. Korea's modern nationalism was born largely under the Japanese occupation when it clearly identified an adversary in consensus, as demonstrated in the March First Protests and the student uprisings. Yet nationalism's full blossom was forcefully blocked by Japan's oppressive colonial rule. Under the circumstances, Korea hardly had any respite to complete the transformation of its rigid doctrine of Confucian individualism into fully functional modern nationalism.

Another chronic problem plaguing the nation was the lack of outstanding political leadership in this period; Korea was without a true national leader that the masses could have rallied around. The problem was partly institutional; the tradition-rich monarchy was demoted by the Japanese and abandoned by Korean political leaders, but the nation was unable to replace the old institution. Koreans discarded their ancient, two thousand year old institution without having any notion of how to fill the leadership vacuum, a much more serious matter than any of the contemporary Korean intellectuals may have anticipated.

Korea's long imprisonment was ended by the surrender of Japan, a tragedy to that nation of intense pride and ambition. For hundreds of millions of oppressed people of East Asia, it was simply belated justice executed. The Asian lands of agony and lament were swept by cheers and hopes of free people. On August 15, 1945, the day it reclaimed its pirated national sovereignty again, Korea too was swept by a giant wave of liberation, filled with shouts of jubilation, joys of free men, and hopes of a new era and a new beginning. Koreans hardly noticed that across the narrow Korea Strait atomic-bombed Japan was suffering its history's most humiliating and costly defeat. Koreans were too busy with their deserved celebration to feel sympathy over their deposed colonial masters.

Oblivious of their geopolitical predicaments, Koreans thought their problems were finally over. The American victors of the Pacific War were committed to the restoration of an independent status for Korea, but required terms that the Koreans were not quite willing to accept. To no one's surprise, Koreans were not free from the manipulation of their fateful geopolitics. Regardless of their preference and benign hope to be free and peaceful, they were destined for another round of human suffering and destruction. The geopolitical curse of the Korean peninsula remained little changed.

Notes

1. Chosun's three royal envoys, sent to Netherlands in June 1907, were not allowed to attend the meeting. Later in Washington, they attempted in vain to meet President Roosevelt.
2. The Korean army was disbanded on August 1, 1907, under Japanese pressure.
3. The total number of Christian churches in Korea reached 1,493 in 1910.
4. Korean residents in Manchuria reached 92,000 in 1910.
5. Hilary Conroy, *The Japanese Seizure of Korea: 1868-1910.* P.25.
6. Ibid., p.41.
7. George Schwarzenberger, *Power Politics, A Study of International Society.* p. 418.
8. Conroy, p.331.
9. Morinosuke Kajima, *The Emergence of Japan as a World Power, 1895-1925,* p. 67.
10. Ibid., p.65.
11. Ibid., p.332.
12. Conroy, p.383.
13. Korea's total population in 1919 was about 20 million.
14. In K. Hwang, *The Korean Reform Movement of the 1880s, A Study of Transition in Intra-Asian Relations.* p. 485.

15. Phillip Darby, *Three Face of imperialism: British and American Approaches to Asia and Africa 1870-1970.* P. 34.

Chapter 9

Postwar US-USSR Rivalry

1. Postwar Settlement

During the late part of the Pacific War, America undertook some significant steps toward the eventual resolution of the Korean question. It publicly stated its intention to grant Korea independence once Japan was defeated, an expected but heartwarming gesture to the Koreans. Yet Washington was unable to specify how soon after the war Korea would recover its sovereignty. Contrary to the wishes of Koreans, who wanted immediate and full recovery of their sovereignty, the American administration was inclined to believe that Korea would need a transition period before it was allowed to manage its own affairs. It was searching for a formula that it and its allies could agree upon.

The resolution of Korea was one of the major postwar questions the victorious Allies had to address. They first endorsed a just solution for liberated Korea at the Cairo Conference, held on December 1, 1943. The leaders of America, Britain, and China declared that "in due course Korea shall become free and independent." They agreed to grant the Korean people their long-sought independence, but no specific method was given except that the recovery of their independence would come "in due course." The Cairo declaration had tremendously encouraged the Korean independence movement, for it was the first open, positive statement made by the Allies over the Korean question. At the same time, the Allies' reservations about Korea's immediate independence were rightfully interpreted in Korea as the West's insult against its long and in many ways accomplished civilization. Although the Rooseveltian view that liberated colonies would benefit from a period of careful political tutelage had merit in some cases, it did represent America's grave insensitivity to the aspirations and political maturity of the Korean people.

America was seeking the collaboration of its allies for its postwar Korean policy, but ironically, it did not solicit any input from the Korean people themselves. It made no attempt to listen to the opinions of the Korean people on their own future, although Syngman Rhee, the representative of the Korean Provisional Government to Washington, had been engaging in individual diplomacy since the 1920s. Washington, which had shunned the Korean people's aspiration for an independence before so as not to contradict Japanese ambition, was, in the waning moments of the war, willing to help Korea recover its sovereignty. Still, America was pursuing an arbitrary policy to resolve the Korean question just as the Middle Kingdom and imperial Japan had done before. Nevertheless, Koreans, who were still under Japanese colonial rule, had scarcely had any suspicion that America, their looming benefactor, was pondering a formula that would lead to the division of their territory into two spheres of contending political ideologies.

The multilateral trusteeship idea was first raised in 1943 as Roosevelt's general approach toward territories soon to be liberated. He specifically suggested that such an arrangement could be applied to both Korea and French Indochina. Predictably, this move was soundly rejected by both Britain and France, the world's premier colonial powers. Upon the Allies' rejection, Washington had dropped its trusteeship plan for the former colonial possessions of both Britain and France. Still, it pursued the trusteeship solution to liberated Korea, on which neither Britain nor France had any established interests.

President Roosevelt decided to grant Korea its coveted independence after the war but only through his trusteeship plan. Although his plan had failed to receive support from the Allies, Roosevelt was convinced that the trusteeship solution was the only political choice acceptable to him. He continued his quest to obtain consent from the Russians and the Allies. The President's plan called for Britain and China, along with Russia, to participate in the plan as the trusteeship members. Significantly, from the incipient stage of the discussion America took a position that Russia was a de facto equal partner in this plan. In a sense, Roosevelt publicly acknowledged through his trusteeship plan that postwar Korea would be of significant political interest to both America and Russia.

America's renewed interest in Korean affairs was by itself a significant development. Yet to most American citizens the Hermit Kingdom had remained as foreign as the outer world; even the location of the country had been virtually unknown to the public. In spite of Korea's status as "a minor ganglion to a secondary enemy," as the Pacific War was nearing its conclusion American policy planners began to contemplate the Korean solution, paying attention to the peninsula's unusual geopolitical properties. Having grasped an increasingly clear prospect of competing with the Russians for postwar hegemony, they began to consider, for the first time, Korea as an integral part of America's postwar global strategy. Thus contrary to the wishes of its inhabitants, emerging postwar international politics would make Korea an international issue. Roosevelt's endeavor to impose a trusteeship plan over Korea well illustrated the internationalized nature of the Korean solution.

Roosevelt, an internationalist who emphasized the virtues of the capitalistic free trade system and representative democracy, was adamant in seeking a multilateral trusteeship for Korea. The President envisioned that a multilateral trusteeship, which would be ministered by the US, USSR, Britain, and China, would rule, replacing the Japanese colonial administration until Korea was ready to manage its own affairs. The trusteeship's obvious merit was that Korea under the scheme would not orient itself against American interests.[1] By imposing a U.S.-sponsored tutorship, the President intended to secure sufficient time to indoctrinate Koreans with a modern democratic system. He was convinced that Korea could govern itself only after it absorbed under the trusteeship the skills and knowledge of running a modern democratic state. In spite of its justifiable logic, it would be difficult to deny that the trusteeship plan had a definite tone of furthering American interests in the region. Although the plan was contradictory to the aspirations of Koreans, the American position concerning the Korean question was definite in this period. On the other hand, the Russian stand on the question remained unclear.

Roosevelt's Korean trusteeship plan was more than a mere political solution for Korea. In a sense, it was the central piece of his strategic plan for postwar Northeast Asia as demonstrated by his inclusion of China as a trusteeship member. It reflected Roosevelt's design to groom China as the region's postwar power replacing Japan. The President was expecting liberated China, in spite of its domestic difficulties in dealing with the communists, to resume the role of the region's premier power by exercising positive influence toward the stability of the region.[2] The President hoped that China, by regaining its Middle Kingdom status, not only would be able to check the revival of Japanese militarism, but also would reclaim its strong political leadership in the region. To achieve those objects, liberated China was expected to retake Manchuria and to regain political influence over Korea.[3] For the President, who had not been fully aware of the ramifications that his high-stake international power play was likely to instigate in twenty million Koreans, the remarkable lack of both sympathy and understanding of Korea's historical struggle against its neighbors was not totally unexpected. In order to secure the political stability of this strategic region under the influence of a political ally, the American administration was actively seeking renewed Chinese domination in the region.

Roosevelt's initial Korean trusteeship plan called for a ten-to-forty year tutelage. Proposing a long indoctrination period, he thoroughly overlooked the Korean people's eagerness to reclaim their free and independent standing at the earliest date. Nor he was aware of the fact that Koreans would reject another foreign rule regardless of who it might be. Yet the President was not willing to listen to the very people whose future would be most directly affected by his policy.

Roosevelt informed Russia of his Korean trusteeship plan on February 8, 1945. Contrary to Roosevelt's plan for a long-term trusteeship, Stalin, who had objected to the plan at first, preferred a short term. In spite of Roosevelt's effort, the Yalta Conference reached no agreement on the issue. America's foreign policy leaned more toward nationalism after President Truman succeeded Roosevelt in April 1945. Still, Washington was pursuing the trusteeship solution for Korea. The Allies failed again to reach an agreement on the plan at the Potsdam Conference on July 22, 1945. When the Pacific War ended, Washington still did not have the support of the Allies for its Korean trusteeship plan.

While America's postwar Korean policy failed to gain support from its allies, postwar Russia's role in Northeast Asia also remained unclear. It was expected that Russia would view the region with more sensitivity and understanding because its interest in Korea had been much more direct and historical than America's. Thus Stalin's objection to Roosevelt's proposal for the Korean trusteeship was interpreted not as a mere difference, but a fundamental disagreement in their postwar Korean policy at the time. Americans expected Russia to challenge their domination in Europe as well as in Northeast Asia; the possibility that Russia would advance and occupy liberated Korea surfaced as a serious concern for State Department planners as early as late 1943. They regarded a Russian occupation of Korea as creating an entirely new strategic situation that would have severe consequences to the security of both China and Japan. Because of this strategic consideration, they began to ponder a scheme of partial or full military occupation of Korea in early 1944.[4]

Washington's Korean policy during this period contained serious dissonances reflecting the administration's two contrasting approaches: Roosevelt's gradual move vs. the State Department's aggressive one. This lack of a cohesive approach was inevitably to create some serious political confusions in Korea later. Nonetheless, America's new interest in the Korean solution meant a drastic turnaround in its strategic evaluation of Korea and the region as a whole. In the waning moments of the war, America had finally made public its intention to seek the status of independent nationhood for Korea, thus reversing its prewar policy to remain silent over Japanese aggression. America's new Korean policy, on the other hand, reflected its new status as the world's most powerful nation, although it still displayed some confusion and naivete. Still, Korea had been transformed into one of Washington's most pressing strategic concern in Northeast Asia.

America's new Korean policy was to lead to some conflicts with Russia, the only Asiatic power among the victorious Allies. China, regardless of its superficial role as the fourth power of the Allies, was in reality more a victim than a victor. As China was not expected to play any significant role in the region for the immediate future, America was left alone to deal with Russia and to overcome some significant strategic disadvantages.

America's new Korean policy suffered a setback almost from its introduction. The hasty termination of the Pacific War, which came much sooner than State Department planners had considered feasible, made the orderly implementation of America's Korean policy virtually impossible. American war planners made a serious miscalculation over Japan's military capacity to resist the Allies. The swift collapse of Japan's Kwangtung Army, deployed in Manchuria and North China, made it impossible for the American military to keep the Russians from entering the Korean peninsula. This unexpected military situation compounded America's Korean policy, which was from the outset characterized with complexities, contradictions, and ambiguities.[5]

American war planners had anticipated that the invasion of the Japanese home islands would be launched around November 1, 1945. Only after Japan's home base was completely subdued was the disarmament of the Japanese forces stationed in Korea and Manchuria expected to take place. Still, not considering the nuclear option, America was planning for much long and bloody fighting before it would be able to overwhelm the fanatic Japanese military. It also expected Japan's mighty Kwangtung Army in Manchuria to continue to resist the Allies longer.

Anticipating a hard struggle to subjugate the Japanese military on the Asian mainland, America sought Russia's military cooperation, which opportunistic Russia readily offered. As a price for Russia's military engagement against Japan, America was willing to yield Manchuria, North China, and northern Korea to Russia. In retrospect it was an improvident deal even though it was made under the assumption that Japan's military in Manchuria would not offer a swift capitulation. America was hoping that Russia would be able to subdue the Kwangtung Army in Manchuria. It did not expect, however, that Japan's mightiest army would crumble so swiftly and hardly offer any contest to the Red Army. Partly because the Russians advanced so quickly and effectively against demoralized Japanese forces in Manchuria, America was stripped of an opportunity to contain the Red Army before it reached the Korean Peninsula. On the contrary, it assured the Russians a virtual monopoly in occupying the strategic region as they wished to. Even the catastrophe of yielding the entire Korean peninsula to Russia was aborted only by some dubious Russian moves. Had the Russian military not exercised restraint in its advance into Korea, Americans could not have been able to claim even the southern half of the Korean peninsula.

2. The Allies' Occupation of Korea

The partition of the Korean peninsula at the thirty-eighth parallel was America's political decision, hastily made only several days before V-J day. Having faced Russia's rapid advance in Korea, America was forced to adopt the partition scheme making the thirty-eighth parallel as the dividing line in order to assure that Seoul, the capital city, remained in the American zone.[6] Although America was doubtful about Russia's willingness to consent to such a divided occupation scheme, Russia agreed to the American proposal and restrained its forces from entering the southern part of the peninsula. It was a significant yield made by Russia, which was fully capable of occupying the whole peninsula, and made its total control an established fact before the American forces were able to reach the peninsula. Russia allowed the Americans to occupy southern Korea, which included the nation's capital city, two-thirds of its population, most of its light industry, and the greater part of its agricultural land. Russia put under its complete control northern Korea, which included most of the nation's heavy industries, large hydroelectric plants, and rich mineral and forest resources.

Stalin's motive to allow American forces to occupy the southern half of Korea was never clear. But several plausible factors are often cited in this regard. First, historically Russia's primary interest in Korea had been its security concerns, as demonstrated by the unsuccessful negotiations with Japan for the division of Korea at the thirty-eighth parallel in 1896 and 1905. In the same way, Stalin may have been interested in installation of a simple buffer zone, northern Korea, against the new rival, America. Russia might have regarded the occupation of the northern half of the peninsula as being sufficient to assure its security concerns in the region. If this interpretation were valid, it could be assumed that Russia had pursued a simple policy of establishing its political domination in northern Korea without provoking powerful America. Russia might have preferred unified Korea under its influence, but it may have also realized that a divided Korea could serve its basic security interests adequately. Second, Stalin took such a reserved attitude in Korea out of a desire to assure American cooperation in postwar politics. Having realized America's growing suspicions and ill-feelings over its communist doctrine, Moscow may have simply decided to show its restraint in Korea as a goodwill gesture toward America.

However, even if the Russian objective were total control of Korea at the time, a gesture to occupy only the northern part of the peninsula was not totally out of its scheme. In view of the overwhelming strength of the communists and their collaborators in the south during the 1945-1947 period, the Russians could easily have concluded that their ambition to subjugate the entire peninsula was not in jeopardy even if it allowed the Americans to occupy the south. Russia may have assumed that it could depend on its powerful and well-organized political allies, the Korean leftists, to finish the rest of the task shortly. In any event, the Russian army entered Korea approximately one month earlier than the American forces did, but halted its advance at the thirty-eighth parallel as agreed upon. The unexpectedly swift collapse of Japan's Kwangtung Army rendered a unique opportunity for Russia to dominate the entire Korean peninsula. Only Russia's uncertain American policy allowed the Americans to move into the country, although only in the southern half of the peninsula.

The unconditional surrender of Japan did not bring immediate, full independence to Korea. In spite of the excitement most common to those liberated from colonial rules, Korea was now occupied by two Western powers. From early September, 1945, the American forces began to arrive in Korea to assume the occupation duty under General Hodge. The occupation command's task was quite formidable; it had to defend the southern half from the Russian-sponsored northern regime while laying out the nation's basic governing system, which had to be democratic and thus distinguishable from the much despised colonial apparatus. Thus its undertaking included both military and civilian affairs. Yet Hodge's occupation force, largely combat oriented, was hardly prepared for the complicated occupation duties, especially civilian affairs. Partly due to the Herculean task of building a new nation from the meager remnants of the colonial rule and partly due to the occupation command's amateurish policies, the political situation in the south became hopelessly tangled. Contrary to the public's ardent expectation for a new era, the nation plunged into the profound confusion that affected every aspect of the society in the southern region. The pressing task of organizing the new nation had begun but on most shaky ground.

The naive but hopeful expectations of the Korean masses had compounded the confusion and disorder the liberation brought to the south. Militant social order maintained throughout the harsh Japanese rule totally disappeared after the colonial administration was disarmed and expelled from Korea. The liberation that in a sense merely exchanged the Japanese colonial masters with the Western military occupation had greatly bewildered the Korean public, who had waited more than four decades to escape the Japanese oppression. Moreover, their new rulers were foreign soldiers who had little knowledge about the country and its long aspiration to be free and independent. Under this uncommon circumstance it was inevitable for the Koreans to experience a great deal of difficulty in organizing the new nation. Neither their lack of political experience in modern democratic systems nor the occupation's lack of civil experience helped the cause. Many quasi-political organizations were born overnight but with no public mandate or legitimacy.

Under the extreme uncertainty and fluid political atmosphere, the left, better organized and peasant-oriented, began to make great strides and rapidly gained political strength in the south. The leftists' political fortunes benefited greatly by the belated arrival of their inherent rivals; Korea's main, non-left independence movements still remained in foreign countries, the Korean Provisional Government in China and Syngman Rhee in America. Even without the participation of its more prominent political institutions, however, Korea indulged in chaotic political competition, this time between the rightists and leftists. The costly political infighting was to continue until a clean break was made between the left and right. Yet in this early period political rivalry among factions in the south had a distinct flavor of nation building. The Western ideologies, both communism and capitalistic democracy, were yet to become the nation's divisive obsession, although both parties were committed to prevail over the competition. In its early post-liberation period the leftists were the dominant political force in both parts of the peninsula as they were enjoying strong political support of the nation's farmers and workers.

The opposing political factions in the south were most clearly separated by their respective anti-Japanese credentials accumulated during the colonial period. The leftists primarily consisted of the nation's many feverish anti-Japanese fighters who had endured the colonial oppression, while the small and poorly organized rightists included many of those who had served the colonial administration or were passive in the independence movement. Nevertheless, in the south the rightists quickly managed to monopolize the new nation's emerging political structures, benefiting largely from the political support given by their new ally, the occupation command. Almost totally excluded from the nation's new bureaucracy, the leftists concentrated their efforts in expanding political support among farmers and workers. The leftists' approach proved to be highly effective, and in a brief time they succeeded in further consolidating their political domination throughout the rural south.

Quickly the left emerged as the most powerful political force in the south in spite of the presence of the American occupation command, which openly supported the right. General Hodge's command was left with no alternative but to combat this rising tide of the left unless willing to surrender the southern half to Russian domination. Simultaneously, the Americans had to maintain a watchful eye on the increasing clashes along the thirty-eighth parallel, the temporary dividing line for the two halves. America was to face its first postwar challenge waged by the left in Korea.

Hodge was an enthusiastic defender of American interests in Korea. His actions as the commander of the occupation force were designed foremost to promote American interests and to neutralize potential problems. Although his actions on the scene in Seoul were often regarded as contradicting Washington's official line, he was the forceful administrator of the American policies in Korea. Hodge's command was, however, not much concerned with the general welfare of Koreans; under the American occupation, Koreans had become the subject of treatment suitable only to conquered enemies. In reality, Korea was far more America's conquered territory than Japan ever was. Through its actions of the occupation command, America displayed its clear preference for Japan over Korea even in this period when memories of the war were still fresh.

In spite of his being a novice in civil-political administration, Hodge was, nonetheless, deeply committed to build a bulwark state out of southern Korea to contain the Russian thrust in the region. Under his persevering efforts, southern Korea was fast becoming a vital link in the American strategic ring. Inevitably, Korea's aspiration for a unified, independent, and free nation had become a secondary issue to America's global strategic interests, which began to take a much clearer image in the context of East-West confrontation. Korea, liberated but occupied by the two postwar superpowers, was helplessly being drawn into the emerging U.S.-USSR rivalry, which had been transforming the peninsula into another prominent stage for a drama of international power politics.

On September 9, 1945, Hodge set up his military occupation command in Seoul. American soldiers were warmly received by the Koreans as their savior. In spite of good intentions, harmony was absent between the occupiers and the occupied from the outset of the new era. The Korean people, underestimating the formidable task they had to overcome, were only too eager in hoping that America would provide quick and constructive guidelines for a new era of nation building. Moreover, Koreans were scarcely informed about the developing international power politics from which the new nation could not depart regardless of its preference. Hodge's occupation command was interested in helping the new nation, but only under the framework of U.S. postwar strategic interests.

The occupation command was hardly prepared to carry out the lofty Korean mission. It even failed fully to appreciate the land and its people. From its very beginning it neglected returning the warm reception shown by the Korean public and was often antagonistic to the citizens of a long and established civilization. Even Hodge, an outspoken field general, did not attempt to hide his low esteem of the Korean people by openly criticizing Koreans as headstrong, unruly, and obstreperous.[7] The occupation's contemptuous insensitivity on local aspirations and traditions was contradictory to the generosity and civil manner shown by his superior, General MacArthur, toward the defeated Japanese. Hodge's occupation force was widely criticized for its treatment of Koreans; it treated Koreans more like surrogates of the Japanese than proud Hahn nationals who fought the long and lonely war against the Japanese colonial rule.[8] The occupation command's disagreeable manner had become a source of great surprise and displeasure to the Korean people. Apparently, the occupation command's perception of the Korean people was not the best, and the Koreans had returned the favor in kind to some extent. The profound hospitality Koreans felt for Americans suffered a slow but significant erosion from the early part of the occupation.

From the early stage of the occupation Hodge pursued two basic policies that bore many decisions crucial in shaping the fundamental political structure of postwar Korea. First, the occupation command provided virtually unrestricted support to Korea's rightist political faction. Using its unlimited freedom in siding with any individuals or political factions, it provided the rightists with direct as well as indirect political support. The ramification of such overt political support was enormous. Under Hodge's protective wing, southern Korea's conservative faction was rapidly achieving political dominance; it managed to monopolize the new army, police, judiciary, and executive bureaucracies created in the south. Hodge had given an extraordinary political boost to Korea's conservative faction, even though some of these politicians' anti-Japanese credentials were less than impressive or downright suspicious. In the end, the occupation command played the role of midwife to Korea's rightist autocracy through its early support of pro-American, anti-communist political figures.

Second, Hodge carried out with determination a variety of measures intended to suppress the popular leftist movements and the communist party activities. By using their often outstanding anti-colonial credentials and worker-farmer backgrounds, the leftists were expanding their influence to all but a few landed classes of the society in the south. The leftists were rapidly consolidating their political control in the rural south when the occupation command launched its systematic suppression, dispatching Korea's new born police force to communist strongholds.

The occupation government's search for a dependable political leadership, capable either of replacing the military government or playing a key role in the trusteeship arrangement, was extended to both Kim Goo, the head of the Korean Provisional Government, and Syngman Rhee, the nation's most celebrated political institution of the time. Although the Korean Democratic Party (KDP) had already consolidated its political power in the emerging new government under the favorable support of the occupation command, it had failed to produce a popular leader with appropriate credentials and political savvy. The KDP embraced only a small number of so-called democratic and pro-American politicians while commanding little public support. On the other hand, the leftist group represented by the People's Republic (PR) continued to attract warm public support and dominated communities of every level in the south.

The conservative KDP failed to win support of the masses, who were enthusiastic about radical social reforms pursued by the leftists. That the political leadership the occupation government was supporting was no more than a product of the occupation command's political interests made Hodge's political maneuver in south Korea risky and difficult. Even after the return of the major political figures associated with the Korean Provisional Government and Syngman Rhee, the political options left to the occupation were not much improved. Neither Rhee nor Kim Goo, the nominal head of KPG, proved to be an immediate answer to the growing strength of the leftists in the south.

In spite of significant political difficulties it encountered in Seoul, America had not abandoned its trusteeship plan, which was believed to best secure America's dominant influence in Korea. During the first five months of its occupation, Washington was still committed to the multilateral trusteeship as its basic position, but was also actively seeking a containment of Russia in Korea. Yet the decisions taken by the occupation government in Seoul were more oriented to the containment approach. Contrary to its actions in Seoul aimed at suppressing the political strength of the Korean leftists and their Russian allies, Washington remained the prime backer of the trusteeship, the arrangement that would assure Russia's sustained political influence in Korea.

Washington finally obtained consent for its cherished trusteeship for Korea from both Russia and Britain at the Moscow Conference held on December 16, 1945. The agreement stipulated that the trusteeship was to be administered by the four powers- the U.S., United Kingdom, China, and the Soviet Union- for up to five years. The fact that Russia would be only one of four equal votes in the trusteeship, thus a manageable threat, may have been a justification for America to reach such an agreement with Russia. Under the trusteeship format it was expected that Russia would be forced to cooperate with America and its allies. The agreement was a clear manifestation that both superpowers were inclined to seek in Korea mutual cooperation, not a confrontation, at least in the near future. Yet it was probable that the agreement was reached under the vastly different assessment of the Korean political situation by both powers; Russia was well aware of the overwhelming strength of the Korean leftists in both halves of Korea while America was counting on its capacity to dominate the trusteeship. Russia, who favored immediate independence for the Korean nation over the trusteeship, had made a notable concession to America in this regard even though the adopted trusteeship plan was much more limited in scope than the Roosevelt plan. Yet the adoption of the trusteeship plan made plain that America and Russia were the powers to seek dominant influence in Korea. As a result, the notion that Britain and China would have a political role in Korea equal to that of America and Russia had largely dissipated. The trusteeship plan finally agreed upon at Moscow barely resembled the one Roosevelt had originally suggested. It did no longer question Korea's competency in self-governing or suggest that Koreans needed a political tutelage. Under the plan the new Korean government was to be installed before the trusteeship was imposed. Thus, the success of the plan was all the more dependent on close American-Russian coordination as well as the full cooperation of the Korean people.

The imposed trusteeship plan was coolly received by the Korean people. The trusteeship scheme had never been popular in Korea ever since it was proposed by Roosevelt. Now liberated although again occupied by the Western forces, Koreans were in no mood to acquiesce to such a humiliating treatment. For most Koreans the shameful memories of the Japanese annexation were still so fresh that they would not assent to another outsider's domination regardless of how it was presented. The rejection of the plan was unanimous, including the nation's left and right factions, who expressed their anger with spontaneous street demonstrations which broke out all over the country. For a while, the anti-trusteeship fever had thus been strong enough even to unite the antagonistic leftists and rightists as they together waged nationwide anti-trusteeship campaigns.

The Korean trusteeship plan was also critically undermined by the American occupation command, which did not bother to conceal its objection to the trusteeship plan. Perhaps aided by on-the-spot observations and persuaded by a military attitude, the occupation command opposed Washington's official plan in which Russia would have a voice. After the Moscow agreement was signed, the occupation openly encouraged Koreans to reject the accord. The occupation's close Korean ally, KDP, spearheaded the anti-trusteeship crusade. Encouraged by the occupation's support and truly angered by the Western powers' blockade of their immediate independence, the Korean people for a short while maintained a rare single voice that said no trusteeship at all.

But inevitably divisive politics intervened in the movement. The south's pro-American faction rejected the multilateral trusteeship but then as an alternative openly advocated an unilateral American tutelage, a clear sign of the growing influence of the rightists in the south. Then the left suddenly reversed its position by supporting the trusteeship; the rightists conveniently exploited the shift by inventing the slogan that "Russia advocates trusteeship, America advocates immediate independence" and made Russia an enemy of the Korean independence. The contention was grossly erroneous because it was America, not Russia, that initially advocated a trusteeship for Korea. On the contrary, Russia had used its influence to weaken the American proposal. Nonetheless, soon the movement evolved into a full-scale anti-communist, anti-Russia campaign bearing Korea's first full-blown anti-communist and anti-Russian movement. In the end, the rightists largely succeeded in sabotaging the trusteeship accord and also were able to illustrate the dangers of international communism in the process. Strengthened by the successful anti-trusteeship campaigns, the rightists commenced a bloody offensive against the leftists, who were still dominant in both the south and north in early 1946. The leftists' sudden shift in favor of the Moscow accord aided the rightists' coloring of the leftists as mere tools for international communism. The right-left split in the anti-trusteeship movement effectively foreclosed any possibility for the two contending factions to reach a compromise.

Unlike the south, the Moscow accord was received favorably in the Russian-occupied north. This meant that Russia had pursued the trusteeship plan at considerable cost to its reputation as a champion of Korean independence and a liberator of the oppressed. The risky Russian gamble could not be adequately explained without examining its position in northern Korea. Unlike the American forces in the south, the Russian occupation in the north remained largely behind the scenes from the beginning. Although their domination in the north should have been nearly absolute, Russia managed the occupation chores largely through its Korean allies. Russia's sensitive scheme was effective in reestablishing the badly-mangled social order while protecting the public image of the Russian occupation command. The Russians successfully projected themselves as liberators of Korea in the north, a notable success in comparison to America's policies that left the south still struggling under extreme political uncertainty. The Russians were confident of their capacity to earn the respect of the Korean people and eager to engage in a political game against their counterparts in the south. After all, the Russians must have felt that the trusteeship could be a useful avenue to reach their ultimate ambition to put unified Korea under their own firm influence. With the northern half under its camp, Russia's favorable expectation may have not been too far off. The Russians were fully capitalizing on their prominent advantages over America - prior experience with Korea and geographical proximity.

The Russian forces entered northern Korea on August 10, 1945, only five days before the Japanese surrender. Scoring a rapid advance against retreating Japanese forces, the Russians managed to occupy most of northern Korea's major cities by August 24th. For the army that was prepared for long and tough battles against Japan's powerful Kwangtung army, the occupation of the northern half of Korea was to a certain extent a simple task. Unlike the American forces that were not able to reach Korea until the early part of September, Russian forces fought against Japanese forces on Korean soil even though Japanese resistance was generally light. The Russians thus entered Korea not only as victors of the Pacific War but also as comrades-in-war to the Koreans and were received favorably by the Korean public. Although Russians were perfectly capable of occupying the entire peninsula, they refrained to advance beyond the thirty-eighth parallel.

Russians squandered no time in implementing their extensive programs to establish a socialist society in northern Korea. Instead of installing a military government, which was the case with Americans in the south, Russians chose to utilize the ubiquitous people's committees, a convenient and popular local political organization, as governing bodies for local administrations ranging from the provincial level to the township level. Through the people's committees the Russian occupation undertook the task of removing the colonial legacies and extracted strong support and respect from the Korean masses. The Soviet decision to forgo a central administration during the early part of the occupation may have been based on the assumption that the north would soon join the south and forge a central government in Seoul. Furthermore, the Russian occupation did not plan for a separate regime in the north at least until early 1946.

Russia's most pronounced success in the early period of its occupation of northern Korea was extensive land reforms, which were greatly aided by the peculiar socioeconomic structure of the northern half. Not only was the presence of landlords and colonial apparatus thinner in the north than in the agricultural and heavily populated south, but also many prominent landlords and high colonial accomplices had already fled to the south after the liberation. The obstacles for the occupation-sponsored reforms were far fewer in the north so that the reforms could be accomplished quickly and with little bloodshed. Contrary to the south under the American occupation, the north was to witness the emergence of a new elite class drawn almost exclusively from the ranks of workers and peasants. In addition, the Russians had brought in a handpicked leader that they had chosen to guide postwar Korea, apparently unified Korea. Through their careful installation of communist leadership and deft manipulation of local politics, Russians firmly established their political influence in northern Korea.

3. Birth of Two Koreas

During the early part of the occupation period two eminent political leaders were introduced to both halves of Korea by their respective backers: Syngman Rhee in the south and Kim Il Sung in the north. They were more pronounced in their dissimilarities than similarities, yet they both were destined to lead the respective halves of Korea with remarkable distinction. Both spent the colonial period in exile waging anti-Japanese campaigns: Kim in armed struggle in the Russia-China-Korea border region, and Rhee in diplomacy in Washington. In spite of their age disadvantages, Kim being too young in his early 30s and Rhee rather old in his 70s, both men fully intended to lead the liberated and unified country. Both men's absolute self-confidence in their noble motives and abilities and their inability to settle matters through democratic compromises were the nation's pride as well as its tragedy.

Syngman Rhee was well known among Koreans associated with independence movements although he had not been in Korea for more than twenty years prior to his return home in September 1945. He thus had not had an opportunity to build a political power base or a large number of followers within Korea until he was able to return home. As a result, for the public he was more of a legendary figure associated with the faraway nation of America. His superb educational achievement, a doctoral degree from Princeton University, and a long exposure to Washington politics made him a strong contender for the political leadership of the new nation under American tutelage. Yet he was shunned by Washington and received by the occupation command with some coolness on his return home. Rhee was a strong-willed, sophisticated figure who well understood the complexities of Washington politics. Largely because of Rhee's headstrong character, the occupation command was anxious to find a more moderate politician instead. However, there were no other political figures who had such a lofty reputation and political savvy comparable to Rhee. Despite the unmistakable reservation shown by the occupation command, he eventually emerged as the most powerful and skillful political leader in the south when he was elected as head of the Representative Democratic Council in early 1946.

Unlike Rhee in the south, Kim was largely unknown except for his legendary name. Much of his background prior to the liberation remains obscure even today. He was believed to be a young, anti-Japanese guerrilla leader who at times commanded several hundred guerrilla fighters. His anti-Japanese activities were well known to the colonial authority, but he was considered a minor figure, partly due to his youth. Considering the extremely limited number of Koreans fighting the Japanese during the 1930s and 1940s, his force still might have been one of the most active Korean resistance movements. Stories of his being a great hero of guerrilla wars and a national leader in his 20s are abundant in North Korea's publications. Yet there is considerable difficulty in separating facts from fancies manufactured later by his followers. Nevertheless, Kim was connected to the Red Army during the early 1940s; his being a Red Army officer in a battalion mainly formed of Korean nationals was correct. The association was presumed to have occurred after his original force was driven out by the Japanese forces to the Russian Maritime Province in 1941.

It is also believed that Kim spent some years with Chinese Communist guerrillas and joined the Chinese Communist Party in the 1930s. Thus Kim was exposed to both Russian and Chinese communists for a considerable period. Through these experiences he had observed the nature of communism first hand and formed his own brand of communism that included various political tactics advocated by both Stalin and Mao. In spite of his enigmatic background, Kim Il Sung's anti-Japanese credentials could be judged formidable compared to that of his many political rivals. Nevertheless, just as Rhee had experienced in the south, Kim initially encountered serious challenges from his communist rivals in the north. Korea is a nation that never lacks aspirants for political power regardless of the high price it often demands.

Kim Il Sung was introduced on October 14, 1945, to the north Korean public by Cho Man-sik, a prominent and revered nationalist leader, with an endorsement identical to General Hodge's welcome for Syngman Rhee on October 20 in the south. Partly by their own desires and each respective occupation command's need to install a political leader who was ideologically compatible to political backers, these two leaders were pushed into the main stage of the Korean political drama and expected to fill the leadership vacuum the liberation had created. Both men, being self-centered, ruthless to their rivals but jealously nationalistic, soon established themselves as the foremost speakers for their respective halves of Korea. Other political contenders - Kim Goo of the Korean Provisional Government, Kim Mu Chong (most celebrated military man in the north due to his high ranking position in the Chinese communist military), Yeo Un Hyung of the moderate left, who was popular in the south - were to fade away as the two men's political domination became nearly complete. By designating a political leader in their respective occupied zones, the occupation commands were ready to allow Koreans to establish two separate governments on both sides of the thirty-eighth parallel.

By the end of 1946, Russia and its Korean allies could have felt considerable satisfaction over their work in the north. The approach to remain behind the scene and to give the Korean collaborators substantial freedom enabled the Russian occupation administration to run economically and perhaps, more importantly, to shield it from criticism of the north Korean public, who were sensitive to interference of a foreign power regardless of its intentions. The north Korean political leadership, consisting of a coalition of the left, struck up a cooperation with the popular people's committees in carrying out fundamental reforms demanded by the public. By the end of the year, the north had created effective police and defense forces. The north's military - contrary to the south's, whose recruits mostly came from the former Japanese police and military ranks - was built exclusively with anti-Japanese fighters with the backbone comprised of members formerly belonging to Kim Il Sung's own guerrilla force.

Political events were evolving much faster in the north than in the south. The credit for the success in the north, however, did not solely belong to the Russian occupation command and the Korean communists. Pyongyang, the capital of the northern half, remained only of secondary importance in Korean politics. The rebuilding tasks in the north were far less complicated and time consuming than those in the south. Therefore, by the end of 1946 the north emerged as a dangerous challenge to the south, where the political situation remained far from clear or settled. So muddled was the political situation in the south that even Kim Il Sung's eagerness to attempt taking over the south had to wait until things were sorted out first.

The trusteeship accord created a wild political storm in the south from which the opportunistic rightists came out winners at the expense of the leftists. The trusteeship issue not only highlighted the widening chasm between anti-trusteeship rightists and pro-trusteeship leftists but served as a fateful trap for the leftists in the south. The left was on the defensive after its sudden shift from the anti-trusteeship to pro-accord stand, and was being accused by the rightists of being a machine controlled by the Russian communists. The left failed to advance a convincing justification for its support of the accord. The leftists' pro-trusteeship stand gave the rightists much needed justification to destroy the incompatible leftists, and on this point the American occupation apparently agreed with the rightists.

While Korea was suffering a profound confusion in the trusteeship issue, America and Russia made the last attempt to salvage the accord by convening two U.S.-Soviet Joint Commission meetings in 1946. Yet no agreement was reached that was acceptable to both halves of Korea and their respective backers. Neither America nor Russia was willing to yield the whole Korean peninsula to the other while the option of keeping half of it was still valid and firm. Moreover, the divided nation would serve the security interests of both America and Russia well, at least for the time being. The failure of the joint commission meetings effectively ended any prospect of establishing a unified government supported by both powers. It also meant the end of the Rooseveltian trusteeship plan that had been America's official policy for postwar Korea since 1943.

After the trusteeship plan totally unraveled, America pursued an avenue intended to grant southern Korea immediate independence as the Korean public had demanded. The U.S. thus turned for the Korean solution to the United Nations, an international organization in which America had exercised an overwhelming influence. As requested by the American delegation, the United Nations General Assembly adopted a resolution that defined procedures to establish a free and democratic government through a general election in both halves of Korea. For supervisory purposes, the United Nations authorized the creation of the United Nations Temporary Commission on Korea. Thus, America had obtained a legal sanction from the world's new police organization to take steps to implement Korea's immediate and unconditional independence.

Although the resolution called for a general election, the UN commission's entry into northern Korea was rejected by the Russian occupation command. Subsequently, the United Nations had authorized the election to be held within the area where it was feasible. Thus the stage was set to install a pro-American, anti-communist government in the territory occupied by the American forces. The UN resolution was not a surprise for either America or its south Korean allies, namely the Korean Democratic Party and Syngman Rhee, for they preferred a separate government to a unified government containing Russian-backed leftists or communists. Against the left-leaning idealists who did not relinquish their bid to unify the nation until the last moment, the realists, Syngman Rhee in the south and Kim Il Sung in the north, prevailed in the end. For over two years the Korean people had yearned and struggled for a free nation tended by a single central government only to be forced to accept the division of their liberated nation along the political spheres of the two world superpowers.

The South Labor Party, which represented communists in the south, waged the most vehement protests against the United Nations' resolution for the general election to be held only in the south. They rightfully criticized the UN sponsored election, saying it would divide the nation forever. To prevent the election, the communists employed brutal riots and guerrilla warfare nationwide. The communists' offense was often spectacular and powerful since it was also intended to demonstrate their strength not only to the rightists in the south but also to communist rivals in the north. The occupation command and South Korea's national Police responded to the communist sabotage with equal determination and effectiveness. Their campaigns against the communist riots were in effect the culmination of their successful suppression of leftists and communists in the south, which had commenced in the pacification of the nationwide leftist riots in late 1946. The South Korean police effectively eradicated communists and their sympathizers who had penetrated into many government organizations, forcing the remnants to go underground. Finally, the leftists and communists that had dominated the rural south during the first two years of the occupation period were effectively subjugated by the American-sponsored rightists in the south. If the American offense against the leftists had not been so decisive, the south would very likely have been won by the communists. Thus the southern region had become America's first successful defense against its rival in the Cold War. The American occupation command was the primary institution that helped to wrestle Korea back from the jaws of the communists, even if it was only a half.

Korea's first general elections took place on May 10, 1948, in areas to which the UN Temporary Commission on Korea had an access, meaning all parts of south Korea under the American occupation. The elections were held as planned even though the leftists and some middle-roaders refused to participate. The rightists and conservatives emerged as the overwhelming majority as expected. The one hundred ninety-eight elected representatives formed Korea's first National Assembly; one hundred seats were left vacant for its northern region, which denoted a rough proportional division of the population at the time. Empty seats in the assembly were a symbolic gesture representing the desire of the Korean people to form a unified government. Under the new constitution signed on July 17, the assembly elected Syngman Rhee as the first president of the Republic of Korea. On August 15, 1948, the third anniversary of the liberation, the Republic was officially proclaimed to be in business. The United Nations duly recognized the Republic of Korea as the only legitimate government in the Korean peninsula.

Upon the establishment of a government in Seoul, the north was left with only two plausible options. It could join the government in the south and compete against anti-communists and conservatives, whom northern communists did not hesitate to call Japanese collaborators and traitors. In the assembly, if the north joined, it would have had a two to one numerical disadvantage, let alone the firmly attached stigma in the south as the Russian puppets and tools of international communist conspiracy. Nonetheless, the north would have exercised considerable power; Kim's communist party with its solid base in the north could have emerged as a strong political force supported by well-organized socialist organizations in the south, including the still powerful South Labor Party under the capable leadership of Park Hun Young. Kim Il Sung should have considered joining the Seoul government, for this could have prevented the division of the nation and enriched the new government with the experience of various reforms he had implemented successfully in the north. Instead, he chose, or was forced to choose, the other option available to him - to establish a separate government in Pyongyang.

The formation of the People's Republic of Korea (North Korea) was proclaimed in September, 1948, in Pyongyang. Almost 1,300 years after Silla's unification of the three kingdoms, the Korean nation had again been divided into two separate entities. Koreans had precious opportunities to bring both halves together and work out the ideological difference in a brotherly manner. Instead, the nation's two leaders, whose personal ambitions and narrowly defined patriotism were smartly disguised with the Western ideologies, had consented to a solution that was to serve the Western interests foremost. The imposed nature of the solution was most ironic because the division of the country was justified by ideological incompatibility, yet the Korean public did not have even a rudimentary knowledge of the contending capitalist and communist ideologies. In any event, Korea's two self-claimed supreme patriots had created two separate governments that were remarkably similar in structure to the government of their respective backers, each insisting his system a true democracy. In a sense, they merely followed a shameful national tradition that governments tend to serve the rulers, not the public.

The ruling class of the South that was dominated by Syngman Rhee and the conservative Korean Democratic Party were never too eager to take genuine steps needed to unite the South with their communist brothers in the North. They would have been receptive to do so only under their own terms. Being fiercely political and typically divisive, they were capable of settling for a short term advantage even at the expense of long term national interests. They were singularly oblivious of the tragedy of court politics of the Chosun dynasty, to which they aspired to succeed. In this regard, Syngman Rhee and his followers may not be exempt from harsh criticism. Yet there is little indication that Kim Il Sung and his followers did differently in the North. On the contrary, their speedy Sovietization of North Korea might have convinced the rightist leaders in the South that a compromise was impractical.

Kim Il Sung and his Russian backers were pursuing a separate government in the North as early as 1946 when the North Korean

Provisional People's Committee was established with Kim Il Sung as its chairman. The People's Committee and its successor remained as the highest administrative organ in North Korea until September 1948. Having established a governmental structure, the communists drafted a constitution in November 1947. Predictably, the new North Korean constitution was much similar to the 1936 Soviet constitution in overall institutional structure.[9] While they were engaging in propaganda wars with the South over the UN resolution to hold a general election in the South, the communists were preparing a general election themselves in the North. The election for the supreme people's assembly was held on August 25, 1948, and the new constitution was ratified by the assembly on September 8. Kim Il Sung was named premier of the People's Republic of Korea on September 10. Thus two Koreas emerged from the occupied zones, sponsored by respective powers, although the support given to Kim and Rhee were by no means identical.

Kim had enjoyed solid Russian support from almost the very beginning of the occupation, while the Americans treated Rhee with a considerable degree of ambivalence. Nevertheless, both superpowers succeeded in creating some rough copy of their own system in their respective occupied zones. Rooseveltian trusteeship proved to be unacceptable to the Korean public, but immediate Sovietization was also resisted. The political systems largely imposed by the occupation powers were to remain foreign to the Korean people for a protracted period of time. Nevertheless, Korea was at long last to become the land of the Koreans although it remained divided.

The political objectives of both America and Russia in postwar Korea were remarkably similar in essence but quite unlike those of the Japanese or Chinese. China had sought Korea's symbolic submission to the cultural superiority of the Middle Kingdom. Korea had learned that the geopolitics of the peninsula dictated its compliance, even if largely superficial. As a result, Sadaeism was born and became the backbone of Chosun's China policy. The long-term damage of such an arrangement was never seriously contemplated. Japanese ambition in Korea was far more extensive and complicated; it attempted to incorporate Korea into Japan's own territorial system. This typical colonial arrangement was insufficient to satisfy the island nation's ambition on the Asian mainland. In contrast, America and Russia, the non-Asiatic powers to dominate Korea for the first time in its history, strove to bolster and support systems that would preserve a continuing political and economic orientation toward themselves. In order to secure a dependable leadership for such a system, they brought Kim - in the Russian case - and invited Rhee - in the American case - and provided them with substantial political support. Within the range of maintaining a proper alignment, they allowed each government a measure of independence and self-government. Yet neither was willing to tolerate Korean independence or unification at the cost of risking their strategic interests in their respective sphere of domination.[10] Both foreign amies were withdrawn from the Korean peninsula at the end of 1949. At long last Korea was without an occupation army, divided but free from outside occupiers.

Notes

1. Bruce Cumings, *The Origins of the Korean War, Liberation and the Emergence of Separate Regimes.* Princeton: Princeton University Press, 1981, p. 103.
2. *Sherwood*, p. 773
3. Cumings, p. 107.
4. *Ibid.*, p. 113.
5. *Ibid.*, p.116.
6. *Collins*, p. 25.
7. *Cumings*, p. 139.
8. Allan Millett, *For the Common Defense, A Military History of the United States of America.* New York: The Free Press, p. 486.
10. Chin Chung, *Pyongyang Between Peking and Moscow: North Korea's Involvement in the Sino-Soviet Dispute*, 1958-1975. p. 21.
11. *Cumings*, p. 437.

Chapter 10

The Korean War: A Civil International Conflict

1. The Origin of the War

The Korean War lasted for only three years. If the period of long stalemate along the eventual truce line is excluded, the actual war period was even shorter. In spite of its short duration, however, this war was one of the deadliest in history, memorable particularly for wanton physical destruction as well as excessive human suffering. From the way it was fought and the international scope of participation one can easily get an impression that it was not a simple civil war. Then, again, it was not a typical international conflict, either. Ironically the war broke out essentially as a civil conflict, a direct result of Japan's colonial occupation of the peninsula. Yet from the very outset, the conflict was heavily colored by the mentality of the postwar East-West confrontation and escalated into an ideological war of an international dimension. Forces participating in the conflict included the United Nations contingent, comprising troops from sixteen member nations, in addition to Korean units representing both halves of the nation. The People's Republic of China later sent its army on behalf of North Korea. Direct and indirect participants in the operations clearly bore out the notion that the Korean conflict was more a small-scale world war than a civil war.

The war could have been won by either side: by the North in the early part of the conflict or by the United Nations forces months later. Yet neither side managed to win a clean victory. By virtue of not being able to score a conventional victory, both sides had lost. Korea gained nothing from the war, in spite of such terrible devastation; it had brought about no major territorial realignment, let alone the unification of the nation. It was a profoundly futile conflict in the sense that it solved no pending questions despite its extensive scope and severity. On the other hand, a "proxy" war that was the first major flare-up of the postwar Cold War period might not have been expected to solve any civil dispute.

For the citizens of the remote Land of Morning Calm the war was just another geopolitical punishment. Then, again, Korea is by no means a country with ordinary geopolitical properties. Like a tree standing in the way of a trade wind, the citizens of the troublesome peninsula were not allowed to remain undisturbed for long. The war was a product of this trade wind, born by the regional externalities that had rarely been kind to docile inhabitants of the Korean peninsula.

The origin of the Korean War still remains controversial to the present day. Yet most available records conclusively indicate that the North initiated the so-called "liberation war." Moreover, it appears that North Korea began the war with no direct prodding from either of its Communist backers. It is equally evident that both the Soviet Union and Communist China willingly cooperated with North Korea once Kim's invasion scheme was presented to them.[1] Before some specific points are discussed, it would be useful to examine the Korean peninsula's postwar geopolitics.

Though it proceeded to occupy southern Korea militarily, the United States had no firm policy toward Korea during the 1945-1950 period. America did play the role of a midwife to the birth of the Republic of Korea (South), a feat engineered under the auspices of the United Nations. Still, during the post-independence period U.S. policy toward Korea remained anything but firm, sending many conflicting signals; at times it appeared to disavow the responsibility to protect the new republic from a probable communist takeover attempt. Vague and noncommittal foreign policy statements made by various American officials left a strong impression that America was unsure of its role in Korea.

Washington's unsettling policy toward Korea was not spontaneous. As early as September 1947, the United States Joint Chiefs of Staff stated that Korea was not essential for the security of the United States.[2] It is worthy to note that the question was whether or not Korea was needed "for" the security of the United States. Furthermore, Secretary of the State Dean Acheson publicly declared, in his Asian policy speech on January 12, 1950, that the American defense perimeter in the Pacific ran from the Aleutians to the Philippines, enclosing Japan. By deliberate omission he managed to leave a strong impression that South Korea was excluded from America's critical defense perimeter. His weak qualification - Washington regarded the security of Korea as the United Nations' responsibility that the U.S. would have to respect - escaped the attention of most observers, including the Communists.[3] The Truman administration's apparent low esteem for the strategic value of South Korea was also shared by the U.S. Congress; on January 19, 1950, the House of Representatives defeated the administration request to provide $60 million in supplementary economic assistance to the Republic of Korea. Even in the light of the bill's subsequent passage, the vacillation was another indication that Washington's support of the Republic of Korea was remarkably soft and uncertain.

During the immediate postwar period the strategic value of the Korean peninsula remained uncertain to the United States largely because it had been experiencing difficulties in establishing a policy that might have clarified its strategic objectives in the region. This ambiguity was partly caused by the region's concomitant political makeup, which raised serious questions over the peninsula's defensibility.[4] Korea's geographic juxtaposition to the Communist-dominated Asian mainland had entirely disparate strategic implications, depending upon the posture of the United States and its new regional rival, the Soviet Union. While Washington's Korean policy remained fluid, the impression proliferated, both in Korea and abroad, that the United States did not consider the survival of the Seoul regime vital to its security. Regardless of its true intentions, which were still unsettled, Washington's lukewarm support of South Korea projected a strong impression that the U.S. would not rush to save South Korea even if a hostile attempt was launched by North Korea.

By 1950 the impression that the United States was prepared to tolerate the loss of South Korea had become pervasive. This view was further strengthened by a number of actions taken by the American military establishment, which, after all, attached a low strategic value to the Korean peninsula. Washington not only had resisted strengthening its military presence in South Korea but also had implemented the early withdrawal of its occupation force. Moreover, after the withdrawal, it had provided South Korea with financial resources suitable only for a limited buildup of its newly-formed military. Both the United States' military establishment and Congress refused to recognize South Korea's legitimate military needs. On the contrary, they supported the Truman administration's stand that objected to the formation of the South Korean defense force comparable to that of its counterpart in the North.[5]

When Washington withdrew its occupation force from Korea in mid-

1949, it left behind equipment barely suitable to arm a 50,000-men force. The armament transferred to South Korea was not only insufficient for the projected South Korean defense force but, more important, consisted mainly of small arms. Tanks and other heavy weapons were all withdrawn based on the judgments of American military advisors in Korea, who had concluded that the Korean terrain, roads, and bridges would make operations of heavy weaponry ineffective. When the cloud of war darkened in the spring of 1950, the Republic of Korea managed to field a hastily assembled force of 98,000 men equipped only with an insufficient number of vintage small arms. The ROK forces had no heavy artillery pieces, no tanks, no anti-tank weapons, and no military aircraft at their disposal. Yet the American military advisory group projected that the Republic of Korea forces were capable of defeating the North Korean People's Army as long as there was no foreign military intervention. Under this erroneous but favorable assumption, Washington rejected President Rhee's urgent requests for more sophisticated weapons. The Rhee regime's domestic difficulties, ranging from a mismanaged economy to coercive politics, also contributed to Washington's reluctance to provide more aggressive support to the Seoul government. By the time the United States' ambassador to Korea made a sharply different assessment that North Korea would have a margin of victory in the event of a full scale war, the actual outbreak of the war was only about two weeks away.

America's intelligence apparatus in South Korea had failed to assess accurately North Korea's rapidly growing military capability, let alone its intentions. Furthermore, Americans failed to grasp the significance of the North Korean leaders' self-imposed mission of unifying the nation, which was repeatedly and openly claimed by both Kim Il Sung and Park Hon Yung. Kim Il Sung made no secret of his ardent desire to unify the peninsula under his initiative. As early as December 1945, Kim made his so-called "democratic base" approach public, revealing a scheme of building a powerful democratic base in the North first in order to use its revolutionary energy in unifying the whole country under communism. In 1949 he repeated the claim in his letter to U.N. Secretary General Trygve Lie, making it clear that he would use any means at his disposal to unify the country under his leadership. However, it is not fair to imply that only the northern leaders harbored such an intense yearning for the unification of the country. South Korean leaders, including Syngman Rhee and the nationalist Kim Goo, shared the same desires and moral obligation for the national unification. For Rhee the unification of Korea under its own independent and pro-Western government was also his lifelong pursuit. Neither Rhee nor Kim would have shied away from using military means to achieve the national unification if given a favorable opportunity.

As of June 1950, South Korea had a defense force that was far from being capable of launching any offense against the North; for an offensive force, the South Korean military lacked experienced officers, heavy equipment, naval ships, military aircraft, and proper training. It was still more suitable for duties such as suppression of local riots and routine, peacetime police activities. It was not even an effective defensive force, particularly against an all-out invasion staged by well-organized and heavily equipped North Korean forces, as the early part of the war demonstrated.

Nor was the United States prepared to make a full-scale military response on behalf of South Korea. In a short five years after the end of World War II, the United States' military forces had been dismantled to such a degree that they were ill-prepared to fight a war even against such a secondary military power as North Korea. By June 1950, the U.S. Army was down to 592,000 men, about one-seventh of its 1945 strength. In the Far East, the U.S. maintained a force of only 83,000, all in Japan. Furthermore, the majority of this contingent was performing duties of the occupation army. The United States possessed in the region neither combat-ready units that had sufficient battle experience nor sufficient heavy weapons that were needed to defeat the heavily armed North Korean forces.[6]

For all practical purposes, Kim Il Sung in his unification drive abandoned a political solution in favor of a military campaign after the South formally established its government in Seoul. Installing his own administration in Pyongyang, he concentrated the regime's energy and resources in building military strength. Ironically, North Korea's military adventure was hastened by the intense Kim Il Sung-Park Hon Yung rivalry over control of the Korean Communist movement. To outflank Park, one of a few political opponents who remained capable of challenging him, Kim needed a decisive move. Another important factor contributing to the early initiation of the conflict was the supposed readiness of the South Korean Labor Party (SKLP), which operated underground. The communists in the North, calculating that SKLP was in control of more than a half million followers in the South, expected the southern communists' full-scale collaboration for their military venture. By the end of 1949 the invasion was a foregone conclusion, leaving only the exact time of the attack undecided.

Unlike in the South, North Korea's military build-up had progressed rapidly with the full support and supervision of the Soviet Union. Since 1946, North Korea had dispatched to the Soviet Union over 10,000 soldiers to train as pilots, aircraft mechanics, and experts in tank warfare and maintenance. Upon their return they had become cadres in the mechanized units of the new North Korean Army. North Korea formed its army with these Soviet-trained soldiers and a core of battle-hardened troops, the latter having fought during the colonial period against the Japanese forces in Manchuria. The North's strength was further augmented by more than 12,000 seasoned soldiers who had been earlier sent to Manchuria to help the Chinese communists' campaign against the Nationalists.

The war preparations undertaken by North Korea and its Russian backers were both extensive and meticulous. The North Korean military filled its commanding officers' positions exclusively with Koreans. Still, the Soviet Union maintained its potent influence; by the end of 1948 the Northern military was fully under the direction of Soviet advisors. Numbering 3,500 by June 1950 and assigned to all North Korean military units above the company level, the Soviet advisors were in charge of training. They were called back only days before the invasion.[7] The Soviet Union was also the sole source of armament for the North Korean military, supplying the North Korean forces with at least 170 fighter planes and attack bombers and some 300 tanks during the short pre-war period. With these extensive supports the North Korean forces had come to enjoy an overwhelming advantage over the South Korean forces in almost every category of heavy weaponry. The Soviet aids also provided the Pyongyang regime with financial resources enabling it to command a two-to-one advantage over the South in military manpower.

In North Korea's extensive war preparations the contributions of the People's Republic of China (PRC) were relatively inconspicuous. Yet the Beijing regime did not remain totally neutral; as the war drew closer, the PRC mobilized many combat units, moving them into Manchuria. In view of the bilateral defense treaty signed by Communist China and North Korea earlier, this troop movement was a significant development.[8] By positioning its huge army in the Sino-Korea border region, the Chinese Communists provided North Korea not only a safe sanctuary for retreat in case the attack failed but also a reserve army when needed. The Chinese leadership had concluded that its force had to intervene if the North Korean military was under pressure.[9]

North Korea's military build-up proceeded with typically totalitarian unity. Yet there is no direct evidence to portray the pre-war Kim Il Sung government as a passive gun for imperial Russia or for a monolithic Soviet system totally subservient to international Communism. Although the extensive involvement of the Soviet Union in North Korea's war preparation efforts cannot be denied, by no means should the launching of the war be depicted as a simple international conspiracy. It would be unfair to deny North Korea the proper credit for having a nationalistic motive, which was the only positive aspect of this ruefully bloody conflict.

Korea had not been divided by foreign powers alone. The division was as much of the Korean people's own making as it was a product of external interference generated by postwar strategic games played by the United States and the Soviet Union. Regardless which side the United Nations supported, both the Seoul and Pyongyang governments could have claimed the same ground as far as legitimacy was concerned. In reality, recognition by the U.N. was no more than a Western formality that either Korean government might have elected to ignore. As for North Korea's nationalistic leaders, a war intended to unify the country should have been a totally justifiable avenue of action. The same rationale could have been applied by South Korea if and when it chose to unify the country by force or other means. The fact that the war initiative was heavily supported by the two communist giants is beside the point.

2. The North on Offense

Early Sunday morning, June 25, 1950, North Korea launched massive frontal attacks along the entire demarcation line, the thirty-eighth parallel. The attack, spearheaded by six well-trained and well-equipped army divisions, caught the South Korean defense forces in total surprise. In spite of warnings and gloomy predictions of eventual eruption of hostilities, neither South Korea nor the United States had anticipated that war would erupt on that quiet Sunday morning.

The invasion quickly threw South Korea into chaotic confusion. The hapless Rhee government only worsened the situation by issuing empty claims that the invaders would be repulsed shortly. On the contrary, the South Korean (ROK) forces, poorly equipped and under-trained, tried to slow the invasion but only proved that they were hopelessly overpowered. Early encounters of the two armies proved that the South Korean forces were grossly inadequate to deal with Kim Il Sung's highly efficient war machine. Their desperate resistance was anything but sufficient to defend the capital city from the North's onslaught. North Korean forces captured Seoul in four days, forcing the Rhee government to evacuate to the southern city of Taejun. The military situation deteriorated hourly as the invasion columns encountered only token resistance. It was evident that the South possessed neither manpower nor equipment to stop the invaders, and the United States alone had the military power to prevent North Korea's complete military victory.

The red army's astonishing drive was what North Korean planners projected; they were confident that the conquest of the South would be accomplished in fifteen days, an arrogance based on their extensive war preparation. It proved to be more than a daydream, however, almost succeeding; within three months after it crossed the demarcation line the North managed to capture the whole territory of the south except for a small pocket around Pusan, the nation's largest port and second largest city, located in the southeast corner of the peninsula. Throughout the early phase of the conflict the surprise was not the South Korean army's ineptitude but the North Korean army's spectacular efficiency.

As the North Korean army began to overpower the South Korean defenders along the front, the United States' policy toward both South Korea and international Communism as a whole met a severe test. Yet neither North Korea nor South Korea was sure of what Washington's reaction might be, having witnessed the United States' conspicuous ambivalence in its Korean role during most of the postwar period. Both were aware that the Truman administration had two entirely contradictory, far-reaching choices: it could write off South Korea and accept the North's military conquest as a punishment for its failure to anticipate the event and to train and equip South Korean forces adequately; or it could intervene militarily by reversing its irresolute Korean policy. Washington had little time to deliberate its options.

The invasion news reached Washington on Saturday, June 24, 1950. Unlike its dubious attitude toward the defense of South Korea, the Truman administration's response to the outbreak of hostility was not only decisive but also expeditious. Those aggressive diplomatic and military initiatives taken by the United States in the first few days of the outbreak made a critical difference for the war itself as well as for Korea's political future.

From the very beginning the United States maneuvered to portray the war as the socialist movement's overt challenge to Western democracy and as North Korea's open contempt of the integrity of the United Nations. Implying that South Korea was founded under the United Nations' explicit mandate, Washington succeeded in characterizing the Korean civil conflict as a communist offense against United Nations' authority. With crafty diplomatic maneuver Washington persuaded the United Nations to assume the responsibility of restoring order and peace in the Korean peninsula, thus making the Korean War the first war fought by the world organization.[10]

The Korean War(1950-1953)

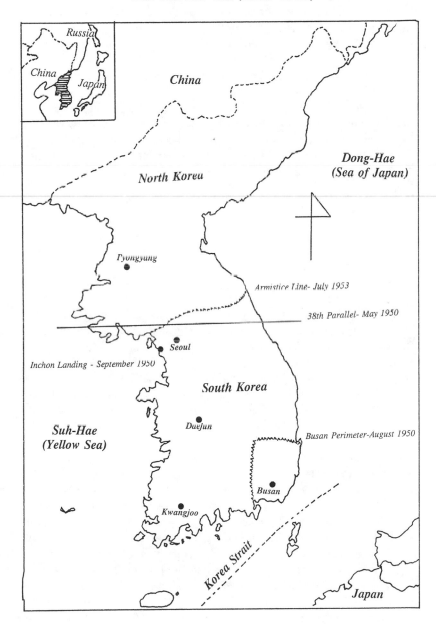

The United Nation's Security Council met on Sunday, the second day of the conflict, and adopted a resolution that accused North Korea of an armed attack and called upon both parties to impose an immediate cease-fire. The next day it passed another resolution recommending that its members furnish assistance to the Republic of Korea to repel the armed attack. Thus, for the first time in history an international organization assumed for itself a role of collective peace enforcer.

The Soviet Union's U.N. delegation did not participate in the Security Council's deliberation on the Korean conflict. It had stayed away from Council activities since January of that year because of a dispute over the Chinese seat at the Council. Thus, Moscow missed the critical opportunity to use its veto power against the U.S.-backed resolution. Had the Soviet delegation been present, it is commonly conjectured, the resolution would not have passed, and the motion to send the United Nations' force to Korea could have been blocked. Instead, without the participation of one of the super powers, the world organization voted to use its own armed forces for a police action in Korea. Remarkably overlooked was the fact that neither party to the hostilities belonged to the organization. Since it was not a dispute between its members, the move was more like an international organization's effort to arrest an outlaw.

With the UN decision to take a collective police action against North Korea, Washington had in reality transformed a civil war into an international conflict. Moreover, as the United Nations was assuming overall military responsibility in Korea, the United States avoided being seen as a super power waging a war against a small third world country alone. Considering that the bulk of the UN force was supplied by the United States, the difference might have been more symbolic than substantial. Nevertheless, it was a significant factor that gave the war a drastically different meaning.

Washington's immediate and strong response to the hostilities represented a notable reversal of its earlier indecision over the defense of South Korea. Its publicized ambiguity over the defense perimeter in the Far East, which might have been a direct source of the fatal North Korean misjudgment, now all but disappeared. Instead, the United States made clear its intention to defend the territorial integrity of South Korea using every means at its disposal. Its sudden policy shift over the Korean defense caused a great deal of bewilderment in both Beijing and Moscow.[11]

The American public hailed the Truman administration's firm response and its drastic reversal of the U.S.'s uncertain role in the Far East. The administration, suspected of being soft on international communism because of the fall of China to the communists in 1949, could ill afford the loss of Korea. Furthermore, Washington regarded the outbreak as part of an orchestrated offensive of international communism that might spread to other spots around the world unless resolutely checked in Korea.[12] To the Truman administration, the Korean War was a Soviet challenge designed to test the will and strength of the Western democracies, and thus it ought to be countered accordingly.[13]

In its successful U.N. diplomacy the United States exploited the argument that the attack was directed against the U.N. itself. This notion was based on the fact that South Korea was established under U.N. supervision while North Korea was not. Thus the decisions taken by the Security Council were defended as necessary in protecting the authority and prestige of the United Nations itself. It is self-evident why higher UN officials were receptive to such an argument.

Having lost the first round to the United States, the Soviets strove to negate the U.S. sponsored U.N. resolution by characterizing the conflict as a domestic dispute provoked by South Korea. Backing North Korea, the Soviet Union rejected any foreign interference in Korea's internal affairs, including that of the United Nations.[14] With the United States holding the Soviets ultimately responsible for the war while the Soviet Union accused South Korea, a protege of the United States, of the provocation, each superpower deliberately implicated the other in the war.

The Korean War was a formal benchmark for the opening of the aggressive Cold War between the United States and the Soviet Union. It represented a serious international challenge to both the world communist movement and Western democracy. From almost the very beginning, therefore, the war ceased to be a simple civil war intended to unify the divided country and instead became a "proxy" war representing the two sides of the East-West rivalry. In this war, fought in Korea predominantly by the Koreans, the Soviets would test the will of their new adversary while America would openly acknowledge the Korean peninsula as its new military frontier. The fact that President Truman justified U.S. involvement by claiming the necessity to prevent a third world war sufficiently illustrated the U.S. disposition toward the war. For the West, the North's military initiative had to be opposed, even if it may have reflected the Korean people's desire to unify the nation. To the United Nations and the United States, a divided Korea was clearly preferable to a unified one under communism.

On June 26, 1950, the United States decided to provide all-out air and naval support to South Korea under the umbrella of the United Nations command. Immediately, massive American military assistance was on the way to save one Korea from another Korea. As United States' troops headed to the Korean peninsula, the Nation of Morning Calm was to become the world's most active military frontier.

The United States was determined to make a point by displaying its will and military might to its communist adversary. Yet the Truman administration was cautious not to provoke a direct military confrontation with either the Soviet Union or Red China. In order to achieve this, Washington adopted the limited war concept, which required that air strikes be restricted to military targets in North Korea but to stay clear of both Chinese and Soviet borders. America was not ready to fight another world war in Asia, even against international communism.

While the United States Army under the command of General Douglas MacArthur was scrambling to assemble reinforcements in Japan, the South Korean defenders continued to engage in desperate holding actions with whatever tactics they could muster. Their ardor unavailing, however, successive defense lines crumbled quickly. On July 4, within ten days after the outbreak, the first detachment of U.S. forces was deployed on the front line.[15] Even after American combat units were introduced, the thrust of the North Korean forces remained overwhelming. Under the attackers' relentless pressure, the defenders were almost continuously in retreat. The North Korean army's blitz-like advance allowed the scrambling South Korean forces no time to regroup. For two months the North's forces successfully denied the defenders any respite needed to build an effective defensive line. Kim's total military victory appeared imminent.

Only when the U.N. and South Korean forces reached the southern province of Kyungsang-Do did North Korean forces begin to encounter serious resistance. By the middle of August, after mostly uninterrupted retreat and futile resistance, the United Nations' forces and their South Korean allies were able to muster enough strength to stall the advancing columns; they finally secured a precious redoubt from which they could regroup and wage counterattacks. Along the Nakdong perimeter the allied forces built a last-ditch defense line in a desperate attempt to escape the fatal predicament of being pushed into the sea altogether.

In addition to the United Nations' rapid troop build-up along the front and the defenders' acquisition of valuable battlefield experience, several other factors contributed in slowing the North Korean forces' march toward total conquest of the peninsula. As it made a rapid thrust in the southern part of the peninsula, the North Korean army encountered a critical challenge in safeguarding its long, exposed line of logistical support. This was partly due to Northern war planners' grave miscalculation of the speed of the advance. They had correctly assessed it to be critical for the North Korean army to finish the campaign as quickly as possible in order to minimize the dangers of external intervention. Thus, they envisioned the whole "liberation war" to be extremely short, a blitzkrieg variety. As a result, the supplies prepared for the campaign did not extend much beyond the amount needed for twenty days. In addition, Northern war planners had expected its "liberation army" to receive full and willing support from the South's farmers and workers, many of whom they had assumed to be communist sympathizers. However, the Southern farmers offered little support to the North and actively engaged in various kinds of sabotage against the invaders.

The second frustration to the North was the unexpected slowdown of their advance. Although the South Korean army was largely ineffectual in resisting the advancing columns of the invaders, the defenders had inflicted serious setbacks here and there to the extent that the advance lagged greatly behind the North's schedule. For example, the South Korean Army's timely destruction of the Han River bridge, which was the only bridge connecting the capital to the southern part of the nation, caused serious problems for the southward movement of tanks and other heavy equipment, and forced the invaders to lose a few precious days.

A third factor was the allied forces' ability to maintain absolute domination in air and naval warfare. As soon as the American forces were introduced into the war, they took unchallenged control of the air and sea. America's air supremacy was particularly deadly to the North Korean forces' logistical movements, restricting operations almost exclusively to the dark hours. The long supply route that had to be maintained to support the advancing columns became for the North Korean Army a logistical nightmare. Likewise, the North Korean positions along the sea coasts became untenable under bombardment of American ship-borne artillery.

A fourth factor was a costly strategic blunder committed by the North Korean military. North Korea's main thrust failed to rush to Busan, the "point of no return" for the defenders; instead, the invading force was dispersed to mop up pockets of resistance throughout the south. It was a costly and time-consuming operation that allowed more time for the UN forces to solidify their last ditch defense line along the Naktong River. The greatest surprise the communist invaders experienced in the South was the cool reception shown by the masses. The political and economic disorders that had engulfed South Korea since its establishment in 1948 were naturally construed as the South Korean public's disenchantment over the extreme-right Rhee government. Moreover, Pyongyang vastly overestimated the political influence of the South Korean Labor Party, its collaborator in the South. Under such an erroneous assumption the North's political leaders expected their advance columns to receive enthusiastic support from the South Korean masses. However, South Koreans treated the communist conquerors with open hostility. Communists did collect the support of the "partisans," the local communist collaborators. Yet by committing wanton violence that was intensely abhorred in the South, the partisans did more harm than good for their communist masters.

The communists' occupation of the South lasted only four months. Nevertheless, it was long enough to allow the Southern citizens who were dismayed and disappointed by the inept and insensitive Rhee government to discover the true meaning of the communist liberation. It was costly in terms of human lives as senseless killings and terror swept the occupied territory. Communist "purification" efforts were no more than elimination of individuals associated with any activities defined as objectionable to their narrow socialist doctrine. Tens of thousands of people were executed without trial. In the process, any faint hope that the communists might salvage the people from the tyranny of the rightist totalitarian regime quickly vanished. The brutal persecution and needless killings the invaders inflicted quickly persuaded the South Korean public that their own system, in spite of many faults, was irrefutably preferable to communist terrorism. The bloody occupation rendered the first opportunity for most South Koreans to learn the hostile nature of the North Korean communists, who descended on the south not as liberators but as brutal oppressors. The North Korean communists allegedly came to the South to "liberate" their Southern brothers from Rhee's oppression but ended up giving the unpopular Rhee regime a moral legitimacy and a new lease on its political life. In the end, the communists proved themselves to be the best teachers of anti-communism.

The stand-off at the Nakdong perimeter was the last defensive ploy for the UN forces. Once the Naktong line was breached there would be no plausible way to oppose the invaders; there were no more defensive lines behind which the U.N. forces could retreat. In all practicality, the next line of defense for the perimeter would have been the Korea Strait, which separates the Japanese islands from the Korean peninsula. When the U.N. forces and their South Korean allies clung to their last toehold in the peninsula, the invaders fully grasped the urgency of breaking through the Naktong defense line for the final blow. They realized that the allies were building up at the most frantic speed behind the line.

The North Korean forces, depleting their dwindling reserves of armor, ammunition, and manpower, carried out ferocious and reckless attacks night after night against the desperate defenders. Their daring drives came perilously close to success time after time, but UN forces managed to avert fatal disasters by the narrowest of margins.[16] Still, the beleaguered United States Eighth Army, commanded by General Walker, and the South Korean forces held the 130-mile defense line with a remarkable tenacity. Throughout the hot summer months of 1950 the UN and South Korean forces fought the desperate war that decided the eventual outcome of the conflict. It was a long and crucial six-weeks for both defenders and invaders. In the end, unable to inflict the last decisive blow on the defenders, the invaders suffered a setback that broke the spine of their southward advance. The allied forces withstood the North's onslaught, gradually gaining confidence and composure. For the first time there appeared some hope of an outcome that might favor the allied force led by the "least professional, least motivated armies America had ever put into the field." [17]

3. Return to the Status Quo Ante

On September 15, 1950, General MacArthur's UN forces made a successful landing at Inchon, a port city southwest of Seoul, commencing one of history's most daring counter-offensives. Having almost totally fooled the North Korean forces, MacArthur's sea-borne forces were highly effective in assaulting the North Korean army from its rear. Simultaneously, the Eighth U.S. Army, having survived the precarious seizure, began its northward push from the Nakdong perimeter. The U.N. forces' effective pincer operation inflicted staggering losses to the North Korean forces, nearly trapping the main body. In addition, the North's overextended supply lines and means of communication became easy prey to the U.N. forces' air and land attacks. Facing the allies' all-out counter-offensive, Kim's exhausted, over-extended war machine had no choice but general retreat, taking heavy losses along the way. The South Korean forces recaptured Seoul on September 28, 1950, shattering Kim's dream of unifying the country under his communist banner.

As the U.N. forces continued to decimate the retreating invaders in the South, they soon faced a momentous decision over the permissible geographic limits of their operation - whether or not to expand operations north of the thirty-eighth parallel. To the Truman administration the decision had to be made with political considerations of global scope, just as in its earlier decision to resist the aggression militarily. The United States was concerned about the possibility that UN forces marching in the north might provoke a military response from China and Russia.[18] Yet taking measures of precaution, the U.S. chose an all-out assault on the North Korean forces, extending the U.N. operation beyond the prewar demarcation line. Washington thus authorized the MacArthur command to extend its military operations north of the thirty-eighth parallel, providing that there was no entry by the Soviet or Chinese communist forces. At the same time, the U.S. administration made it clear that U.N. forces would not cross the Chinese or Soviet borders under any circumstances.

As the war was reversing its course, President Truman publicly reaffirmed Korea's right to have a free, independent, and unified government. In reality, his declaration meant that Washington intended to pursue the unification of the Korean peninsula under the U.N. banner. That it had just barely managed to frustrate Kim Il Sung's ambition to unify the country was conveniently buried. In the era of growing East-West competition, the unification of Korea itself was no longer an issue. The paramount issue was, however, under whose domination the unification would be achieved. Ironically, the Western ideologies, of which the Korean masses had little understanding, emerged as the most decisive factor in Korea's struggle for national unification. Both Kim and Rhee were unwittingly collaborating with the Western powers' global power game.

The U.N. decision to eradicate the North Korean forces could have been justified only under the assumption that the Northern regime was illegitimate. Otherwise, neither the United Nations nor the United States could have a mandate to destroy the North Korean forces. The North Korean army invaded no foreign country but its own country with an intent to rectify the division that had been a byproduct of superpower politics. The two extraordinarily nationalistic but uncompromising political figures who had come to dominate politics of divided Korea were both interested in unifying the nation. However, the peculiar postwar power politics had turned that simple desire into an epochal political event of global dimension. No longer did the matter concern the aspirations of the Korean people.

U.N. forces and the South Korean army made a rapid advance toward the northern half of the peninsula, encountering only scant resistance from by then totally demoralized North Korean forces. On October 9, 1950, the allied forces crossed the thirty-eighth parallel. On October 19, Pyongyang, North Korea's capital city, fell to ROK forces. The allies continued their northward drive, allowing the North Korean army no time to regroup. On October 25, spearheading the allied forces, the ROK army's first division reached the Amrok River, the Korean border with China. The unification of Korea was just a few steps away, not by the communists but by U.N. forces. The prospect of U.N.-imposed unification was a solution quite unexpected but nevertheless received with enthusiasm and joy by South Koreans as well as most North Koreans.

The end of the war had been widely touted as imminent when suddenly the Chinese Communists committed their military might against U.N. forces. Again, both the character and the course of the war took a wild turn as the Middle Kingdom refused to accept the U.N. victory against its Communist neighbor. The MacArthur command not only failed to prepare for the contingency but refused to believe in the early period of the intervention that there were Chinese forces fighting on behalf of North Korea, a delusion resulting from the incorrect assumption that Beijing would not or could not operate independently of Moscow.[19] The Chinese intervention was by no means a simple intelligence misfire but rather manifestation of complex regional politics that preordained the unique outcome of the conflict. The MacArthur command's dramatic failure to anticipate Chinese intervention later became the subject of widespread discussion in the United States.

The Chinese intervention was a quintessential element along with the U.S. intervention in characterizing the Korean War as an international conflict. If the American intervention represented U.S postwar political preoccupation to contain international Communism, China's intervention demonstrated its firm persuasion that its legitimate geopolitical interests extended into the Korean peninsula. Ming China responded to the Japanese invasion of Korea by sending a large contingent of troops in the sixteenth century; Ching China reacted in similar fashion again in the early nineteenth century when the Japanese influence grew to threaten its position in Korea. Historically, there had been unmistakable geopolitical precedents for China to resort to military actions in defense of its influence in Korea. From this historical perspective alone the U.N. command should have expected a hostile reaction from the Chinese when its forces reached the Korea-China border.

Yet there is considerable disagreement among observers over how eager the Chinese communists were to engage the United Nations forces in Korea. Chinese intervention should have been expected, considering the treaty obligation incurred by the China-North Korea mutual defense pact. On the other hand, it was an unlikely venture for the People's Republic of

China, which was suffering a myriad of domestic problems. In fact, the Chinese communists were facing the most awesome task of rebuilding and stabilizing their war-torn society when the North Korean forces were cornered by the U.N. and South Korean forces. China's domestic situation remained volatile to the extent that even its military leaders had serious reservations about sending the People's Liberation Army to the Korean front.[20] Besides, Chinese communists lacked quality forces for the Korean operation except for essentially a guerrilla army that was poorly equipped and trained.

Notwithstanding domestic difficulties, the Chinese communists were compelled to intervene in the war. China felt uncomfortable to have United States forces in north Korea in close proximity to its industrial center in the northeast.   Strategic considerations such as the United States' open commitment to protect Taiwan from the Chinese communists was also a factor. Mao and his colleagues had concluded that the liberation of Taiwan, their life-long ambition, could not be achieved without curbing U.S. influence in the region.[21] Thus defeating the United States, all the more an incompatible power because of its military involvement in Korea, would have served many strategic purposes for the Chinese communists. Still, Mao agonized long over the prospect of fielding his lighly equipped force against Western forces; his final decision to confront the United States in Korea was heavily influenced by the proddings of Stalin, who promised logistical support but believed that US-Soviet confrontation should be avoided at any cost. At any rate, the leading wave of the Chinese People's Volunteers, consisting of four corps and three artillery divisions commanded by Pen Dehuai, crossed the Amrok River on October 19, 1950.[22]

In the harsh winter months of 1950 the Chinese forces, effectively utilizing their absolute numerical superiority, waged savage battles against the U.N. forces with telling impact. Numbering more than 130,000 seasoned fighters, the Chinese quickly pushed the allied forces back along the entire front.[23] Night after night the Chinese soldiers launched unending frontal attacks, usually accompanied by yelling and blowing horns, terrifying the demoralized defenders. Initial results proved that engagement in the rugged mountain terrain at the peak of a harsh Korean winter was decisively favorable to the fresh, lightly equipped Chinese. The allied forces that had made a miraculous comeback and pursued the retreating North Korean invaders with supreme confidence and ardor were now forced to surrender their captured territories in general retreat. They abandoned Pyongyang on December 5, 1950.

Chinese intervention single-handedly unraveled the Korean peoples' second opportunity to unify their divided nation as the U.S.-led allied forces had done earlier. Neither the West nor the East was willing to allow the nation to unify itself. Like Korea's division, its unification had become a major East-West tug of war. Washington by then realized that the unification of two Koreas could not be accomplished without defeating the Chinese communists first, perhaps at the price of entering a general war with China. Facing the risk of a global war, Washington chose to abandon its months-old position to bring about the unification of Korea through military means. The unification of the Korean peninsula was not worth of risking war against China or the Soviets, who were providing most of the arms and replacement ammunition for the Chinese army fighting in Korea.

Encountering unexpected Chinese intervention, the United States and its UN backers retreated to their original position, the restoration of the status quo that had existed prior to the outbreak of the war. Accordingly, the United Nations abandoned its resolution to unify Korea by force and instead adopted a policy to remove its forces from Korea as soon as it was able to terminate the fighting.[24] The sudden turnabout clearly illustrated that the Korean people's desire for the unification of their country remained only an incidental issue to America's priority global strategy: the containment of the Soviet Union and the defense of Western Europe. Moreover, Washington's new position reflected the growing discontent of its Western European allies, who feared that the Korean conflict might evolve into a worldwide military confrontation between the East and West, most of which would be fought in Europe.[25]

The UN forces failed in establishing a successful defense line in Northern Korea. As the Chinese forces continued their southward thrust, the U.S. Joint Chiefs of Staff conceded that Communist China did possess the military capability to defeat the UN forces in Korea. Under this unfavorable assessment, Washington then began to consider strategic evacuation of the UN forces from Korea. Ferocious contests against a numerically superior Chinese army meant further troop losses. Furthermore, without large scale reinforcement it was estimated that the expected losses could endanger the Eighth Army itself. On the other hand, appropriating its remaining forces stationed in Japan for reinforcement would have left Japan defenseless. Washington had no attractive options.

MacArthur opposed the Joint Chiefs' pessimism and proposed taking broad retaliatory measures that would severely cripple the Chinese military capability at home. They included a naval blockade of the Chinese coast, air raids on China's major strategic targets, the reinforcement of the U.N. forces with Nationalist Chinese, and diversionary actions by Chiang

Kai-Shek's forces against mainland China.[26] MacArthur reasoned that without attacking the very source of the enemy's strength, the war could not be won; thus he wanted to expand the sphere of his military operations to China itself. The Joint Chiefs rejected MacArthur's recommendations and instead ordered the general to defend his forces until the losses of men and materiel forced him to evacuate.

It is important to note that President Truman saw the Korean War entirely from the perspective of an anti-communist campaign. He was waging the campaign to repel the invaders but only in order to frustrate the communists' international conspiracy.[27] The United States was fighting its first anti-communist war against the Korean invaders, not a Korean war against the communist invaders. The difference was by no means subtle and the ramifications far reaching. For President Truman, the unification of Korea, perhaps the only justifiable cause for the war in the first place, was not the primary reason to employ American troops in the action. Rather he was demonstrating his determination to contain international communism, even in the remote Korean peninsula. Having done that, he had less motive to insist upon a military victory that might have precipitated another global war. Moreover, under the critical military situation in which even the restoration of the status quo, a divided nation, looked futile during the dark winter months of 1950, Washington was swept by a strong surge of isolationism. America was prepared to accept a draw.

The allied forces evacuated Seoul on January 4, 1951. Yet their humiliating retreat continued, covering more than three hundred miles. It was not until they had reached the defensive line close to the thirty-seventh parallel that they were able to halt the communist columns in late January. However, the end of this long and humiliating retreat was another turning point; not only was the immediate crisis successfully averted, but the allied forces launched yet another counteroffensive that liberated Seoul for the second time.

General Matthew Ridgway's Eighth Army began its counteroffensive on January 25. Although the U.N. advance was slow and difficult this time, it managed to reclaim the capital city on March 24. By the middle of April the U.N. forces had advanced to establish a new defensive line above the thirty-eighth parallel. In spite of Ridgway's desire to send his troops further into North Korea, his advance was not allowed much beyond the thirty-eighth parallel. Unlike the previous drive, Washington prohibited any military operation that might become detrimental to arranging a cease-fire agreement and the restoration of the status quo ante of June 25, 1950. The thirty-eighth parallel was a political demarcation line in 1945; it had become again acceptable to America in 1951, even under vastly different circumstances. America's global political considerations superseded any military consideration when U.N. forces established a new defense line along the thirty-eighth parallel, a success that only inaugurated a war of attrition for the next two years.

While UN forces engaged in their second counter-offensive in the early months of 1951, a movement to end the costly and unpopular "police action" in Korea had been gathering strong popular support in the United States. A war in a faraway nation scarcely known to the American public was never popular. There was another critical undercurrent for Washington's apparent willingness to compromise, a fear of a nuclear confrontation with the Soviet Union. Korea was a convenient place to make a point, and it was also a convenient place to make a compromise. The army rejected the compromise overture, but when General MacArthur, who still insisted upon the unification of Korea by military means, was fired on April 11, the road for a negotiated settlement of the conflict was paved.

General MacArthur's insistence on pursuing a clean military victory, either a Chinese surrender on the battlefield or a total destruction of their homeland, was contradictory to the administration's limited-war, limited-objective policy. Yet MacArthur was well aware of the global implications of the Korean war, as he maintained that America had to resist communist aggression in Korea to save Europe and Asia. He was correct and had the courage to speak out the reality that America was fighting Europe's war in Korea.[28]

Moscow responded positively to the American proposal for a negotiated conclusion of the Korean civil war, a conflict in which both powers had been instrumental in elevating to an international war. Despite the superpowers' manifested eagerness to terminate the military contest, the looming prospect of an imposed armistice alarmed the South Koreans. It was a mystery for them that America would abandon the war effort while the cause of the conflict remained unresolved. South Koreans wished to settle conclusively the unification problem, for they had paid the price with enormous destruction and human suffering. It was a grave injustice to waste such incalculable sacrifices by signing a simple armistice without settling the very cause of the war. It was grossly unfair for tens of thousands of those who lost their lives and for millions of those who lost their homes to return to the status quo ante, even if a no-win solution was dictated by global considerations. The nation was full of emotion, and the public demanded that its voice be heard over how the war should be terminated. Regardless, a minor state like Korea rarely has that luxury, even if it is their own affair.

South Korea's response to a negotiated settlement was an empathetic "Buk Jin," or northward advance, at any cost. The vehement objection to an armistice underscored the South Korean people's desire to correct the very source of the internal conflict, the national division. They could scarcely fathom America's sudden unwillingness to repeat the march to the Amrok River only a few months after it almost assured the total destruction of the North Korean army. America's drastic policy shift, which was affected by the fact that the war was being fought in the shadow of nuclear destruction, was beyond the comprehension of the South Korean public. To South Koreans, who had little knowledge of the Korean War's growing unpopularity in the United States but had undying affection for America's courageous stand for freedom and righteousness, Washington's insistence on ending the war unfinished was deeply frustrating. At the end, South Korea had to yield to America's multiple pressures. The cease-fire negotiations were conducted by the representatives of North Korea and the United Nations command. South Korea, the primary victim of the war, was allowed to participate only as an observer.

America's resolve to end the conflict "with or without the Republic of Korea's government" overcame South Korean objections. In return, the United States made pledges to South Korea for a mutual defense pact and economic and military aid. As far as America was concerned, the war had been lost at the banks of the Chosin Reservoir when the Chinese volunteer force successfully ejected the allies. On July 27, 1953, the armistice was signed, and the fateful Demilitarized Zone(DMZ) along the thirty-eighth parallel fell silent. Yet there was no one who could rightfully claim a victory. After three years destruction, the war resolved nothing at all; the nation's unnatural but de facto demarcation line, established in 1945, remained about the thirty-eighth parallel, although heavy bombardments greatly defaced the natural landscape and methodically removed vegetation throughout the central part of the peninsula.

The Korean people had witnessed one of history's most ironic geopolitical episodes; North Korea's ambition to unify the motherland under the Communist banner was repulsed by the United States. In return, the opportunity to unify the country under the initiative of Western democracy was also frustrated by the People's Republic of China. The war's incalculable destruction and human suffering only underscored the reality that Korea's unruly geopolitics remained explosive even in a nuclear age.

However ironic it may seem, the war served the political purpose of the United States, a new superpower. As in earlier centuries and in recent decades, Korea merely lent a stage where the world's ideological rivals settled their differences and made a few clear points: the Communists did not hesitate to exploit a weak link of the United States' containment effort, while the United States made plain that it was willing to use military power to contain international communism. Yet each was equally reluctant to confront the other militarily or to use nuclear arms to achieve a total victory even in this surrogate war. In reality, hapless Korea again had been drawn in as a stage for a geopolitical drama that helped the United States the most to globalize the postwar Cold War.[29] After the war the United States undertook an extensive program to link free world countries with various political and military pacts to strengthen its containment ring around the Soviet Union.

The Korean War was postwar America's Rubicon in confronting the communist menace in broad global terms rather than in European terms alone. From this perspective, it could be judged a successful war for the United States. Having faced the unique geopolitical reality of the region, Washington had to settle for a limited war for which political objectives would have global implications for a long time. The outcome showed that in an age of nuclear weapons, an acceptable conclusion of a war did not have to be limited to a solution that could be interpreted as successful only in a conventional sense. Nonetheless, for the Koreans it was a cruel, cynical war in which the human suffering has lingered on even to today.

Notes

1. Nikita Khrushchev, *Khrushchev Remembers*. Boston: Little, Brown and Company, 1990. p.369.
2. John W. Spanier, *The Truman-MacArthur Controversy and the Korean War*. p. 120.
3. Allan R. Millett and Peter Maslowski, *For the Common Defense, A Military History of the United States of America*. p. 486.
4. The question was raised by Senator Connally, Chairman of the Senate Foreign Relations Committee.
5. Glenn D. Paige, *The Korean Decision*, p.69.
6. Robert T. Oliver, *Syngman Rhee and American Involvement in Korea, 1942-1960*, p. 289.
7. Khrushchev, p.370.
8. The People's Republic of China-North Korea defense treaty was signed in March 1949.

9.Sergei N. Goncharov, John W. Lewis, and Xue Litai, *Uncertain Partners; Stalin, Mao, and the Korean War, p.171.*

10. The only other very recent such case is the Gulf War of 1991.

11. Max Hastings, *The Korean War.* p.60.

12. Ibid., p.59.

13. Dean Acheson, *The Korean War.* p.248.

14. Burton I. Kaufman, *The Korean War, Challenges in Crisis, Credibility, and Command,* p.38.

15. The South Korean government transferred the command of its forces to the UN Command at this time. The arrangement remains valid at the present, although it now applies to only war situations.

16. Hastings, p.85.

17. Ibid., p.98.

18. The People's Republic of China did warn the UN force not to cross the 38th parallel through the Indian government. Refer to Sergei N. Goncharov.

19. Ibid., p.131.

20. Ibid., p.133.

21. Gittings, p.43.

22.Mao assigned the force under the jurisdiction of the Chinese People's Volunteers through his official order issued on October 8, 1950. Sergei N. Goncharov, p. 184.

23.Chinese People's Volunteers were units of the regular army, contrary to the impression the Chinese Communists might have intended. They were picked by Mao Zedong, Chairman of Central Military Commission, for the Korean task.

24. Kaufman, p.109.

25. Ibid., p.110.

26. Spanier, p.140.

27. Ibid., p.143.

28. Refer to MacArthur's farewell speech to the Congress.

29. Kaufman, p.356.

Chapter 11

Legacies of the Korean War

1. Postwar Period

In 1953, the entire Korean peninsula was buried under the ruins of the war, a mere eight years after its long-sought liberation from Japan. The Korean War, an odd combination of civil, regional, and international conflicts, had devastated the small nation as thoroughly as a wild fire. Raging from the northern tip to most of the south, the war not only disfigured the nation's moving natural beauty but quashed the aspirations and desires of liberated Koreans. It ushered in human sufferings of historical dimensions. When the guns finally fell silent, there was no victor but only victims on both sides of the monstrous thirty-eighth parallel. Fate bestowed once again its cruelty to the people of the Korean peninsula.

Over the years the physical damages of the war were mended, and out of the devastated ruins modern cities have emerged. Yet the emotional scars of the war are still lingering in witness to the paradoxical nature of humanity. Millions of those who fled to the south during the war have not been able to return to their families in the north. The Demilitarized Zone that separates the two Koreas remains the world's most heavily guarded frontier.

The Korean War was a peculiar incident in the sense that its outcome was calculated to be inconclusive by the superpowers' own political interests. By the time the truce was arranged, even the very character of the conflict was transformed into a "police action" in which restoration of the status quo and peace would be an acceptable objective.

The armistice silenced one of the most destructive civil wars in history and brought the nation a respite, although tentative at best. The war, in every aspect a futile exercise of misguided political ambition, solved nothing but wiped out the nation's meager infrastructure. The small peninsula remained divided into two military camps in spite of the astronomical material and human costs, which included almost two million killed or wounded soldiers, more than a million civilian casualties, and millions of refugees and homeless.

The cease-fire achieved nothing but a temporary cessation of military engagement; the situation along the truce line remained tense. Each side was compelled to maintain nervous vigilance over the other, while the arduous task of rebuilding the ravaged country lay before them. Neither the North nor the South had any illusion that the armistice would keep the other side from making another try to unify the nation, militarily or otherwise. Under unabated mutual suspicion and distrust, the cease-fire has never evolved into a major step toward the permanent resolution of the national division; it in a sense helped in prolonging the confrontation, although in the most acute cold war style. The current thawing of the icy North-South relations is a recent phenomenon of the 1990s.

The war created a deeper chasm between the two Korean states. The vague animosity existing during the prewar period between peoples of both sides of the thirty-eighth parallel had been transformed into more concrete personal feelings of enmity and incompatibility. The Communists remained committed to the unification of the country under their own red banner. In the North, an antagonistic attitude was born, based on categoric aversion to the United States, a power that had frustrated the Communists' attempt to "liberate" the motherland and that since has been condemned as a threat to its security. Along with the anti-American sentiment, the "liberation" of the southern brothers from "American imperialism" became the North's paranoiac obsession, a zealotry maintained for decades which categorically rejected any moderation whatsoever. In their uncompromising drive for a relentless anti-America and anti-South Korea campaign, however, the North Korean rulers demanded the public bear endless sacrifices.

The North's obsessive unification fervor has allowed the citizens of the South little comfort when they needed calmer intra-national relations to heal the deep scars of war. On the contrary, the North's unabated militancy has further convinced the South that the Communists are totally incompatible to its way of life. In the South, the prewar-period's open yearning for the unification of the nation had shifted to the firm belief that the unification had to be done, when and if feasible, without Communism. Filled with painful memories of the war and mindful of the abusive northern regime, still ruled by the same leader who sent down the invasion force, the South embarked on systematic efforts to turn the country into a modern-day fortress. In the South, anti-Communism had become not a mere ideological choice but a bare necessity for survival. To that end, the public has willingly accepted enormous sacrifices, both as individuals and as a state.

When the guns fell silent, both Koreas undertook the task of rebuilding their military forces, as if their primary objective was to eliminate each other militarily from the face of the earth. More than ever, the threat posed by the other side was each nation's foremost concern - a classic demonstration of Korean temperament. A national compromise was beyond the realm of an acceptable alternative; the slightest deviation from the official line was judged traitorous. For the following forty years Koreans have spent a disproportionate amount of their resources and creative energies just to fortify and penetrate the small real estate called the Demilitarized Zone (DMZ). On both sides of that ugly 155-mile long demarcation line that replaced the thirty-eighth parallel, two separate Korean states have faced each other with the world's best-trained armies. Filled with a thick wall of mines and barbed-wire entanglements, these conspicuous legacies of the Korean war still represent the world's most heavily fortified but absolutely useless piece of land. To Koreans, the fact that such an extreme absurdity was caused by the postwar East-West rivalry has been of little consolation.

The inconclusive war taught Koreans that the resolution of the nation's unnatural division has to be found by themselves. The national self-destruction was contrary to the fact that the nation of the Hahn people was entering the period of its long-delayed maturity after a protracted incubation period, which goes back to the late Koryo period. It should have been a clear warning for Koreans to outgrow the traps the Western ideologies created and for which they had already paid an extraordinary price. Yet the years that followed the armistice had shown anything but such national awakening. On the contrary, the nation was destined to suffer a dark period of unproductive internal struggle for decades to come.

Among the many adjustments the two Korean states had to make during the postwar period, North Korea's external relations were most significant. As an occupation force, the Soviet Union had established its dominant influence in the North as early as 1945. The withdrawal of Soviet forces that followed the formal establishment of the North Korean regime in 1948 did not diminish Moscow's overwhelming political influence there.

In order to counterbalance the preeminent influence of each other in its respective sphere, the United States and the Soviet Union maintained their unchallenged supremacy in both halves of the peninsula throughout the prewar period. Meantime, China and Japan, who had been Korea's enemies as well as backers at times, were both preoccupied with their own domestic chores of rebuilding war-torn nations.

The armistice was expected to signal the return of the region's prewar external equilibrium, a standoff between two superpowers. Yet the war introduced an element that quickly proved to be a significant barrier in the North's returning to its prewar external relations: the Soviet Union's overwhelming influence. The rise of the political leverage of Communist China in North Korea, a direct result of its effective military intervention in the Korean war, was to complicate North Korea's external relations and to some notable extent the postwar relations of the two Communist giants in the region. It was an interesting turn of events that the conflict facilitated by the rivalry between two occidental powers had enabled Oriental China to emerge as a threat to the Soviet Union's influence in North Korea. As postwar North Korea was obliged to accommodate the rising prestige of Communist China, its closest comrade-in-arms during the war, the Soviet Union, lost some of its preeminent influence in North Korea. In that sense, North Korea's problematic relations with its two powerful Communist neighbors were preordained when Chinese soldiers crossed the Yalu River in late 1950.

In comparison to the North, the South's postwar external relations remained stable, at least in the sense that the United States continued to be the only major foreign ally of the Seoul government. Japan's rise to regional power, as a logical successor to the United States, had to wait much longer. Accordingly, South Korea's postwar recovery was almost exclusively dependent upon generous military and economic support from the United States. South Korea in general has been able to maintain a close rapport with the United States in spite of the periodic difficulties it encountered.

2. Kim Il Sung and the Sino-Russian Rivalry

During the 1945-1950 period the Soviet Union's political influence in North Korea was nearly absolute. There was no competition for the victorious occupation force. This fact is what contradicts the assertion that the Korean War was ignited solely by North Korea's initiative, though there is no direct evidence to indicate the Soviet Union's involvement in Kim's premeditation for launching the war. Still, the fact that Kim's war plan was presented to and approved by Stalin before the outbreak illustrates the overwhelming dimension of the Soviet influence over North Korea.[1] From the very beginning of its occupation the Soviet Union vigorously pursued the Sovietization of North Korea. The task, carried out primarily by the occupation force, the Red Army's 25th Division under the command of General Ivan M. Chistiako, produced generally successful results in not only political but also socio-economic spheres. In this process the Soviet Union secured its dominating leverage over North Korea's economic and commercial interests in addition to its political-military domination.

The Soviet Union's extensive post-World War II political and economic support of the Kim Il Sung government had its price. North Korea was no exception from the Soviets' standard practice of extensive economic exploitation of occupied territories. Just as in most East European countries, North Korea was compelled to pay partially for the Soviet support and occupation by arranging its natural resources and productive capacity in such a way so as to subsidize its benefactor.[2] Despite the obvious drawbacks, the North Korean Communists strove to maintain close relations with the Russians, the only ally with enough economic and military muscle to support their ambitious economic and military programs. Even after the Chinese Communists had completed their conquest of the mainland in 1949, Moscow's dominant position in North Korea was neither diminished nor challenged, as domestic problems still preoccupied the new Chinese government.

The Soviet Union continued to be North Korea's primary source of economic and military support during the postwar period. It was still the only power capable of providing political support for the Pyongyang regime on the international stage. However, Communist China began to project itself as Russia's chief rival in North Korea during the early postwar period. In spite of the Soviet Union's prestige and power, Beijing had considerable advantages over Moscow in Korean matters, which it was willing to fully employ. Kim Il Sung's political longevity owed a great deal to his willingness and skill in eliminating his potential rivals. Kim had consolidated his political power by purging numerous opponents of right, left, and even moderate persuasion, thereby demonstrating his brutal political philosophy. His failure to achieve national unification did not alter either his political ambition or his ruthless campaign against potential rivals. His relentless purge of rivals resumed when the truce was arranged.

The most serious political challenges Kim faced during the early postwar period came from the Yennan faction, a group of mostly military figures closely associated with the Chinese Communists. The socialist Yennan faction, once outnumbering and outweighing Kim's faction, was still powerful enough to challenge Kim for the nation's political leadership. Particularly because of growing Chinese influence, this danger was real and worsening for Kim and his followers. His response to this pro-Chinese rival was both sweeping and severe. Those who did not escape Kim's political purge included Kim Mu Chong, a prominent military figure and the leader of the Yennan faction, whose close association with the Chinese military was publicly known. Destroying him under the pretext of poor military leadership during the war, Kim Il Sung singularly ignored the political cost of such drastic moves, which were clearly against the wishes of the Chinese Communists. Kim Il Sung chose this risky course with full understanding that his attempt to make Kim Mu Chong a scapegoat for his military defeat might have serious political repercussions. Kim, however, refused to yield to the growing prestige of the Chinese and made only a meaningless concession by transferring the victim to the Chinese after a strong Chinese protest. Kim's open challenge to Chinese prestige occurred when a large number of Chinese soldiers were still participating in his nation's various rebuilding programs. More than anything, Kim demonstrated through the successive purges his willingness to risk his essential external support to remove domestic rivals. His political gambles during the early postwar period set the tone for his uncompromising stand even toward his most potent benefactors.

Kim Il Sung's adventurous purge of his pro-Chinese rivals was not without precedent. During the prewar period he demonstrated his willingness to defy the Soviets, an even more domineering power at the time than the postwar Chinese, by eliminating Ho Ka-i, the leader of the Soviet-Koreans and a rumored favorite of the Soviets for the leadership of the new nation. In fact, Kim had waged a compaign to eliminate his pro-Soviets rivals when the Soviets' influence over his regime was nearly absolute, and he did the same against his Chinese-supported rivals after his regime had been salvaged by Chinese forces. His other strong challenger for the leadership, Park Hon Yong, who headed the leftist South Korean Labor Party with intimidating organizational strength, was also eliminated in July 1953. He was Kim's other eminent scapegoat for the failure of the war. Kim's relentless purge of his rivals, apparently disregarding the potentially grave political costs, best illustrated his venturesome and ruthless political style.

Although Kim Il Sung ruthlessly removed his major domestic political rivals, his control of the Communist Party was anything but complete. His vindictive purge of pro-Soviet and pro-China factions in the party and governmental hierarchies continued for some time. In spite of his crafty and brutal drive for absolute control of North Korea, his leadership was often challenged by determined adversaries who still had strong ties with the Chinese or the Russians. Such incidents, which signified North Korea's dilemma of being a neighbor of the two competing Communist giants, helped Kim to forge the measured diplomatic style that had been the mainstay of the regime's relations with its Communist neighbors for so long. By 1958, Kim had managed to secure undisputed leadership of both the Workers' (communist) Party and the government of North Korea.

Regardless of his uncompromising politics, it was inevitable for Kim Il Sung to tolerate the much expanded postwar influence of the Chinese Communists. Even Kim could not refute the fact that the North owed its survival to the intervention of millions of Chinese "people's volunteers." The Chinese had not intervened in the war from just a neighborly obligation or as a friendly gesture of socialist fellowship. Undoubtedly, the costly intervention represented the Chinese Communists' new political posture in the region; the Chinese intended to maintain a close political rapport with North Korea even if that meant encroaching on Soviet domination. The rise of Chinese political leverage over the Kim regime meant a corresponding decline of the Soviets' domination. An inevitable diplomatic competition between these Communist superpowers followed. Kim was not too alarmed by the development but instead was interested in taking advantage of it.

Kim Il Sung had every reason to be thankful for the Chinese intervention. The Chinese Communists' military intervention was a sharp contrast to the Soviets' refusal to commit infantry forces against the allied forces. The Soviet Union, in spite of its favorable approval of the war plan, was not willing to rescue the Kim regime from the verge of a total collapse during the pivotal winter months of 1950. On the other hand, the Chinese Communists' intervention, although greatly encouraged and supported by the Soviets, was the key to its survival. After the armistice the Chinese Communists impressed the North Korean regime further with its generous economic assistance for costly rebuilding programs. China not only waived all the debts incurred by North Korea during the war period but also granted a substantial sum of funds to be used during the early reconstruction period. Considering the fact that China was in dire need of financial resources for its own reconstruction programs, its generosity toward North Korea's reconstruction efforts was remarkably benevolent. In addition to economic aid, the Chinese "people's volunteers" had provided extensive manpower in rebuilding North Korea's decimated infrastructures until their total withdrawal at the end of 1958. North Korea duly acknowledged the Chinese goodwill, which not only saved the regime but helped to overcome its most difficult postwar period.

In providing postwar economic assistance to North Korea, the Chinese Communists were discreet and deliberate. A case in point was the Chinese "volunteers" who were ordered to participate in North Korea's reconstruction programs after the armistice was signed. These soldiers behaved quite amiably particularly in comparison with the Soviet occupation forces in the prewar period. Although racist acts against the Korean people were perpetrated more by the American occupation troops in the South, it was known that the worst offenses had been committed in the North by the Russians. Unlike these Western occupation forces, the Chinese "people's volunteers" were under strict orders from the Beijing leadership not to commit criminal outrages in North Korea.

For the first time in history the Chinese behavior reflected their correct understanding of the Korean temperament and sensitivity; they recognized that Korea no longer wished to be treated as China's junior partner regardless of the cause and circumstance. Accordingly, the Chinese soldiers were careful not to commit any public relations disaster that would be detrimental in building a close rapport with North Korea. Through concerted efforts of generous economic cooperation and exemplary conduct, the Chinese Communists earned the confidence of the Kim regime and, more importantly, of the North Korean public. Long after its political influence was forcefully ejected by the Japanese in 1904, the Chinese were succeeding in building their influence back in Korea, though only in the northern half.

Chinese influence in the North grew but it was not yet pervasive enough to sway the basically Soviet-oriented North Korean leadership. Kim Il Sung still remained unwilling to accord the Chinese the eminent leadership role in the international socialist movement, a status monopolized by the Soviet Union. As China continued its drive to reclaim its traditional close collaboration with North Korea, it inevitably caused conflicts with securely entrenched Soviet interests. Neither China nor the Soviets was willing to surrender its influence to the other. Although North Korea was not in a position to side with either power, its extensive economic and military dependence on the Soviet Union had deepened even after the war. The pitfalls of siding with either Communist giant became apparent to the North Korean leadership, who needed ever more external assistance. The only alternative left for the North was a peculiar diplomacy based on a deliberate balancing act.

The Soviet Union's influence over postwar North Korea was paramount; Russia was not only the predominant supplier of the North Korean military but also continued to be its largest economic donor. Moscow's economic leverage over the North reached a peak when the Kim regime adopted the Soviet-style agricultural collectivization system during the 1953-1957 period. In general, North Korea employed more of the Soviets' economic system than that of China and undertook its industrial reconstruction along the Soviet pattern during the 1953-1958 period. During this time North Korea's trade relationship also leaned heavily toward the Soviet Union, surpassing its trade with the Chinese.

The war damage inflicted on North Korea was by any yardstick excessive; most major industrial facilities as well as infrastructures were either destroyed or severely damaged during the war. The fact that the nation's gross industrial production in 1953 remained only thirty-six percent of that of the prewar period underscored the severity of its awesome war loss. In some industries more than ninety percent of the production capacity was lost. North Korea's task of rebuilding the country out of the war debris was overwhelming, and accordingly the process was slow and tedious. By the end of 1955, it had recovered only fifty-six percent of its prewar industrial capacity. Massive foreign aid provided by the Soviet Union, China, and East European countries played a major role in this extensive rebuilding process. North Korea's sluggish reconstruction efforts, in spite of the goodwill of its fellow socialist brothers, must have convinced its leaders of the pitfalls and limitations of foreign dependence.

The flow of foreign aid to North Korea was by no means adequate for its herculean tasks. Worse yet, it started to dwindle quickly. The European socialists were not able to render North Korea sustained assistance as they faced equally formidable reconstruction chores at home. In addition, the North's wavering stand in the Sino-Soviet rivalry had a direct impact on the amount of foreign aid the nation was receiving. The generosity of fellow Communist brothers was contingent on Pyongyang's political submission to the Soviet Union. Even under such pressing circumstances, however, Kim and his colleagues displayed their extreme uneasiness for taking sides with either of the two contending Communist super powers. Instead, Kim Il Sung elected to pursue the policy of *juche,* an ideology of independence and self-reliance that includes the doctrine of *jaju* (political independence), *jarip* (economic self-sustenance), and *jawi* (military self-defense).[3] In essence, Kim had declared ideological independence from his chief and dominating benefactors and, simultaneously, had made it clear to the masses of North Korea that their economic recovery had to be completed through their own hard work and sacrifice.

Regardless of its uncertain acceptability to the world socialist movement, the declaration of the *juche* ideology was a momentous development for the Korean nation.[4] It was fresh and highly symbolic for this nation that had historically been dominated by its stronger neighbors and was able to maintain its precarious survival only by adopting Sadaeism (open appeasement). Notwithstanding its outmoded nature in this increasingly interdependent world, the North Korean regime has maintained the idea of *juche* as the national doctrine to date.[5] In spite of its emphasis on the doctrine of *jarip* or self-sustenance, an economic branch of the *juche* ideology, North Korea's formidable reconstruction task was still heavily dependent on assistance from its two powerful benefactors. Economic necessities were not all; Pyongyang also needed the goodwill of the two Communist giants for political and diplomatic support in the international forum. Because of these pressing needs, North Korea could hardly have afforded to alienate either of its primary backers. Nevertheless, as the Chinese continued to challenge Moscow's role as the undisputed leader and arbiter of doctrine in the world Communist movement, the relations between the two were bound to deteriorate. Accordingly, North Korea's ability to remain as a benign third party in the dispute was increasingly undermined. Regardless of its desire to be neutral in the dispute, North Korea was not able to distance itself far enough from this socialist-block squabbling.

Realizing that he could not afford to antagonize either backer, Kim initially pursued a strategy of pleasing both of his competing backers simultaneously. He preferred the Soviets for the leadership of the world socialist camp, but he adopted most of China's economic models for his new economic development strategy. Not surprisingly, so dismal was the result of this unusual approach that he was shortly forced to take a more assertive stand.

The Chinese effort to build a stronger rapport with North Korea intensified after 1958. High-level visits were exchanged, and both sides made pledges for a close mutual relationship that was often described as "sealed in blood." Both nations were truly interested in strengthening their "flesh and blood" relation. Under this favorable atmosphere, filled with friendship and a renewed spirit of comradeship-in-arms, the Chinese Communists extended further economic assistance for North Korea's reconstruction efforts; along with additional commercial credits, closer cooperation in joint scientific and technical projects were also promised. The assistance Beijing offered in this period was extensive.

North Korea's leadership must have appreciated the generous aid China extended. But the North's response was not always predictable. At times it showed its gratitude in a most peculiar manner; for example, North Korea officially banned the use of Chinese characters in its written language.[6] Through this highly symbolic gesture, Kim made a point that friendship and economic cooperation should not cost his independence from his partners. The incident was one of a string of events that might have been interpreted as Kim's deliberate attempts to demonstrate his independent stand to his imposing neighbors.

Except for the occupation period North Korea had always exercised a full measure of its independence from the Soviet Union, even in matters of ideology; it had never been a docile Soviet satellite, contrary to the Western tendency to include it in such a category. North Korea's independent pursuit was even more plainly demonstrated when it adopted in 1958 a series of economic policies championed by China. The most conspicuous Chinese approach adopted by North Korea was an industrial development scheme based on the concept of cottage industries, a Chinese experimentation of setting up a series of small and conventional factories in rural areas to utilize local resources. It is self-evident why North Korea was attracted to such a labor-intensive industrial development scheme at the time.

In addition, Pyongyang had adopted an agricultural collectivization program, one that closely resembled many of the principal features of the Chinese commune system, which the Soviets had previously announced to be unacceptable. Another initiative adopted by North Korea in this period was the Flying Horse Movement, which paralleled China's Great Leap Forward Movement. Both programs were designed to accelerate the pace of economic development and recovery of war damages by utilizing human labor to the maximum. Shunning the Soviet Union's more machine-oriented approach, North Korea followed the Chinese Communists' approach that required compulsory appropriation of public labor; under the scheme the North Korean public was forced to participate in various construction projects from dawn to dusk.[7] During this period, Kim Il Sung at least by implication embraced the Chinese claim that its brand of economic development approach was more effective in helping Asian countries more rapidly achieve socialism and Communism. It was also Kim's tacit but plain rejection of the Soviets' economic development model.

North Korea was aware of the probable repercussions of siding with China even in economic policy matters. Kim's adoption of the Chinese economic methods was more based on his conviction that China's Asiatic economic solutions would expedite his economic development drive. Kim might have felt confident to make such a judgment because of his long acquaintance with both Communist countries. While it pursued close collaboration with China, North Korea was paying equally keen attention to the Soviet Union, trying not to offend its most powerful benefactor. The North reaffirmed that it still accorded the Soviet Union the role of foremost leader in the international socialist movement. However, North Korea's efforts were not sufficient in curbing the Soviets' growing uneasiness over the Sino-North Korean collaboration. Moscow's intensified pressure on Pyongyang was unavoidable.

The Soviets' display of displeasure over the North Korean regime was indirect but unmistakable. By the end of 1958 the Soviets had escalated their open criticism of Chinese economic policies, particularly castigating China's commune and Great Leap Forward programs as distortions of the teachings of Marxism-Leninism. It must have been plain to Kim that Moscow's harsh criticism of the Chinese Communists was also directed at him. He neither accepted the Soviets' verdict nor remained quiet. Kim publicly criticized the Soviets' zealous objection to the Chinese-inspired economic policies. Still, North Korea's initial response to the Soviets' criticism was ambivalent. On one hand, Pyongyang praised the Soviet Union's economic success and leadership of the international socialist movement, thus indicating that the North still intended to follow the Soviet line in general; but on the other hand, North Korean leaders made clear that Soviet pressure was unacceptable to a regime that had adopted the idea of *juche* as the nation's foremost political ideology.

North Korea rejected the Soviet Union's demand for an implicit following of its policies, citing the need to apply the Marxism-Leninism doctrine according to national peculiarities. Thus, it indirectly repudiated the Soviet Union's universal approach. Furthermore, Kim argued that the Russo-North Korean relationship should be based on the principles of equality and non-interference in each other's domestic affairs. He openly embraced a solidarity with the Soviet Union but emphatically rejected submitting to Moscow.[8] Kim's firm protests were duly noticed by Soviet leaders, who, instead of punishing, rewarded its stubborn beneficiary with substantial favors. Along with other cooperation such as an extended trade agreement and cultural programs, the Soviet Union agreed to provide atomic technology to North Korea for its "peaceful use." This agreement was particularly significant because it was reached right after Moscow unilaterally abrogated the Sino-Soviet atomic agreement in 1959. The Soviet Union was determined to recover its eroded influence in North

Korea.

Kim Il Sung's carefully weighed neutrality in the Sino-Soviet dispute was severely tested by the Soviet Union's new peaceful coexistence doctrine. Khrushchev, who led the world's socialist superpower for the 1958-1964 period, not only radically departed from Stalin's militant standoff but adopted a doctrine of peaceful coexistence as his nation's fundamental Western policy by proclaiming his intention to pursue competition against the West through peaceful means. He justified his new foreign policy as a rational choice between peaceful coexistence and nuclear confrontation. Publicly embracing peaceful competition instead of risky nuclear confrontation as the basic framework of its foreign policy, Moscow gave East-West competition a new dimension. Although the Soviets' new overture was perceived in the West more as a reflection of the evolving age of nuclear warfare than as any fundamental shift in the Russians' world view, it was nevertheless a major hurdle for the rigid North Korean regime to overcome.[9]

Khrushchev's new doctrine was categorically rejected by the People's Republic of China, the world's most populous agrarian state that did not possess atomic weapons at the time. Thus, the two Communist superpowers exposed their most serious philosophical difference in their posture to the West. Unlike Communist China, however, North Korea came out to support Khrushchev's peaceful coexistence policy, but with a major reservation-Kim adamantly refused to apply it to intra-Korean relations. He claimed to prefer the peaceful unification of Korea but not peaceful coexistence for two Koreas.

Kim had interpreted Khrushchev's peaceful coexistence doctrine as an umbrella policy favoring the permanent division of Korea. Kim's southern rivals must also have rejected the doctrine if peaceful coexistence meant the permanent division of the country. In fact, neither Germany nor Vietnam, the other countries suffering similar national division at the time, would have accepted the permanent division of their countries in exchange for peace. In this regard, Kim's unfavorable reaction to Khrushchev's peaceful coexistence doctrine would have been predictable. Nevertheless, Kim's refusal to apply the Khrushchev doctrine in intra-Korea matters was interpreted as an indication that he was willing to launch another attack on South Korea. Kim's outspoken stand over the policy was so inflammatory that Khrushchev was compelled to warn him publicly not to start another military adventure against South Korea. Regardless, it was apparent that Khrushchev's doctrine meant little as far as the volatile Korean situation was concerned.

Throughout the 1950s Kim maintained his militant stand toward South Korea. He continued to accuse South Korea and the United States of planning a new war, thereby justifying his rebuilding of armed forces and accepting Soviet military aid. If Khrushchev's mildly mellowed anti-West stance was a source of Kim's deepening anxiety, Mao's deepening animosity toward the United States might have been a source of comfort to Kim. The Chinese-North Korean relations were further solidified by their sharing a common enemy, the United States, which blocked the unification of Korea under Communism and prevented Mao's subjugation of Taiwan. In the middle of these contradictory interests, North Korea was, nevertheless, careful not to make itself appear to be too closely aligned with either of its two powerful Communist backers. The ultimate objective of Kim's unique diplomacy remained valid, which was to maintain a benign neutrality so that neither the Soviets' economic and military assistance nor China's ideological support was jeopardized. Unfolding events in the early 1960s demonstrated that Kim's unique equidistance diplomacy, however idealistic, was more hazardous and demanding than he might have expected.

3. Syngman Rhee and the Reluctant American Shield

South Korea's tasks in the postwar period were no less challenging than that of its northern counterpart. Like Kim's North Korea, South Korea's immediate economic survival was deeply intertwined with its diplomatic relations. Although Syngman Rhee's regime did not face the knotty diplomatic dilemma North Korea had to manage, its rebuilding task was no less formidable.

Rhee's postwar diplomatic activity was almost exclusively limited to managing relations with the United States. Rhee was no stranger to American politics; he had spent most of his adult life in the America that became the savior of his country and of his regime from Kim's "liberation war." Like Kim with the Soviets and the Chinese, Rhee was mindful of the critical importance of American support for the survival of his beleaguered republic. Facing the pressing reality, Rhee refused to remain a passive partner; he was too knowledgeable and experienced about American politics. He was greatly interested in swaying Washington politics to his liking by any means possible. The diplomatic games he had almost constantly waged against the United States were, however, quite different from Kim's balancing act between China and the Soviet Union.

Rhee's bid for the unification of Korea by military means was turned down by the West at the end of the war. In spite of the nation-wide protests against the imposed cease-fire, Rhee had to be content, in the end, with a series of concessions from America: an agreement for the U.S. to supply him with military aid to rebuild his armed forces (but with a condition not to build an attack force); a mutual defense treaty as a long-term security measure for his nation; and generous economic assistance for reconstruction of his shattered nation. It was a substantial achievement even for Rhee, whose diplomatic savvy was well known by then. Yet he was still preoccupied by the desire to win a pledge from the United States to renew military initiatives unless the Communists would agree to a free, fair, and democratic election. His drive, however, produced no results whatsoever. The Geneva Conference, with a remarkably naive provision required by the armistice, had failed to produce anything at all toward a political settlement. Both the West and the East were willing to forget the stipulation of the armistice for a political resolution of the war. The prospect of Korean unification in the near future was growing remote, but the president never gave up his dream of unifying the nation under his initiative.

In 1954, Rhee undertook some significant steps, such as dropping his demand for renewed military action, in an effort to amend his turbulent relations with the United States. Yet he did not forsake his unique diplomacy of friendly confrontation, leaving the Seoul-Washington relationship uneasy at best. His incessant assault on rising American isolationism remained a source of a bitter dispute between the two allies. Nevertheless, he was not afraid to denounce U.S. global policies, which he considered a virtual surrender to Communist imperialism. As South Korea's American financed reconstruction programs were under way, Rhee and Washington engaged in another thorny disagreement; he demanded a greater voice for his government in the execution of the aid programs.

President Rhee's early postwar efforts centered around securing Washington's economic as well as political support critical to resuscitating the nation's lethargic economy. Once the aid packages were arranged, however, he demanded that the United States allow him discretionary power over the funds. Although this endeavor was often met by outright hostility in Washington, Rhee was determined so to persuade the American administration, which in his judgement showed a growing prejudice against his nation. Rhee was definitely more than a Korean "egomaniac" with whom Washington preferred not to deal. The task the president faced was forbidding; the nation's economic recovery from the war ruins required his immediate attention even as there still was uncertain military confrontation along the new truce line. Under the press of circumstances it was quite natural for the intensely nationalistic Rhee to employ his utmost diplomatic skills to convince America to pay greater attention to Korea. Rhee was too well informed about Washington politics to overlook the fact that only his continuous prodding could move the reluctant United States government to provide him the necessary support.

Rhee's stubborn diplomacy was by no means the only cause of the United States-South Korean disharmony. Korea had never been popular with the American public. The "wrong place" which had staged a "wrong war" became even more remote to the public as American interests in Asia shifted south to Indo-China in 1954. Moreover, after the signing of the armistice, still volatile European security questions and neglected domestic issues had reclaimed their traditional high priority in Washington. Naturally, the American public resented giving away billions of dollars to this faraway country where thousands of its young men had already been sacrificed. The sentiments were genuine, and President Rhee's outspoken approach only aggravated the situation.

The United States' aid to South Korea was channelled through several organizations. The United Nations Korea Reconstruction Agency (UNKRA), founded in 1950 with support of forty-seven U.N. members and six non-member nations, handled funds for investments in construction, production facilities, and industrial projects. Almost all other economic aid, however, was dealt with by the International Cooperation Administration (ICA), a United States agency. The mainstay of the early American aid was food items. From 1956 the United States began to send food to South Korea under Public Law 480, the Food for Peace Program, which was established to serve a multitude of functions using surplus agricultural commodities. The total aid to South Korea during the 1945-1961 period reached about 3.1 billion dollars, which amounted to twelve percent of South Korea's national gross product during the period. These generous contributions helped South Korea to overcome severe food shortages and to revive its war-torn economy to some extent.

America's aid programs for South Korea were quite controversial in several ways. First, they were administrated directly by American officials who sought very little cooperation from the Korean government. This practice was hotly contested by the Rhee administration. In retrospect, the practice was poorly conceived, although hardly a surprise. It was consistent with the disdainful American attitude, a leftover from the occupation period, that Korea was not able to manage its own affairs. Washington's open contempt for the Korean people's ability was erroneous and reproachable, yet it persisted more or less for decades to come.

Second, the aid was basically intended for the relief of immediate problems such as food shortages, not for rebuilding the nation's ruined productive capacity. The funds for reconstruction or expansion of productive capacity, more capital-intensive ventures that were needed to build a self-sustaining economy, amounted to only 1.2 billion dollars, a sum insufficient even to replace the war damages, which reached about three billion dollars. Instead of laying down a foundation for long-term economic growth, American aid only created an extensive "aid economy," one dominated by consumption rather than production.

Third, the aid of food items under Public Law 480 proved to be effective in the short run, but highly addictive in the long run. Although it helped the nation to overcome the immediate crisis of calamitous food shortages, aid through the Food for Peace program rendered little long-term assistance to the staggering South Korean economy. On the contrary, it created some major negative consequences; the availability of low-priced or free foods, the PL 480 items, effectively deterred Korean farmers from planting the aid items, thereby making the nation perpetually dependent upon foreign sources. The massive food aid, intended to rectify a catastrophic food shortage, also became a contributing factor in the nation's hyper-urbanization. As the nation's agricultural prices remained artificially low with the continuing influx of U.S. food aid, a large number of marginal farmers were driven out of farm work and moved to the nation's overcrowded major urban centers to seek non-agricultural employment. The premature rural-urban shift had created massive urban unemployment; this remained a serious social problem until the 1970s when South Korea's industrial and service-sector economy grew to generate an increasing amount of urban-oriented employment. Numerous shanty-towns created by both war refugees and urban migrants in major cities were a source of severe social and political problems for many years to come.

South Korea's economic recovery was slow and difficult. Massive infusion of American aid was almost solely directed to the immediate relief of shortages which were caused by war-related loss of production capacity and the influx of war refugees. Because of the nation's pressing needs and the commodity-oriented American aid, the rebuilding of the nation's decimated production capacity remained a secondary objective for the Rhee administration. Industrial rebuilding programs remained more an ambition than a reality throughout the 1950s, while pressure for greater non-agricultural employment intensified, particularly in the nation's major urban areas.

In the South, industrial infrastructure was pitifully weak even before it suffered extensive war damage. Korea's industrial structure during the colonial period had been built with Japan's imperial ambition in mind: the merging of the Korean economy into the Imperial Japanese economy. Under this scheme Korean industry was dominated by mostly extractive and processing-oriented operations, while final processing or more sophisticated operations were done in Japan. Furthermore, industrial structure was sharply dissimilar between the South and North; in the more densely populated South it was heavy with agriculture and light-consumer-items industries, while in the resource-rich North heavy, energy-related industries dominated. As a whole, the prewar South Korean industry could function best only when it was fully integrated with the operations of both North Korea and Japan. Liberation had severed the functional linkage with Japan, and the thirty-eighth parallel soon blocked critical intra-Korea industrial cooperation. The war destroyed most of the remaining production capacity except for those few factories processing some basic consumer products, mostly in the Pusan area. South Korea's peculiar prewar industrial structure made the reconstruction of its manufacturing industry even more formidable.

President Rhee spared no pains in articulating his profound suspicion that Washington was disoriented in its battle against international communism. More than anything, his outspoken admonition was a reflection of his deep conviction that the Western democracy had to fight communist imperialism to save the world from socialist tyranny. Rhee was convinced that South Korea, as the Western democracy's frontier against international communism, deserved priority attention. He was quite disappointed by the West's lack of a concerted effort to help him in rebuilding his country, although he did not harbor any irreconcilable animosity. His relationship with the United states remained less than desirable, but he was aware that there was no fundamental incompatibility but only tactical differences between his regime and Washington. Periodic disagreements and some open disharmony aside, Rhee remained adamantly pro-American.

In contrast, Rhee's relations with postwar Japan were full of mistrust to the extent that a logical dissolution of the past relationship was virtually impossible. Although the nation's lack of a formal diplomatic tie with Japan, let alone friendly cooperation, had been of deep concern to Washington, President Rhee refused to take any steps toward a rapprochement with Japan. Like his anti-Communism, his antipathy toward Japan was a deeply rooted and undying passion. His more pressing concern was America's apparent intention to restore Japan to major power status in Asia. He questioned the wisdom of building up Japan and pressed Washington to take measures to prevent Japanese domination of its neighbors. He also unequivocally rejected the notion that it was necessary to strengthen Japan economically and militarily to ensure that it would stay out of the communist orbit. Although Rhee was the most prominent practitioner of true anti-Japanism, by no means was he alone. The majority of Korea's educated class would have belonged to that same category. History taught the Korean people to be wary of their neighbors regardless of temporal appearances.

The Rhee government's ill feelings toward Japan were further aggravated by the arrogant and irrational statements of the Japanese Foreign Ministry, which implied that eighty-five percent of all the developed property in Korea rightfully belonged to the Japanese and that Korea should compensate for these properties.[10] Japan might have appeared repentant to the victorious America, but it remained quite insolent to Korea. Rhee was also alarmed by the Japanese efforts to establish trade and diplomatic relations with the communist governments of China and North Korea.

The South Korean government rightfully demanded that Japan renounce all her property claims and rescind the old Treaties of Protectorate and Annexation, the legal justification for Japan's colonial control of Korea. President Rhee's militant anti-Japanism was well expressed in the administration's forceful protection of the Korean waters from Japanese fishing boats. Rhee made clear that short of full and unconditional Japanese apology, he would not even talk with the loathed former colonial masters. The public remained solidly behind the president's obstinate stand. The Japan-South Korean relations remained thorny; no normalization procedures were even contemplated under the Rhee administration.

The United State's consistent drive to restore Japan as a preeminent power in the region was a source of constant irritation for President Rhee. However, America's high esteem of Japan was not a new phenomenon. Having fallen into a fatal assumption that it would be in its best interest to install Japan as the leader in the East Asia, America had openly endorsed Japan's earlier annexation of Korea early 1900s. It had ignored the Korean people's pleas for help, only to have to fight the Pacific War. Yet after the war the United States resumed its basic prewar policy of supporting and encouraging Japan to reemerge as the regional leader. This peculiar attitude might have reflected a historical pattern that the United States had never been comfortable with exercising a dominant political influence in the region. Washington's pro-Japan stand hardly pleased a single soul in Korea.

Regardless, Washington continued the pro-Japan policy, hardly paying attention to the Korean people's strong objection. Under the so-called "regional integration plan," the United States forces stationed in Korea had to procure all supplies from Japan, though South Korea was producing many of these items with the same or better quality. Washington's single-minded drive to make South Korea dependent on Japan's growing industrial power was an ultimate source of the dispute between Rhee and Washington. South Koreans were dismayed by the fact that postwar Japan had benefitted immensely by the Korean War and that it would continue to benefit after the war, at their expense.

The United States withdrew four of its remaining six combat divisions from South Korea in 1956. By then the South Korean military had expanded to about 700,000 men. Yet the withdrawal greatly disturbed the public because most "Chinese People's Volunteers" still remained in North Korea. Moreover, the public was aware that the modernization of the South Korean military had not been sufficiently completed to substitute for the departing United States forces. Nonetheless, with the withdrawal, the attention of the American public as well as the government was still further drifting away from Korea. Washington's disdain for Rhee remained unabated, mostly due to his authoritarian rule over vocal domestic opponents and his exhausting diplomatic feud against Washington. The latter virtually undercut the president's efforts to forge closer relations with the United States. Syngman Rhee was not unlike Kim Il Sung, as far as his dominating personality was concerned. Both men's credentials as profound nationalists were outstanding, although they owed a great deal to foreign powers for their eventual ascension. Neither man tolerated opposition; each ruthlessly suppressed plitical rivals. While they vigorously pursued an absolute internal control, they resisted any interference from foreign powers, even when the survival of the regime was at stake. Both men exploited convenient, readily available excuses to monopolize near dictatorial power: Kim's political legitimacy was based on the national imperative of unification, while Rhee's principal justification for his authoritarian rule was anti-Communism and anti-Japanism. In fact, each man provided the other with easily defensible reasons for a long rule.

In spite of substantial differences in age and background, the two shared basically identical aspirations, the unification of the nation under one banner. Yet neither was interested in negotiated settlement; each sought a military solution. Kim had never advocated peaceful means in his drive to unify the nation under his brand of socialism.[11] After the war, Rhee also emphasized a military solution for the unification question. In the end, both leaders themselves became a large part of the Korean problem. In all fairness, both men must share the dread responsibility for the polarization of national politics and thus the prolongation of national division. Both Rhee and Kim were capable politicians with extraordinary nationalistic fervor, and to some extent they were successful in performing the role of the deposed Chosun monarchy. It is ironic that these two men both sought monarchial power in a nation where such an institution had been deliberately abolished only three decades before.

Rhee's extensive dependency on the United States, which resulted both from choice and sheer necessity to compete against North Korea, did not mean that his rule was based on an American system. In reality, his brand of democracy was far from the one advocated by the United States. In spite of his familiarity and frequent contacts with that nation, he had been a poor student of the plural democratic system with which America was often identified. Still, the president was absolutely confident of his loyalty and ability to lead the troubled nation. To support his political appetite, his Liberal Party adopted many questionable measures solely designed to assure his continuing rule. Naturally, his authoritarian rule was of constant concern to the United States; it was opposed by his vocal domestic rivals in the national assembly, whom Rhee did not hesitate to suppress by force. Rhee had one overwhelming and convenient excuse for taking such an unpopular road: constant military threat posed by the North.

The specter of another war was often deliberately invoked to remind the public that the government was in fact in a wartime situation. Using the convenient pretext of the North-South confrontation, Rhee was determined to extend his rule as long as possible. His Liberal Party spared no means to secure him absolute power, oblivious to the fact that even the president's genuine patriotism could be harmful if it was wrongfully employed. On the other hand, the nation's economy was making no tangible progress. The consumption economy, fueled by massive aid of American commodities, was suffering from hyper-inflation and excessive unemployment, which created growing social unrest among the urban as well as rural population. President Rhee's nationalistic enthusiasm could not provide solutions for multiple economic problems.

The 1960 presidential election ended President Rhee's twelve-year rule. The election results that brought about a fourth term for the eighty-five year-old President Rhee were prefabricated in some areas in order to secure victory for ruling-party candidates. The president himself was still popular enough to win an election against perhaps any opposition. The fraud was committed to help his unpopular vice presidential running mate, but without Rhee's personal knowledge. The nation was quickly swept by student demonstrations demanding a new election. In the end, the nation's college professors joined the protest, effectively bringing down the Rhee regime. It was April 26, 1960, when the president, a man of integrity and conviction, announced his resignation. Few had questioned his good intentions and his dedicated service to the nation. Yet more had wondered if the president were able to distinguish good intentions from bad conduct. Syngman Rhee was a tragic victim of the myth of his own indispensability. Unfortunately, he was neither the first nor the last to suffer such a fatal disease in the Korean political landscape.

The "4.19 Revolution," the two-month-long nationwide protest that brought down President Rhee, was a spontaneous but clear expression of the public's desire to install a new leadership for the nation. Students, the most vocal representatives of the public since the colonial period, did make their points abundantly clear; they demanded a democratic government that would be honest and fair. The spirit of the Hahn people was, after all, still young and hopeful.

The sudden departure of Syngman Rhee left a political vacuum that endangered South Korea's national security. The transition government was unable to calm the chaotic social disorder, which heightened the nation's vulnerability to the North's military adventure. Yet the country continued, even after the installation of the Second Republic led by the Democratic Party, to drift into rampant social disorder that came close to total anarchy. The collapse of rigid political control led to the rise of various political persuasions, including the resurfaced leftists and reformists, dismaying the public who were still led by conservative political ideology.

These reformists, the most radical spectrum in South Korean politics, focused their attention on issues the right-wing political factions had deliberately avoided: negotiated national unification, the Korea-United States relationship, and the security laws. They boldly proposed establishing trade relations between two Koreas and demanded a revision of the U.S.-Korean economic relations, which they contended were unfair and one-sided. The reformists' unification movement was quickly labelled "pro-Communist" by the nation's conservative factions, which had dominated South Korean politics ever since the liberation in 1945. For these radical proposals the new administration of the Democratic Party responded with a policy of "economic development first, unification second." To the ruling Democratic Party, which deviated little from the stand held by Rhee's Liberal Party in its conservative politics, the unification of the nation had to be accomplished under the democratic banner. Interestingly, in this chaotic period the idea of national unification under neutrality was resurrected by some reformists.

South Korea's social unrest continued as the Democratic Party government remained largely ineffective. To the great disappointment of the public, the freely elected leadership proved to be inept and disoriented; it failed to restore not only the social order but also the nation's faltering economy. South Koreans were learning a bitter lesson that their problems were not rectifiable by simply replacing the authoritarian president with a more democratic-minded prime minister. The new government's political wandering continued until May 1961, when the military took over the government through a bloodless coup.

The short-lived government of the Democratic Party might have been a casualty of the post-Rhee political transition. In a sense, it was more than a transition problem; it was an inevitable result of a weak leadership that could not fill the nation's historical legacy of monarchy. Postwar Korea was more receptive to a charismatic, authoritarian leader than a low-key leader, regardless of his intention and ability. It was not merely a coincidence that South Korea has long been ruled by strong-willed, authoritarian leaders. North Korea had been ruled until 1994 by the same person, whose authoritarian character was beyond any dispute. In reality, these leaders filled the vacuum created by the abolition of its tradition-rich monarchy. Like old Korean monarchs, new Korean rulers were preoccupied with consolidating their power, and they did not tolerate any dissension. The nation's transition from absolute monarchy to modern democratic government should never have been expected to be quick and uneventful.

President Rhee's administration was heavily burdened by numerous problems that had not been created by him or his administration. In any event, the arduous task of rebuilding the war-torn nation required more than one capable leader. Furthermore, Rhee was not an experienced manager and could not alone effectively lead the administrative efforts of rebuilding the nation. Most of all, he was preoccupied with Washington, which was at best reluctant to commit itself to the Korean cause for anything not absolutely necessary. Rhee expended his creative energy to retain Washington's commitment to Korea. This was much different from Kim's predicament in the North, where China and the Soviet Union competed for an alliance with North Korea. Another distracting problem was Japan's rise under the special tutelage of the United States. Rhee's government had to compete against America's traditional favorite, Japan, for Washington's attention and support. He was quite successful in that regard, considering the circumstances, but his success did not compensate for his cardinal failure-his inability to forge a national unity in the South during the postwar reconstruction period. Had he been able to draw upon national unity, this man of outstanding diplomatic skills and charisma would have served his country with much greater distinction.

Notes

1. Nikita Khrushchev, *Khrushchev Remembers,* Boston: Litte, Brown, p.487.
2. Chin Chung, *Pyongyang Between Peking and Moscow: North Korea's Involvement in the Sino-Soviet Dispute,* University: The University of Alabama Press, p. 12.
3. Dae Suh, pp. 300-302.
4. Suh argues that the "juche" idea is contradictory to the socialist ideology that rejects nationalism. He claims that the juche idea is nothing more than xenophobic nationalism that has little ideological relevance to communism. Refer to Suh, Dae-Sook, pp. 301-313.
5. The North Korean government refers to the doctrine as Kimilsungism,an effort to promote it as an idea invented by its leader. The thought system includes the idea of juche (self-reliance) in ideology, the idea of jaju (independence) in political work, the idea of jarip (self-sustenance) in economic endeavors, and the idea of Jawi (self-defense) in military affairs. Refer to Suh, p. 302.
6. Koreans have used Chinese characters with its own alphabet, Hahn Geul. Currently some 2,000 Chinese characters are being used officially in South Korea.
7. Dae Suh, p. 347.
8. Ibid., p.38.
9. In 1960 in a highly publicized incident Russia shot down an American U-2 spy plane over its territory. In 1962 Khrushchev engaged in the adventure of trying to install Soviet missiles in Cuba, provoking the "Cuban Missile Crisis."
10. Robert Oliver, *Syngman Rhee and American Involvement in Korea, 1942-1960,* New York: The Free Press, p. 462.
11. Dae Suh, p. 113.

Chapter 12

The Coup to Economic Take-off

1. The 5.16 Coup

After the collapse of the authoritarian Rhee government, South Koreans placed high expectations on their second republic. Amid the jubilation, everyone overlooked the fact that the new ruling Democratic Party, quarrelsome but ideologically impoverished, had neither the experience nor the preparation to lead the nation. Prime Minister Chang Myun's new administration soon proved that it was not ready even for the task of restoring the nation's badly shaken law and order. Political and emotional buoyancy aside, the nation continued to suffer political drift that had begun during Huh Chung's interim government and remained unabated in the Chang administration. South Koreans successfully drove out Rhee's authoritarian government but had little idea what the next steps should be.

The Chang administration's mounting political difficulty was caused mainly by its inability to devise effective post-Rhee policies. These ought to have represented a careful balance between the nation's deep security concerns and immediate socioeconomic democracy. In addition, the new leaders failed to provide an alternative to the public's distorted sense of freedom and democracy; the streets of the nation's cities continued to be filled with protest marches promoting every imaginable cause. Inevitably, the prolonged political paralysis caused many citizens to begin to fear that the situation would become a fatal invitation for the North to launch another military adventure. Such apprehension was particularly strong among South Korea's armed forces, the only organized entity left unaffected by the ongoing unrest.

As political instability worsened, some of the nation's conservatives openly advocated military intervention. Others adamantly rejected such a notion. The issue reflected seemingly contradictory perspectives regarding the proper role of the powerful national defense force in South Korean politics. Despite the common sense reality that the military should avoid civilian politics, the fact remained that even the military had an inherent right to exercise political options. Whether this political right included radical intervention was debatable, but the notion that the military ought to shun civilian politics under every circumstance was without logic and practicality. Naturally, the South Korean generals did not concede to the view that they should avoid civilian politics.

As the civilian government continued to suffer from destructive futility, the nation was losing the plausible argument against its armed forces' political intervention. The notion that the military should remain idle was losing validity, while the society dashed toward a point of internal disintegration. Many realized that the military was the only cohesive organization still capable of halting the disastrous civilian politics and restoring law and order.

In 1961, the South Korean military launched a coup, using national salvation as its sole justification. The generals portrayed themselves as saviors of the nation rather than as usurpers of power. Eager to salvage the country from chaotic social disorder and political drift, they immediately undertook a number of corrective measures in military fashion. Unlike the professional politicians they had just replaced, military leaders were able to overcome obstructions and barriers that might have stalled a civilian political process. Thus began the first period of South Korea's extensive military rule.

As in most developing countries, South Korea possessed a large standing army. Thus the threat of a military takeover of the civilian government was almost inherent in South Korean politics. In a sense, South Korea was an ideal setting for such a undertaking due to several factors. First, military intervention could be readily justifiable on the ground that it would save the nation from the threat of a North Korean attack. As long as the hostile North-South confrontation persisted, the pretext of national security would remain credible. Second, South Korea's small geographic size made the political utilization of armed forces very effective and convenient. Seoul, the capital city, was defended by reinforced crack troops, which, ironically but realistically, could be used to topple a civilian government. Third, South Korea's officer corps was a close-knit group, most of whom shared a background of having attended the same service academies. Thus, a consensus could be attained quickly once they felt political intervention to be justified. Fourth, South Korea's civilian government had categorically failed to establish a democratic tradition or to provide effective political leadership. When civilian politics failed to provide effective leadership and thus caused protracted social instability, South Korea's young officers easily found excuses to take over civilian politics.

The South Korean military's political appetite surfaced clandestinely during the Rhee administration; it was close to staging a coup against the Rhee government under the pretext of rectifying chronic corruption in its own ranks. The attempt was, however, preempted by the 4.19 Student Uprising and the subsequent collapse of the Rhee administration.[1] Under the ineffective government of Prime Minister Chang Myun, the nation had reached a point where social disorder and political impotence were threatening the nation's cardinal concern, the survival of the non-communist system. This situation provided the military with a second opportunity to push for political control of the nation. South Korea's prolonged social chaos served as an invitation not only for the North to launch another military adventure but for the takeover of the civilian government by its own military. In a sense, the coup preempted the North's ambition, but perhaps barely.

The South Korean military ended Chang's ineffective and seemingly disoriented administration. Yet the coup received neither instant approval nor immediate rejection from the public. Even after suffering chaotic social disorder and political instability under the Chang administration, the public was reluctant to give the military solution instantaneous approval; only gradually did it recognize the reality, however, paying scant attention to the long term ramifications of the development.

By proclaiming "anti-Communism" to be the nation's foremost priority, the coup's collective leadership effectively exploited public sentiment. Under a renewed anti-Communist frenzy, an extensive crackdown on the pro-left and reform factions proceeded. The nation's rare ideological experimentation, which had flourished because the Chang administration was unable to contain the nationwide unrest, was summarily banned. Along with its strong anti-Communist stand, the governing junta, with militaristic speed and method, adopted various measures designed to remedy the social-economic maladies that had plagued both the Rhee and Chang administrations. These measures encompassed extensive political purification measures; most politicians and entrepreneurs who were identified with impropriety and corruption were either prosecuted or banned from political participation in the new society. The military government also exerted pressure for conformity on the press and on student activists. The young and energetic military leadership was undertaking drastic measures that it regarded essential in building a just society, free from corruption and impropriety.

The coup left some lingering questions regarding the role of the United States. The United States officially and openly registered its disapproval of the South Korean military's removal of a constitutional government. Nevertheless, America had implicated itself in the coup indirectly; the commander of the United States forces in Korea, a U.S. general, was in charge of operations of all Korean army units, a wartime arrangement that had survived. As far as the command structure was concerned, the Commander of the UN forces in Korea had operational authority over the units that participated in the coup. But individual South Korean military units were led by Korean comanders. In reality, the UN command had only a limited capacity to prevent South Korean units' unauthorized short-duration deployment because the command structure left the responsibility of their common maintenance operations to South Korean commanders. In addition, there was no indication that the UN command had any prior knowledge of the impending coup. Equally, there was no evidence that the UN command did intervene to thwart the coup during its early stage.

In response to the Western criticism of its abolishing a duly elected government, the military junta promised that a civilian government would be installed in mid-1963. Two years later the South Korean military complied with its own promise by transferring power to a civilian government as scheduled. However, the transfer of military rule to a civilian government did not mean the military's total withdrawal from politics. Instead, the junta chose to remain the nation's ruling political force in the new civilian government. In the ensuing general election, the junta leader, General Park Chung Hee, was elected as the nation's fifth president.

The South Korean public halfheartedly elected this retired army general as its president. In spite of the all-out efforts of the military government, Park won only forty-seven percent of the popular vote, while his opponent, former President Yun Po Sun, received forty-five percent. Although the public's support for Park's rule was tentative at best, the nation's military earned an opportunity to prove its insistent claim that only Park was capable of salvaging the ruined economy and strengthening its defense to discourage a North Korean military adventure. In a sense, Park's pledge for a decisive and honest government represented new hope and expectation for a nation that had survived the corrupt and ineffective government of Syngman Rhee and the turbulent social disorder of the Chang administration. South Korea's third republic was installed on December 17, 1963.

2. Normalized Relations with Japan

The political tasks facing South Korea's third republic were formidable even for the highly dedicated and energetic President Park. In addition to the nation's faltering economy, which demanded not only immediate but also comprehensive attention, the new administration had to confront several major tasks in both domestic and international areas. Foremost, it had to devise a long term strategy for the ever present military threat of North Korea. In foreign relations, it had to revise its relations with the United States to fit the evolving international political climate. In addition, it had to find an acceptable formula, both emotionally and politically, to resolve its diplomatic stalemate with Japan. The new government faced such intimidating problems without matching national strength. Moreover, it could expect no outpouring of international goodwill from the Western community, to which South Korea remained a hermit kingdom representing nothing but bitter memories of the war and poverty.

The Park administration's first and most urgent priority went to normalizing its relations with Japan. The junta realized that normalized relations with Japan were a matter of critical importance for South Korea in political, economic, diplomatic, and security dimensions. Unlike emotional President Rhee, the nation's new leaders approached the task of establishing normal diplomatic ties with the nation's former colonial master with a realistic assessment of South Korea's overall strategic requirements.

There were many factors that promoted the consummation of the South Korea-Japan rapprochement; some were of a domestic nature, but others were regional and international in scope. One of the most compelling factors that helped complete the normalization of the Japan-Korea relation was the strong political pressure exerted by the United States. Although well justified, Washington's earlier effort to persuade the two countries to come to a settlement had been frustrated by Rhee's uncompromising stand. With a far more receptive and eager military government in power, Washington renewed its effort for an early completion of the negotiations, hoping to establish normal diplomatic ties between its two principal East Asian allies. This was vital to America's strategic interests in the Far East.

The United States made it clear to the Park administration, which was in dire need of Washington's goodwill and support for its ambitious economic and modernization programs, that its political support would be contingent on the settlement of Korea-Japan disputes.[2] Also, an agreement would remind Japan that to a significant extent its security depended upon South Korea's ability to remain an independent nation, strong enough to resist Communist threats.[3]

The United States had another equally pressing motive for pursuing normalization of Korean-Japanese relations. Washington had poured over three billion dollars into South Korea's struggling economy during the 1945-1964 period. In spite of this massive aid, however, that economy was still suffering from shortages, excessive unemployment, hyper-inflation, negligible growth performance, and increasing import dependency. As South Korea remained far from reaching a self-sustaining economy, Washington was eager to share the cost with an increasingly prosperous Japan. In a sense, the United States was anxious to relinquish its role as South Korea's sole financial supporter. Thus, Washington actively pursued an avenue for placing South Korea under the joint custody of the United States and Japan. On the other hand, Japan was hardly in a position to overlook Washington's wish, as its rapidly expanding industrial economy needed continuing access to the vast consumer market as well as the capital and technology pool in America.

Another important factor that greatly motivated South Korea's new administration in its quest for normalized relations with Japan was the emergence of Communist China as a major military-political power. China's growing prestige, stemming from its rapid economic recovery and achievement of nuclear capability, profoundly changed the power equation in the Far East. The drastic ascension of Communist China in the world power hierarchy implied by association the elevation of North Korea's image in the region. Under this ominous development, South Koreans feared that they might have to face, alone, a militant North Korea supported by Communist China and the Soviet Union while the Vietnam conflict preoccupied the United States. The South realized that a close rapport with Japan was the best route for preventing its political-military isolation. The rising stature of China's Communists left South Korea with few alternatives but the pursuit of reconciliation with Japan.

South Korean leaders recognized the fact that military cooperation between the two nations was a remote possibility in the near future.[4] However, they understood the critical importance of securing Japanese support in both economic and diplomatic spheres. Japan's neutrality or collaboration with the region's communist regimes would make South Korea an island surrounded by hostile neighbors. Having their principal supporter across the Pacific, they were keenly aware of the nation's vulnerability. In spite of its understandable ill feeling toward and distrust of Japan, South Korea badly needed Japan's friendship in the early 1960s.

The South Korean economy had been a major disappointment for the Rhee government as well as for the United States. During the 1953-1964 period the nation's GNP grew at the rate of 4.5 percent per year, while its per capita income reached only 104 dollars in 1964. In spite of the massive U.S. aid, the South Korean economy performed most woefully, unable to cope with a mounting burden of heavy military spending and reconstuction projects. Although the nature of the aid had some important bearing on the poor economic performance, it was nevertheless evident that the nation desperately needed new blood and direction to renew its efforts to build a viable economic foundation.

South Korea's heavy military spending was a serious burden that contributed greatly to a stagnant economy; it was spending over thirty-three percent of its annual budget for national defense during the 1960-1964 period. Moreover, the U.S. economic aid began its downward spiral when the nation's need to expand and upgrade its production facilities remained unfulfilled. This forced South Korea to look for other sources for economic cooperation, including the West European countries. Yet it was evident to the military leaders that Japan was the most ideal source for the substantial capital and technical cooperation needed to carry out the nation's first Five-Year Economic Development Plan, adopted in 1962. For its ambitious economic development programs, the Park government identified the funds related to the property claims settlement and others that would be available at the conclusion of its normalization talk with Japan. In addition, the government was hoping that normalized relations would help to correct its growing trade deficit against Japan.

Both Park's and Sato's administrations desired to resolve the unpleasant past by opening a new chapter of neighborly cooperation. In this regard both governments' desire was consistent with that of powerful business communities in Japan and South Korea. The South Korean business community was eager to establish normal relations with Japan, hoping to expand its business horizon by utilizing Japanese capital, technology, and marketing skills. On the other hand, the Japanese were anxious to secure the Korean market for their industrial products. They were also observant of the opportunity to exploit South Korea's abundant but highly educated labor force. Aggressive business leaders of both countries exerted pressure on their respective governments for an early conclusion of normalization talks. The ensuing developments proved that the judgment of these business communities was generally correct and justifiable.

In spite of sufficient justifications for the normalized relations with Japan, the majority of South Koreans rejected the Park government's accord. The public agreed with Park's political opponents that the settlement of the $800 million package was not a just compensation for Japan's harsh, forty-year colonial repression and exploitation. Yet, significantly, the opposition was concerned more with the symbolic and long-term economic-political implications of the agreement than with the monetary amount; it pointed out that the nation's rightful property claims for colonial exploitation should not be settled by "economic cooperation" but by "reparation." The Koreans demanded a just and fair resolution of Japan's transgressions. Even when the nation desperately needed foreign capital to revive its faltering economy and a regional ally for its security considerations, the Koreans did not overlook Japan's unwillingness to admit fully its past indiscretions. Koreans were angry that Japan insisted on "helping" their country with economic cooperation rather than "suffering" a reparation it so richly deserved. The opposition also raised grave doubts about the Japanese motive for entering the treaty settlement; they feared that economic cooperation would lead to renewed Japanese economic and political aggression. The specter of another Japanese incursion was obsessive and constant; also the distrust of Japan's political past remained deep and rampant among the Hahn people.

The Park government was firm in its decision to conclude the treaty negotiation successfully. Because it made the conclusion of normalization talks such a high priority, the regime's very survival was at stake. Yet the activist students and the regime's political opposition were equally resolute in objecting to the ratification of the "sell-out" treaty. Mainly because of Japan's insolent attitude, the talks provoked intense nationalistic emotion among Korea's young citizens. In the end, the Park government resorted to a decree of "garrison state" of a martial law variety to contain the nationwide protests. The National Assembly adopted the South Korea-Japan normalization bill on August 14, 1965, though the opposition did not participate in the deliberation. The Park government thus established a legal ground for its close cooperation with Japan in both economic and political spheres. On the other hand, enterprising Japan had acquired an official sanction for reentering the South Korean market scarcely twenty years after it was forced to withdraw from the peninsula at the end of the Pacific War.

3. The Nixon Doctrine

The Park government's most prominent accommodation to U.S. desires was the conclusion of its normalization talks with Japan. Yet this was only the beginning of extensive Seoul-Washington collaboration that flourished during the early part of the Park administration. In 1965, South Korea entered active military cooperation with the United States by sending its combat troops to South Vietnam. This was the first time in Korea's modern history that the Hahn nation dispatched a military force to another country. South Korea's Vietnam war participation, which lasted almost to the end of the conflict, involved two army combat divisions and one marine brigade, along with their customary supporting units.

Although the South Korean military was the second largest among those participating in the Vietnam war, the Americans refused to equip these allies with either an air wing or a tank corps, units that South Korea could ill afford to take out from its own inventory along the DMZ front. Even under such a disadvantageous arrangement, Korean soldiers proved to be the finest fighting force. Along with other allies that dared to participate in the unpopular war, the South Korean forces made significant contributions to the United States war effort in Vietnam.

The Park regime's decision to send its combat troops to faraway Vietnam was extremely unpopular with most South Koreans, who were not comfortable with sending troops to a nation of no historical connection. Moreover, they were unsure of North Korea's reaction to the South's overt association in an anti-communist campaign elsewhere. Yet President Park remained firm with his decision to collaborate with the United States in Vietnam.

The South Korean leaders believed that North Vietnam's unequivocal victory, supported by Communist China and Russia, would have serious implications for the military balance in the Korean peninsula. They feared that victorious Communists might launch a similar venture against South Korea. It was an oversimplified analogy but a powerful argument to the security-conscious South Korean government. In addition, the Johnson administration exerted considerable pressure on the Park administration; in return for South Korean commitment it promised assistance in upgrading the South Korean military and postponment for the scheduled transfer of its military aid to the Korean government. The other concessions Washington made, such as financial assistance to the South Korean forces in South Vietnam, might have been a substantial incentive for the Park government, which was seeking a large sum of foreign exchange for its extensive economic development programs.

South Korea's participation in the Vietnam war was openly criticized in Western Europe; the nation had to suffer some diplomatic censure as a result. Nevertheless, its Vietnam participation was an important juncture for modern and confident South Korea, which was bidding for a full membership in the society of the Western industrial democracies. President Park intended to make a point that South Korea was a worthy ally, willing to take risks and to suffer for the interests of the anti-communist world. In return, South Korean leaders hoped that the United States would honor its security commitment to their country.

President Park's aggressive drive was evident not only in his Vietnam involvement but also in his economic policies. In his early drive for economic development, the priority went to building an industrial infrastructure for a self-sustained, growth-oriented economy. His plan called for extensive utilization of foreign input, including capital, raw materials, and technology. In order to facilitate the free movement of capital and technology, he initiated many new fiscal policies, including participation in GATT and the adjustment of exchange rates. The government was mobilizing every available resource to accelerate the nation's economic revitalization.

South Korea's economy entered its take-off stage by the late 1960s. Led by Park's focused leadership, it undertook a rapid import-substitution drive as its export-led industrial expansion was shaping up. During this period multinational corporations started to enter the South Korean market, providing the domestic economy with a growing influx of foreign capital and technology transfer. The nation's industrial development proceeded at such a rate and scope that it even changed the people's pessimistic attitude. Suddenly the society was filled with self-assurance and a rosy expectation of building a "Hahn River Miracle." The new promising chapter of a modern, industrial Korea was beginning to unfold. By the early 1970s the South Korean export economy had passed its incubation period and entered the world market, concentrating on its strategic sector of labor intensive, low technology products.

The close United States-South Korea collaboration in Vietnam and warm bilateral relations encountered a sudden chill with the inauguration of the Nixon presidency in 1969. President Nixon's new diplomatic initiative, known as the Nixon Doctrine, profoundly affected South Korea's domestic politics as well as its relations with America. The Park government had done its utmost to accommodate Washington's aspiration in East Asia; therefore, the Nixon Doctrine, which included the withdrawal of the remaining United States ground forces from South Korea, was more than a great concern. The full implementation of the doctrine, a complete withdrawal of American ground forces from Asia, meant that the United States' East Asian policy was undergoing a fundamental shift; no longer could any nation expect a full and automatic intervention by United States forces against communist aggression in the region. Under the framework of "Asian defense by Asian forces," Washington was willing to offer its Asian allies only logistical support.

President Nixon's new initiative gave America's Asian allies a strong impression that the United States was getting out of Asia. The South Koreans particularly received the new doctrine with a great deal of apprehension and suspicion. Just as they had wondered if Washington really understood the strategic importance of the Korean peninsula when it hastily removed its occupation force from defenseless South Korea in 1949, so South Koreans again had to agonize over the dependability of the American commitment. They wondered if the United States had sufficient determination to protect South Korea from aggressors. Nixon's assertion that his country would maintain its nuclear deterrent in the region did not calm the nerves of South Koreans.

South Koreans had not expected the American forces to become a permanent fixture of the Korean landscape. Yet they earnestly wished the United States military to remain until the South's military completed an extensive modernization program, which was needed to strengthen its still inadequately equipped forces to a level at which they could face the North's forces alone. The modernization of South Korean forces, a pledge that the Johnson administration made in 1965, had not progressed much by 1969.

The Nixon Doctrine was born against the backdrop of political uncertainty in East Asia. By then the United States was not expected to achieve a clean victory in Vietnam; the nation with the most modern weaponry and tactics but which was politically divided and unsure of its mission in the region failed to subjugate the ill-equipped but determined Vietnamese guerrilla force. Confronted by the prospect of a long military stalemate and worsening anti-war sentiments at home, Washington was anxious to end the war by withdrawing its forces.

The fact that the new initiative reflected the Nixon administration's strong interest in improving its relations with Communist China further perturbed the South Koreans. They suspected that Washington was making a dangerous gesture- a drastic reduction in its security commitment in the region- to pursue the opening of the People's Republic of China. There was even a fear among South Koreans that the U.S. might use South Korea as a bargaining chip for a Sino-American rapprochement. The Park government's suspicion over retreating American resolve against the communists was traced back to the United States' non-response to North Korea's provocative attacks on its intelligence-gathering operations: North Korea's attacks included the incidents of the Pueblo in February 1968, and the EC-121 in April 1969.

South Korea's strong objection to the implementation of the Nixon Doctrine caused a growing strain between the two close allies. Nevertheless, over South Korean protests the Nixon administration had withdrawn its 20,000 combat troops from South Korea by early 1971. The withdrawal forced the South Korean army to assume the defense of the entire western front along the DMZ, thus making the Koreanization of the South Korean defense in the front almost complete. However, as the Nixon administration had assured, it did not radically alter the military balance along the DMZ; the United States left one last combat division in South Korea as a symbol of its security commitment over the peninsula.

The Nixon Doctrine and the subsequent withdrawal of United States combat troops had not caused an immediate weakening of South Korean defense capability. The departed divisions transferred some heavy equipment to the South Korean army to compensate for troop reduction. In addition to its air wings in South Korea, the U.S. continued to maintain its strategic force in the region, including a strong naval and air presence in the Philippines and Japan. Nevertheless, the sudden shift in Washington's Asian policy profoundly changed South Korea's domestic political climate as it further deepened the peninsula's security anxiety.

South Korea's paranoia over North Korea's militancy was greatly exacerbated when North Korea attempted the assassination of President Park; the North's guerrillas almost succeeded in reaching the Blue House, the South Korean presidential mansion, when the police spotted and neutralized them on January 21, 1968. This incident, one of the most disturbing security concerns even for the citizens of this violence-ridden peninsula, graphically illustrated South Korea's vulnerability and North Korea's determination to disrupt life of its southern brothers.

The immediate effects of North Korea's guerrilla attempt on the Blue House were more political than military. The incident provided the Park government and its supporters an excuse to grope for a scheme to prolong the presidency of Park Chung Hee, who had just begun his second and last presidential term under the constitution. The primary argument the pro-government faction advanced was that the nation's security crisis demanded a strong and stable leadership, the kind of patriotism and devotion only

General Park could provide. Although President Park himself had favored such an arrangement, the public overwhelmingly rejected the scheme. Nevertheless, over the public's unambiguous objection, the Park government and its followers instigated the adoption of a constitutional amendment that enabled President Park to run for a third term.

The argument that there was no alternative leader to replace Park might have been correct. Yet the situation was largely a product of the Park regime itself. Throughout his rule President Park did not tolerate any potential threat within his own political faction, not to mention grooming a successor. In reality, the president was unwilling to tolerate his replacement until the nation completed its rejuvenation process; in this sense he was a most convinced and equally dedicated leader. Thus monopolizing the South Korean political process, he deliberately created a deplorable leadership vacuum allowing no viable political leader who was capable to challenge him.

In many ways the 1971 presidential election was an epochal point in South Korea's political maturity. For the first time in history, the government permitted open political forums, although in a limited fashion. It even engaged in a public discussion of the merits of nationalistic unification, the notion that the nation should undertake steps toward the unification process unfettered by political ideology. The new approach represented a radical departure from the stereotypical ideological unification doctrine pursued by the governments on both sides of the DMZ - unification in each side's image. The main opposition candidate, Kim Dae-jung, insisted that national unification was feasible not by military means but by the political guaranty of the four powers, namely China, Japan, the United States, and the Soviet Union. Kim's peaceful unification proposal, which called for the regional powers' support and consent to succeed, was far too drastic for the governments of North and South Korea, both of whom had been repeating nothing but combative unification rhetoric since the division. Nevertheless, it was the first solution that had substantial practical value in the sense that it was based on the region's political reality. Kim's bold idea was, in spirit, compatible with Nixon's East Asian approach, which argued that the justified interests of the four powers be respected. Kim's unification method, though it stirred South Korean society, was far too drastic to be politically acceptable. Still, the fact that such a far-reaching proposal was publicly debated illustrated the region's changing political climate and the maturing of South Korean politics.

Ever since the failure of the North-South reconciliation talks in 1946, each Korea had totally rejected even discussing any unification scheme that did not conform to its own ideological preference. Unification under Western capitalism remained unacceptable to North Korea as much as unification under the communist banner was unacceptable to South Korea. Kim's "four power guaranty" approach implied that Korea's internal political structure should be respected by the four powers regardless of ideological orientation. It implied, by virtue of the four power involvement, that a unified Korea would accept the form of an ideological mix that would be far from both the extreme right and the extreme left. Neither the North nor the South was even close to accepting such a compromise at the time. In the sense that it required collective support, the method was somewhat similar to the old Rooseveltian trusteeship idea. Yet the proposal was more practical than any ideological one was; it represented the reality that Korea's unification, like its independence, could be achieved only when it somehow accommodated the political interests of the four regional powers.

Kim's progressive proposal was largely election material more than a serious political proposal. Yet the fact that such a revolutionary idea had surfaced in a nation where extreme rightists prevailed was a significant development. The "four power guaranty" solution, along with Kim's other proposals, such as non-political North-South exchanges, helped encourage the Park government to take a more progressive attitude toward its northern counterpart.

4. The North-South Dialogue

On July 4, 1972, the governments in Seoul and Pyongyang simultaneously issued an extraordinary joint communique. In it both governments declared that they would seek national unification in a spirit of independence, peaceful unification, and greater national unity. Furthermore, they agreed to expand the bilateral exchanges and talks through a North-South committee to be established. After nearly three decades of military confrontation, the world's most antagonistic rivals, though blood brothers, agreed to pursue the unification of the fatherland through "dialogues" rather than "military means." It was the first meaningful North-South dialogue after the signing of the armistice almost twenty years before. The fact that both sides agreed to talk was itself an exciting development in Korea, although no one underestimated the portentous obstacles that had to be cleared for the eventual unification. Yet the historic euphoria was to belittle the extraordinary complexity of the unification problem.

However, intermittent talks that followed the joint communique produced no tangible results. Neither the North nor the South was ready to negotiate anything of substantial value. Talks did not even contribute to the stability of the peninsula's military confrontation. Despite the lack of progress, the talks did raise a hopeful expectation that the national unification might not have to resort to military means. Dialogue served the political purpose of the dictatorial regimes on both sides of the DMZ.

Apparently, President Park felt that the South Korean political system was at a disadvantage in a prolonged political contest with the North. He regarded South Korea's open society, in contrast to the North's totalitarianism, as a significant drawback. Park also feared that South Korea's loose political system, often marred by divisive politics, could become a substantial burden in his negotiation with Kim's closely controlled communist regime. Whether Kim's imposing political stature was an added incentive was not clear, but Park began to seek a long-term political mandate during this period.

Against his pledge not to run for another term, Park continued to seek for a way to extend further his presidential tenure. This time Park's followers actively engaged in devising a way to bypass the already-revised constitution for his long-term rule. President Park desired a clear, unlimited political mandate for the completion of his self-imposed mission: building the nation's self-sufficient defense and mature industrial economy. Driven by the lofty task of national security and economic prosperity, President Park and his followers ignored the fact that such a political monopoly would ruin any hope for a peaceful transition of political power, a necessity in building the foundation for the nation's democratic tradition. South Koreans wondered aloud if those lofty tasks Park believed to be his mission could not be carried out by other leaders through a more free and open political process. In spite of Park's assertion, which was not totally self-serving, South Koreans remained reluctant to bestow such an open political mandate upon him.

In October 1972, President Park suspended the nation's constitution and all political activities by proclaiming martial law. Through this emergency measure the president sought not only a political mandate, but also a fundamental restructuring of South Korea's governing system. As his legal framework, Park adopted the new system of Yushin, or Revitalizing Reform, through a referendum. Under the Yushin Constitution, Park was eligible to serve in the presidency for an indefinite number of six-year terms. Moreover, unlike the old constitution that stipulated direct presidential election, the Yushin constitution allowed indirect presidential election; the president was to be chosen by a popularly-elected body known as the National Conference for Unification, which was otherwise a largely symbolic institution with the dubious task of discussing unification matters. The overwhelmingly pro-government conference, from which partisan politics were officially barred, was given the prerogative of selecting the nation's president.

By bestowing the power of selecting the nation's supreme political leader on the new institution, the Yushin system assured President Park an unlimited term to rule. On the other hand, it greatly reduced the power of the often defiant National Assembly; the president was given an extraordinary power to nominate one-third of the total membership of the National Assembly and to dissolve the assembly at will. Ostensibly, the new government would be a government for national unification. In essence, however, it was a constitutional dictatorship designed to confer on Park the complete political mandate he believed he needed to handle the unification issue with the communist dictatorship in the North. Under the Yushin Constitution, Park easily secured his election to the presidency, a position that yielded unprecedented power.

President Park Chung Hee enunciated the Yushin Reforms as a step to assure South Korea's resolve to pursue national survival and security. Under this pretext he claimed that his amassing awesome political power was a necessary measure to deal effectively with the nation's security concerns and to push for the unification of the nation.[5] Having secured his political power, the president pushed for extensive national reforms, which extended to most aspects of South Korean society. This vast revitalizing movement was, the president rationalized, an imperative for the nation's survival, prosperity, and unity.

President Park justified his government's constitutional revision and the Yushin Reforms with domestic and international political considerations. Yet his increasingly vocal opposition accused him of imposing premeditated dictatorship. Regardless, he had a compelling motive: rapidly shifting regional politics. President Nixon's China visit, a consummation of Washington's rapprochement attempt, along with Japan's constant overtures to China and the Soviet Union, seriously disturbed Park's sense of acceptable checks and balances among international powers in the Far East. The looming new strategic order convinced Park that South Korea's only viable road to national survival and peaceful unification was by means of building national strength. The Park administration's desperation had a valid ground; when the Nixon administration announced the withdrawal of one of the two remaining U.S. infantry divisions, the

South Korean military had not even fully embarked on its long-delayed modernization drive. Whether Yushin was the best answer to South Korea's pressing political-defense problems remained debatable, however.

Suspicions over the Yushin system were widespread among the South Korean populace. The ruling party's abuses of virtual political carte blanche were also substantial. Nevertheless, Park's obsession with defense buildup and industrial development had a solid basis. Furthermore, the nation's dramatic success in both its defense industry and civilian manufacturing sector during the 1970s proved the validity and unselfishness of his drive. Yet the public remained skeptical of the Yushin system as it charted the nation's most ambitious journey; in 1973 South Koreans expressed through the election for the national assembly their grave displeasure over the Park government by casting forty-two percent of the votes for opposition parties as compared to thirty-nine percent for the ruling party. Undeterred by the obvious public rebuke, Park implemented, with single-minded devotion, the new Yushin programs, which he defended as "nation saving" measures.

The Yushin Reform's most conspicuous instrument was Saemaul Undong, or the New Village Movement. It was a government-led campaign to create an improved general environment by maximizing self-help and cooperation among the local people. It originally started from and targeted rural villages where living amenities were in many aspects less than desirable. Later, the movement spread to cities and factories nationwide. As its application extended to urban areas, the movement's mission also progressively evolved to include the propagation of new ethics for all of the society. The Park government endeavored with extensive administrative assistance to make the movement instrumental in achieving both physical remodeling and spiritual revitalization of the nation. The New Village Movement was successful to some significant extent in improving the nation's rural living environment. Yet the results might have been more effective with a systematic, cohesive national plan rather than with a piecemeal, semi-volunteer approach. Nevertheless, the movement was one of the nation's most publicly enforced volunteer movements during the Park administration.

5. Park and Defense Build-up

President Park's most profound contribution to his country was his successful expansion and upgrading of the nation's defense industry. His quest for a self-sustained defense industry was firm and consistent, eventually providing South Korea to a significant extent with a confident national defense capability. The president was convinced that the United States would be an unreliable partner as far as the modernization of the South Korean armed forces was concerned. Such skepticism grew from the Johnson administration's breach of its pledge. Park remained doubtful of the Nixon administration's promise for the same reason.

The modernization of their armed forces was a matter of critical importance for South Koreans. When it became evident that United States assistance would remain insufficient to achieve the overall goal, the South Koreans realized that the most dependable road to achieving the national desire was to build their own defense industry. Thus, President Park initiated his systematic drive for a self-sustained defense industry soon after the Yushin government was established, and he encouraged the participation of South Korea's energetic and resourceful private sector in his programs.

The Park administration provided the nation's infant defense industry with every possible assistance to expedite its expansion and sophistication. In many instances, the president himself assumed the role of a floor leader for the gigantic crash drive, seeking funds from every available source, both external and domestic. In addition, the nation's growing industrial sector economy and the availability of quality scientists trained in Western industrial countries were a great help to the rapid growth of the defense programs. As the 1970s drew to an end, President Park's drive for building the nation's self-sustained defense industry became even more feverish, as if his political mandate were about to expire. By overcoming numerous obstacles, Park's defense programs recorded phenomenal success, transforming South Korea into a nation of virtual self-sufficiency in arms, except in some high technology areas. President Park had achieved beyond what South Koreans believed to be possible. Through his crash defense programs he successfully demonstrated the spirit of his proud motto, "We can do it."

In conjunction with the nation's defense programs in conventional arms, President Park also pursued the nation's nuclear capability. His yearning for nuclear arms attracted favorable public support; South Koreans remained, in general, boldly candid and knowledgeable about nuclear weapons. Some having been survivors of Nagasaki and Hiroshima, they understood the awesome destructive power of the weapons. Yet they were realistic enough to concede that these weapons could be used, under certain circumstances, against their own nation, i.e., the North, but they were supportive of such an application if the military situation so dictated. Their fear of another destructive war with the North overcame even the specter of having to use nuclear weapons.

When the Nixon Doctrine raised the possibility of pulling out U.S. infantry divisions and tactical nuclear weapons from the South, the two most highly regarded deterrents to North Korea's military adventurism, the Park administration was convinced that the development of "Korean nuclear weapons" was the only alternative. Most South Korean leaders regarded the nuclear option as the only approach that could safeguard the nation's security when and if the American security commitment were withdrawn. The fear of Northern military superiority that this withdrawal would likely create was so overwhelming that even Park's antagonistic opposition tacitly approved the program. Although Park apparently pursued the program with his typical devotion, the extent of his success in this area has not been disclosed at this time. Officially, South Korea suspended its nuclear program in 1974 because of President Ford's persuasion and his pledge to maintain the U.S. nuclear umbrella in the region.

Whether Washington's pressure forced President Park to cancel entirely his nuclear weapons program cannot be determined at the present time. There were indications that under United States pressure South Korea's resolution to achieve its own nuclear deterrent hardened, albeit in total secrecy. One telling indication of this was that Washington did not trust South Korea's official stand over its nuclear intentions, as illustrated by the United States' tight surveillance of South Korea's major research facilities and scientists during the period.

South Korea's nuclear weapons capability, if it had been realized, could have been a significant setback to the nuclear non-proliferation effort the world's nuclear powers were undertaking. On the other hand, to South Korea it was not a matter of a treaty obligation but of national survival. Many Koreans felt that their country had a right to build a weapon system against an international treaty, however loathsome that may be, to protect itself from external threats. The Park administration insisted that as a sovereign state it had a right to build any weapon system required to safeguard its own survival.[6]

Vietnam played a major role in South Korea's security panic in the late 1970s. The United State's unwillingness to retaliate against North Vietnam's treaty violations and the subsequent collapse of the South Vietnam regime sent a chilling message: the United States had lost its passion to fight against Asian Communists. Dramatically improving China-United States relations and the stream of Southeast Asian refugees caused the South Koreans confusion as well as apprehension over their own national security.

Their fear of possible fallout from North Vietnam's victory was genuine and extensive; they openly wondered if the Vietnam fiasco would serve as a promising reference for Kim's North Korean regime. The South Koreans were aware that their national security arrangement was unlike that of South Vietnam, but they could not help noticing certain parallels. The region's growing political uncertainty, which transpired because of the tarnished image of the United States in the region, all the more convinced South Koreans of the need to develop their own defense capability, including nuclear arms.

South Korea's security panic reached its peak when Jimmy Carter, the Democratic presidential candidate, openly insisted on the withdrawal of the remaining U.S. ground forces from South Korea. South Koreans felt that their worst fear was materializing even before the early phase of their defense industry program was completed. The Park administration resisted Carter's withdrawal plan, pushing simultaneously its weapons programs with maximum efforts. The Carter administration eventually discarded its withdrawal plan under the intense pressure applied by Congress and the military establishment. However, the misgivings the proposal aroused within the Park administration lingered on throughout the Carter presidency.

The Park government's conflict with the Carter administration was not limited to the ground forces issue. The liberal Carter administration and ultra-conservative Park administration tangled over human rights issues, developing severe diplomatic conflicts. Security-conscious South Koreans rejected President Carter's singular emphasis on political human rights, which transcended all other considerations. They insisted that human rights ought to include not only customary political rights but the even more fundamental right of living in a secure nation. The Park administration responded to Carter's pressure for political liberalization with outspoken antagonism, opening an abyss that was never fully closed during the Carter presidency. Despite his noble intent, President Carter's approach to South Korea revealed his lack of proper appreciation of the nation's unique security concerns. The American leader's campaign did not transform the authoritarian Park administration, but instead Carter became the most unpopular U.S. president to South Koreans.

In spite of his single-minded pursuit, President Park did not complete his ambitious defense and industrial programs; he was assassinated by his long-time confidant and security chief Kim Jae Kyu on October 26, 1979. Yet by presiding over the most crucial period in the South Korean security and economic development, the general won a unique place in Korean history. As the nation's driving force toward economic development, he built the foundation for one of the world's most spectacular industrial economies. Under his militaristic leadership South Koreans widened their business horizons to the global level. His drive was bold and consistent; he earned much-needed foreign currencies in South Vietnam, the Middle East, and international markets. As a career military man he transformed the corrupt and inefficient government into a virtual military organization by emphasizing and rewarding efficiency and forceful leadership. Furthermore, he was the mastermind of South Korea's powerful defense industry. Some may feel that his farsighted, strong leadership might have been significant enough to compensate for his conspicuous failure to establish a peaceful political transition. To General Park, the welfare of the Hahn nation apparently superseded mundane politics. In many ways, he was the right leader for South Korea during the period when its economic foundation had to be laid.

Park was by nature an authoritarian leader of iron conviction, a man of unselfish motive and unbending loyalty to his nation. He was an honest and clean politician. Yet he invented a political system only to accommodate his own agenda of national rebuilding. By choosing not to tolerate any rival, regardless of affiliation, he failed to establish a democratic political tradition. His foreign policy was neither creative nor bold, but firm and consistent. Nevertheless, he did not hesitate to gamble when he was convinced that it was in the national interest. At the price of deliberately sacrificing the democratic political process, Park provided South Koreans with relative political-military stability and economic development.

Pursuing the nation's security and economic development as the nation's highest priority, President Park often castigated partisan politics. The public, however, remained doubtful of his forceful politics. He responded to growing vocal opposition with measures of harsh oppression by issuing Emergency Decree Number 9 in 1975. This measure, which forbade all criticism of the Yushin Constitution, and thus his rule, remained effective until his downfall. As a result, when he met with a tragic end, the nation's political process was frozen deep.

In spite of his willful delinquency regarding political democracy, his positive legacy will prevail in history. The general did not have enough time to complete what he intended to achieve for his country: the status of an industrialized nation with defense strong enough to discourage any North Korean military temptation. Nonetheless, his accomplishment was remarkable by any yardstick.

President Park's assassination brought South Korea the "Spring of

Seoul," a euphoria filled with a sense of freedom from authoritarian oppression and a new hope for open, democratic politics. The nation seemed to demonstrate its political maturity in overcoming the sudden political upheaval; a new government was duly installed under the existing Yushin Constitution. The public was eager to see the political legacy of the Park government completely removed by installing a new, democratic leadership. Democracy had been a prominent victim of Park's persistent claim that the nation could not afford political experimentation while the needs for economic development and national security were pressing. Now, however, many believed this the opportune time to put democracy in motion after a long postponement. Only a few would anticipate that the military would reinstate its influence over the civilian government and maintain General Park's legacy.

President Choe, the interim figure installed under the Yushin Constitution, held responsibility for leading the nation until the new government was formally installed. That meant the adoption of a new constitution and an election that the constitution would specify. The government of President Choe, a career bureaucrat, was, however, quickly overrun by some of the nation's junior generals who had held key positions under the Park presidency. By early 1980 the military usurped most of the Choe administration's political power. This unexpected development disappointed the public in general and activist students in particular, and they resorted to nationwide protests demanding a democratic government. The most bloody protest, led by student activists but participated in by a large number of civilians, occurred in the City of Kwangju, one of the nation's major provincial capitals in the southwestern region. The protesters instantly earned the support of the public not only in the city but in most of the region's smaller cities and towns.

The citizens of Kwangju thus decided to challenge the military for the nation's political democratization. The conscience of the new era briefly prevailed as the protesters controlled the city. The military, however, forcefully crushed the civilian protests. Paratroopers sent by military leaders brutally suppressed the heroic struggle, causing hundreds of casualties.[7] History will find a deserving place for the uprising, which was, contrary to the military's claim, not incited by North Korean agents or opposition political leaders but staged by the "common people." It was a serious display of ordinary people's yearning for an open, democratic society, one that did not deserve the military's harsh suppression. The Kwangju uprising, another chapter in the consciousness and sorrow of the Hahn people, left rueful wounds on the nation's process of political development.

By suppressing the Kwangju uprising by force, the military retired President Choe's fourth republic. Led by General Chun Doo Hwan, the military took over political power; the hopeful "Spring of Seoul" died without bearing a flower of democracy. The vicious circle of military rule set into motion by Park was running its natural course in spite of the public's bloody rejection. South Korea's fifth republic was formally installed in August of 1981 after General Chun Doo Hwan managed to be elected as the president for a single seven-year term by the Yushin's presidential electoral college. Thus, Park's military government was succeeded by another military government.

Like his predecessor Syngman Rhee, General Park knowingly played the role of a Korean monarch. His heavy-handed politics earned public disdain although his noble intentions were well received in general. General Chun was a part of Park's inner military circle; he had witnessed the drive and rationale of Park's rule. Not deterred by the public rejection Park had to take, Chun, who was much similar to Park in his make-up, decided to appropriate power by ambushing the public's overwhelming yearning for democratic political process. Chun, like Park, his military predecessor, used the threat of North Korean military aggression as his primary justification for usurping political power. Naturally, the public, which had shown great reluctance in supporting General Park in 1964, was even more reluctant to support General Chun's presidency. Regardless of the urgent security concerns he cited for his intervention, President Chun's alleged involvement with the bloody suppression of the Kwangju uprising unequivocally and permanently marred the integrity of his presidency. Chun's political ambition aside, the real cause of South Korea's recurring political setback was its security problem. The rise of the Chun regime, defying the public's desire to keep the military in the barracks, underscored again the reality that South Korea's true political democratization may be achieved only when the nation successfully deals with the peninsula's overwhelming political question, the North-South confrontation.

Notes

1. The student revolt of April 19, 1960, was officially known as the 4.19 Revolution in South Korea.
2. Kwan Kim, *The Korea-Japan Treaty Crisis and the Instability of the Korean Political System.* New York: Praeger Publishers, 1971, p. 80.

3. Ibid., p. 79.

4.South Korea's naval fleet visited Japan in December 1994 for the first time in history. A systematic military cooperation of the two neighbors still remains remote.

5. Park Chung Hee, p. 50.

6. Hyun Dae Moon Hwa Sa, *Jae Sam Gong Hwa Gook.* vol. 8, DaeGoo, Korea: Hyun Dae Moon Hwa Sa, 1986, pp. 13-91.

7. The total number of reported casualties ranges from a few hundred to a few thousand.

Chapter 13

Transitions and Intra-Korea Relations

1. Political Apathy and Global Marchantship

General Chun succeeded the late General Park in 1981 by assuming the presidency of the nation's fifth republic. Despite incessant public protests against its heavy-handed rule, the nation's military prevailed again over civilian politics. With the Chun presidency it extended the power it had held since the early 1960s; the nation's military legacy and the public's open disdain of it were certain to continue.

General Chun's elevation to the presidency was much more controversial than that of his predecessor. More than anything, the public's yearning for more open, free politics had grown stronger when Chun intervened in civilian politics. In addition, unlike Park, who had a credible excuse for his coup - the restoration of law and order - Chun offered no comparable justifications for his usurpation of power. Park's coup was in a sense regarded as national salvation, whereas Chun's takeover was criticized as political violence which dashed the dreams of the "Spring of Seoul." Chun failed to present to the public any altruistic motives for his disrupting civilian politics with ruthless intervention and thwarting the rare opportunity to install a democratic government.

General Chun added another sad chapter to South Korea's already tainted history of political transition, one that had earned the hermit kingdom a much disparaged reputation in the eyes of the world community. Inevitably, the public's ubiquitous protests and his harsh, predictable reprisals marred his seven-year tenure. The chronic confrontation between Chun's military regime and the citizens of more aggressive persuasion -

radical student activists, and militant labor -was a fixture of South Korea's political landscape throughout the 1980s.

Chun Doo Hwan, a junior general with minor exposure to the public until his craftily staged ascension to the presidency, was a very enigmatic figure. To a great extent he remained so to the public throughout his rule. As president he proved to be energetic and ambitious. Like President Park, he was convinced that even political democratization can be suspended if it is needed in achieving the nation's economic development and maintaining the national security. His political domination was not much different from that of Park's in the sense that he sought an absolute political authority in the nation. Nevertheless, unlike Park he remained insecure in his power, largely due to his failure to win public support; he was much preoccupied with maintaining total political domination throughout his tenure.

The majority of the public remained uncommitted to the Chun regime, although they hesitated to topple it mainly for fear of inciting destructive social instability. In reality, the public elected to acquiesce to the Chun administration's serving as a long transition government, thereby denying Chun the support he needed in pursuing the ambitious programs with confidence. Because he lacked a public political mandate and because of the lingering question over the legitimacy of his rule, President Chun failed to pursue a cohesive national agenda in spite of his sincere desire to do so.

Like General Park, Chun exploited the public's fear of weakening national defense and their desire to continue the nation's economic expansion. These two overriding concerns still remained decisive, although it was debatable whether they were sufficient to give Chun an excuse for dashing the nation's long-standing desire to move toward the democratization of political process. No one should have failed to discern that the situation Chun manipulated was by no means as critical as the one that General Park and his followers confronted in the early 1960s. Therefore, South Koreans, with their unique psychology toward the divided nation and their military-economic concerns, gave Chun a grudging consent to finish his term. The nation's general public, losing confidence in political institutions, was increasingly more concerned with enjoying improving economic fortunes. Rising political apathy was another phenomenon notable in the Chun rule.

President Chun's largely negative domestic perception did not, however, correspond to his extraordinarily good fortune in the regime's external relations. During his tenure South Korea enjoyed its most successful economic growth; it was also blessed with solid political support from the United States. Along with unabated tension along the DMZ, the nation's robust export economy provided a justifiable shelter for the unpopular Chun regime. Whether the nation's rapid industrial growth and trade expansion was led by the Chun government was beside the point. The public was understandably less critical of the ruling regime when the economy continued to expand.

The election of Ronald Reagan as President of the United States was Chun's other good fortune. The conservative U.S. president provided Chun with consistent, significant political support. Throughout his tenure Reagan highly regarded Chun's role as the strong ruler of a faraway frontier against the Soviet Union. Because Chun's South Korea served as a critical link for his strong anti-Soviet campaign, Reagan readily overlooked Chun's domestic politics. Inevitably, Washington's support of the Chun regime was openly opposed by the South Korean public in general and by Chun's political opposition in particular.

Even the nation's unprecedented economic prosperity and Washington's unequivocal political support did not mollify the public's aversion toward the Chun regime. Chun had never been able to completely overcome the public's hostility; public support was so thin that at the end it even scuttled Chun's attempt to install his colleague as his successor. Having faced nationwide protests, Chun was forced to negate this scheme and to agree to amend the constitution to allow a direct presidential election. Although he managed to leave behind one positive legacy - a peaceful political transition - his presidency is likely to be remembered as a political detour that squashed the people's democratic aspirations.

Throughout his rule Chun had to battle the nation's most militant student activism. Born during the Rhee regime, student activism escalated in the later period of the Chun rule to nationwide protests to which the nation's labor and religious circles rendered increasing support. Throughout his tenure protests calling for his immediate ouster were as common as Seoul's worsening traffic jams. Chun responded to the opposition in an equally combative manner, stationing the anti-riot police force at almost every corner of most major cities. The cat-and-mouse confrontation continued uninterrupted while the majority of the public remained callous. Yet Chun never resorted to a negotiated settlement with his opposition, partly because the opposition demanded no cosmetic reforms but the ouster of the president himself. Unable to win the public trust and support even with his near dictatorial power, he gradually became the prisoner of his own power, relying on the military that remained his sole constituency and the bulwark of the regime.

The survival of the Chun presidency itself was the irony and sorrow of South Korean politics. To a great extent, Chun served out his term because of the political delinquency of the South Korean public. Ever since independence, the people had shown a great deal of reluctance to exercise their sovereign right to drive out dictators. Even the public's extensive discontent had never become a serious threat to Syngman Rhee, Park Chung Hee, or Chun Doo Hwan. Except for a few incidents in which the public accorded some symbolic support to the efforts of student activists, it had assumed, in general, the role of bystander, acquiescing to dictatorship. Moreover, it often submitted to the dictatorial pressure by validating the rule of authoritarian leaders through the electoral process.

The foremost cause for South Korea's political split personality is its security concerns. The fear of another North-South military confrontation had always played a key role in greatly restricting the people's maneuvering room in the political arena. Through the electoral process South Koreans had traditionally endorsed the rightist notion that even at the price of deferred political democratization, another intra-Korean bloodshed had to be prevented. As the public preferred to play safe, only radical student activists continued to challenge the military government. Student activism, firmly established unfortunately as the nation's political tradition, was considered a beacon of South Korea's political conscience.

Contrary to its generally negative political image, the Chun administration provided focused leadership in the nation's drive for economic development. During President Chun's tenure the nation experienced its first true economic buoyancy, illustrated in the milestone of its first current account surplus in 1986. Under the guidance of the Chun regime the exuberant export sector spearheaded the nation's hyperactive economic expansion.

South Korea had effectively departed from its humble reputation of being a hermit kingdom in the 1980s. Not only did it refuse to continue the isolationist tradition but actively pursued global merchantship, which has been instrumental in elevating South Korea to one of the world's largest trading nations. It also secured a coveted place among a small band of nations by being recognized as one of the newly industrialized countries (NICs) and one of Asia's economic "tigers." Its rise to the status of a blossoming industrial nation deserved high accolades, particularly considering its meager resource bases and the crushing burden of maintaining one of the world's largest standing armies. As the nation's export drive continued to overcome barriers and utilize its increasingly sophisticated global merchantship, it inevitably faced growing competition worldwide. South Korea has responded to the challenge with an ambitious quest for technological independence and sophistication.

By the early 1980s South Korea had made further positive corrections in its export economy. It reduced its heavy export dependence on predominantly low-technology, labor intensive products by expanding the strategic export sectors to medium-technology, capital intensive products including automobiles, electronics, and supertankers. Entering the last decade of the twentieth century, South Korea's export economy was performing at a pace that should enable the hermit kingdom to achieve the desired status of a mature industrial power by the early 21st century.[1]

In South Korea's drive for export-led economic development, the central government's leadership has been quintessential. Equally profound in this regard were the efforts of its young, passionate business leaders. Confident in their abilities to penetrate faraway markets and to compete against Western industrial states and Japan, South Korea's aggressive business leaders rarely hesitated to take even unusual risks, practicing President Park's "Can Do" spirit. The nation's remarkable success in global export competition prompted the rise of many world-class business conglomerations, known locally as *Jaebul*. With the ability to mobilize huge capital and personnel assets quickly and cohesively, these mammoth corporations have been the driving force of South Korea's export machine.

South Korea's recent success in international export markets has given its citizens confidence in their ability to build a modern industrial state. The public is increasingly aware of the fact that they have finally found a viable solution to escape from the historical conditions of isolation and passivity that kept the nation backward for so long. Economic success has finally given the citizens of the hermit kingdom a worldly view and participation that would help them to gain a new political status in East Asia. Having paid a stiff price for its unique geopolitical properties for centuries, Korea, albeit only its southern half, finally reached the threshold of national maturity.

In trade volume, South Korea ranked 101st among the nations of the world in 1961. The war-torn economy continued to stagnate under the burdens of growing defense expenditure and a high population growth rate. Having abundant human capital but a meager endowment of natural resources, South Korea's economic recovery depended solely upon its ability to produce industrial consumer items for international markets. In order to build an industrial economy, the Park government adopted highly effective industrial growth policies: aggressive and innovative export promotion policies along with a comprehensive incentive system to channel the nation's limited resources into export-oriented activities. Considering the nation's poor natural resource endowments, the Park government's commitment to export-oriented national development was an economic imperative. The South effected an epochal shift from the basic survival strategy that had dominated the postwar period. For the first time in its history, the hermit kingdom undertook an outward-oriented development strategy, departing from an inward, isolated approach of traditional practice. The Park government was in fact pursuing the nation's first economic independence, an ambition in which the nation could not afford to fail.

South Korea entered the 1980s with its export sector performing at a rate surpassing that of most developed countries. However, it had not alleviated the nation's major industrial deficiencies: its export economy was still overly dependent upon borrowed capital and imported technologies. In addition, the economy was yet to recover from the costly mid-stream policy shifts primarily dictated by the Park government's political-military considerations. In the midst of tumultuous strategic cross-currents prompted by the normalization of Sino-U.S. relations and by the expected withdrawal of American troops from South Korea under the Nixon doctrine, the Park government in the early 1970s redirected its industrial priority to areas needed in building up industrial bases for an independent defense capability. This shift meant major sectoral adjustments in favor of industries of high strategic value: various basic machinery and foundry industries plus heavy and chemical industries indispensable in building the nation's self-sustaining defense industry. Such sectoral adjustments required additional capital and technology input, further straining the economy. Rising income aside, industrial independence was still far from a reality.

Despite the difficulties entailed, the revised industrial development drive proved to be highly beneficial to the Chun government. As its exports of labor intensive, low technology items found growing acceptance mainly in the markets in the United States and Western Europe, South Korea met increasing global competition. The most stiff competition came from China and other labor-rich Asian countries. Growing competition in international markets forced South Korea to further revise its industrial strategy by gradually upgrading its industrial hierarchy to compete with Japan and other industrialized countries for production of middle-level technology items. Without the Park government's emphasis on defense-related heavy industries such as naphtha-cracking, steel, metal products, shipbuilding, machinery, and automobile production, South Korea would not have been able to adjust and maintain its strong export economy. Both Park's sectoral adjustments and Chun's hierarchical adjustments served the nation well in the end.

President Park's single-minded drive for the development of heavy industries was not without some disturbing drawbacks. The nation's preoccupation in developing capital-intensive industries caused serious structural imbalances and subsequent financial losses in the nation's overall economic development program. Furthermore, by neglecting small and medium-size industries, the backbone of its profitable export sectors, it seriously damaged the export economy. The nation's sudden export slump in 1979 underscored this structural problem, although it was vastly aggravated by the worldwide oil crisis and political uncertainty after the assassination of President Park.

The Chun government moved quickly to redress the nation's industrial disorders, laying the groundwork for the march toward industrial maturity. The government's emphasis shifted back to a broader industrial spectrum, emphasizing small and medium-size firms. At the same time, it adopted more of an indicative planning approach by allowing a greater role for the private sector. This timely policy adjustment was effective as the nation's export economy regained its momentum with an even broader export base. By providing steady guidance and support, General Chun's fifth republic made a significant contribution to the nation's global export sector.

By the late 1980s South Korea agreed to accommodate the increasingly vocal demands of its major trading partners. As a step toward import liberalization, it reduced the rate of import protection by about sixty-nine percent in 1980; by 1988 import protection had declined ninety-five percent. By the end of 1990, the rate was further reduced to ninety-eight percent, thus greatly opening domestic markets to foreign products. The nation's average tariff rate was also drastically lowered during the late 1980s, reaching about ten percent in 1992. The Uruguay Round, the GATT negotiation of 1994, forced the nation to open even its strategic domestic market, the foremost product being rice, to foreign products. In spite of gross misgivings of the nation's farmers over the opening of its rice market to outsiders, the government remained confident that the new international trade order would benefit the nation more in the long run.

South Korea is expected to maintain its highly successful export-oriented approaches as its basic economic framework for years to come. Its global marketing will be led by the nation's major *Jaebuls*. To bolster its global competitiveness, the nation plans to allocate even more resources to research and development activities. Both the government and the business community are cognizant of the fact that vigorous pursuit of R&D is a prerequisite for entering head-on in the competition against Japan and the

Western industrial economies. The government greatly expanded its R&D commitment throughout the 1980s, with its science and technology investment reaching 2.5 percent of GNP in 1990.   Private R&D expenditures are also expanding rapidly. The limited availability of risk capital in the nation is being compensated for by the presence of aggressive business conglomerates. The trend is likely to continue as the nation will be pressured further to rely on its own technology in international markets.

Historically, the rivalry among the nation's most prominent conglomerates, or *Jaebuls*, has been extremely intense in every aspect of business activity. As the South embarked upon entry into an advanced industrial economy, competition among the *Jaebuls* has expanded to most R&D activities, which include all potentially profitable fields. Because of high costs for advanced R&D activities, the involvement of the *Jaebul* groups is vital in Korea's achieving the desired technological leap for technology- intensive, productivity-sensitive fields. A growing trend in South Korea is the major *Jaebuls'* assembling of large R&D teams after the successful Japanese model. It is expected that breakthroughs in the commercial application of advanced technologies will accord the nation a cutting edge advantage in worldwide industrial competition. South Korea's all-out endeavor for R&D breakthroughs reflects that it believes that there will be increasing difficulty in importing advanced technologies from mature industrial countries.

South Korea's export sector was particularly strong during the latter half of the 1980s. The country recorded its first trade surplus in the 1986-1987 period in which its export volume grew at a phenomenal rate of twenty-six percent per year. Its total export reached $60 billion with a positive trade balance of over $11 billion in 1988. This accomplishment was assisted by favorable macroeconomic conditions: the decline of oil prices, the diminution of the worldwide interest rate, a high exchange rate for the Japanese yen, and a stable economic performance in industrialized countries. Since then, due to shifting external factors and growing imports, South Korea's trade balance has experienced drastic fluctuation: the surplus reduced to $10 billion in 1990 and it turned to a deficit in 1991. But a favorable trade balance was back in 1993. South Korea's stable export performance during the 1980s and the early 1990s was largely responsible for the nation's reaching its economic objectives: a high growth rate with price stability, and a current account surplus. The vigorous export sector is expected to continue spearheading the high growth performance of the national economy for years to come.[2]

The pattern of South Korea's trade development was much similar to that of Japan. It was primarily fueled by the adroit utilization of its favorable accessibility to the giant consumer market in the United States. Only after accumulating experience and confidence in the American markets did South Korean industries venture to expand their trade horizons to Europe and elsewhere. In the sense that its capital and technological cooperation was not limited to the United States. With   normalized relations, South Korea actively sought Japanese cooperation in capital and technology transfers, an invaluable help to its export-oriented, industrial development drive.

Despite its heavy dependency on Japan's semi-produced and capital goods, South Korea has been only marginally successful until recent years in penetrating Japan's growing consumer market. Japan's jealous protection of its domestic market from South Korean products resulted in a virtual one-way trade pattern and a huge trade deficit for Koreans with respect to Japan.[3] Although there has been some improvement in this regard in recent years, this anomalous trade imbalance still remains as long as Japan is unwilling to remove its extensive non-tariff trade barriers against South Korean products.

To mitigate the exacerbating trade conflicts with the United States, South Korea undertook an ambitious trade diversification campaign throughout the 1980s. Its expanding trade ties include the nations of southeast Asia, eastern Europe, and the Middle East. The historic shifts in the international political atmosphere, inaugurated by China's limited experimentation with a market economy, a brainchild of Deng- and *perestroika,* a bold initiative of Soviet President Gorbachev, provided further momentum to South Korea's drive. In 1990 South Korea's two-way trade with the East bloc countries and China reached $5 billion, recording a yearly growth rate of over twenty-three percent. Its trade with China has grown to $10 billion by 1994, making China South Korea's third largest trade partner.

With its diversified trade practices, South Korea reduced its export dependency on the United States market to thirty percent in 1990, a marked improvement from thirty-five percent in 1988. At the same time, its import dependency on American products has risen to twenty-five percent, thus narrowing the trade imbalance to less than $1 billion by the end of 1990. South Korea's export share to the United States continues to decline: it was twenty-three percent in 1992. As a result, it is expected that South Korea will run small trade deficits against the United States in years to come. Having made significant trade adjustments to eliminate their huge trade surplus - over $9 billion, which was a mere seven percent of America's total trade deficit of over $120 billion in 1988- South Koreans remain confident that their trade relations with the United States will continue to be mutually productive and cooperative.

South Korea's efforts to redress its trade imbalance with Japan had remained less than desirable, however. Compounded by the yen's weakness against the dollar, the South's trade deficit against Japan worsened in 1989, reaching over $10 billion. The deficit for the 1990-1994 period remained at the same level with small fluctuation. South Korea's dependence on imports from Japan remained about thirty percent, while its export to Japan reached only seven percent of Japan's total imports. Japan is South Korea's only trade partner that has consistently run a trade surplus against Koreans. This pattern is not expected to change much for the foreseeable future.

The South Korean economy is projected to grow at an annual rate of seven percent for the 1992-1996 period. Its per capita GNP will reach $10,190 in 1996, compared with an estimated $7,244 in 1993. By 1996, the nation's merchandise exports, estimated to top $112 billion, will generate some current account surplus. The South is expected to become a top ten trading nation before this century expires. These glowing projections represent South Koreans' confidence in their ability to carry out the historic task of transforming the resource-poor nation into an industrial power by the turn of the twenty-first century.

2. Hyper Growth and Labor

South Korea's phenomenal economic expansion in recent years has been instrumental in laying a solid foundation vital for its expected joining the club of developed industrial economies. However, success has presented the nation with a number of serious social problems, ranging from growing inequality in income distribution to the widening development gap between rural and urban communities.

For the last three decades, the South Korean government has maintained a low wage policy to keep its industrial products competitive in the world market. The nation's success in global export markets owes greatly to a quality labor force who accepted difficult sacrifices. The South being a technological youth and upstart, full utilization of the inexpensive labor force was not only an imperative but also the most effective and perhaps the only alternative for the nation in its struggle to enter world markets. It was workers' willingness to tolerate subsistence wages and to work long hours in less desirable conditions that made the publicized economic take-off possible. As a whole, labor has been remarkably cooperative with ambitious management in the cause of national economic development.

Nonetheless, labor's altruistic motives were showing rapid erosion when the nation, emphasizing the further expansion of an export-oriented economy, continued to neglect measures to ensure more equitable distribution of the benefits brought by economic buoyancy. Persuaded by industry's urging for facility expansion and for maintenance of competitiveness in the international markets, the government was reluctant to side with labor, which in turn sought militant confrontation against management. Many major industries have been affected by long and destructive strikes. However, the public remained unconvinced by labor's militant demands. Since the late 1980s the nation's radical student activists and the political left increasingly have shown their support of labor unions.

Labor's contentious demand for more equitable distribution of wealth was significant. Labor openly declared its unwillingness to further tolerate subsistence wages and other sacrifices while the small upper-class monopolized the fruits of remarkable economic expansion. Moreover, the militant labor movement took an increasingly political tone as a growing number of young and poorly paid factory workers were participating in student-led anti-government protests. As a result, labor-management disharmony has become an explosive social-political issue.

Under the Rho administration South Korean labor has become even more bold and militant as it gained political support from powerful opposition parties. Even the skeptical general public became more sympathetic to workers' demands as the nation's business community compounded its tarnished image of extreme selfishness with much castigated business practices including real estate speculation and excessive competition in non-productive activities. Pernicious labor unrest, which has often closed down the nation's major manufacturing industries, endangering economic progress and sociopolitical stability, still remains volatile and destructive to some industries. The nation is yet to find an acceptable middle ground, a solution that may placate the increasingly vocal workers while ensuring the needs of entrepreneurs to expand and improve their production facilities to stay competitive in the world's global marketing race. For South Korea's labor movement, it is crucial to find a proper role that is appropriate and constructive in the nation's unique economic system.

The underlying cause of South Korea's labor unrest is the widening gap in living standards between the upper class and the rest of the society. The nation's remarkable success in the global export race has primarily benefitted its urban upper-classes, leaving the majority working classes further disadvantaged. The nation has so far failed to adopt effective economic filtering-down mechanisms that might have ensured more equitable distribution of the wealth. The nettlesome income gap is also present in rural communities, as farmers' incomes continue to fall back to that of non-agricultural workers. As a consequence, the rural regions are left with little improvement while major urban centers, particularly Seoul and a few others, have undergone an impressive transformation, achieving the status of being modern metropolitan areas with advanced living amenities.

In spite of its continuing urban expansion, South Korea's agricultural labor force is still much larger than that of advanced industrial economies. In Western Europe and America, economic development has been accompanied by a gradual reduction of the farm labor force; the stable growth of non-agricultural employment was needed to make the farm-urban transition possible. South Korea's farm labor force, 15.6 percent of the total in 1992, is too large to ensure it a living standard comparable to that of the nation's manufacturing and service sector workers.

South Korea's agrarian tradition still runs deep. As long as the government pursues a low agricultural price policy to protect its industrial sector economy, it will remain imperative for South Korea to increase its low per-farmer-acreage to bolster farm income. This can be achieved only through further reduction of the agricultural population. Yet it is critical that the rural to urban migration be gradual to avoid excessive urban unemployment and to allow the urban economy time to create gainful employment for marginal farm workers who will be displaced. Even under the best circumstances, therefore, the rural economy is expected to improve only slowly, forcing the nation to suffer urban-rural disparity for a prolonged period.[4]

In spite of the problems of inequitable distribution of wealth, the steady growth of the confident middle class has greatly contributed to the stabilization of South Korean society. As a whole, the middle class, whose definition is not precise although the majority of moderate income groups tend to designate themselves as being in it, was not much different from other members of the society in objecting to Chun's authoritarian rule. However, having a larger stake in the order and stability of the society, the middle class has shown more reluctance than lower income groups in supporting the opposition's eagerness to topple the regime. While yearning for democratic reforms, the middle class had been unwilling to risk its newly-earned status by opposing the Chun regime until the very last moment, albeit passively. With vastly improved material well-being, South

Korea's middle class remains strongly anti-communist and generally prefers the conservative status quo to a radical political shift. Sociopolitical stability and continuing economic progress, which are inseparable components particularly in South Korea, are so paramount that the middle class chose to tolerate Chun's unpopular and authoritarian rule as a lesser evil.

3. The 1988 Summer Olympic: A Korean Showcase

The International Olympic Committee (IOC) awarded the 1988 Summer Olympic games to Seoul. It was a dramatic juncture for the Hahn nation, which had survived numerous foreign interventions and dominations, to be selected by the world community as the nation to hold the largest peacetime pageantry. It was the first such international recognition for the Hahn nation in history.

The IOC decision galvanized South Koreans. At the same time, it was a bitter defeat for North Korea, which had long sought world recognition for its leadership among third world countries. Realizing the far-reaching political implications, the North demanded from the IOC and the Seoul government a concession to permit it to co-host the games. However, the South was not willing to share the games on an equal basis, in spite of North Korea's open threat to disrupt the proceedings if its demands were rejected. Nevertheless, incessant negotiations followed. In the end, neither South Korea nor the IOC submitted to North Korea's demands. Moreover, the North's demands won little support from the international community; in spite of Pyongyang's diplomatic pressure, only a few socialist nations sided with North Korea in boycotting the games. The North-South impasse over the Olympic games again illustrated that the Korean predicament was not to be resolved by simple negotiations. Had both sides committed to utilize the rare occasion to build mutual trust and cooperation, it could have been an unusually opportune time to advance national reconciliation.

South Korea spent over three billion dollars to construct ultra-modern Olympic facilities in Seoul. North Korea also built major stadiums in Pyongyang. Being eager to fully exploit the rare opportunity, both Korean states poured in resources to make the Olympics a showcase. Both states were determined to display what they had accomplished over the ruins of war. Indeed, it was a most fitting stage.

In 1986, using the new facilities, the Seoul government staged the Asian games, which were supposed to be a simple pre-run of the 1988 for Seoul. The games were overwhelmed by the far-reaching political ramifications of the participation of the People's Republic of China, which sent a large delegation to Seoul unhampered by the lack of diplomatic relations between the two nations. It was the communist giant's first open indication that it was serious in upgrading its relations with South Korea. The Chinese participation totally eclipsed North Korea's absence from the games and was the first tangible success for South Korea's persistent pursuit of non-political contacts with China. The PRC's careful endeavor to mend its relations with South Korea had been notable throughout the 1980s. Yet it remained in the shadow with only intermittent commercial contacts until China made the grand gesture of sending its delegation to the 1986 Seoul Asian games. Understandably, Chinese participation was deeply appreciated by the Seoul government, for it greatly helped the success of the event and more importantly it virtually assured China's participation in the 1988 Summer Olympic games. Once the Chinese stand was known, the remaining question was whether the Soviet Union and its East European allies would participate in the games. In spite of the Chinese precedent, there were considerable obstacles; not only did most of the East bloc countries not have diplomatic relations with the Seoul government, but Pyongyang was exerting its utmost pressure on its European Communist brothers not to participate in the games unless it was allowed to stage the games as a co-sponsor. The participation of the socialist countries, essentially a political decision, remained unsettled for a while.

In the end, most East European communist nations and the Soviet Union decided to participate in the games. Except for a few minor countries, the overwhelming majority of the world community, one-hundred sixty nations, participated, making the games the most successful in the history of the Olympic movement. Without doubt, the event served to enhance the prestige and international recognition of South Korea, and this managed to dampen the North's dream of sharing the world's center stage. Yet in spite of the remarkable rewards, the Hahn nation failed to utilize the event for advancing its most pressing task, the unification of the nation.

As did the 1964 Tokyo Olympics for postwar Japan, so did the Seoul Olympics help elevate the prestige of industrial South Korea worldwide. The hermit kingdom had staged the games with unparalleled grandeur and professionalism. Unlike their forebears who hopelessly procrastinated in opening the nation to the West, contemporary Koreans were eager to show their progress and success to the world community. They were sanguine about their accomplishment of conquering age-old poverty and rebuilding the nation over devastated war ruins in less than three decades. They were rightfully proud of their "Miracle of the Hahn River."

In a sense, the world community was obliged to come to this small and historically impoverished nation to celebrate the will and dedication of the people who had survived thousands years of hardships and foreign intervention to finally build their own productive industrial culture. There could be no better setting for the Hahn nation than the Olympic Games for displaying the hard-won success before the world community. The world community in turn accorded the Koreans many deserving compliments, along with a new identity. On this stage the Hahn nation officially bid farewell to its old image, that of a passive victim of regional geopolitics.

The sole political loser of the 1988 Olympic games was North Korea. Most of all, the North disclosed its weak strategic sense by failing to harness the unusual opportunity to advance its own cause. Its strong appeal to boycott the games went unheeded even by its most trusted socialist brother countries. Unwittingly North Korea demonstrated that it was but a lone wolf even in the international socialist camp, and Kim's international prestige suffered damage. Despite Kim's long and hard campaign for third world leadership, the Olympic Games had revealed Pyongyang's non-existent political clout even in the third world. His inability to sway the eastern bloc countries conclusively illustrated his regime's distance from the mainstream socialist world.

North Korea did manage to extract some positive dividends by boycotting the games, however. It demonstrated to the world its highly uncompromising nature even under worldwide pressure. Kim had once again let the world realize that his regime would withstand world opinion if deemed necessary. He was still willing to risk isolation from the entire socialist camp to make his point. By refraining from interrupting the games, on the other hand, North Korea had displayed its willingness to behave as a responsible member of the world community. To some extent, North Korea's quiet behavior during the games won sympathy not only from the world community but also from its southern adversary. The ensuing dialogue between the two Koreas could not have come about without the favorable atmosphere generated by the North's appeasement during the games. Thus, the games failed to provide a direct and immediate channel toward an intra-Korean detente, but nevertheless they had helped to lay a positive foundation for a new and positive atmosphere in North-South relations.

4. The Signs of the Times

The election of President Ronald Reagan in 1981 was heartily welcomed in Seoul. South Koreans expected the conservative president to be more supportive of their cause than President Carter. Having endured Carter's controversial Korean policy, which was generally identified with unremitting human rights campaigns and an aborted attempt to withdraw U.S. ground forces, the South welcomed Reagan's steadfast stand against international communism. Despite incessant domestic political squabbles, South Korea's commitment to anti-communism remained a most compelling, even transcending political affiliation.

President Chun made deliberate overtures to win the friendship of the new Reagan administration. His efforts, which included sparing the life of his most potent political opponent, Kim Dae-jung, won him the honor of becoming one of a few foreign guests entertained by Reagan right after his inauguration. Through his ultra-conservative politics that served Reagan's anti-communist objectives well and his deliberate fence-mending measures, Chun successfully extracted Reagan's political support, which lasted until Reagan's term expired in February 1988. The U.S. President's strong political support was one of the most critical factors in sustaining the Chun regime.

Although the Reagan administration's support of the Chun government might have been more a part of an overall strategic maneuver in maintaining its worldwide containment ring against the Soviet Union rather than patronage for Chun's harsh domestic repression, this U.S. support attracted sharp disapproval from South Korea's political opposition and student activists. They were disturbed by the United States' recurring patronage for South Korea's military dictatorships, the regimes of both Park and Chun. Many realized that the U.S. policy had an element of inherent contradictions; Washington needed to maintain a firm stand against the communist adventure, but to do so it supported dictatorships against the will of the South Korean people. What South Koreans did not fully comprehend about the American stand in Korea was that Reagan's policies were not deliberately intended to ensure the survival of the oppressive regime. Still, the Chun regime portrayed the Reagan administration's support as its legitimacy on the international stage.

The suspicion that Washington was behind the empowerment of both Park and Chun had been pervasive in Seoul. Notwithstanding repeated U.S. denials, South Korean skeptics pointed out that both coups were carried out by the South Korean military units under the U.N. Command. Because the command was headed by a U.S. general, many assumed that Washington was capable of thwarting the coup attempts, if it desired. They also reasoned that it would have been almost impossible for the coup plans to completely escape the detection of the U.S. military authority in Seoul. Moreover, they suspected that by placing South Korea's political stability foremost, i.e., strong rule by a rightist regime, Washington had no real incentive to frustrate the coups staged by "dependable" generals.

The opposition's contention that the United States had exercised an enormous political influence over South Korean affairs had some valid reference; it is widely believed that Washington's unequivocal objection had dissuaded the South Korean military from staging another coup in 1987. The alleged U.S. involvement or acquiescence in Chun's bloody suppression of the Kwangjoo Uprising and the subsequent coup had been the most polemical aspect exploited by the opposition and student activists. Regardless, Chun's opposition had ample political motive to implicate the U.S. in the birth and survival of South Korea's unpopular military governments; even if overly simplistic, the insinuation that American forces had been co-conspirators or collaborators with Chun's dictatorial rule was a powerful political weapon for the opposition.

From the rising radical view that American political interests in South Korea were contradictory to the people's wishes, anti-American sentiments were surfaced; those who held this view, the student activists and liberal intellectuals, protested the presence of the U.S. forces in South Korea. Such a negative reaction, however, was not an occurrence unique to South Korea; provided the same allegation were present, most nations of pro-American standing might suffer a similar public reaction. The irony was that the U.S. was known to have exercised its utmost influence to encourage the military government to democratize its policies.

The South Korean public's recent display of anti-American sentiment, although it was scant and restricted to a particular segment of the public, was an open message to Washington that its support of the military government would entail damaging consequences. Focusing on the dangers of becoming accomplices of the unpopular military government, South Koreans reminded the United States that the best defense of its Far Eastern flank is not a right-wing military dictatorship but a democratic government that enjoys the public support.

As Washington's support of the Chun administration provoked severe irritation nationwide, the debate over the proper role of the U.S. military in South Korea surfaced. Ever since President Rhee put the South Korean military under the command of the U.N. commander in 1950, the wartime arrangement has remained intact; the Korea-U.S. forces in South Korea are under the command of U.S. generals who customarily assume the commanding post of the United Nations Forces in Korea.[5] The lingering suspicion over the role of the American forces in coups had given a powerful boost to the still-minority view that the decision of the wartime arrangement was long overdue and that the nation's sovereign right to command its own military must return to the Korean government.

Another source adding significant momentum to the rise of anti-American sentiment in South Korea was Washington's heavy pressure to open South Korea's domestic markets to American products. Mindful of Japan's monstrous trade surplus against it, Washington applied considerable political pressure to the South Korean government to open its still infant consumer markets. South Koreans are well informed of their responsibility to safeguard the free-trade system, which has been most propitious to their own economic well-being, but regarded the U.S. pressure as excessive. They were quick to point out that South Korea's trade surplus against the U.S. has been realized only since 1986 and that the amount had never surpassed $10 billion, approximately eight percent of the U.S. total trade deficit.[6] South Koreans openly questioned whether the U.S. intended to make South Korea a scapegoat in its trade problem while a much bigger and damaging partner, Japan, was generally overlooked. They were resentful of Washington's singling out the nation as a perpetrator of unacceptable trade practice, particularly when they have made significant adjustments to achieve a reasonable trade balance with the United States.[7] The public has remained sympathetic to the domestic industries' demand for extended protection from the onslaught of highly sophisticated U.S. products, pointing out that a much stronger Japanese market had long been successfully protected from U.S. penetration.

The rising anti-American sentiment in South Korea, although feeble and limited in scope, was more than anything a sign of the time. It was a part of South Korea's emerging desire to reevaluate its role in the community of nations. The call for the rectification of the old legacy, including its one-sided relationship with Washington, represented the South's aspiration to project the new image of a confident, modern, industrial democracy. South Koreans believed that their nation had matured enough to demand a more equitable treatment from the world community, which includes the United States.

In the era of global experimentation in political pluralism, Washington may have expected such a nationalistic sentiment to arise in South Korea. At the moment, the emotion is neither widely spread nor intense enough to provoke a full-scale anti-American movement. Yet the trend is likely to accelerate as the nation continues to widen its international horizons with its newly earned status as an industrially advancing nation.

A vast majority of South Koreans still take North Korea's military threat with extreme seriousness and categorically oppose any weakening of the nation's defense capabilities. At the same time, they are also aware of the fact that the nation's military regimes have exploited the North-South confrontation for selfish political purposes. President Chun, like his predecessor President Park, liberally invoked national security concerns in mobilizing the nation's vast police force to contain all vocal opposition. As long as South Korea's political democracy remained a hostage of the security pretext, even the Reagan administration's plodding efforts for political liberalization had little effect on the Chun regime.

However, Washington did mobilize its influence to avoid another irregular leadership change unacceptable to the Korean public after Chun actively concocted a scheme to transfer the presidency to his confidant at the end of his seven-year term. At this time the U.S. publicly urged the Chun government to undertake "constitutional and legislative reforms," and, preempting the customary security pretext, renewed its defense commitment to the nation with a "reliable shield against aggression." Washington not only advocated "civilianization" of South Korean politics but, more importantly, demanded that the Korean military "devote their full concentration on defense against external threats." Washington intended to avoid the rise of another military dictatorship in South Korea.

Pressure for democratization of South Korean politics was building not only externally but also internally. In 1987, South Korea's militant student activists staged nationwide protests opposing President Chun's scheme to transfer the presidency through an indirect election in which the government candidate was in all practicality assured of election. Unlike previous anti-government protests, however, the succession of protests soon attracted a growing number of middle class citizens. The nationwide outcry left the Chun government with the ultimate dilemma of either giving in to public defiance or else declaring martial law, an act jeopardizing the scheduled Summer Olympic Games of 1988. In the end, Chun had to accept the public's unkind de facto verdict on his rule, and he consented to write a new constitution. The people's power finally defeated the nation's entrenched military politics.

On December 16, 1987, South Korea held its first direct presidential election in sixteen years. Over ninety percent of the eligible voters went to the polls and gave Roh Tae Woo, the candidate for the ruling party, a victory, but with a mere thirty-six percent of the total vote. Thus, South Korea's remarkable 1987 political revolution completed its initial chapter. The nation achieved its first peaceful political transition, laying the foundation for its long-delayed democratic tradition.

The election was highly crucial both for substance and symbolism. It signaled the official ending of military rule. Furthermore, in the sense that the nation's democratic political process had been successfully carried out, the election connoted the nation's growing political maturity and was an auspicious indicator of its deferred political awakening.

Despite its profound positive effects, the election created a baffling political landscape. The people seemed to express their preference quite clearly when they gave fifty-three percent of the votes to the opposition. Yet they managed to elect the government candidate, Roh Tae Woo, Chun's close associate in the coup, because the majority of votes were split among Roh's three opposition candidates. The public, extremely disappointed, blamed the opposition parties, who had failed to field one single consensus candidate to run against Roh despite intense public appeals. Thus the remarkable political evolution of 1987 resulted in an administration that lacked strong political mandate. The election results again illustrated Korea's chronic political misfortune- lack of far-sighted, magnanimous political leadership. Being a nation of conscientious people has never been sufficient to overcome such misfortune.

In April 1988 South Korea held a parliamentary election to complete the nation's first peaceful political transition. Like the presidential election, the opposition split into three major parties. Yet the South Korean voters again sided with the opposition and denied Roh's ruling party a parliamentary majority. By granting it a scant thirty-three percent of the popular vote, the public inflicted a severe defeat on the ruling party for the first time in history. It was a display of the public's clear intention not to grant a full mandate to the party that had succeeded the Chun regime. Therefore, the nation's desire to bury the military legacy was left unfinished.

Despite the controversy, a popularly elected regime was in place. Moreover, for the first time in history the opposition held a majority of seats in the parliament. With the opposition capable of challenging the executive branch and led by the nation's most celebrated opposition leader, Kim Dae-jung, a vigorous parliamentary democracy was finally realized. The dictatorial administrations of the past had taught the South Korean public the virtues of a political system based on checks and balances.

The free direct elections themselves were an extraordinary political development both in scope and speed. Only the nation's improved self-image and political maturity made the feat possible. Even the peculiar election results proved to be quite effective; due to its scant mandate, the Roh administration was more conciliatory toward the opposition than were its predecessors. Yet the new administration was slow in adopting necessary democratic reforms, displaying its considerable reluctance to depart from a strong military orientation.

The grand finale of the shift came in 1992, when the nation elected Kim Young Sam as its president. President Kim is the first non-military president in three decades. The election of a civilian president who had been a life-time opposition leader signified the beginning of South Korea's long march toward full democratic reforms. President Kim's "New Korea" movement entails the systematic abolishment of the military's arbitrary political practices. The ambitious vision notwithstanding, the long and harsh military legacies will be hard to eradicate overnight. Difficult adjustments will be needed as the South navigates along its new and fresh route, one the nation hopes will lead to mature democratic power with a globally recognized industrial economy.

5. Winds of Change and Defiance

During the 1989-1991 period most socialist countries underwent revolutionary political transformations. The epochal developments were spurred by Gorbachev's bold reform programs, *glasnost* and *perestroika*, which helped to release the eastern block countries from the long Kremlin control. In turn, freed former Soviet block countries adopted various political measures pursuing society-wide democratization and institutional pluralism. This effectively terminated not only the Soviet-led socialism movement in the world but also the traditional East-West rivalry.

Before Gorbachev's historic reform initiative, China's Deng Xiaoping had adopted economic liberalization programs. Deng's limited and controlled market economy was intended to revive the middle kingdom's feeble economy, thus demonstrating his unusual political flexibility and at the same time exposing the desperate state of the Chinese economy. Similarly, Gorbachev's belated reform drive reaffirmed the grave economic difficulties in the workers' paradise. It was an open admission that economic stagnation in the socialist camp reached a point where it threatened national survival itself. The signs of the times were abundant throughout the socialist world.

Kim Il Sung's North Korea greeted the emerging political reality in the socialist world with typical disdain. Naturally, the dictatorial regime, which had pursued the highly unrealistic dream of building a socialist paradise with the self-sufficient *Juche* idea, saw the revolutions in eastern block countries as more of a threat than a benevolent transformation. Having enforced rigid political regimentation for most of the postwar period, the Kim Il Sung regime harbored an intense fear of reforms that might eventually cause its own demise. Categorically rejecting the seemingly irresistible currency of wholesale reforms in the socialist camp, the North Korean leadership elected to continue the course maintained for decades, namely its own brand of isolated socialism. It showed no inclination of modifying its dictatorial leadership, which was characterized by the intense personality cult of Kim Il Sung and his family. Even the historic developments in Eastern Bloc countries failed to persuade the Pyongyang regime, which is still firmly attached to its archaic system of an anti-foreign *Juche* ideology, a centralized command economy, and excessive political and ideological regimentation. [8]

In a sense, Kim's uncompromising stand illustrated the unique background of North Korea's socialism, which is much different from that of Eastern Europe. Unlike East Europe's socialism that was essentially imposed by the Soviet Union during the postwar period, North Korea's socialism has many features of a home-grown ideology. The Soviet Union and the People's Republic of China had exerted a profound influence on Kim's socialism during its infancy, but later Kim's own *Juche* ideology and intense personality cult had replaced it, making the North Korean socialism predominately a domain of Kim Il Sung's ideology. Thus, the collapse of Moscow-led intranational socialism had only a limited immediate impact on North Korea.

Even during this tumultuous globe-wide transition period, Kim's dictatorial rule remained intact, providing Kim and his son, the designated successor, maneuvering room against any sentiment for Deng- or Gorbachev-style reforms. Relying on its total political control as its shelter, the regime successfully resisted the global wind of changes. While other Eastern Block new countries raced to adopt democracy and a market economy, Pyongyang was determined to ignore history's most far-reaching political reform movement. In fact, Kim and his colleagues successfully shielded North Korea from the global trend of political democracy and economic liberalization.

North Korea's leadership not only stubbornly refused to heed but even disparaged socialist reforms, calling them the imperialists' "frantic efforts to undermine socialism, the bulwark of peace and progress."[9] Shunning the democratization trend embraced by most of his socialist colleagues, Kim maintained highly dogmatic policies both in international relations and domestic affairs. Unabated was his self-imposed mission to unite the peninsula under a socialist banner. Furthermore, Kim pursued to no avail the dream of attaining the foremost leadership status in the third world. Still being confident and sure of his own indispensability, Kim chose to distance himself from cold reality. Even at the Chinese vocal prodding, Pyongyang remained one of only a few countries that refused to join the globalized reform trend, largely unwilling to forsake its unbending loyalty to Kimilsungism - Kim's own socialism.

Nothing is more characteristic of Kim's old-fashioned politics than his succession scheme. Since the early 1970s Kim undertook various political maneuvers to gain a legal as well as political sanction to designate his son, Kim Jong Il, a man known for limited experience and unknown leadership quality, as his successor. The elder Kim's archaic succession scheme, deftly packaged on the pretext of "carrying through the revolution generation after generation," was to ensure the survival of his political legacy. His scheme to perpetuate his family's political monopoly encountered little domestic resistance, at least in public. Kim's brutal politics in treating potential opponents may have been the primary reason for this apparent acquiescence.

As early as 1974 North Korea's Kim Dynasty was already operational; Kim Jong Il took over the daily operation of the Workers' Party, but under his father's close supervision. Nevertheless, the elder Kim continued a relentless, highly organized campaign to consolidate his son's political power throughout the 1970s. By the time the Sixth Congress of the North Korean Workers' Party was held in 1980, Kim had clearly obtained the political support needed to openly force through his anachronistic undertaking. Shortly, the elder Kim made the son the second most powerful man in the nation by naming the younger Kim as secretary of the party's secretariat, the fourth highest position in the politburo. Kim also appointed his heir-apparent to the third highest position in the party's military commission.[10]

As Kim Il Sung became confident of his son's chance for succession, he gradually pushed the young man to the trenches of North Korean party politics. Yet the elder Kim did not surrender his own dominant power in administrative functions, for he continued to launch various administrative ploys to assure Kim Jong Il as his heir. The political developments in other socialist countries did not deter Kim: he was not just defying the winds of change but was daring to reverse the direction. He singularly ignored the inevitable truth that nepotistic succession is an anachronism for a civilized country in this era of democratic reforms. To extend his own dynasty in North Korea, Kim was determined to overlook even the open displeasure of the socialist camp.

By the early 1980s the North Korean press began to acclaim the younger Kim as the "great thinker and theoretician, outstanding genius of leadership, boundlessly benevolent teacher of the people, and the great leader of the century," clearly indicating that the systematic transfer of the Pyongyang regime's leadership was under way. The elder Kim turned the political spotlight toward his son, gradually transferring more authority for affairs of the state and the party to his son. The elder Kim's succession plot was nearly completed by 1993 when young Kim assumed the nation's highest military positions, chairman of the military commission of the party, and commander-in-chief of armed forces.

The North Korean leadership remained unwilling to accommodate the global winds of change toward social and political pluralism. Kim's total repudiation of the reform movements in the socialist camp stood firm as the national policy. He was apparently prepared to defy the winds, however strong it may be, alone if necessary. The sacrifices and lost opportunities the public would have to suffer eventually did not concern the *beloved father.*

Kim Il Sung, the only leader North Korea ever knew, died in July 1994, leaving behind even more questions about the secretive regime. The world knew little about Kim, and even less about the inner workings of the Pyongyang government. Still, North Korea without Kim Il Sung was expected to be quite different, yet what his sudden death meant to intra-Korean relations remained unclear. Consequently, the question of whether Kim Jong Il could someday gain the power and prestige his father had monopolized in North Korea was unanswered for a while.

Kim died in the midst of two critical talks underway: his government was negotiating with the United States for a solution to the nation's alleged nuclear program, and he and South Korea's President Kim were to have the first-ever summit meeting shortly in Pyongyang. Kim missed the rare opportunity to finally use his prestige and power in improving the troublesome intra-Korean relations. Despite his towering stature in the North, he failed even to initiate a dialogue toward an eventual resolution of the national division and the lingering anguish of the war, in both of which matters he was a principal player.

Gradually Kim Jong Il succeeded his father to the leadership of North Korea. His ascendancy, although he was unable to claim the presidency outright, was greatly benefitted by the fact that there is no political faction in North Korea capable of foiling the succession scheme the two Kims worked for so long and hard. Whether young Kim is able to consolidate the power so that he succeeds his father fully and for a prolonged period remains, however, an open question at the present.[11]

Kim may still need the armed services' continuing supports before he claims the nation's undisputed political leadership. He needs extraordinary persuasion to satisfy his military, known for its hard line approach to the South and the West; ironically the military holds key cards in Kim's surviving the unprecedented food shortages and general collapse of the economy. The armed forces' reservations were suspected to be major barriers to his assuming the presidency. But unless he is successful in reviving the economy that is antiquated and hovering near total collapse, Kim Jong Il is likely to face challenges from a number of sources, including a nationwide protest staged by the disgruntled public.

Kim Jong Il in the North-South equation presents a dimension that is quite different from the one his father represented. He lacks the charisma and revolutionary credentials his father had and used so effectively. On the other hand, he is not burdened by the lofty reputation of his father so that he may be able to exercise more flexibility and be open to new approaches. How these factors will affect the intra-Korea relations remains uncertain at the moment.

With its antiquated political structure still in place, North Korea faces a new era that is profoundly more complex and challenging. Kim's unparalleled succession scheme, in reality not a transition but a simple extension of the existing power structure, holds firm at the moment. However, it may take a while for the new leader to collect enough political support that will be critical for the long-term survival of the post-Kim politics. Despite the worsening food shortage and collapse of manufacturing sectors, Kim Jong Il has demonstrated his unwillingness to depart from the late leader's disastrous idealism at least for the time being. In public the state still pursues the self-reliant Kimilsungism, or *Juche* ideology, while seeking food aid from the international community and South Korea. Nor has it abandoned its quick fix in its relations with the United States and Japan. The North's relations with its traditional allies, China and Russia, suffered a severe deterioration as these reformed powers increasingly strengthened their commercial and diplomatic ties with South Korea. Kim has to deploy truly skillful maneuvers to restore the close relations with these irreplaceable backers. The North continues to apply a manipulative diplomacy to South Korea, apparently keeping a military option as a last resort. Domestically the government of Kim Jong Il is known to undertake some limited and measured reform measures, the successful outcome of which will become the key to his long-term political survival.

6. The Kim Dynasty and the South

North Korea's foremost political doctrine, the *Juche* idea or Kimilsungism, was to some extent the product of the regime's bi-directional postwar predicament. Despite its overtone of an economic doctrine, the *Juche* ideology was essentially Kim's political statement of independence against the feared Soviet and Chinese influence. The *Juche* ideology originated from the term *Juche*, an idea long used in Korea that extolled the virtues of self-reliance and resistance to external influence. Thus *Juche* can be regarded as an abstract form of a political thought, meaning to act in accord with one's own judgement. Particularly during the post-colonial period, the term was often used to express the nation's desire to instill a new attitude away from its profound tendency to indulge in Sadeism, a form of colonial submission.

The North Koreans insist that the *Juche* doctrine was initiated by Kim in the 1930s. Yet the spirit of the *Juche* idea cannot be considered Kim's sole invention, at least in its general form. During the Japanese colonial rule Koreans had often emphasized the very concept to express their strong yearning for national independence. It may be correct, however, that Kim had upgraded it to a multi-dimensional political doctrine by adding to it a sectoral dimension. The North Korean version of the *Juche* extends to three areas: the concept of *jaju,* the doctrine of political independence; *jarip,* the doctrine of economic self-sustenance; and *jawi,* the doctrine of military self-defense. North Korea adopted the three-dimensional *Juche* doctrine as the nation's fundamental governing philosophy in its 1972 constitution.

Kim had used the *Juche* doctrine as the regime's ideological shield against its two dominating socialist backers. Considering the pre-modern Hahn states' long ineptitude in harnessing the peninsula's troublesome geopolitics, Kim's *jaju* political stand was not only appropriate but highly meaningful. For that, however, the North Koreans had to pay an exorbitant price: rigid application of *jarip* economic doctrine ensured that Kim's socialist kingdom be relegated to no more than a nation of perpetual economic stagnation and worsening privation even with reasonable harvest. Contrary to the regime's public claim of being the real and only paradise in the world, its self-reliance doctrine has not only failed to mitigate its economic woes in this highly interdependent and technological era, but has almost completely isolated the nation from the world community. Pyongyang will certainly have to reconsider the rigid application of the *Juche* ideology. Well intended as it may have been, the approach is counterproductive and impractical for the era of deepening globalization. Its lofty, noble intentions do not have to be totally discarded, but Kimilsungism is gravely unfit for a nation with a faltering economy and an archaic political structure.

Kim Il Sung's provision for the future by designating his successor, albeit in the person of his own son, was not only a cosmetic but also a self-serving political evasion. His nepotistic succession scheme is viewed in the South and elsewhere as a path likely to delay the inevitable society-wide transformation which the post-Kim Il Sung regime must undertake in the future. Kim Jong Il's succession ignored a global trend for democratic government by simply extending Kim Il Sung's legacy, one of the world's longest dictatorships characterized by economic stagnation and political suppression.

North Korea should discard the archaic political philosophy Kim Il Sung left behind and boldly adopt a democratic form of government which will spearhead the nation's drive for political stability and economic expansion. Instead, its answer to the time of unprecedented reform worldwide was succession in a family. Kim Jong Il is certain to encounter serious opposition although he and his followers have solidified their grip on power. Yet it is still possible that the Kim Dynasty will prove to be a mere fantasy of the old revolutionary dictator. Only when Kim's political legacy is dislodged will the winds of change start to penetrate xenophobic North Korea with force. Whether or not Kim Jong Il has political skills and courage to undertake such regime-unsettling reforms is yet to be evident.

The Korean peninsula's two regimes have yet to dismantle the cold war legacies they have built and sustained for the last five decades. Nevertheless, intra-Korean relations entered a new and promising phase during the first half of the 1990s. In the North, Kim's iron rule that had lasted until 1994 was replaced by his son as his anachronistic succession scheme intended. On the other hand, the South has just completed its political democratization, initiated in the late 1980s. These historic developments appeared at least to offer the Hahn nation a new opportunity to strive toward mutual reconciliation and eventual unification. However, the tension along the 155 mile DMZ remained unabated, proving the road to unification will be harder than even most pessimists predicted.

In addition to Kim Il Sung's death, the1990s were the most challenging period for North Korea. Its nuclear program attracted suspicious attention from the world community while extensive food shortage, outcome of an unfortunate mix of man-made and natural disasters, made the *Juche* ideology a mockery. The Pyongyang regime, had, however maintained its hardline against the West and the South probably because its appearance of submission could have been fatal to the regime. In spite of its combative rhetoric, Kim Jong Il's regime has exposed its two profound weaknesses: it has no realistic answer to the West's pressure to dismantle its nuclear program, and it can not survive without massive outside food aids.

The intra-Korea relations of the 1990s showed marked improvement from the more sharp confrontation of the 1953-1980 period. Although the consummation of the nation's foremost challenge, peaceful reconciliation and unification, remains distant at the present, the mere fact that the antagonistic parties finally saw the benefits in maintaining channels for dialogue, sporadic at best, was by no means trivial. The intermittent North-South talks had produced little tangible progress, although they might have helped improve mutual understanding somewhat. Shared mistrust and suspicion accumulated over the past five decades were not to be resolved overnight.

In spite of open professions in favor of national unification, both Korean regimes have yet to agree on even the nature of the unification they wish to pursue, the most fundamental prerequisite of any unification proceeding. Lacking the basic framework to which all unification measures should be fitted, the proposals launched by both sides remain mostly cursory and tactical in nature. They reflect more of the confrontation-oriented past than the harmonious future they must cooperate to build. In reality, the sporadic proposals intended more to accommodate their own domestic politics than to set a long-term itinerary the Hahn nation must travel to reach its third unification. The lack of tangible progress in core areas make the prospect of producing any workable agreement in the near future poor and uncertain at best.

Notwithstanding the scant progress in finding common ground for mutual cooperation and eventual unification, in recent years both sides have succeeded in improving the general state of intra-Korean relations. Vanished East-West confrontation and the democratic political evolution in Eastern Bloc countries might have contributed to the development. South Korea's economic success and North Korea's faltering economy were also critical factors. More importantly, the nation's rising political maturity was a driving force.

The signs of the Korean peoples' political maturity are abundant. For the first time in history the South earned international recognition for its single-minded drive for a confident, competitive industrial economy. The North withstood the super powers' incessant attempt to dominate even at the expense of enduring hardships and discomfort. In reality, the Korean nation is about to reach its long delayed political adulthood. Such late blossoming maturity will eventually enable the Koreans to solve the current problems in a civil way and to finally take full advantage of Korea's unique geopolitics in building a politically confident and economically competitive nation. Yet the first step continues to be nurturing mutual confidence and renewing the spirit of oneness on both sides of the DMZ.

The inauguration of the Roh administration in 1986 was an important juncture for intra-Korean relations. Unlike its predecessors, the new administration was much more active and flexible in its dealings with the North. Not only did it launch extensive initiatives to improve intra-Korean relations, but it also introduced the so-called "Northern Diplomacy," deftly taking advantage of the evolving new world order and the drastic melt-down of the East-West confrontation. President Roh's initiative for a dialogue with not only North Korea but also the world's two most powerful socialist nations, China and the Soviet Union, was a drastic departure from the passive diplomacy South Korea had long practiced. For the first time, South Korea took aggressive measures to outmaneuver North Korea's recurrent diplomatic offenses, active ever since the signing of the armistice in 1953.

North Korea maintained its militant "liberation" policy toward South Korea for most of the post-Korean war period. Its self-imposed crusade to expel the "American imperialists" from the South and to achieve unification, using unspecified methods but under the socialist banner, was Pyongyang's foremost justification for its harsh dictatorship. It was not until 1980 that the North launched its first peace offensive by proposing a peaceful unification formula. The South duly noted that the North's shifting stand was more symbolic than substantial, although the fact that the North came up with a peaceful unification formula itself was a positive development. Nevertheless, South Koreans suspected the North's new proposal as a diversionary scheme which may have been devised to facilitate its militant conquest of the South.

The sixth meeting of the North Korean Workers' Party, held on October 10, 1980, adopted North Korea's new unification formula known as the "Confederal Republic of Koryo." The new initiative, an umbrella formula made of various demands the North had insisted upon during the 1970s, primarily served Pyongyang's political propaganda objective. As preconditions, it demanded the South abolish its anti-Communism law and security apparatus, replace the present government with a "democratic" one, and persuade the U.S. to withdraw forces. In addition, it demanded a peace agreement with the United States. These demands were regarded by the South merely propaganda ploys and contained no new initiatives. South Koreans failed to see any changes in the North's militant approach to intra-Korean relations.

The plan did contain a cosmetic concession on Kim's part in the sense that he was willing to resolve political differences through future discussions. Yet the South rejected the proposal outright, labeling it as Pyongyang's tactical ploy to incite subversion and to a create a pro-North Korean faction in the South for eventual takeover.[12] Seoul viewed with customary skepticism and doubts Kim's largely self-serving argument that each side should form a government based on the current political ideology which would be coordinated by a neutral federal government. The North's plan must have been influenced by Khrushchev's new "peaceful coexistence" doctrine and the regime's worsening economic crunch. But in the South where a budding industrial economy had further convinced the public of the validity of anti-communism, Kim's old formula found few supporters.

Its negative reception in the South notwithstanding, Kim's new peace offensive opened a new chapter in intra-Korean relations. To the Chun administration, which succeeded the conservative Park administration but remained far more flexible than Park's no-contact, hard-line stand, it was a glimmer of hope for a peaceful resolution of the national tragedy. Despite a hiatus created by the 1972 joint communique, President Park was too committed an anti-communist to risk a political solution that was believed only to serve the purposes of the North Korean regime. President Chun largely resumed the Park administration's hard-line stand against North Korea, but after Kim's new peace offensive his conservative tone was somewhat relaxed. In 1982, Chun proposed the Formula for National Reconciliation and Democratic Unification, which called for the formation of a Korean Unification Council with participants from the two sides charged with the responsibility of writing a constitution for a unified democratic republic. The North rejected this initiative.

Under the rule of two obstinate nationalists, the intramittent intra-Korea dialogues were given little chance to produce significant results. Merely playing political games with no real intention to commit to a step that might necessitate some serious compromises, they failed even to lessen the military tensions along the DMZ. On the contrary, both sides strove to modernize their armed forces with the most advanced weaponry the superpowers were willing to provide, and the explosive tension along the DMZ remained as a fixture of the Peninsula's painful landscape.

During the 1980s South Korea's widely publicized success in economic development emerged as a powerful variable in intra-Korean relations. It is presumed that the North obtained its first factual understanding of the South's robust economic growth only in the early 1970s when both sides exchanged officials for visits. The somber realization that the South had outperformed by a large margin the ossified *Juche* economy may have motivated the North's disdainful leadership to reassess its policy toward the South. This development validated the effectiveness of President Park's "economic self-sufficiency first, unification later" approach.

North Korea's Confederal Republic of Koryo approach could have underscored its political naivete that the two Koreas could be unified simply by tolerating and recognizing each other's opposing systems. But the confederal scheme could have been a deliberate, far-reaching deception;[13] South Koreans regarded Kim's formula as a deft maneuver designed to agitate the society and derail their successful economic development programs. Thus Kim's new plan not only failed to dissipate but rather intensified suspicion over the North's ultimate objective: conquering the southern half through a premeditated scheme. It was suspected to be a repackaged version of his long-standing, three-step unification drive: the withdrawal of U.S. forces, political domination by South Korea's socialist factions, and eventual unification of the two socialist nations under the control of the communists. Kim's confederal formula still stands as North Korea's official unification plan although it has no prospect of gaining any support in the South.

Wary of Kim's confederal unification proposal, South Korea maintained a cautious approach. Committed to the export-led national rebuilding drive, Seoul had favored a gradual unification method, one which may be described as "reconciliation first, political unification later." Even under North Korea's incessant political pressure, often expressed by abrupt suspension of the scheduled dialogue, the South had not altered its quest for the gradual reduction of intra-Korean tensions with normalized relations in commercial, cultural, and humane concerns. South Koreans were more than ever aware of the growing advantages of an open society over the North's closed society and of their overwhelming economic strength over the pulverized economy of the competition. The South's democratization drive in the late 1980s produced a government that was more open and responsive to the public. The successful Summer Olympic games of 1988 helped the nation to achieve a de facto admission to the world's elite club of industrialized democracies. As the South's economy continued to expand at one of the highest growth rates in the world, there were ample justifications for South Koreans' growing confidence in dealing with the North.

South Korea's move to improve its relations with the Eastern Bloc countries and North Korea was momentous. This new foreign policy initiative by the Roh administration, known as "Northern Diplomacy" or Nordpolitik, was intended to establish trade and economic relations with socialist countries, thereby forcing the North to modify its militant isolation. The unprecedented diplomatic overtures to Eastern bloc countries and North Korea, to which the public rendered strong support, had quickly borne some important results. South Korea concluded diplomatic relations with Hungary, Poland, Czechoslovakia, and others in east Europe during the 1989-1990 period. It established formal diplomatic ties with the Soviet Union in 1990 and with the People's Republic of China in 1992, upgrading its trade offices. Overcoming North Korea's strenuous objections, South Korea thus had completed its great reconciliation with the region's two socialist giants, China and Russia, in addition to most former Eastern Bloc countries. As South Korea's diplomatic and commercial ties with former socialist countries grew, North Korea witnessed a rapid erosion of its political prestige even in its own backyard. South Korea's successful rapprochement with the Soviet Union and the People's Republic of China must have been most dismaying to the North Korean leadership.[14] As an apparent response to the South's aggressive diplomatic campaign, the North initiated contacts with the United States in 1990 under the pretext of discussing mutual concerns: returning the remains of American soldiers lost during the Korean War and sending North Korean scholars to academic conferences in the United States. The North also reversed its long-standing objection to cross recognition, seeking Japan's and the United States' recognition of its government in exchange for China's and the Soviet Union's recognition of South Korea. To this end North Korea also took tentative steps to establish formal diplomatic relations with Japan. Still, North Korea's new diplomatic initiatives were largely uncertain and whimsical.

Despite the North's calculated agitation, the South maintained Roh's unification proposal as its official policy, a counter to the North's Confederal Republic of Koryo. Roh's plan called for creation of a Korean Commonwealth and relevant administrative organs as an interim stage toward a unified democratic republic. Though similar in terminology, there were some significant and perhaps fundamental differences between the two plans. Both sides recognized the contradictory reality of their systems; yet the South's plan represented a notion that the extant barriers could be removed only through a careful reconciliation process, while the North's proposal epitomized the view that the emotional and ideological gap existing between the two Koreas could be overcome by immediate structural adjustments.

North Korea reconfirmed its confederal unification formula in 1990 through Kim Il Sung's new five-point proposal. Though failing to narrow the differences in both sides' unification approaches, it reaffirmed the North's steadfast quest: to drive out the American forces and to "liberate" the people of the South. Kim Il Sung still sounded as if only he and his impoverished, isolated regime could carry out the lofty task of national unification. He was never willing to face reality, although the signs of change were overwhelming worldwide. On the other hand, even under the growing political pressure exerted by nationalistic student activists and leftist intellectuals, the South felt the most practical route to national unification was to continue its gradual approach, which favored incremental opening of the North Korean society to the South and to the world.

Unification approaches advanced by both sides thus far have reflected their own individual political interests. The North must have realized that the future for it does not hold a great promise and is thus forced to insist on an immediate political solution - the only plausible alternative open to diehard communists. The South, on the other hand, is convinced that unification will be realized under its leadership in due course. Growing international prestige and its powerful industrial economy have given the South unprecedented confidence. Nevertheless, the North has remained unwilling to negate its long-standing quest for the national unification under its own system, an increasingly remote possibility. Meantime, the South continued to employ tactful maneuvers so as not to provoke the isolated, militant North. Notwithstanding the significance of exploring each other's unification approaches, the third   national unification was still not an immediate prospect.

South Korea's rapprochement efforts to both China and Russia have had a diverse background. The most powerful motive for the "northern diplomacy," the Roh government's foremost diplomatic doctrine, was the South's desire to isolate the North politically, in order to soften its militancy and to pave a way for national unification. At the same time, South Koreans realized that the dreaded communists could provide much needed consumer markets as well as rich natural resources for their expanding industrial economy. The public was solidly behind the efforts of both the government and the business community to establish close commercial ties with their northern neighbors. The initiatives were an intricate but far-sighted undertaking based on an assessment that Russia, despite the demise of the Soviet Union, will emerge again as a major power in the future, particularly in nuclear armament and industrial resources. South Korea recognized that Russia, while it had lost the premier leadership as a super power, still had uncommon potential to become a major industrial power in the near future. Moreover, South Korea expected that Russia would eventually exercise a powerful influence in northeast Asia. Yet Seoul did not anticipate that the Soviets would readily sacrifice long-standing relations with the Pyongyang regime, even though the South had much to offer to the crumbled Soviet Union and Russia. Thus, Gorbachev's eager response to South Korea's diplomatic overtures startled the Seoul government. The normalization of their relations proceeded at a rapid speed as the Soviets primarily sought South Korea's economic cooperation.

Seoul's initial overtures to Moscow provoked no immediate responses. Moscow was restraining its desire to improve the bilateral relations with Seoul out of concern for North Korea's reaction, yet Russia's participation in the 1988 Summer Olympic games in Seoul served as a harbinger of a rapid diplomatic thaw. These Olympic-related high-level contacts led to the little-publicized Roh-Gorbachev meeting in San Francisco, which was followed shortly by the establishment of formal diplomatic relations.

In many ways the establishment of the Soviet-South Korean diplomatic tie was significant. More than anything, the way it was achieved and the hostile reaction shown by the Pyongyang regime left the impression that the Soviets had abandoned a long-time ally and were subscribing, in essence, to the unification method pursued by the South. The Soviet Union conferred upon South Korea its long-coveted diplomatic recognition even though there was no tangible reduction of tensions along the DMZ nor a reconciliation of the two Koreas. It is equally significant that the breakthrough may have reflected Moscow's new Korean policy in the context of Gorbachev's new, nuclear-free Far East concept. Russia's political intention in the region was, however, not yet clear. Nevertheless, for North Korea, Moscow's sudden warmth toward the Seoul government should have been a chilling reminder that the intra-Korea relations had entered a new era. Pyongyang's political isolation was also completed by its loss of the Soviets' traditional support. With the establishment of its tie with the Soviets, South Korea almost completed its drive to establish diplomatic relations with most of the former Eastern block countries. It was the Roh regime's most prominent diplomatic achievement and potentially one of the most critical dimensions in the nation's strategic alignment in the looming twenty-first century.

Seoul's quest to establish formal ties with China was equally earnest in spite of its tediously slow progress. China in the 1980s remained essentially a monolithic socialist country, although Deng's cautious experimentation with a market economy earned the nation some liberal images abroad. It was widely assumed that China, the last major socialist empire, would defy the worldwide trend as long as feasible. Naturally, it desired to maintain its close relations with North Korea, a traditional ally and a buffer against both the United States and Japan. Reflecting historic, strategic considerations, China was reluctant to agree on full diplomatic ties with South Korea even when its unofficial commercial relations were expanding rapidly. South Korea duly took account of the predicament the Chinese government faced. Setting aside completing political-diplomatic ties, Seoul made expanding commercial ties to China a top priority. South Korea did not wait for the establishment of formal diplomatic relations; its industrial conglomerates began to build factories in China even in the absence of formal diplomatic agreements. Commercial cooperation between the two nations expanded rapidly, leading the former adversaries to establish formal diplomatic ties.[15] China, an entrepreneurial realist by nature, thus publicly recognized the government of South Korea for the first time in history.

Despite the major obstacle of North Korea, there were unmistakable signs of enthusiasm in both South Korea and China for diplomatic relations. Considering the recent history of their being mutual ideological adversaries, such an open desire for normalization was by itself remarkable. More importantly, the Chinese, through the willingness to deal with the Seoul government, made plain their intention to distinguish political support for Pyongyang from economic cooperation with South Korea. Regardless of its unwillingness to heed the trend that brought political liberalization to most former socialist countries, China adopted a new diplomatic posture toward the Korean Peninsula - recognition of two Koreas. China could no longer ignore the Seoul government's growing prestige and industrial might. At the same time, it was unwilling to sever its ties to the North. For South Korea, extracting China's diplomatic recognition successfully completed its first major diplomatic initiative toward the region's two perennial powers.

South Korea's rapprochement attempt toward North Korea had been even more delicate and wearisome, primarily because Kim Il Sung was still pursuing his drive for national unification under his red banner. He maintained his long, dictatorial rule, showing no willingness to heed the ongoing political liberalization trend in the socialist world. At the end, he was about the only leader in the world who deliberately shunned the prevailing global trend with only Fidel Castro, a comparable but somewhat lesser anachronism. In spite of its willingness to explore the South's position through intermittent high-level contacts, North Korea was yet to demonstrate the flexibility and sincerity that may lead to genuine national reconciliation, a prerequisite to the unification. South Korea's northern diplomacy proved potent and timely, but inadequate in bringing the North Korean regime to negotiating table.

Like its remarkable success in establishing diplomatic ties with the socialist bloc countries, South Korea's attempt to reduce the military tension along the 155-mile demilitarized zone had been earnest. Initiatives were undertaken in the unusually favorable international political climate of the 1980s, a climate which South Koreans construed as international consent to their northern policy. In addition, the Roh administration encountered intense pressure from the nation's radical student activists and the political left for a new approach in the South-North dialogue. Bolstered by their historic triumph over the military government, the nation's student activists turned their attention to intra-Korean relations and thus to the unification question. Students demanded that unconditional unification talks be held, even though the general public remained uncommitted. As the student activists, armed with simplistic but ardent nationalistic zeal, assumed the role of the driving force, the unification question no longer remained an abstract policy matter.

President Roh's six-point plan, announced on July 7, 1988, is the nation's most comprehensive policy toward the eventual goal of national unification. The plan called for measures to change both sides' antagonistic relations: unrestricted personnel exchanges, open trade, the South's acceptance of the allies' trading non-military goods with the North, an end to adversarial relations, and the South's cooperation with Pyongyang's attempt to improve its relations with the United States and Japan. Roh's new initiative reflected more than anything else the nation's growing awareness of the necessity to overcome the stalemate with peaceful means. Yet such a bold proposal would not have been possible without the rapid improvement in the South's political confidence in dealing with a now largely isolated North. By pursuing economic cooperation with the North first, leaving the political solution secondary as a long-term objective, the Roh administration clearly intended to exploit its main strength, the growing industrial economy.

North Korea had not responded to the proposal both Roh and Kim, his successor, made. South Korea's assistance is desirable and perhaps inevitable in the long run for the North's gravely ossified economy. But openly accepting the South's assistance may be construed as the North's admission of failure and thus the fatal weakness of Kimilsungism. Pyongyang had avoided such a predicament even at the price of national deprivation. Instead, Kim kept reiterating his long-standing political solution, the establishment of the Confederal Republic of Koryo.

General Park's presidency in the 1960s made Kim's drive for national unification through military means virtually unrealistic. Yet Kim did not alter his pursuit of immediate and complete unification under his leadership. His only concession, albeit never formally declared, was restraint in launching another military venture. No Koreans would object to the noble cause of reuniting the two Koreas. But many South Koreans have qualms about the method of unification. In fact, the two nations have to resolve the issue of unification procedure first before negotiating the details. Kim's confederal scheme does not provide a timetable for eventual unification; it simply implies that two nations, two systems under one federal government, could last for an undetermined period of time. Such a system is not likely effective in forging a cohesive national sentiment in a short period of time. This approach is consistent with the North's unwillingness to recognize the socio-political chasm that developed between the two halves of the Hahn nation. Kim's unification approach failed to include an institutional arrangement through which the issue of incompatibility in two opposing ideologies can be properly addressed. Kim's plan was based on the assumption that the unified Korea would be governed by his own system, the defunct Kimilsungism.

North-South relations had made some significant progress during the early part of 1990s. Seoul and Pyongyang signed a Non-Aggression Agreement in 1991, raising a hope that decades-old hostility between the two was subsiding. Meetings at the cabinet and prime minister levels were held. More importantly, perfunctory meetings seemed to have turned into sessions for serious negotiations. As a result, some economic cooperation measures were being implemented, including restored intra-Korea direct trade that had been barred since 1948. Contrary to some success in trade relations, the two Koreas had not been able to take any meaningful measures toward reducing military tensions along the DMZ. Still, when the meeting between Kim Il Sung and Kim Young Sam, the president of the South, was scheduled, the nation was sensing some breakthrough.

Kim passed away in 1994, snapping the thread of hope in national reconciliation. The North-South relations entered another long winter recess. When heir-apparent Kim Jong Il's ability to take over the government was seriously questioned, any meaningful contacts could not proceed. Kim Il Sung, one of the political giants in Korea's modern history, held extraordinary power and authority capable of making even the most drastic decisions. His death could have been a major loss in opening a new chapter in the North-South relations.

7. Pyongyang's Nuclear Ambition

In August 1994 North Korea agreed to receive international inspection of its nuclear facilities, reversing its steadfast refusal to do so for two years. The long-running America-North Korea negotiation also extracted North Korea's promise not to reprocess arms-grade plutonium from nuclear power plants' spent rods. In return, America offered to provide North Korea safer reactors and diplomatic concessions. This agreement, which successfully resolved the two-year long crisis, was accepted in the West and South Korea as North Korea's new direction taken by the administration of Kim Jong Il, North Korea's new leader. Regardless of who initiated this far-reaching North Korean policy shift, it was a positive development for worldwide efforts to contain nuclear proliferation and could add a new momentum to intra-Korean relations.

The crisis began when North Korea openly challenged the International Atomic Energy Commission in 1992 and threatened to formally withdraw from the Nuclear Non-Proliferation Treaty of which it was a member. Its open rejection of the IAEC's on-site inspection of nuclear facilities caused a serious concern in the West and among North Korea's neighbors. The specter of a region-wide nuclear arms race was real and troublesome. But an even more important aspect was the likelihood that the world's acquiescence to North Korea's nuclear program would encourage other aspiring countries to rush for the development of nuclear weapons.

Neither the West nor South Korea had an accurate assessment of Pyongyang's nuclear program. What was clear to them was that the North did have operating nuclear facilities which regularly produced spent rods and that it had acquired reprocessing technology to extract weapons grade plutonium from the rods. The best estimation was that North Korea might already have two nuclear bombs and could produce more shortly. Washington made it a state policy that North Korea should not be allowed to become a nuclear power.

The Kim Il Sung regime was quite evasive over its nuclear program. It insisted that it had no nuclear arms program but at the same time refused to open the suspected facilities to the international inspectors. Long, difficult negotiation followed, often accompanied by North Korea's abrupt shifts in position. Washington did not exclude a possible military option to remove the suspected facilities. North Korea's three other neighbors - China, Japan, and Russia - all insisted North Korea return to NPT and accept the international inspection. Kim was all alone in fighting against the entire Western world, insisting that North Korea was not a nuclear power and did not intend to be one. Until his death the world community had no reliable information whether his statement was true.

In spite of its categorical denial, a nuclear bomb program was the only and last card North Korea possessed to extract any meaningful concessions from the United States and South Korea. Kim apparently intended to use it to the fullest extent; the final outcome illustrated that North Korea's gamble had succeeded to some extent. The negotiations with the United States put the isolated, lone remaining Stalinist regime on a world stage when Kim's envoys sat with those of the United States, the power that North Korea has called its mortal enemy since 1948. By virtue of being a negotiation partner, North Korea obtained a measure of recognition for which it had long yearned from the world's only remaining superpower. In the process, however, it risked a major military confrontation in which it had no chance to prevail. Even if it was his last resort, Kim's nuclear gamble was gravely dangerous. Kim's stand may have reflected North Korea's dire desperation to enter the community of the world by using the United States as its usher.

North Korea's nuclear program had some valid motives which the West and the South Koreans summarily ignored. In the Far East, all major countries already possess nuclear weapons or were nuclear-capable by the 1980s with the exception of North Korea. This region, of course, houses two premier nuclear powers, Russia and China.   While Japan is not technically a nuclear power, it is fully capable of producing any number of bombs on short notice, including sophisticated delivery systems. Only South Korea is an exception. Even South Korea should be able to develop a nuclear program quite easily if it is needed. Surrounded by these powers and the United States, North Korea could well have felt isolated and helpless and might have concluded that nuclear arms were a necessity for its own defense. The problem was that North Korea had been known as an aggressor who, it was feared, would be willing to use the weapons if they were available. The West regards any nuclear arms that North Korea might have as purely offensive.

To Washington, North Korea's nuclear arms meant Japan's probable nuclearization, which might well be followed by a nuclear South Korea and Taiwan. The likely result would be a shifting balance of power which might cause a region-wide nuclear arms race. Such a development could be a nightmare for America, the world's only real police power. The world's nuclear club and America have valid reasons not to allow North Korea to become an official nuclear power.

Pyongyang's nuclear concession was more than the termination of its costly program. It implied that Kim Jong Il was pursuing a reconciliation with America. North Korea, lacking its founder Kim Il Sung or at least out of old Kim's long and dark shadow, may have signaled that it was ready to join the global community. Perhaps it was too late to do that, for its economy may have by now crossed the point of no return. But the fact that it began to reassess its position was a hopeful sign for the security of the region in particular and the world as a whole.

8. Peninsula - Wide Crisis: Road to the Unification

In the late 1990s Korea's eventful nation building drive encountered an unexpected yet prophetic setbacks, which served as defining events in drastically changing the intra-Korea relations. The irony was that these developments took place almost simultaneously on both sides of the DMZ, although their nature was fundamentally different. North Korea's devastating food shortages, a result of both man-made and natural disasters, became known to the outside in 1995 after the nation experienced a severe drought and flood alternatively. While the "workers' paradise" transformed into a global emergency aid case and a subject for unprecedented international humiliation, the South's ambitious industrial development was derailed in 1997 by a massive foreign debt crisis. Thus the two Koreas found themselves facing severe national challenges that threatened the nations' integrity and honor. Paradoxically, however, the crises came to serve as a new turning point toward the intra-Korean reconciliation, a first step to the national unification.

North Korea is a nation of limited capacity in food production even when nature cooperates. Inadequate planting acreage, poor soil quality, and a short growing season continue to be serious obstacles toward its food sufficiency. To compensate for the natural limitations and traditional means of farming it employs, North Korea had expanded its planting to areas mostly unsuitable for stable cultivation. North Korea's natural calamities during the 1994-1996 period, severe flood and drought, were destructive to the marginal acreage and exacerbated the nation's food sufficiency. Its gravity even compelled the reclusive Pyongyang regime to resort to appealing to South Korea and the West for extensive food aid. Predictably the international community's initial response was widespread skepticism and indifference reflecting the fact that there were few nations sympathetic to North Korea's anachronistic behavior. In addition, Pyongyang was less than forthright to those who sought its promise to restrict the aid to civilian use only. The world community including South Korea was slow to respond to the tragic food shortage in the last Stalinist nation in the region. After months of usual disputes South Korea and international agencies did ship food to North Korea although their donations were not even close to what North Korea had asked for.[16] In a sense, the world community conveyed to the Pyongyang regime a stern message that it remained troubled by its highly anti-social behavior. It was North Korea's populace, particularly those rural residents, who suffered most from the outside world's lukewarm enthusiasm in food aid. A North Korean defector speculated that there were 500,000 starvation deaths in 1995 alone. He further argued that death could have reached 1 million in 1996 and 2 million in 1997.[17]

North Korea's chronic food shortage is not to be solved by external aid alone. It must be overcome by improved domestic production while leaving the door open so that imports meet the deficiency. In short, the North must seek a solution in a market economy, an idea that remained largely unacceptable to *juche*-oriented Pyongyang regime. Significant improvement in food production is not likely possible under the highly centralized *jarip* economy the North is still unable to discard. North Korea still utilizes as its economic main engine collective farms, a method proved to be ruefully ineffective in socialist countries elsewhere. This bureaucratic system, which is perhaps most effective only in achieving complete political control, is wasteful and highly ineffective, for it provides farmers with little incentive to be creative and assertive. Still Pyongyang has shown no sign of abandoning the anachronic juche-system Kim Il Sung left behind as his lasting legacy. Since assuming the leadership post, Kim Jong Il has adopted a few cosmetic reforms and programs intended more for foreign consumption. He remains committed to the tightly controlled socialist system of central planning, demonstrating that his foremost concern continues to be the regime's own political survival even at the intolerable price of human suffering. Kim's survival drive at any cost appears effective at the moment. Even though the food shortage and the catastrophic failure of the national economy as a whole was serious enough to cause the downfall of the political leader in any democratic society, Kim's political leadership remains safe. His pursuit of full control of the government including the assumption of the presidency was completed in late 1998.

In 1992 South Korea elected as its fourteenth president Kim Young Sam, a prominent opposition leader to the governments headed by former generals. By replacing, through a democratic process, the last military leader, General Noh, who succeeded General Chun, the nation rightfully rejoiced in the dawning of the "civil government" era. The fact that the 30-year long military rule had ended by a peaceful transfer of power was a cause enough to celebrate. The public accorded Kim's civil government overwhelming support. In response, the government announced its priority policies that included continuing the democratization process, an anti-corruption campaign for high ethical conduct for the nation's elite society, economic growth, and globalization. President Kim issued on August 12, 1993 a presidential emergency order that banned all financial transactions using false names, one of his most celebrated and substantial achievements.

Kim Young Sam's bold initiative, which could have had a major bearing on the North-South relations, was derailed by Kim Il Sung's death on July 8, 1994. Although President Kim remained interested in intra-Korea dialogue and made overtures to the new leader, the North was either unable or unwilling to respond to them throughout his term. Not Kim's approaches but the North's domestic politics, which were in transition, might have been the major cause for this lack of response. In spite of the North's rejection to dialogue, President Kim dispatched food aid and undertook steps to fulfill the provisions of the U.S.-North Korea Nuclear Agreement signed in 1994, the construction of a light-water reactor(LWR) power plant that is to replace North Korea's graphite-moderated reactors. South Korea had accepted the large share of financial burden in constructing a new nuclear power plant. The public was largely behind the government's decision, underlining its serious concerns over the North's nuclear ambition.

Kim's presidency appeared to be solid enough to leave behind a favorable impression in spite of its setbacks in the intra-Korean relations and controversies related to his "history-correction" measures that resulted in incarceration of his two predecessors, former presidents Chun and Roh. South Korea's economy was expanding at the yearly growth rate of 7-9 percent, elevating the resource-poor nation to the world's tenth largest trader. The world community readily acknowledged that South Korea had finally graduated from developing country status when it was admitted in 1996 to the Organization for Economic and Cultural Development, an exclusive club of developed industrial nations. South Koreans even began to debate the merits of a German-style unification method, absorption of nearly bankrupted North Korea.

If North Korea proved to be more resilient than the world community believed it to be, South Korea's rosy self-portrait turned out to be premature. Kim, an old-fashioned and highly effective political tactician, was far from being a capable manager for the nation's economy. He was poorly prepared in dealing with the issues related to the rapidly expanding, overly ambitious industrial economy, which faced increasingly strong challenges in the global market place in the 1990s. In an environment of all-out competition, the medium-technology based South Korean economy was under worsening wage pressures and needed most an experienced navigator just to survive. The signs of approaching trouble were abundant when some large business groups went under in early 1997. Yet Kim's government was unable to properly fathom the impending disaster, thus squandering the narrowest window of opportunity to seek a remedy. To make matters worse, in addition to a struggling Japanese economy, Southeast Asia was engulfed by severe financial difficulties, raising serious doubts over the stability of the regional economy as a whole. Still, Kim's civil government remained essentially a bystander, erroneously maintaining that its economy was on a strong foundation. To the contrary, the South Korean economy shortly faced a catastrophic foreign exchange crisis when foreign investors, losing confidence over the economy, withdrew their portfolio investments. When the government became aware of the seriousness of the crisis that had overnight thwarted Korea's ambition to rise as a serious industrial power, it was too late. The crisis, which hit South Korea hard and extensively, left the government no alternative but to seek IMF's massive intervention and its stern disciplinary measures.

South Koreans did not place the whole responsibility for the destructive exchange crisis to Kim Young Sam's civil government. However, they were in unison in blaming the government's amateurish handling of the crisis, which turned the common notion of their being a middle class into a mere illusion. The nation had no choice but to accept the cold and painful reality of being a member of globalized market economy. As the nation entered a period of a painful reform and restructuring, its only hope was that the miracle of the Hahn River could be rekindled and restored within a few years. Being aware that the recovery was to be long and difficult, the public rejected the ruling party at the 1997 presidential election. Yet to be apparent to most citizens was the extensive fallout of the crisis, but most remained unwilling to forgive both public and private sectors' wanton mismanagement that wiped out their hard earn prosperity. A few realized the fact that the nation had to accept the inevitable adjustment process with grace.

South Korea's debt crisis was unique in a sense that it was caused by neither depression in any leading industrial sector nor acute weakness in the fundamentals of the national economy. However, it had two rather unusual but coincidental contributors: domestic shortcomings and external developments. The most damaging domestic failure was its flawed banking system, which led to unorthodox financial practices. The banking system, which was the product of political needs and convenience, precipitated the uncontrolled borrowing by the nation's irrationally expansion-oriented jaebuls, or business conglomerates. Jaebuls' monopoly of funds, however, did not solve but exacerbated the loss suffered by the already struggling industrial sector, victims of "4 highs and 3 lows": high wage, high interest, high land price, and high transportation costs plus low technology, low value-added, and low managerial efficiency.[18]   When this led to the accumulation of debts, the banks should have forced the industries to go under as a market economy dictates. Yet the jaebuls, the heroes of spectacular economic expansion in the 80s, used their political influence, often in the form of illegal political contributions, to gain more funds just to keep the unprofitable businesses afloat. This polluted financial practice led to the eventual feebleness of the entire financial system, a source of loss of confidence by foreign investors.

Kim Young Sam's government was aware that the nation's banking systems and the jaebul-oriented market structure that made the overall financial sector of the nation unstable should undergo a major overhaul. Yet its reform initiatives were ineffective from the outset as the opposition mobilized its formidable political influence. Still, the globalization pressures were ever increasing, forcing the government to liberalize its capital market. The result was unprecedented inflow of foreign portfolio investment. At the same time, banks and finance companies began to borrow short-term loans abroad for long-term physical investments or portfolio investments abroad, forcing the nation's gross foreign debt up threefold during the 1990-1996 period.

Foreign investors, alarmed by the widespread banking and other business transaction irregularities, reacted quickly to the foreign exchange crisis in the Southeast Asia and the deepening recession in Japan by dumping Korean stocks and bonds and refusing to roll over loans. Overnight the Korean won lost 60 percent of its value against the dollar, effectively and unceremoniously terminating South Korea's   jaebul-dominated high growth period. The shock for which no one was prepared to accept put South Korea into the most severe challenge since the end of the war in 1953. It was an ironic but befitting coincidence that Kim Young Sam's troubled presidency expired in the midst of this foreign exchange crisis.

In 1998 South Korea chose for its fifteenth president Kim Dae-jung, another prominent opposition leader under the long military leadership. In spite of his narrow victory margin and a limited power base South Koreans were quick to place desperate hope and expectation on the new president. Known for his steely motivation and extensive knowledge over wide subjects, he was regarded as the right person to lead the nation, which was dispirited and in need of clear, farsighted direction to survive the "IMF era."

Wholesale reform and restructuring measures mandated by the IMF quickly led to massive unemployment and worsening hardship in general. Guided by the president's unwavering determination the new government still adopted initiatives that both the defiant business community and the reluctant bureaucracy accorded reluctant consent in order to put the nation's economy on the long road to a recovery. In a sense, it was a fitting trial, for South Korea's economy had to undergo a revolutionary rebirth process like its hard-won democracy. An economy recklessly polluted by party politics could not survive and prosper in a democratic society in a globalized world.

South Korea faces a daunting task of surviving the IMF prescription, which included a high rate of unemployment and drastically eroded purchasing power. Even under the most effective leadership President Kim is able to muster, the recovery is projected to take 3 to 5 years. Yet, if the reform and restructuring measures are successful in overcoming the mistakes committed in the past, South Korea could emerge as an economy leaner, stronger, and more democratic.

President Kim Dae-jung's "people's government" adopted bold policy initiatives on all fronts. Reform and restructuring of the nations's economy was the bastion of the initiatives reflecting his intense desire: quick and successful graduation from the IMF era. Kim's presidency will be most likely judged by its success in the economic front. A more long-term oriented but no less significant initiative the new people's government adopted was the "sunshine policy," its new open, pragmatic policy toward North Korea.

President Kim incorporated into his new "sunshine policy" the spirits of Kim Young Sam's northern policy: not taking advantage of the North's economic difficulties, agreeing to the North's joining the international community, and a peaceful unification of the peninsula without either side imposing its will on the other. The new government stressed in its "sunshine policy" a willingness not to tolerate the North's military provocation, its interest in pursuing a peaceful unification rather than absorption of North Korea, and promotion of reconciliation and exchange. President Kim made clear that he would promote cultural, economic exchanges apart from the political reconciliation, leaving the door open to improve intra-Korean relations even without the benefits of political-military thaw.

Kim Jung Il, the general secretary of the worker's party and the president, has yet to make a formal, comprehensive response to the new Seoul government's initiatives. Yet the early indications were fairly promising. For the first time since the 1953 armistice, two Koreas were to engage private-sector cooperation including joint ventures on tourism and manufacturing. Although tentative and less than spectacular, this commercial cooperation is likely to serve as a vanguard to the meaningful yet slow political reconciliation.[19]

In spite of President Kim's sunshine policy, the North-South confrontation remained little abated. Still the DMZ continues to be the world's most heavily guarded frontier. As of the end of 1997 the two sides maintained 1.7 million heavily armed troops defending Korean territories from Koreans. The apparent shift in a political paradigm, from the cold war ideology to politico-economic nationalism, is yet to affect meaningfully the old fashioned mentality of the Pyongyang leadership.

North Korea's military superiority over South Korea in terms of both troop and weapon strength remains intact.[20] The North's persistent attempts to deal with the United States directly and thus isolate the South is also counterproductive and scandalous. Yet the North is likely to maintain such a defiant attitude toward the more populous and economically powerful South as long as the narcissistic Pyongyang leadership remains in power. The North is expected not to abandon its irrational quest to conquer the South militarily even though the nation struggles to avoid a total collapse of its economy; it is yet to show signs of shifting from a road of militant defiance that may end in a sudden collapse to that of gradual reform and thus active interaction with the global community. But it may not be able to resist long. Just as the IMF intervention has forced South Korea to assume a more pragmatic road toward unification, the food crisis and anemic economy will necessitate North Korea to choose reform and restructuring instead of defunct socialism and untenable militancy. Ironically, the crisis that brought to the populace unprecedented suffering and humiliation may serve as a call for rational approaches toward unification.

The Korean peninsula has entered a final chapter in its internal division. Koreans are no more interested in borrowed foreign ideologies. And the peninsula's regional geopolitics is also favorable to unification. Only Pyongyang's anachronism remains a serious obstacle in closing the final chapter of the division, which after all was imposed by now defunct cold war politics. The unification process, arduous and slow as it may be, is currently under way, and even those who willfully ignore the irreversible current cannot block it long. By the early part of twenty-first century, the Korean peninsula will be tended by one unified government as the Hahn nation finally assumes the proper role in the historic and critical Far East region. It will mean the grand finale of the long, demanding drive of the "white cloth people's" nation building undertaking.

Notes

1. The state-run Korea Institute for Intranational Economic Policy projects that by 1996 South Korea's total trade will reach $240 billion, making the nation one of the world's top ten trade nations.

2. South Korea's Economic Planning Board projects that its trade surplus will reach a modest $5.5 billion in 1996 after a negligible amount in 1991-1992 period.

3. Since 1988 South Korea's annual trade deficit against Japan has remained over $10 billion. The deficit size has changed little over the last six years.

4. The Government projection shows a gradual decline in the nation's primary sector, from 19.1 percent in 1990 to 13.5 percent in 1995, and 9.2 percent in 2000. *Newsreview,* July 14, 1990.p. 13.

5. The U.S. transferred peacetime operational control of South Korean military forces to the South Korean government on November 30, 1994. The Combined Forces Command, which is under the control of a U.S. officer, resumes authority over Korean forces in the event of war and joint military operations.

6. The U.S. trade deficit in 1988 reached over $120 billion. Since then the figure has shown some fluctuation, ranging from $120 billion to less than $100 billion. In 1994, in which the U.S. trade deficiet climbed to over $120 billion, the trade flow between South Korea and the U.S. has remained roughly in balance.

7. South Korea's National Assembly approved legislation for the country's membership in the World Trade Organization, the new multilateral trade association that replaced the GATT on January 1, 1995.

8. Gahb-Chol Kim, 'North Korea's changing Socialist System and its Juche Ideology," *vantage Point 13* (January, 1990),p.6.

9. "Summary of Kim Il Sung's New Year Message," *Vantage Point 1* (January, 1990), p.16.

10. Suh dae Sook, *Korean Communism,* 1945-1980, (Honolulu: university of Hawaii Press, 1981), p.281

11. Kim Jong Il holds posts of the North Korean Worker's party secretary, the commander of armed forces, and the presidency as of late 1998.

12. Sinn Rinn-Sup, "Democratic Confederal Republic of Koryo," *Korea and world Affairs* (Wintra, 1990),p.632.

13.*Ibid.*, p.635.

14.Suh Dae Sook, *Korea communism*, 1945-1980 (Honolulu: University of Hawaii Press, 1981), p.616

15.The People's republic of China rose to be South Korea's third largest trading partner, after the united States and Japan, in 1994.

16. South Korea's rice donation to the North in 1995 was $252 million.

17. Claims were made by Hwang Jang-Yop, former secretary of North Korea's Worker's Party Central Committee, who defected to the South in 1977.

18. Duck-Woo Nam, "The financial crisis in Korea," *Korea Economic Update*, January 1998:1

19.Total intra-Korean trade reached $252 million in 1996 after the limited trade relationship began in 1988.

20.North Korea's significant military superiority in quantity includes troop strength and virtually all categories of weapons such as tanks, field artillery, combat ships, and tactical as well as support aircraft.

Bibliography

Books in English

Acheson, Dean. *The Korean War.* New York: W.W. Norton, 1971.
An, Tai Sung. *North Korea in Transition.* Westport: Greenwood Press, 1983.
Baik, Bong. *Kim Il Sung, Biography.* Tokyo: Miraisha, 1969.
Bishop, Isabella B. *Korea and Her Neighbors.* Seoul: Yonsei University Press, 1988.
Bridges, Brian. *Korea and the West.* New York: Routledge & Kegan, 1986.
Chai, Chu and Winberg Chai. *Confucianism.* New York: Barron's Educational Series, Inc., 1973.
Choe, Ching Y. *The Rule of the Taewongun, 1864-1873, Restoration in Yi Korea.* Cambridge: Harvard East Asian Monographs, 1972.
Chung, Chin O. *Pyongyang Between Peking and Moscow: North Korea's Involvement in the Sino-Soviet Dispute, 1958-1975.* University, Alabama: The University of Alabama Press, 1978.
Chung, Chin Wee. *Korea and Japan in World Politics.* Seoul: Seoul Computer Press, 1985.
Cohen, Raymond. *Theatre of Power: The Art of Diplomatic Signalling.* New York: Longman, 1987.
Collins, Lawton J. *War in Peace.* New York: Houghton Mifflin, 1969.
Conroy, Hilary. *The Japanese Seizure of Korea:1868-1910.* Philadelphia: University of Pennsylvania Press, 1960.
Crowley, James B. Edt. *Modern East Asia, Essays in Interpretation.* New York: Harcourt, Brace & World, Inc., 1970.
Cumings, Bruce. *The Origins of the Korean War, Liberation and the Emergence of Separate Regimes, 1945-1947.* Princeton: Princeton University Press, 1981.
Darby, Phillip. *Three Faces of Imperialism, British and American Approaches to Asia and Africa, 1870-1970.* New Haven: Yale University Press, 1987.
Dennett, Tyler. *Americans in Eastern Asia.* New York: Barnes & Noble, Inc., 1941.
Deuchler, Martina. *Confucian Gentlemen and Barbarian Envoys, the Opening of Korea, 1875-1885.* Seattle: University of Washington Press, 1977.

Fairbank, John King. *The United States and China.* 3rd Edition.Cambridge: Harvard University Press, 1971.

---------. *The Great Chinese Revolution, 1800-1985.* New York: Harper & Row, Publishers, 1986.

Foot, Rosemary. *The Wrong War: American Policy and the Dimensions of the Korean Conflict, 1950-1953.* New York, Ithaca: Cornell University Press, 1985.

Fukuda, Tsuneari. *Future of Japan and the Korean Peninsula.* Seoul: Hollym International Corp., 1978.

Gernet, Jacques. Translated by J.R. Foster. *A History of Chinese Civilization.* New York: Cambridge University Press, 1982.

Goncharov, Sergei N., John W. Lewis, and Xue Litai. *Uncertain Partners, Stalin, Mao, and the Korean War.* Stanford: Stanford University Press, 1993.

Griffis, William E. *Corea, The Hermit Nation.* New York: Charles Scribner's Sons, 1911.

Grousset, Rene. *The Rise and Splendour of the Chinese Empire.* Berkely: University of California Press, 1953.

Ha, Young Sun. *Nuclear Proliferation: World Order and Korea.* Seoul: Seoul National University Press, 1983.

Hahm, Sung Deuk, L. Christopher Plein. *After Development: The Transformation of the Korean Presidency and Bureaucracy,* Washington, D.C.: Georgetown University Press, 1997.

Han, Woo Keun. *The History of Korea.* Seoul: The Eul-Yoo Publishing Company, 1970.

Hastings, Max. *The Korean War.* New York: Simon and Schuster, 1987.

Higgins, Trumbull. *Korea and the Fall of MacArthur.* New York: Oxford University Press, 1960.

Hinton, Harold C. *Korea Under New Leadership, the Fifth Republic.* New York: Praeger Publishers, 1983.

Hoyt, Edwin P. *The Pusan Perimeter, Korea, 1950.* New York: Stein and Day, 1984.

Hsu, Immanuel C. Y. *The Rise of Modern China.* New York: Oxford University Press, 1970.

Hwang, In K. *The Korean Reform Movement of the 1880's, A Study of Transition in Intra-Asian Relations.* Cambridge: Schenkman Publishing Company, 1978.

Joe, Wanne J. *Traditional Korea: A Cultural History.* Seoul: Chung Ang University Press, 1972.

Kajima, Morinosuke. *The Emergence of Japan as A World Power, 1895-*

1925. Vermont: Chales E. Tuttle Co., 1968.

Kaufman, Burton I. *The Korean War, Challenges in Crisis, Credibility, and Command.* Philadelphia: Temple University Press, 1986.

Khrushchev, Nikita. *Khrushchev Remembers, The Glasnost Tapes.* Translated and Edited by Jerrold Schecter with Vyacheslav Luchkov. Boston: Little, Brown and Company, 1990.

Kihl, Young Whan. *Politics and Policies in Divided Korea: Regimes in Contest.* Boulder: Westview Press, 1984.

Kim, Haeng Jung. *The Cycle of Maturity.* Seoul: Jung Ang Publishing Co., 1981.

Kim, Jai-Hyup. *The Garrison State in Pre-War Japan and Post War Korea: A Comparative Analysis of Military Politics.* Washington, D.C.: University Press of America, 1978.

Kim, Jch Young. *Toward a Unified Korea.* Seoul: Research Center for Peace and Unification, 1987.

Kim, Kwan Bong. *The Korea-Japan Treaty Crisis and the Instability of the Korean Political System.* New York: Praeger Publishers, 1971.

Kiyosaki, Wayne S. *North Korea's Foreign Relations, the Politics of Accommodation, 1945-1975.* New York: Praeger Publishers, 1976.

Koo, Youngnok and Sungjoo Han, eds. *The Foreign Policy of the Republic of Korea.* New York: Columbia University Press, 1985.

Ku, Dae Yeol. *Korea Under Colonialism.* Seoul: Royal Asiatic Society, 1985.

Kwak, Tac Hwan, Wayne Patterson and Edward A. Olson. *The Two Koreas in World Politics.* Masan: Kyungnam University Press, 1983.

Langer, William L. *The Diplomacy of Imperialism, 1890-1902.* New York: Alfred A. Knopf, 1935.

Lee, Chae-Jin. *China and Korea: Dynamic Relations.* New York: Hoover Institute Press, 1996.

Lee, Ki Baik. *A New History of Korea.* Translated by Edward Wagner and Edward Shultz. Cambridge: Harvard University Press, 1984.

Lee, Suck Ho. *Party-Military Relations in North Korea.* Seoul: Research Center for Peace and Unification, 1989.

Lensen, George A. *Balance of Intrigue, International Rivalry in Korea & Manchuria, 1884-1899, Volume I and II.* Tallahassee: University Presses of Florida, 1982.

McAleavy, Henry, *The Modern History of China.* New York: Frederick A. Praeger, 1967.

May, Ernest R. and James C. Thompson, eds. *American-East Asian Relations: A Survey.* Cambridge: Harvard University Press, 1972.

McAleavy, Henry. *The Modern History of China.* New York: Frederick A. Praeger, 1967.

Millet, Allan R. and Peter Maslowski. *For the Common Defense, A Military History of the United States of America.* New York: The Free Press, 1984.

Modelski, George. *Principles of World Politics.* New York: The Free Press, 1985.

Morgenthau, Hans J. *Politics among Nations, the Struggle for Power and Peace,* 3rd edition. New York: Alfred A. Knopf, 1960.

Nam, Koon Woo. *The North Korean Communist Leadership, 1945-1965.* University, Alabama: The University of Alabama Press, 1974.

Nish, Ian. *The Origins of the Russo-Japanese War.* New York: Longman, 1985.

Oliver, Robert T. *Syngman Rhee and American Involvement in Korea, 1942-1960.* Seoul: Panmun Book Company, Ltd., 1978.

Paige, Glenn D. *The Korean Decision.* New York: The Free Press, 1968.

Park, Jae Kyu, ed. *The Foreign Relations of North Korea: New Perspectives.* Boulder: Westview Press, 1987.

Park, Chung Hee. *Korea Reborn, A Model for Development.* Englewood Cliffs: Prentice-Hall, Inc., 1979.

Roberson, John R. *Japan, from Shogun to Sony, 1543-1984.* New York: Atheneum, 1985.

Scalapino, Robert A. *North Korea Today.* New York: Praeger, 1963.

Scalapino, Robert A. and Chong-Sik Lee. *Communism in Korea, Part 1: The Movement.* Berkeley: University of California Press, 1972.

Segal, Gerald, ed. *The Soviet Union in East Asia, Predicaments of Power.* Boulder: Westview Press, 1983.

Shin, Jung Hyun. *Northeast Asian Security and Peace: Toward the 1990s.* Seoul: Kyung Hee University Press, 1988.

Simmons, Robert R. *The Strained Alliance.* New York: The Free Press, 1975.

Sohn, Pow-Key. *The History of Korea.* Seoul: Korean National Commission for UNESCO, 1970.

Stueck, William. *The Road to Conflict: U.S. Policy Towards China and Korea.* University of North Carolina Press, 1981.

Suh, Dae Sook. *The Korean Communist Movement.* Princeton: Princeton University Press, 1967.

--------, *Korean Communism, 1945-1980.* Honolulu: University of Hawaii Press, 1981.

--------- *Kim Il Sung, The North Korean Leader.* New York: Columbia

University Press, 1988.

Spanier, John W. *The Truman-MacArthur Controversy and the Korean War.* New York: W.W. Norton & Company, 1965.

Storry, Richard. *Japan and the Decline of the West in Asia, 1894-1943.* New York: St. Martin's Press, 1978.

Swartout, Robert R. *Mandarins, Gunboats, and Power Politics: Owen Nickerson Denny and the International Rivalries in Korea.* Hawaii: The University Press of Hawaii, 1980.

Talbott, Strobe. Translator. *Khrushchev Remembers.* Boston: Little, Brown and Company, 1970.

Vinacke, Harold M. *A History of the Far East in Modern Times.* New York: Appleton-Century-Crofts, 1959.

Walton, Richard J. *The United States and the Far East.* New York: The Seabury Press, 1974.

Weems, C.N. Edt. *Hulbert's History of Korea.* London: Routledge & Kegan Paul, 1962.

Weiner, Myron and Samuel P. Huntington., eds. *Understanding Political Development.* Boston: Little, Brown and Company, 1987.

Whiting, Allan. *China Crosses the Yalu: The Decision to Enter the Korean War.* Berkeley: University of California Press, 1970.

Books in Korean

Baik, Gyung Nam. *Guk Je Gwan Ge Sa (History of International Relations).* Seoul: Bup Ji Sa, 1987.

Chindan Hakhoe. *Hahn Guk Sa (History of Korea).* Seoul: Eul-Yoo Publishing Co., 1959-1965.
  Vol. 1: Ancient History, Lee Byung Do
  Vol. 2: Medieval History, Lee Byung Do
  Vol. 3 & 4: Modern History, Lee Sang Baek
  Vol. 5 & 6: Recent and Contemporary History, Lee Sun Guen

Cho, Ki Jong. *Hahn Guk Gyong Je Sa (Economic History of Korea).* Seoul: Il Sin Sa, 1962.

Hahn Guk Min Joong Sa Yeon Goo Hoe. *Hahn Guk Min Joong Sa (History of Korean People). Vol. 1, 2, 3, 4.* Seoul: Hahn Guk Min Joong Sa Yeon Goo Hoe, 1986.

Hyun Dae Moon Hwa Sa. *Jae Sam Gong Hwa Gook,(The Third Republic). Vol. 1-8.* DaeGoo: Hyun Dae Moon Hwa Sa, 1986.

Hyun, Sang Yun. *Chosun Yuhak Sa (History of Korean Confucianism).*

Seoul: Minjungsogwan, 1949.

Jeonjang Sa Up Hoi. *Hankuk Joenjang (History of the Korean War)*. Seoul, 1990.

Kim, Byung Ha. *Yijo Joonggi Deil Muyuk Yongu (A study of Chosun's Trade with Japan)*. Seoul: Korea Research Center, 1969.

Lee, Byung Do. *Koryo Sidae ui Yongu (A Study of Koryo Period)*. Seoul: Eul-Yoo Publishing Co., 1948.

Lee, Han Gi. *Hahnguk ui Yungto (The territory of Korea)*. Seoul: Seoul University Press, 1969.

Lee, Hyong Jong. *Yijo Joonggi Hahn-Il Gyosop Sa Yongu (A Study of Korea-Japan Relations During Chosun's Intermediate Period)*. Seoul: Korea Research Center, 1964.

Lee, In Yong. *Hahnguk Manju Gwange-Sa ui Yongu (A Study of Korea-Manchuria Relations)*. Seoul: Eul-Yoo Publishing Co., 1954.

Lee, Ki Baek. *Koryo Byungje-Sa Yongu (A Study of Koryo Military System)*. Seoul: Ilchogak, 1968.

Park, Joon Gyu. *Hahn Ban Do Guk Je Jung Chee Sa Lon (International Political History of Korean Peninsula)*. Seoul: Seoul University Press, 1984.

Park, Myung - Lim. *Hankuk Joenjiangui Balbalgwa Giwon (Outbreak and Origin of Korean War)*. Seoul: Nanam Press, 1996

Son, Jin Tae. *Chosun Minjok Munhwa ui Yongu (A Study of Korean Culture)*. Seoul: Eul-Yoo Publishing Co., 1948.

Song, Gun Ho. *Hahn Guk Hyun Dae Sa (Modern History of Korea)*. Seoul: Doo Rae Press, 1986.

Yoo, Won Dong. *Yijo Hoogi Sang-Gongup-Sa Yongu (A Study of Commerce and Industry in Chosun's Later Period)*. Seoul: Korea Research Center, 1968.

INDEX